Postadoption EXPERIENCE

Adoptive Families' Service Needs and Service Outcomes

Edited by Martha Morrison Dore, PhD

Child Welfare League of America • Washington, DC

CWLA Press is an imprint of the Child Welfare League of America. The Child Welfare League of America is the nation's oldest and largest membership-based child welfare organization. We are committed to engaging people everywhere in promoting the well-being of children, youth, and their families, and protecting every child from harm. All proceeds from the sale of this book support CWLA's programs in behalf of children and families.

CHILD WELFARE LEAGUE OF AMERICA, INC.
HEADQUARTERS
440 First Street, NW, Third Floor, Washington, DC 20001-2085
E-mail: books@cwla.org

CURRENT PRINTING (last digit)
10 9 8 7 6 5 4 3 2 1

Cover and text design by Jennifer R. Geanakos
Edited by Tim Sniffin

Printed in the United States of America

ISBN-13: 978-1-58760-077-7
ISBN-10: 1-58760-077-3

Library of Congress Cataloging-in-Publication Data

The postadopton experience : adoptive families' service needs and service outcomes / edited by Martha Morrison Dore.

   p. cm.

  Casey Family Services commissioned the papers in this report to share knowledge and esperience in the ara of post-adoption services"--Introd.

   ISBN-13: 978-1-58760-077-7 (pbk. : alk. paper)

   ISBN-10: 1-58760-077-3 (pbk. : alk. paper)

  1. Adopted children--Services for--United States. 2. Adoptive parents--Services for--United States. 3. Foster children--Services for--United States. 4. Adoption--United States. 5. Family services--United States--Evaluation. 6. Evaluation research (Social action programs)--United States. I. Dore, Martha Morrison, 1943- ii. Casey Family Services. iii. Title.

HV875.55P68 2006

362.7340973   2006028135

Contents

7 The Development of Postadoption Services in Massachusetts 135

Christopher G. Hudson, Patricia Cedeño-Zamor, Cheryl Springer,
Marguerite Rosenthal, Sharon C. Silvia, Steve Alexander, and Loretta Kowal

8 The Nature of Effective Adoption Preservation Services: A Qualitative Study 159

Susan Livingston Smith

9 Factors Affecting Recent Adoption Support Levels in the Washington State Adoption Support Program 197

David Fine, Lee Doran, Lucy Berliner, and Roxanne Lieb

Introduction

Casey Family Services, the direct service agency of the Annie E. Casey Foundation, believes that every child needs—and deserves—a lifelong connection to a caring, nurturing, stable family and to a strong community. For children unable to live with their biological families, adoption can provide the permanent, stable environment needed for healthy growth and development. Ironically, supporting and preserving adoptive families traditionally receives less attention than the adoption process itself.

Over the past decade, the need to provide permanence for foster children has been widely recognized, and due to a variety of public policy initiatives, the adoption of foster children has grown substantially. In 2004, 51,000 children were adopted through the child welfare system. This is nearly twice the number since 1996. Studies indicate that many, if not most, foster children who are adopted continue to face various physical and mental health challenges as a result of their histories of traumatic abuse, neglect and/or abandonment. Similar research makes it clear that these children and their adoptive families need a variety of postadoption services—short- and long-term—to ensure that the adoption is a success.

The significant increase in the numbers of adoptions of children from the public welfare system has illuminated something that has been well known among the adoption community: Signing the legal adoption papers is just one step toward a successful adoption. Adoptive families report that services and supports have been critical to their adjustment to the lifelong process of adoption. Families considering the adoption of special needs children are more likely to make the commitment to adopt when they know postadoption services are available.

Although the need for postadoption services is generally agreed upon, there is not consensus on fundamental issues, including:

- What services are most effective,

- How to make services accessible to children and family,

- How to fund services,

- How to judge the effectiveness of services, and

- Where to direct research on postadoption services.

Casey Family Services requested the papers for this book to share knowledge and experience in the area of postadoption services, including services needs, effectiveness of those services and research issues.

The first three chapters examine the needs of adoptive families and children. Jeanne Howard's research in Illinois compares the services needs and challenges faced by families formed through foster parent adoption, kinship adoption, and matched adoption. Trudy Festinger's survey of parents who adopted children through the New York City Administration for Children's Services (ACS) examines the needs of these families and the services they received. Michael Grand's review of two studies of adult adoptees provides evidence of the services likely to be needed at the various developmental stages.

The next six chapters review a variety of postadoption services and evaluate their effectiveness. Susan Livingston Smith examines the experiences of families served by the Illinois Adoption Preservation Program. She later identifies characteristics of effective postadoption services through an analysis of adoptive families from Illinois who received services. A team from Casey Family Services, the Research Triangle Institute, and the University of North Carolina School of Social Work track the experiences of more than 400 families in six sites who participated in postadoption services. Michael Lahti describes how the Maine Adoption Guides Project has supported families adopting children with special needs. A team of social workers and academics from Salem State College describes the evolution and effectiveness of Massachusetts's Adoption Crossroads, which provides post-adoption services. Finally, a team from Seattle investigates Washington's Adoption Support Program to determine the level of financial support families received through this program to encourage the adoption of children with special needs from the state child welfare system.

Postadoption services are relatively new, and research is both limited and important. The final two papers focus on frameworks for effective research. Jeffrey Haugaaard of Cornell University analyzes methodological and design issues and identifies research criteria for the further study of postadoption services, while a team from Florida State University describes how concept mapping of qualitative data can identify barriers to post-adoption services and solutions to overcome these barriers.

Working in foster care and other family-based programs since 1976, Casey Family Services has found that postadoption services are essential to helping children and families build successful relationships. The organization and the studies' authors hope this book helps to shed light on successful and achievable approaches.

SECTION ONE

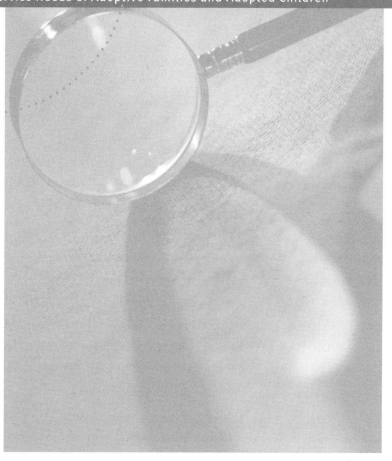

Service Needs of Adoptive Families and Adopted Children

AN EXAMINATION OF
Postadoption Functioning
AND THE NEEDS OF Kin, Foster, AND
Matched Adoptive Families

Jeanne Howard

D ramatic changes in adoption policy and practice have led to large increases in the number of children gaining permanency through adoption. In several states the numbers of children receiving adoption subsidies has surpassed the number of children in foster care (Wulczyn & Hislop, 2002). As the numbers of adoptions of children with special needs increased, so did recognition of the need to support families after adoption was finalized. Yet little is known about how to serve these families best.

The movement to develop services supporting adoptive families is based on a general understanding of their likely needs. Yet, adoptive families differ in the nature and type of their postadoption concerns. Services for families must fit the range of families who adopt.

This study examined the postadoption functioning and identified service needs of 1,343 families receiving Adoption Assistance in Illinois, a state with one of the largest populations of adopted children in the United States. Data were analyzed by type of adoptive family: kin families (in which relatives have adopted), foster adoptive families (in which children's former foster parents have adopted them), and matched adoptive families (in which a child was placed with a designated family for the purpose of adoption). There were significant differences across the three types of adoptive families in child functioning, parental satisfaction, and the need for additional support. This chapter discusses differences in child functioning and parent satisfaction by type, and raises questions for further research.

Method

The goal of this study was to assess how children and their families fared after adoption. The study examined child functioning in home, school, and community, as well as children's general health and mental health; preparation for adoption; and family service needs after adoption. Survey items included 65 forced choice questions, including the Behavior Problem Index. Open-ended responses were sought by several questions. For example, adoptive parents were asked, "Do you have concerns about your child getting along in your neighborhood or community?" If they answered yes, they were asked to describe their concerns and to identify what they thought would help. In addition, adoptive parents were asked two general open-ended questions. The first was "Please describe the best things about your child," and the second (and final) question of the survey was "What other recommendations, if any, do you have for improving services to adopted children and their families?" The survey was modified in response to the suggestions of 12 volunteer respondents and then was evaluated for reading level. Using the Flesch-Kincaid measure, the survey was assessed as understandable by individuals at a grade reading level of 4.8.

The survey was targeted to families with children of school age in Illinois. Previous research has indicated that problems among adoptive families of children with special needs escalate over time, with school problems leading to significant family stress. Thus, only families with children ages 6 to 18 were included in the sample. Many adoptive families in Illinois include more than one adopted child. In order to increase the return rate, parents were asked to complete the lengthy survey only on their oldest child.

Surveys were sent to 3,993 families randomly selected from the list of children receiving Adoption Assistance in Illinois. Thirty-four percent of the surveys that were successfully delivered were returned and were useable, yielding data on 1,343 families.

The Findings

The findings from the study are presented in four areas: characteristics of the responding families and their children and differences by adoptive family type, children's adjustment by adoptive family type, preparation for adoption, and service needs and recommendations.

Description of Responding Families and their Children and Differences by Type

In this study, most adoptions (83%) resulted from preexisting relationships between the parent and child, with the parent being either a former foster parent for the child (44%) or a relative (39%). Fourteen percent of those responding had been matched with children for the specific purpose of adoption. (The remaining 3% of respondents did not complete this item.)

Illinois has moved rapidly to kin foster care and adoption. As a result, a large number of the respondents unsurprisingly were kin adopters. In 1995, 41% of finalized adoptions of children in foster care were by kin, 46% by foster parents, and 13% by matched parents. By 1999, 57% of these adoptions were by kin, 41% by foster parents, and only 2% by matched adopters (Illinois Department of Children and Family Services, 2001). Kin adoption, however, has not progressed as rapidly nationwide. Although adoptions by kin are increasing nationally, only 16% of adoptions of children in foster care in 1999 were by kin (U.S. Children's Bureau, 2001).

Characteristics of adoptive families

Analysis of the data revealed that there were significant differences across the three types of adoptive families. Kin adopters were much more likely to be members of minority racial or ethnic groups (chi square = 268.13, p < .001). Eighty-two percent of kin adopters were minorities, and of this group, most were African Americans. By contrast, the majority of foster parents who adopted (62%) and the majority of matched adoptive parents (73%) were Caucasian.

One clear difference across adoptive family types was income level: For a number of factors, kin adopters had much lower incomes than their foster and matched counterparts. In addition to the income differences associated with race, kin adopters were much more likely to be single parents and have less education than either foster or matched adoptive parents. More than 60% of kin adopters were single, compared to 29% of foster adopters and 21% of matched adoptive parents. The majority of matched parents (52%) had completed college, compared to 33% of foster parents and 15% of kin adopters. Forty-three percent of the kin adopters had a high school education or less.

The difference in family income was dramatic. Kin adopters were far more likely to have low family income, followed by foster adopters and them by matched adoptive parents. The great majority of kin adopters (79%) reported annual incomes (exclusive of subsidy) of less than $35,000, slightly less than half (47%) of foster adopters and 25% of matched adopters. In addition, many kin adopters had extremely low incomes. Thirty-eight percent reported incomes of less than $15,000 a year. By contrast, only 13% of foster parent adopters and 6% of matched adopters had annual incomes that low. Further, kin adoptive families were likely to contain more children than the other family types, perhaps as a result of the greater tendency for relatives to adopt sibling groups.

In summary, kin adopters were likely to be single-headed, African American families with limited education and low income. Foster parent adopters were likely to be dual-headed, Caucasian families, with more education than kin adoptive families and low to moderate income. Families formed through matches were generally dual-headed and Caucasian, with moderate to higher incomes.

Characteristics of the children

As might be expected given that the majority of kin adopters were African American, children adopted by kin were much more likely to be African American (76%) than children adopted by foster parents (48%) or matched parents (38%) (chi square = 109.94, p < .001).

Children adopted by kin and by foster parents were somewhat younger at the time of survey completion than children in matched homes (F = 228.42, p < .001). The overall mean age of children at the time of survey completion was 12 years. Children adopted by relatives had a mean age of 11.8 years, while those adopted by foster parent adopters had a mean age of 12 and by matched parents a mean age of 13.

There was no statistically significant difference in age at the time of the children's placement with their adoptive families. The great majority of the children, irrespective of adoptive family type, were 5 years old or younger when placed in their current homes. There was a difference, however, in their ages at time of entry into foster care, with children adopted by kin being older at entry. Children adopted by kin were, on average, 3.2 years old at entry, compared to 2.2 years for children adopted by foster parents and 1.8 years for children matched with adoptive parents (F = 369.87, p < .001).

Perhaps the most important difference across adoptive family type was the length of time children spent in foster care before being placed with their eventual adoptive families. Children adopted by kin were placed with their relatives much more quickly than children placed with matched adoptive parents, and somewhat more quickly than children adopted by foster parents (F = 210.81, p < .001). Children adopted by kin spent a mean of 9.8 months in foster care before being placed with their relatives who would adopt them, compared to 1.1 years for children adopted by foster parents and 2.1 years for children placed with matched adoptive parents.

Although they spent less time in foster care before being placed with their eventual adoptive families, children adopted by kin took much longer to be adopted (F = 1046.75, p < .001). Children adopted by kin averaged 4 years between their placements and the finalization of their adoptions. Children adopted by their foster parents waited nearly as long (3.5 years). Because matched homes are preadoptive homes by definition, it is not surprising that these children waited far less time from placement to finalization, an average of 1.1 years.

The survey presented parents with a list of maltreatment types and other risk factors for later adjustment problems, for example whether the child had moved back and forth from home to foster care or had a history of psychiatric hospitalization. In general, matched adoptive parents were the least likely of the groups to report they knew important aspects of their child's history. Foster parents were more likely to know important aspects of their children's backgrounds, and kin reported having the most information about their children's pasts. When parents knew about central aspects of their child's history, foster parent adopters were the most likely to report the existence of previous maltreatment and related problems, as indicated in Table 1.1. However, in two categories—serious neglect and prenatal substance abuse—kin families reported a higher incidence than did matched families. On no item did kin parents report the highest incidence of a type of maltreatment or other risk factor.

In terms of current problems, matched adopters were more likely to report the presence of a range of special needs than were foster or kin adopters, with the exception of behavior problems, an area in which foster parents reported a slightly higher percentage. Table 1.2 provides the percentages of adoptive families by type who reported that their children had certain special needs.

In terms of both current special needs and problematic aspects of the children's histories, kin adopters were likely to report fewer difficulties. Further, they knew more about their children's lives, particularly their exposure to various types of harm.

Children's Adjustment by Family Type

Overall, children were reported to be doing well after adoption despite their complicated backgrounds. Although kin adopters had many fewer financial resources; they were more likely to report that their children were doing either satisfactorily or well in the home, community and school; and they had fewer health and mental health problems. In each category, matched parents reported the most difficulty, although on several dimensions, matched and foster parents answered similarly.

TABLE 1–1

Previous Difficult Life Experiences by Type of Adoption

Nature	Kin	Foster	Matched
Serious neglect***	59%	69%	56%
Prenatal substance exposure***	59%	63%	51%
Two or more prior placements***	18%	45%	50%
Physical abuse***	23%	40%	35%
Sexual abuse***	12%	19%	20%
Back and forth/ home and foster care	16%	19%	22%
Previous adoptive placement**	11%	13%	23%
Pre adoption psychiatric hospitalization/ residential treatment	8%	11%	9%

**p<.01. ***p<.001

TABLE 1–2

Special Needs by Adoption Type*

Type of Need	Kin	Foster	Matched
Learning disabilities	37%	54%	57%
Emotional disturbance	24%	42%	46%
Behavior problems	43%	57%	55%
Developmental delays	17%	39%	51%
Vision/ hearing impairment	26%	35%	45%
Chronic medical problems	11%	21%	24%
Mental Retardation	3%	10%	17%
Physical Disability	2%	8%	15%

*p<.001 for each chi square

The large majority of kin adopters (91%) rated children's overall functioning at home as excellent or good. Foster and matched parents likewise responded positively to this question: 88% of foster parents and 83% of matched adopters rated their children's functioning as excellent or good. Certain aspects of home life, however, showed greater difference. Parents were asked to what extent their child's behavior made it difficult for them to find someone to watch their child. Twenty-six percent of matched adopters reported that their child's behavior made it "very difficult," compared to 22% of foster adopters and 12% of kin (chi square = 14.14, $p < .05$). Matched adopters (9%) were more likely to report that their child had had a negative impact on the family than were foster parents (4.5%) or kin (1.4%) (chi square = 27.98, $p < .001$).

Parents in all adoptive family types reported that the school setting was more problematic for children than the home. Again, children placed with matched adoptive parents had more difficulty across the board than children adopted by their former foster parents. In all areas except repeating a grade, children adopted by foster parents had more difficulty than kin children (Table 1-3). Although children adopted by kin appeared to be doing better in school, there was no difference across family type in terms of parents' identification of unmet educational needs. All parents most often cited concerns about tutoring, after school programs, and appropriate educational placements for their children.

As with school issues, there were differences in child health and mental health by adoptive family type. Children adopted by matched adoptive parents (40%) were more likely to be identified as having special medical needs than were children adopted by their former foster parents (33%) or by kin (19%). Kin adopters (79%) were most likely to rely on Medicaid to meet their children's health needs, a finding that is not surprising given their low average incomes. Despite having to rely on Medicaid, kin parents were less likely than foster and matched parents to report difficulties in getting adequate medical services.

Parents also evaluated the mental health of children and, once again, matched parents reported the greatest concerns (Table 1-4). Although the majority of parents in all family types reported their children had excellent or good mental health, 35% of matched adopters rated their child's mental health as fair or poor as did 28% of foster adopters and 13% of kin adopters.

Parents' assessment of their children's overall mental health also was reflected in their ratings of their children on the Behavior Problem Index (BPI). Once again, kin rated their children as having the fewest problems in behavior—that is, their children received the lowest mean scores on the BPI (Table 1-5). Children adopted by foster parents and by matched adoptive parents had identical scores—scores that were, on average, higher by 4 points than the score of children adopted by kin (chi square = 122.02, p < .001).

Nicholas Zill (1990), creator of the BPI, had reported that the mean score for children receiving or needing psychological help was 14.82. Extrapolating from Zill, we assessed differences among children with serious behavior problems by type of adoption by looking at children with scores of 15 and higher. While 27% of children adopted by kin had a score of 15 and above, this was true for 47% adopted by foster parents and 45% adopted by matched adoptive parents (chi square = 38.67, p < .001).

Another measure of the seriousness of children's problems is their placement in a residential treatment facility. Although few children required residential placement after adoption, there were differences by adoptive family type. Children adopted by matched adoptive parents were the most likely to have been in residential treatment (11%). This was true for 7% of children adopted by foster parents and just 2% adopted by kin.

The pattern of more positive response by kin adopters was evident in the parents' rating of how difficult the child was to raise (Table 1-6). Kin adopters were more likely to see their child as not at all difficult or a little difficult to raise. Only 6% of kin stated that their child was very difficult to raise compared to 14% of foster parent adopters and slightly more than one-fifth (21 %) of matched adopters (chi square = 87.05, p < .001).

TABLE 1–3

Factors Related to School Adjustment

PROBLEM TYPE	KIN	FOSTER	MATCHED
Special Education/ Learning problems***	29%	46%	53%
Medication for behavior***	16%	39%	46%
Repeating a grade*	24%	24%	35%
Teacher complaints about behavior	50%	54%	61%
Poor grades (mostly Ds and Fs)*	14%	18%	23%

*p<.05, **p<.01, ***p<.001

TABLE 1–4

Overall Mental Health by Adoption Type

RATING	KIN	FOSTER	MATCHED
Excellent	38%	25%	22%
Good	44%	47%	43%
Fair	16%	22%	25%
Poor	2%	6%	10%

TABLE 1–5

Behavior Problem Score by Adoptive Family Type

[MAXIMUM SCORE = 18]

Kin	9.76
Foster	13.12
Matched	13.12

TABLE 1–6

Difficulty of Child to Raise by Adoption Type*

RATING	KIN	FOSTER	MATCHED
Not at all difficult	38%	22%	22%
A little difficult	37%	27%	27%
Moderately difficult	19%	33%	31%
Very difficult	6%	14%	21%

*Chi square = 87.05, p,.001

Although parents reported that some children were difficult to raise and had mental health problems (as assessed by the BPI), a significant majority in all family types felt close to their children (Table 1-7) and were satisfied with the adoption experience (Table 1-8). The pattern of more positive responses by kin, however, held for both of these factors.

A final measure of parents' feelings about the child and the adoption was tested in the question, "Knowing everything you now know, if you had it to do over again would you adopt this child?" Very few parents (all of whom were foster parent adopters) reported that they *definitely* would not. Once again, foster and matched parents were less positive than kin. Ten percent of matched adopters, 8% of foster adopters, and 4% of kin reported that they probably would not adopt this child again.

Preparation for Adoption

The nature of preparation for adoption and the service needs identified also varied by type of adoptive family. Kin adopters were much less likely to receive formal preparation, perhaps because children were in their care longer prior to the formal adoption. Nevertheless, they were the most positive of the three groups about training when they received it. Despite receiving less training, kin were the most likely of the groups to believe that they and their children were well prepared. Foster parents were less positive but generally felt good about preparation. Fifty-one percent reported that they felt fully prepared to adopt and 60% reported that their children were fully prepared for adoption. For matched parents, 40% felt fully prepared, and 31% felt their children had been fully prepared.

Nonetheless, 20% of kin, 34% of foster parent adopters, and 42% of matched adopters felt that they and their children could have been better prepared for what was to come after adoption (chi square = 44.42, p < .001). Parents in all family types most commonly stated that adoption preparation could be improved through full disclosure about the child's history and background. Parents, as the following comments reflect, spoke powerfully about both the satisfactions of adoption and their need to know everything possible in order to help their children achieve healthy adulthood:

- "If parents adopt a child with substance abuse exposure, tell them—repeat and warn them about the slow learning of the child."

- "Parents deserve every scrap of information about the harm that has come to their child and need to know everything about their child's past. Don't hold anything back! Tell us what it all means so we can help our children make sense of it all."

- "My recommendation is to have birth parents fill out a family medical history to let us know what possible illness our child may be in danger of having. Also, let the adoptive parents know if the birth parents used drugs while being pregnant."

TABLE 1–7

Closeness to Child by Adoption Type*

Rating	Kin	Foster	Matched
Very close	90%	80%	73%
Somewhat close	10%	17%	23%
Not at all close		3%	5%

*Chi square = 37.87, p<.001

TABLE 1–8

Satisfaction with Adoption Experience by Adoption Type*

Rating	Kin	Foster	Matched
Very satisfied	66%	55%	54%
Satisfied	30%	35%	32%
Dissatisfied/ very dissatisfied**	4%	10%	14%

*Chi square = 28.68, p<.001

** categories collapsed due to small numbers

- "The best thing you can do is to tell us everything you know. We deserve to have all the facts so we can raise this child."

Kin adopters raised similar concerns:

- "Adoption by grandparents is confusing for the child, and the natural parents never go away. [We needed help] knowing how to explain all this to them and figuring out how this would all work."

- "We adopted my nephew (the child of the husband's brother) and don't really know anything about his birth mother. There's this big gaping hole in our information. Does she have mental illness? Health problems? What do I tell him about her? And how do I found out what I need to know to help him as he grows up?"

Parents often offered specific suggestions for preparing for certain kinds of issues. A review of the responses to open-ended questions revealed that kin adopters sought more information about their new roles (such as how to explain shifting relationships to the child and how to set boundaries on the interaction between the birthparent and the child). Foster and matched parents sought preparation related to specific child problems or characteristics such as Fetal Alcohol Syndrome, attachment problems, and behavior management.

When asked about the specific techniques used to prepare them for adoption, many adoptive parents apparently did not receive the "basics." For example, 45% of parents across all family types reported they did not receive written background information about their child. Further, only 25% of all parents reported that their child had a lifebook (a compilation of pictures, documents, and explanations commonly used to help a child make sense of the past and prepare for adoptive placement) or related information. Matched adopters, however, were most likely to receive written background information on their children, and children adopted by matched adoptive parents were most likely to have completed a lifebook.

Service Needs and Recommendations

In terms of service needs, kin adoptive parents identified fewer needs despite their overall lower incomes. Not surprisingly, many of their concerns related to concrete service needs (such as larger subsidy, better housing, childcare assistance, recreational programs, and ongoing support and help), as the following comments illustrate:

- "We need medication, clothes, beds, dressers. And a home in a safer neighborhood."

- "Subsidy is a great help, but it is not enough. All I have [besides subsidy] is my Social Security check and after the bills are paid, there just isn't enough left, even with the subsidy, to get him the things he needs. Low-income families are at a severe disadvantage."

- "Now that my boy is 10 years old, I need more money to feed him and for his clothes. I am retired. I use my money on him."

- "The subsidy helps; childcare while I work is needed. I do not qualify for help from public assistance. Childcare alone is anywhere from $100 to $200 a week!"

- "No one will watch my child. I can barely get a break. I hurt so bad and so long from this situation. I almost lost my husband of 30 years (because of these children's problems and the stresses of raising them). It took me two months to fill out this form because I didn't like what was happening to by family but I didn't want to lie…"

Several parents noted the difficulty of paying for childcare. At the time of the survey, foster parents in Illinois received assistance for childcare expenses, but adoptive parents received such assistance only when there was an identified need for therapeutic care to meet the child's needs. As a result, most adoptive families assumed the cost of childcare after adoption. Although the state viewed subsidy as sufficient to cover childcare costs, comments by parents indicate they did not agree. A recent change in policy allows adoptive parents who are working or in school to receive financial support for postadoption childcare for children up to age 3, when childcare costs are highest.

Foster and matched adopters also raised concerns about concrete needs, but their comments, like those that follow, were more likely to include suggestions about linkage to community services, helping parents understand the impact of their child's past maltreatment, and developing the skills to respond to challenging behavioral and emotional problems:

- "We knew that things might get complicated as time went on, but we didn't know how difficult it would get. Parents need to know where to get help and when to get it."

- "We need better and easier access to information about adoption issues, adopted children's issues, parenting skills, etc. Internet access would help—DCFS should send out a list of good websites. Also, adoptive parents should be informed of all services available and how to reach them."

- "Parents need to know they can contact the agency to get information and help. And not feel like a failure when they do. We need many resources that you know about that we have to dig to find. There must be a way for this to be easier!"

Is kinship protective?

The study indicates that kinship adoption may have a protective aspect for adopted children. That is, children adopted by kin had fewer reported behavior problems than their peers adopted by foster parents or matched parents. Further, their parents perceived them as functioning better in the home, school, and community, as well as having better health and mental health. Can readers conclude that kinship adoption lead to better child adjustment and more positive later functioning? From this study alone, they cannot.

Several differences between kin adoptive families and others confound the picture. First, kin-adopted children were more likely to be older than other children when entering foster care, and the data from this study do not explain the reasons for this dynamic. Children adopted by kin may receive better nurture in the first years of life than other children or suffer fewer breaks in attachment relationships at very young ages. Second, kin-adopted children spent less time adrift in foster care. Although they were technically "in the system" longer than other children, they were placed with the families who eventually adopted them more quickly than were children in either foster or matched homes. Third, children adopted by kin are far more likely to have contact with their birth parents and other family members than the two other groups of children. Such ongoing contact may reduce children's vulnerability to emotional and behavioral problems. Fourth, children adopted by relatives were largely children of color. In this study, African American children in each type of adoptive home averaged fewer behavior problems than non-African American children. Other studies on racial differences in child welfare adoption reported that minority children have fewer behavior problems and a higher level of social functioning than their Caucasian counterparts (Pinderhughes, 1998; Rosenthal and Groze, 1992). Finally, children adopted by family members appear to have fewer risk factors in their backgrounds. Because of this array of factors, it cannot be simply said, "kin adopted children do better."

The study's data were analyzed further in an attempt to tease out some of the issues. First, differences in BPI scores by race of child and adoption type were examined. The results are presented in Figure 1-1. African American children, whether adopted by

FIGURE 1–1

Mean BPI Scores by Race and Relationship

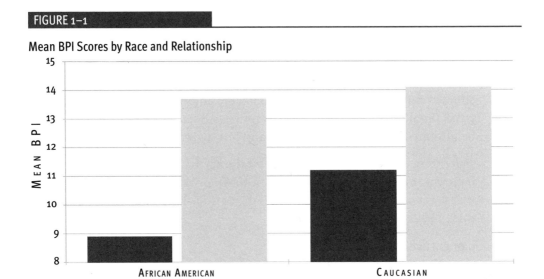

Relative: AA n = 268, Caucasian n = 76   Nonrelative: AA n = 181, Caucasian n = 411

relatives or nonrelatives, had fewer behavior problems as measured by the BPI than did Caucasian children (F = 35.34, p = .000).

Given that most of the kin adopted children were African American, race rather than kinship adoption may be the protective factor for children. This possibility was examined by comparing African American children adopted by relatives with African American children adopted by nonrelatives, with a focus on the number of different types of maltreatment and mean BPI score. As is indicated in Figure 1-2, African American children who have no or only one type of maltreatment in their history and were adopted by relatives have lower BPI scores than African American children adopted by non-relatives with either no or one type of maltreatment (F = 6.53, p = .01). The power of the protection offered by kinship adoption, however, diminishes as the number of different maltreatment types increases. These data suggest that kinship adoption for children who have experienced fewer types of maltreatment provides protection as measured by the BPI score.

Finally, focus was placed on children who had high BPI scores (15 or above) to determine if relatives and nonrelative adopters had different attitudes toward these challenging children. Adoptive parents' closeness to their child, their perception of difficulty in raising the child, and their level of satisfaction with the adoption were examined. Consistently, relatives were more positive than nonrelatives. They reported that they felt closer to their child than did foster or matched adopters (chi square = 16.68; p < .001) and that they were more satisfied with the adoption experience (chi square = 7.6; p < .05). Kin adopters of these challenging children were less likely to rate their child as difficult to raise (chi square = 21.34, p < .001). Although some children in each adoptive family type presented many problems, relative adopters perceived their children more positively despite these problems.

FIGURE 1–2

African American Children BPI Score by Relationship

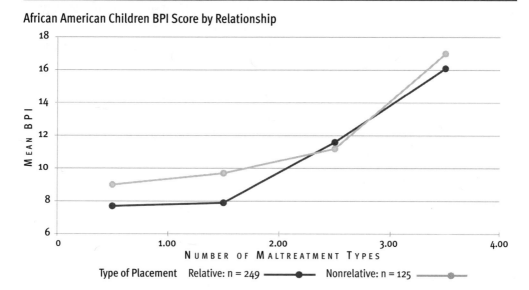

Type of Placement   Relative: n = 249 ●   Nonrelative: n = 125 ●

Discussion

As often with a new area of inquiry, the study raises more questions than it answers. This research, however, can provide the basis for a more careful examination of the postadoption supports provided to adoptive families and the preparation that adoptive parents receive. The good news is that most adoptive families are doing well. Kin families, when compared to foster and matched adopters, said that their children were functioning better and that they had more positive relationships with their children. Nonetheless, the majority of matched families (who appeared to struggle most) reported feeling very close to their children, were certain that they would adopt again, and were satisfied with their adoption experience.

Despite these positive results, some families were struggling greatly, and many families desired additional information and assistance. The information obtained from families in this survey raised the following questions:

- How can matched adopters, who appear to have the most complex family needs after adoption, be better prepared and supported?

- How can the preparation of foster and kin parents be tailored to meet their specific needs? How can kin adopters be prepared for changing family roles after adoption?

- What mechanisms can be put in place to help families quickly (and without a stigma) seek resources for their children after adoption?

- What postadoption services will best meet the needs of kin, foster, and matched adoptive families?

A final concern is the considerable difference in family income across adoption types. Kin adopters typically have very low incomes. Although children adopted by relatives generally fare better than children in foster or matched adoptive families, adoption by relatives may reduce their life opportunities. These realities raise the logical question of whether subsidy determinations should consider the child's needs alone or should include, as one factor, the financial situation of the adopting family.

As is the case with so many aspects of postadoption services, research needs to better inform the preparation and support of different kinds of families who adopt waiting children. As foster care caseloads decline and the number of children adopted from the child welfare system continues to rise, considerably more research is in order to design postadoption services that fit the varying needs of children and families.

References

Illinois Department of Children and Family Services (2000). *Signs of progress in child welfare reform.* Springfield, IL: Author.

Pinderhughes, E. E. (1998). Short term placement outcomes for children adopted after age 5. *Children and Youth Services Review, 20*(3), 223–249.

Rosenthal, J. A., & Groze, V. (1992). *Special needs adoption: A study of intact families.* Westport, CT: Praeger.

U.S. Children's Bureau (2001). *The AFCARS report.* Washington, DC: Author.

Wulczyn. F. & Hislop, K. B. (2002). *Growth in the adoption population.* Washington, DC: U.S. Department of Health and Human Services.

Zill, N. (1990). *Behavior problem index based on parent report.* Washington, DC: Child Trends.

ADOPTION AND AFTER:
Adoptive Parents'
Service Needs

Trudy Festinger

There have been widespread changes in practices and attitudes toward the adoption of children in foster care in the United States. One of the more noticeable changes in recent years has been the increase in the number of such adoptions. According to federal estimates, the number of adoptions of children in out-of-home care between 1983 and 1995 remained quite flat, at between 17,000 and 20,000 each year (Maza, 2000). Since then, the numbers have risen considerably in response to various federal legislative initiatives, including most recently the Adoption Incentive Program of the Adoption and Safe Families Act of 1997. For fiscal year 1999, there were an estimated 46,000 children adopted from the public child welfare system nationwide (U.S. Children's Bureau, 2000). New York City began emphasizing the adoption of children in foster care prior to the latest federal initiative. There was a dramatic rise in the number of finalized adoptions between 1990—when 1,212 adoptions were finalized (New York State Department of Social Services, 1991)—and 1995, when 3,996 adoptions were finalized, a trend that continued through 1998 when the adoptions of 3,820 children in foster care were finalized (Festinger, 1996; Festinger, 1999).

With the increase in the number of adoptions, attention increasingly has focused on postadoption services as a support to prevent and ameliorate problems. Although much has been written regarding the likely need for such services after adoptions are finalized, there is scant systematic information that addresses this concern. This study addresses this gap in knowledge. Data were collected on the nature of service use and families' perceptions of their own service needs following adoption.

This study was made possible through a grant from the W.F. Kellogg Foundation to the New York City Administration for Children's Services. I am grateful to former Commissioner Nicholas Scoppetta, former Assistant Commissioner Jenny Czyrko, and Rachel Pratt for their support. Also, my sincere thanks to the ACS Subsidy Department for their help, as well as Jane Chapline and Renee Ford. Special thanks to Isabel Villegas and the staff of the project for their care, good work, and persistence, and to the many adoptive parents for their thoughtful contributions. Without them this project would not have been possible.

A Review of the Literature

The empirical literature* on postadoption services is quite sparse, yet dotted with a small group of adoptive parent surveys in various states, asking about their service needs, and, in some cases, their use of such services. Although yielding a great deal of information that is useful for planning purposes, many of these surveys suffer from low response rates. This problem raises questions about whether the service needs of parents who responded differed in some essential but unknown ways from the needs of families who were not reached or chose not to respond. Nonetheless, the following descriptions of several studies reflect the general nature of the findings.

In 1989, questionnaires were mailed to a random sample of 1,000 families who had adopted special needs children in Illinois (Walsh, 1991). Families were asked about service needs, use, and access, and families with more than one adopted child were asked to focus on "the child they believed had more problems and needed more services" (p. 5). The responses from 395 (40%) usable surveys showed that families' greatest needs were for special education (50%), medical services (35%), money, other than subsidy (33%), family counseling (30%), and after-school activities (30%). In each of these five service areas, the service use percentage was lower than the need percentage, thus showing a discrepancy between what these families felt they needed and the services they used during the preceding year.

In 1992 and 1993, adoption agency personnel in New York distributed questionnaires to parents at the time of adoption finalization (Avery, 1995). Usable responses were received from 258 parents, a 7.6% response rate. Over 80% were very or somewhat happy with the overall level of service they had received from agencies. When asked about support services for families after adoption, most families offered no suggestions. The 32% with suggestions spoke of various needs, including support groups, counseling, and ongoing training.

In 1993, questionnaires were mailed to 1,200 families who had adopted between 1987 and 1991 in Kentucky (Commonwealth of Kentucky, 1993). Among the 24% who responded, the four most used services and the proportion of families who had used these services were counseling for the child (50%), a contact person for help or advice (36%), family counseling (32%), and specialized therapy (26%). Services not used but needed included respite care, support groups, advocates, and recreational activities. The report noted that these "are, by and large, not 'professional' kinds of services being requested by parents" (p. 43).

---

*   This review was submitted in 2001. It therefore omits a number of writings on postadoption service needs that were not available at the time such as : Reilly, T. & Platz, L. (2004). Postadoption service needs of families with special needs children: Use, helpfulness, and unmet needs. Journal of Social Service Research, 30(4), 51-67; Freundlich, M. & Wright, L. (2003). Post-permanency services. Washington, DC: Casey Family Programs; Egbert, S. C. (2001). Parents' views of special needs adoption in Utah. Utah: University of Utah: Barth, R. P., Gibbs, D. A., & Siebnaler, K. (2001). Assessing the field of Post-adoption services: Family needs, program models, and evaluation issues. Washington, DC: U.S. Department of Health and Human Services.

A 1996 paper reported the results of 562 responses to a mail survey of adoptive families in Illinois, Oklahoma, and Iowa (Rosenthal, Groze, & Morgan, 1996). Many had adopted children with special needs through public agencies. The response rate varied by state, ranging from 49% to 76%. Beyond financial and medical subsidies, the largest percentage of families had received (possibly in the form of prefinalization services) medical and dental services (67%), educational assessment (47%), special education (42%), and counseling for the child (42%).

Families who did not receive a service were asked about their needs. Families most often listed support groups for children (52%), time with other adoptive families (49%) or other adopted children (48%), counseling (39%–52%) and social work service coordination (46%). The data show that in a number of areas, a lower proportion of families received the service than the percentage of families who felt that they needed that service.

Surveys by mail and telephone interviews were conducted with families 18 to 24 months after they had adopted children in state custody in 1995 in Kansas (McDonald, Propp, & Murphy, 2001). Of the families contacted, 159 parents participated, representing a 52% response rate. Although the focus was on adjustment to adoption, the research also produced some data on families' service needs from the time that their adopted children "had come to live with them" (p. 83). Overall satisfaction with the adoption process is reported, although satisfaction levels were lowest in connection with the adequacy of support services for adoptive families. Parents were presented with a 33-item checklist on service needs and use. Items needed by more than one-half of the parents concerned classroom, medical, financial, and legal needs. Because agencies in Kansas must "follow families who adopt for 18 months after adoption, providing them with needed services" (p. 90), it is not surprising that most needs were met. Most families reported no problems in accessing services. At the same time, many "indicated that more services and resources should be available to families" (p. 85).

In 1999, the Michigan Federation of Private Child and Family Agencies (1999) mailed roughly 2,000 surveys to families who had adopted from private agencies in Michigan within the preceding five years. Responses were received from 634 respondents (a response rate of 31.7%). Of these respondents, 41 % had adopted a child with special needs. Although a majority of the families had not used any of the services that the survey listed, psychological counseling, special education, and parent support groups were most frequently used by the parents, respectively cited by 28.2%, 24%, and 23.2%. Families generally were more likely to turn to informal systems of support than formal professional service systems. A summary of written comments concludes that families were sending a message regarding a "lack of postadoption services, lack of information about existing services, the inaccessibility of services and the need for a range of services" (p.11).

In 1999, questionnaires were mailed to a statewide random sample of adoptive families in Oregon (Fine, 2000). Of the 391 valid cases, 195 (50%) responses were received. When these families had adopted is not clear. In addition to the most frequently cited special education services, which were received by children in 43% of the families, the services that families most often listed as having received during the preceding year were individual counseling for a child (30%), respite care (17%), general support group (15%), and professional advice about rights or services (15%). Although 52% reported accessing none of the nine listed services, when they were asked about likely needs in the next 12 months, 69% viewed one or more services as important for their families.

Other articles on postadoption services, either based on professional experience or research, note the import of fostering support systems for adoptive families, including the use of parent groups, individual and family counseling, retreats, and help lines (Daly & Sobol, 1994; Hairston & Williams, 1989; Smith & Howard, 1999; Spencer, 1985; Zill, 1996). Some of these articles have highlighted respite services (Marcenko & Smith, 1991), the provision of concrete information via reading and electronic materials and skills training (Berry, 1997), and general case management services to help families connect to various resources (Ashton, 2000). Educational tutoring and special education has also been mentioned as a needed resource, especially when adopted children have special needs (Watson, 1992). One summary (Barth & Miller, 2000) grouped postadoption services into three categories: "(a) educational and informational, (b) clinical, and (c) material services" (p. 450). The availability of these services, however, has been questioned. One study (Barth, Berry, Goodfield, & Carson, 1987), for example, noted that nearly two-thirds of families claimed that agencies did not remain in contact with them.

In summary, the available data on postadoption service needs are limited, but growing. The survey data are scant and hobbled by response rate problems. Many do not address adoptions of children in out-of-home care. Much information on the need for these services has been based on the observations of caseworkers, and although some studies have asked adoptive parents what they see as their service needs and what services they have actually used, much remains to be understood about service needs and utilization after the finalization of adoption. This study is an attempt to provide such feedback.

Methods

This project was financially supported by a grant from the W.K. Kellogg Foundation to the New York City Administration for Children's Services (ACS) and was housed at ACS. A project manager was hired and a variety of management tools were developed, such as interview tracking sheets and telephone logs. An interview schedule was developed and piloted with the help of a few volunteer adoptive families. After changes were made, the interview was translated into Spanish. Six interviewers were hired and trained in June and July 2000. Interviews began on July 19, 2000, and continued through December 18, 2000. The following discussion describes the methods of the project: the population and sample selection, study procedures, and respondent/nonrespondent differences.

The Population and Sample

The population consisted of 3,074 children in out-of-home care who were adopted in New York City between January 1 and December 31, 1996 and who were residing at the time of the study in New York, New Jersey, or Connecticut. This list was based on information in the Child Care Review Service database (CCRS), a New York State child-tracking system. Using the Statistical Package for the Social Sciences (SPSS), random number generator, a 20% random sample of children was selected (n = 614). Nine of these children were excluded because they either had not been adopted (n = 3) or because three or four siblings in a family were randomly selected (n = 6). When two siblings in a family were randomly selected, both children were included in the study, but when three or four siblings were selected, the number was randomly reduced to two children, as the project staff felt that a parent might find completing the interview instrument on the telephone difficult with any more.

It was necessary to confirm the addresses and telephone numbers of the adoptive parents, because the contact information had been listed in CCRS in 1996—four years earlier. The project staff discovered that 89 children were living in states other than New York, New Jersey, or Connecticut, because their families moved after the adoption in 1996. These cases were excluded because the project focus was on adoptive families living in New York State and two adjacent states. Over time, the project staff also learned of 19 children whose adoptive parent had passed away since adoption finalization. Hence, the eligible sample of children—children whose parents were invited to participate in the interviews—consisted of 497 children. The project staff were able to interview the adoptive parents of 450 children (90.5%). The remaining refused to participate (2.5%) or could not found or contacted (2.2%) in spite of many attempts to locate them. Table 2-1 displays the eligible sample of 497 children, showing essentially no differences in study participation of kinship adoptive families and nonkin adoptive families.

Locating the Sample

The names, addresses, and total number of children adopted in 1996 were checked against card files and subsidy case records at ACS. Once correct addresses were established, letters signed by the assistant commissioner of adoption at ACS were sent to adoptive parents. The letter described the project purpose and sample selection and that the adoptive parent would receive a telephone call from project staff in a week or two. It promised complete protection of the family's privacy. The letter requested their cooperation and gave them the principal investigator's name and a telephone number to call if they had any questions. At most, two or three calls were received.

These letters were mailed out roughly over a three-month time period, with the number of letters mailed each week tied to interview staff availability. The goal was to ensure that the time interval between a letter's arrival and the interviewer's call was not too lengthy. Although addresses were available in card files and subsidy case records, telephone numbers were usually not available. The telephone numbers available from the 1996 CCRS files frequently were no longer correct. Project staff used telephone information services and directories and Internet searches in an attempt to find current telephone numbers. Unlisted numbers were a constant problem. When a telephone number could not be established but an address was verified (as was the case for families who received subsidy checks), the project staff sent additional letters asking the families to telephone us. Some families did telephone, but many did not. Staff called days and evenings, week days and weekends. When staff exhausted all alternatives in

TABLE 2–1

Eligible Sample of Children (N = 497)

OUTCOME	KIN		NONKIN		TOTAL	
	N	%	N	%	N	%
Interview	230	89.1	220	92.1	450	90.5
Nonresponse	13	5.0	9	3.8	22	4.4
Refusal	15	5.8	10	4.2	25	5.0
Total	258	100.0	239	100.0	497	100.0

their attempts to make contact directly with families, they sought out relatives who might give a message to the adoptive parents. The process was time-consuming and frequently frustrating, and it often involved many outreach efforts over time. Throughout, staff consulted with and supported one another. The average time between first call and actual interview was 16 days, the range starting from zero (when parents were interviewed on the same day they were called) to more than four months. One-fifth of the 405 parents were interviewed on the first day they were called, and almost 60% were reached and interviewed within seven days of the first call to them.

These extensive efforts to locate adoptive parents might suggest that families resisted participation. No doubt some families did avoid contact, but in a large majority of cases, families were very positive once staff reached them. Often, they spoke of not receiving the mailings. On further reflection, the mailings with official looking envelopes may not have captured their attention. In fact, at one point, the project staff bought colored (pink) envelopes in which they enclosed matching colored cards, return envelopes, and even creative artwork, asking adoptive parents to please send their telephone numbers. The project staff sent these to parents in those cases in which staff were completely stymied—unable to reach a parent or relative or locate a telephone number and lacking other available alternatives. The response was astonishing: Of the 45 families to whom pink cards sent, 33 (73.3%) responded.

The Telephone Interviews

The telephone interview instrument was devised over time. A core part of this instrument required developing a list of services and questions about each service to capture the needs of children and parents. In addition to a review of past studies of service use, there were many consultations with professionals and adoptive parents. The 26 services listed in the final instrument were the product of the thinking of many individuals. A major limiting factor in the content of the interview instrument was the need to keep it short so that it would not be too taxing on the phone, parents would cooperate, and the instrument could be completed in one interview. As a result, additional content beyond the questions about the 26 services had to be kept to bare essentials. The aim was to keep the time for completion to within 20 minutes, while providing adoptive parents with an opportunity to express their thinking. The average interview time was slightly over 23 minutes (with a median of 21 minutes). Of 448 interviews, interview time ranged from eight minutes to slightly over one hour.

The interview instrument and all letters were translated into Spanish. Letters to Latino families were sent out in both languages, and parents were asked their language preference at the time of the interviews. Of the 117 interviews about children in Latino homes, 57 (48.7%) were conducted in Spanish.

At the end of each interview parents were invited to add any comments they wished. There were occasions when a parent requested information about speaking with a caseworker or obtaining a service. Research staff provided relevant telephone numbers as requested and frequently mailed informational packets to parents about postadoption services.

Refusal and Nonresponse Groups

As shown in Table 2-1, the parents of 25 children (5%) refused to participate and it was not possible to make contact with the parents of 22 other children (4.4%) in spite of many attempts to do so. Many parents who refused to participate said they felt that what they had to say "would not do any good" because "the survey won't be taken seriously." Some parents felt that the survey was too personal, whereas others indicated that their adopted children were no longer in the home or stated that "I adopted a long time ago and just want to move on . . . and that's it." The parents of six children apologized, saying they felt too ill to complete an interview. All parents who refused to participate were asked whether they would be willing to answer several questions about the whereabouts and kinship status of the children they adopted in 1996, and all but one parent agreed to do so. In addition, the research staff searched CCRS and reviewed the subsidy files of all children of parents who refused to participate and all children of nonrespondents to learn of any changes in the number of children in these adoptive homes.

To determine whether the interviewed sample differed from the refusers and nonrespondents, the project staff examined many variables. The three groups were alike in terms of the adoptive parents' ethnicity, their level of formal education, and their adoption by either kin or nonkin. There also were no differences with respect to whether the parent adopted from ACS or from one of ACS's contract foster care agencies, nor were there differences in the number of children that the three groups adopted in 1996. The children of nonrespondents, however, were older at adoption (mean = 12.0 years) than the interview sample (mean = 8.1 years), and the mean age of children of the refusal group was between that of the other two groups (mean = 9.6 years). Also, adoptive parents in the refusal group were older at the time of adoption (mean = 57.7 years) than the interviewed group (mean = 50.7 years) and the nonrespondent group (mean = 47.1 years). Perhaps most noteworthy, in the refusal group (n = 25), 20% of the children were out of the home at the time of the interview, compared to 9.1% in the nonresponse group (n = 22) and 4.4% in the interviewed group (n = 450).

A key question was the status of sample children who were out of the home at the time of the interview. When this issue was examined, it became clear that when the refusal and nonresponse groups were considered together and compared to the interviewed group, proportionately more of the youths in the refuser and nonresponder group were living independently after reaching the age of majority or were living away from home with a sibling or other adoptive relative. More than half (57.2%) of the youth refuser and nonrespondent group were living in these situations, compared to 30% of the interviewed group. There may be some error in this regard, however, particularly with regard to the location of the 22 children in the nonresponse group. The staff did not speak with the adoptive parents of these children and relied instead on information in the subsidy files and records and information recorded in CCRS. Among the nonrespondents, therefore, an undercount of youths who were living independently or with another relative at the time of the study may exist. A foster care or other type of placement, however, probably was not missed because these placements would likely be recorded in CCRS or the subsidy case record.

In any event, a refusal to participate or a nonresponse from some families may have occurred because the adopted children were not in the home when the parents were contacted. If children were living independently or living with a relative, the adoptive parent may have felt that participation was less relevant.

Data Entry

Interview data were coded and entered into SPSS by three current or former New York University students. Data entry included ongoing intercoder reliability assessments. Over time, a total of 85 of the 450 interviews were independently entered twice. There were very few errors (only 10 cases had one or two), and whatever errors occurred were discussed with data entry personnel. Data analysis was completed using SPSS, using a two-tailed .05 criterion throughout.

Children in the Home

The following discussion focuses on the random sample of 450 children adopted in 1996 and the 405 adoptive parents (393 mothers, 12 fathers) who were interviewed. Background information about these families and their children is provided. The discussion then turns to central questions in this study: the services that adoptive families used and the services that adoptive parents felt they needed for their children and themselves after the adoption was finalized.

The 405 Homes

At the time of the interviews, 86.7% of the families were living in one of the five boroughs of New York City, and only 8.9% were living in Long Island, 5.2% in Westchester and upstate New York, and 1.2% in New Jersey. Roughly one-half of the adoptive parents were relatives (49.4%), with the majority being grandparents or aunts and uncles. The remaining parents were nonrelatives (50.6%). Most homes (84.4%) had been supervised by one of 59 contract agencies rather than by ACS (15.6%). As shown in Table 2-2, ACS supervised a larger proportion of kinship homes (25.5%) than nonkin homes (5.9%).

TABLE 2-2

Characteristics of Interviewed Families (N = 405)

	Kin (N=200)*	Nonkin (N=205)*	Total (N=405)*
% Supervised by ACS	25.5	5.9**	15.6
Age at interview (mean years)	56.2	53.8**	55.0
Age at adoption (mean years)	51.9	49.6**	50.8
% Black	72.0	55.1**	63.5
% Latino	21.0	32.7**	26.9
% White	5.0	9.8	7.4
Education (mean years)	11.0	11.9**	11.5
% High school or more	52.8	66.2**	59.6
% Ever married	78.9	84.9	81.9
% Married/with partner at interview	31.1	46.4**	38.9
% Employed	28.6	41.0**	34.9
Number of children adopted in 1996 (mean)	2.2	1.7**	2.0
% Living alone with children	41.4	30.2	35.7

* N's may vary slightly because of missing information

** p < .05

At the time of the interviews, the adoptive parents were, on average, 55 years old (their ages ranged from 30.7 to 80.9 years). At that time, kin were somewhat older on average (mean = 56.2 years) than nonkin (mean = 53.8 years), paralleling the difference in their ages at the time they adopted the children. A large majority of the families were black (63.5%) or Latino (26.9%), and smaller percentages were Caucasian (7.4%) or mixed heritage (2.2%). Kin were more likely to be black. Adoptive parents ranged in formal education from essentially none to having completed three years of graduate work, averaging 11.5 years of formal education. More than one-third (33.7%) had completed high school, and another 25.8% had completed at least some college. A higher proportion of nonkin (66.2%) than kin (52.8%) had completed high school or obtained additional formal education. Nearly 40% of the adoptive parents, both kin and nonkin, stated that they had received additional training, most commonly in such areas as computer work, office and clerical work, nursing and home health care, and cosmetology.

A majority of the adoptive parents (81.9%) had been married in the past. At the time of the interviews, a lower proportion (38.9%) were still married or living with a partner. Nonkin (46.4%) were more likely to be married or living with a partner than kin (31.1 %).

Adoptive parents also were asked whether they were currently employed and, if so, the nature of their employment. As shown in Table 2-2, nearly 35% were employed. Nonkin (41%) were more likely to be employed than kin (28.6%). For both nonkin and kin, employment was more likely to be full time (25.2%) than part time (9.7%). On the whole, a higher proportion of nonkin held professional or technical positions (32.1 %)

than kin (14.3%), whereas kin were more likely to be employed in the service sector (51.8%) than nonkin (38.1 %).

To roughly estimate personal income, a 50% random sample of parents (n = 202) was selected, and staff obtained, to the extent possible, information that had been used for subsidy determinations at the time of the families' adoptions. In light of agency variations in what was reported as income and how income was recorded, as well as the passage of some years, there were undoubtedly errors in this information. The data, however, can provide a rough picture of the financial situation of the adoptive parents. With regard to the 193 parents on whom information was available, the median annual gross income was $11,700, with income widely varying from less than $7,000 to more than $90,000. Nonkin annual gross income was higher on average (median = $17,000) than the income of kin (median = $8,000). Income sources were many and reflected the disparity between kin and nonkin. Proportionately more kin were dependent on public support, primarily public assistance or social security benefits, than were nonkin.

In 1996, the 405 parents had adopted 768 children—the 450 children in the sample and 318 other children who were, for the most part, these children's siblings. Slightly more than 75% of the parents adopted one (45.2%) or two (32.6%) children, and a small percentage adopted five or more (3.5%). Kin, on average, adopted more children in 1996 than nonkin. Because some families had adopted children earlier than 1996 and others after 1996, the number of adoptees in these homes was larger than the figure for 1996 would suggest. At the time of the interviews, there were from 2 to 13 people living in the households, with a median of five people (including both adults and children). On average, two adults were living in these households (including the adoptive parent), while ranging between one to seven adults. At the same time, 35.7% of these parents were living alone with their adoptive child or children.

Adoptive parents were asked whether they felt they had "many, some, a few, or no" friends or family if they needed to turn to others for help and social support. More than 40%, kin and nonkin alike, felt they had no one or just a few individuals to whom they could turn, including 7.7% who felt they had no one. In large measure, these individuals were not among the 35.7% who were living alone with their adoptive children. Thus, having other adults in the household did not shield many of these adoptive parents from feeling that they had little or no social support from friends or family. When asked about people or organizations in the community to whom they could turn for support, most adoptive parents felt they had no (28%) or only a few (35.1%) such supports.

The 450 Children

The random sample of 450 children adopted in 1996 included 45 sibling pairs who were selected for the interviews. As Table 2-3 shows, kin had adopted slightly more than one-half (51.1%) of the children and nonkin slightly less one-half (48.1%).

At the time of the interviews, the 450 children were, on average, 12.3 years old, with ages ranging from 5.2 to 23.8 years. Almost 22% were under age 9, and another 22.2% were age 15 or older. As Table 2-3 shows, children adopted by kin were older on average (mean = 13.3 years) than children adopted by nonkin (mean = 11.3 years).

TABLE 2–3

Characteristics of the Adopted Children (N=450)

	KIN (N=230)*	NONKIN (N=220)*	TOTAL (N=450)*
Age at interview (mean years)	13.3	11.3**	12.3
Age at adoption (mean years)	9.0	7.1**	8.1
At adoption: time in the adoptive home (mean years)	5.6	4.4**	5.0
Age at adoptive home placement (mean years)	3.4	2.6**	3.0
Age at entry into foster care (mean years)	2.5	1.2**	1.8
% adopted as sibling group	67.8	50.5**	59.3
% With 1+ moderate/severe problem	37.0	49.1**	42.9

* N's may vary slightly because of missing information

** $p < .05$

Because the children all were adopted in 1996, their ages at adoption parallel these differences. They were, on average, 8.1 years old at the time of adoption, with an age range from 1.2 to 19.8 years. Children in kinship homes were, at the time of adoption, 9 years old on average, compared to 7.1 years for children in nonkin homes. At the time they were adopted, most children had been with their adoptive families for some time—an average of five years, with range between 6 months to 10.2 years. Children adopted by relatives had been with their adoptive families for a longer period of time (mean = 5.6 years) than children in nonkin homes (mean = 4.4 years). At the time that children were placed with the families who eventually adopted them, they were on average 3 years old. One-half of the children were 1.7 years old or younger. As Table 2-3 shows, children in kinship homes were, on average, older at the time of the adoptive placement (mean = 3.4 years) than children adopted by nonkin (mean = 2.6 years). Children adopted by kin ranged in age from a few days old to 14 years at the time that they were initially placed. One-half of those children were 4 months or younger at the initial placement. Children adopted by kin also were on average older when they entered foster care (mean = 2.5 years) than children adopted by nonkin (mean = 1.2 years).

For a large majority of the children (92.2%), the entry into care resulting in their adoptions was their only spell in care. For 35 children (7.8%), the initial entry was the first of two, three, or four entries, and as would be expected, with each reentry into foster care, their average age at time of placement with the family who eventually adopted them increased. Children with one spell were, on average, 2.8 years old at the time of placement with the families who would adopt them; children with two spells (n = 29), 4.8 years old; and children with three or more spells (n = 6), 8.2 years old.

At the time of their adoption in 1996, most of the 450 children (59.3%) were adopted along with two to six of their siblings rather than as single children (40.7%). As Table 2-3 shows, adoption with siblings was more likely for children adopted by kin than nonkin.

Adoptive parents were presented with six problem areas that may affect their children: physical health problem, physical handicap, neurological problem, learning disability, emotional problem, and behavioral problem. They were asked whether their child had had a problem in each area since the adoption in 1996, and, if so, whether they considered the problem to be "mild," "moderate," or "severe." They also were asked about any other problems exhibited by the child selected for the sample. When all problem areas were taken together, 69.6% of the children were considered to have one or more "mild" to "severe" problems, including 42.9% of whom were described as having one or more "moderate" or "severe" problems. It was more likely that children adopted by nonkin (49.1%) than by kin (37%) were described as having one or more "moderate" or "severe" problems (Table 2-3).

The following percentages of children were described as having one or more problems in each of the six listed areas: health problems (23.8%), physical handicap (6.7%), neurological problems (10.2%), learning disability (36.7%), emotional problems (33.6%), and behavioral problems (40.4%). In addition, 1.3% of the children were described as having another issue, such as mental retardation or a speech problem like stuttering. A child's age at adoption or the time of the interview was not associated with the number of problems, nor was there any association between age and specific problem areas, with the exception of emotional problems. Older children were more likely to be rated as exhibiting emotional problems in the years since their adoptions. Emotional problems were reported for 39.2% of children ages 12 or older at the time of the interview, compared to 28.1% of children under 12. In the age 15-and-older group, a higher proportion (17%) was thought to have severe emotional problems than those who were younger (6%). Behavioral problems, on the other hand, were not associated with age. For example, 41.9% of children ages 12 or older at the time of the interview, compared to 39% of the under-12 group, were described as exhibiting behavioral problems since their adoptions.

Contact with the Agency of Adoption

Adoptive parents were asked to think back to the first six months following their adoption of a particular child and to recall whether they had any contact with the agency that arranged the adoption. The parents of only 22.9% (n = 103) of the 450 children recalled some contact. When asked about the amount of contact during those first six months, 100 parents were able to recall the extent. The reports of contact can be roughly classified into three groupings. About 37% of the parents recalled that contact occurred once a month or more frequently. In the case of several of the children, the parents reported that the contact with the agency had extended over a year. A second group, consisting of roughly 39%, stated that they had had between two to four contacts with the agency during the first six months following the adoption. Finally, close to one-quarter mentioned recalling only one contact during the first six months following the adoption. This group included parents who spoke of only "one contact during the first year" and parents who mentioned that the only contact was a letter (which, in some cases, was described as mentioning postadoption services). The last group also included a number of adoptive parents who spoke warmly about receiving, at an earlier point in time, written invitations to various social events such as picnics or holiday parties. As one adoptive mother wistfully remarked, however, "The invitations stopped...they don't want to talk to us and we miss that."

Services Received and Services Needed Following Adoption

In view of the large proportion of children who were thought to have one or more problems, it was not surprising that the adoptive families spoke of their needs for many kinds of services and supports.

To capture whether they or their adopted child needed or were provided various services, the survey presented adoptive parents with 26 services or supports and posed a series of questions with respect to each service. Adoptive parents were asked whether or not a particular service or support was provided to them or their child during the four years since they adopted that child. If a particular service had not been provided, they were asked whether it was something they or their child needed or could have used. If the answer was affirmative, adoptive parents were asked how much the service was needed: a little, some, or a lot.

It is important to emphasize that the survey questions did not assess sufficiency, that is, whether "enough" of a service was provided. The survey also did not address the extent to which adoptive parents received various services or supports from many different organizations in the community that may have related to adoption agency services. Finally, it is important to note that some adoptive parents took issue with the word "provided" and quickly pointed out that "nothing was provided...I found out where to go and got it myself" or "it wasn't provided...I paid for it myself."

Table 2-4 lists the 26 services and supports and indicated whether adoptive parents stated that these services and supports were provided, not provided but needed, or not needed. The three most commonly provided services (i.e., identified by the largest proportion of adoptive parents) were medical services (49.3%), special education programs (32.4%), and information about after-school activities (32.2%). The three needs that adoptive parents judged to be most "unmet" (not provided, yet needed) were a telephone hotline (57.1%), information about summer activities (52.2%), and tutoring help (51.3%).

In addition to questions about the services listed in Table 2-4, adoptive parents also were asked whether there were any other services they could have used since adoption. About 10% of the adoptive parents mentioned services that fell within three principal areas: (1) the need to increase subsidy payments as children become older (with some adoptive parents asking about the possibility of a clothing allowance for children), (2) the need for more background information about their child's birthfamily history, and (3) their wish for more follow-up contacts from the adoption agency.

The list of 26 services and supports included overlapping or related domains. As an example, a number of items concerned informational needs and other items addressed after-school needs. To better understand parents' needs with respect to the roster of 26 services, the research staff grouped the services into eight domains, or service clusters, which will be discussed shortly. The total picture with regard to services and supports, however, is presented first.

When the 26 services and supports are considered as a whole, the adoptive parents said that since their adoptions in 1996, they had used from 0 to 20 services for themselves or their adopted children, with a median of 3 services. With services needed but not provided, the adoptive parents' needs ranged from 0 to 24 services, with a median of 8

TABLE 2-4

Individual Services and Supports Provided and Needed

Interview Items*	Provided %	Not Provided		Total Number
		Needed %	Not Needed %	
a. Information about services available	30.7	46.4	22.9	450
b. Assistance connecting to services	21.4	45.0	33.6	449
c. Help with transportation to services	13.1	40.0	46.9	450
d. Individual or family counseling	22.3	32.3	45.4	449
e. Medical services (beyond ordinary well-child care)	49.3	12.0	38.7	450
f. Child guidance and mental health services	26.0	30.9	43.1	450
g. Help for alcohol or drug use exposure	4.4	6.2	89.3	450
h. Information about after-school activities	32.2	48.7	19.1	450
i. Information about summer activities	31.1	52.2	16.7	450
j. Parenting education or training	23.4	20.5	56.1	449
k. Homemaker assistance	2.2	31.3	66.4	450
l. Vocational/employment training	3.3	25.6	71.1	450
m. Housing assistance	6.4	28.4	65.1	450
n. Legal assistance (excluding adoption)	6.4	16.7	76.9	450
o. Names of other adoptive parents to call about adoption issues	12.0	31.3	56.7	450
p. Information about adoptive parent group to meet with	19.1	38.7	42.2	450
q. Information about a group of adopted children	6.7	39.8	53.6	450
r. Parent aides at home now and then, for rest	2.4	45.8	51.8	450
s. Someone/place to leave child now and then—respite	6.9	39.8	53.3	450
t. Someone to help with crises	12.9	34.4	52.7	450
u. A mentoring program	5.6	45.0	49.4	449
v. Handicap aids (hearing, wheelchair, etc)	1.3	2.2	96.4	450
w. Special education programs	32.4	15.8	51.8	450
x. Day care or after-school care	20.4	32.4	47.1	450
y. Tutoring for child	15.3	51.3	33.3	450
z. Telephone hotline for information about services, etc.	14.4	57.1	28.4	450

* Not always exact wording in order to conserve space. Also, in a number of items the child's name was mentioned.

services. On the assumption that service use or provision meant there was a need, the number of total needs was calculated. This calculation yielded a median of 13 needs, with the number ranging from 0 to 25 total service needs during the four years (Table 2-5).

An analysis was completed of factors associated with the total number of service needs. Although many characteristics of the children and their adoptive parents were examined, only a few characteristics proved to be significant. Factors that were not

TABLE 2–5

Services Provided and Services Needed (N= 450)

	MEDIAN	MEAN	STANDARD DEVIATION	RANGE
Services provided	3.0	4.22	3.71	0-20
Services not provided, but needed	8.0	8.69	6.06	0-24
Total services needed	13.0	12.91	5.59	0-25

related included the ages of the children at the time of the interviews or adoption, their gender, whether the placement was with kin or nonkin, and whether the agency that had arranged the adoption was ACS or a private contract agency. On the other hand, the number of children's problems, regardless of whether they were considered mild, moderate, or severe, was associated with the number of total services needed ($r = .39$). When parents who perceived their children as having no particular problem with respect to health, learning, or behavior reported that their children needed fewer services (mean = 10.8) than parents who perceived their children as exhibiting problems (mean = 13.9).

Higher total service needs were, on average, voiced by parents who identified themselves as black (mean = 13.8), compared to those who identified themselves as Latino (mean = 10.7). This difference may be related to the fact that black parents, on average, had adopted more children in 1996 than Latino parents. A higher number of adopted children was associated, although weakly, with more service needs ($r = .15$). Viewed somewhat differently, parents who adopted sibling groups spoke of more needs, on average, than parents who adopted one child in 1996. In addition, black parents, on average, had more formal education than Latino parents, and higher education was associated with the identification of more service needs ($r = .22$).

Finally, there was a weak negative relationship between parents' age at the time of the interview and the number of total services needed ($r = -.12$). Older parents voiced fewer service needs than younger parents.

Five factors—number of perceived children's problems, number of adopted children, self-identification as black as opposed to Latino, level of education, and age of adoptive parent—were included in a multiple regression analysis to assess which factors, if any, were independent predictors of the total number of service needs. Four factors independently contributed toward an explanation of the total number of services needed ($F = 25.19$, $p < .000$). They were in order of importance: higher number of problems, self-identification as black rather than Latino, greater number of children adopted in 1996, and higher level of education. These four factors accounted for 26% of the variance of total services needed ($R^2 = .260$).

Service Clusters and Total Needs

To better understand all of the needs and to reduce the 26 services to more manageable dimensions, a series of service clusters was created based on an examination of intercorrelations and a review of relevant literature (Brooks, Allen, & Barth, 2000; Staudt,

1999; Stroul & Friedman, 1986). Each item was given one point if the service was provided since adoption or, if not provided, was needed. Items within each cluster were summated so that each child's case had a score according to the number of items endorsed. Six service clusters were created, leaving three items that did not link together with other service need items: vocational services, housing assistance, and legal assistance. The six service clusters and three individual items are shown in Table 2-6 (with letter references to the services listed in Table 2-4). Table 2-6 also presents the proportion of parents who said they needed one or more of the items that comprised each cluster.

The six service clusters should be viewed as rough indicators only. The makeup of each item cluster, although not arbitrary, is not definitive, and items within each item cluster are not necessarily substantively equivalent. Furthermore, as Table 2-6 indicates, the clusters consist of different item totals and, therefore, are not comparable. To address this problem, average (mean) scores were calculated so that it was possible to compare the clusters. The mean score for each cluster ranged from 0 to 1, with higher mean scores signifying that a higher average number of items in the cluster were rated as needed since adoption. When a parent stated that more items in a service cluster were needed, the need may have been greater for that set of services or supports. Nonetheless, caution should be taken in interpreting these data.

After-school service

These services (consisting of after-school activities, summer activities, mentoring needs, and day care or after-school care) ranked relatively high. On a scale of zero to one, adoptive parents reported, on average, that .67 of the four items was needed since they adopted in 1996. Nearly 93% of the parents stated that one or more of the four items was needed since 1996. These 93% needed 2.9 items on average within the four-item after-school service cluster. Many parents needed information about activities for children when they were not in school, and some parents needed mentoring services for their children. The need for this set of services was more frequently endorsed for children whose adoptive parents identified themselves as black rather than Latino, parents with higher formal education, and parents who were younger at the time of the interview (and who were also more likely to be employed). The need for these services also was greater for children rated as having emotional problems, children adopted as a sibling group, and children whose parents were currently not married or living with a partner. A multiple regression analysis showed that all of these factors, with the exception of parent education, were significant predictors, but they accounted for only 14.9% of the variance ($R^2 = .149$) in the need for after-school services.

Informational services

This service cluster consisted of seven needs for information, including the need for information via a hotline, information through parenting education or an adoptive parent group, and information that specifically addresses available services or service connections. On average, .58 of the seven items were considered needed. Because of multiple items in this cluster, it was more likely that a parent would endorse one or another item, and as a result, 94.2% of parents unsurprisingly stated that at least one of the items was

TABLE 2–6

Service Clusters and Needs (Means) (N = 450)

SERVICE CLUSTERS	% NEEDED ONE OR MORE SERVICES	MEAN ITEMS NEEDED	STANDARD DEVIATION
After-school services: h, i, u, x	92.7	.67	.30
Informational services: a, b, j, o, p, q, z	94.2	.58	.29
Educational services: w, y	77.8	.57	.38
Home assistance: c, k, r, s	76.0	.45	.35
Clinical services: d, f, g, t	77.3	.42	.31
Health services: e, v	62.0	.32	.27
Housing assistance: m	34.9	.35	.48
Vocational services: 1	28.9	.29	.45
Legal assistance (not adoption): n	23.1	.23	.42

needed, including 62.7% who endorsed four or more of these items. The need for informational services was more frequently endorsed by parents of children who had more problems, parents with more formal education, younger parents, parents who felt they had more community support (and who were apt to be more educated and younger), and parents who identified themselves as black rather than Latino. A multiple regression analysis showed that these five factors accounted for 19.3% of the variance (R^2 = .193), with the number of child problems, parents' higher formal education level, and self-identification as black as the three significant predictors of the need for informational services.

Educational services

This service cluster consisted of two items: a need for tutoring and for special education programs. On average, .57 items were considered needed. More than three-quarters of the parents (77.8%) stated that they needed at least one of the items since 1996, for an average endorsement of 1.5 items. A higher cluster score, not surprisingly, was associated with adoptive parents' rating of their child as having a mild, moderate, or severe learning disability. A higher cluster score also was found for males. Finally, parents with higher educational levels, younger parents, and parents who identified themselves as black as opposed to Latino had higher cluster scores. A multiple regression analysis showed that these five factors accounted for 25.5% of the variance (R^2 = .255). A learning disability and self-identification as black were the only significant predictors of the need for educational services.

Home assistance

These services consisted of assistance with transportation to services, homemaker assistance, parent aid services, and respite care. On a zero to one scale, parents considered an average of .45 of the four items as needed since 1996. Slightly more than three-quarters (76%) of the adoptive parents stated that one or more of these services were needed since they adopted. This group of parents needed 2.4 items on average. Parents with children rated as having more problems, parents who adopted more children in 1996, parents who identified themselves as black rather than Latino, and parents with more formal education more frequently endorsed the need for this cluster of services. A multiple regression analysis showed that these four factors accounted for 18.4% of the variance ($R^2 = .184$). All of the factors with the exception of parents' educational level were significant predictors of the need for home assistance.

Clinical services

This service cluster included four items: individual or family counseling, child guidance and mental health services, help for alcohol or drug use exposure, and "someone to help with crises." On average, .42 of these items were considered needed. More than three-fourths (77.3%) of the parents felt that they needed one or more of these services, including 31% who endorsed three or four items. Those parents who expressed needs in this area reported that they needed, on average, 2.2 items of the four services in this service cluster. A higher cluster score was, not surprisingly, related to more child problems ($r = .40$), a child's older age at the time of the interview, a sibling group placement, parents' self-identification as black rather than Latino, and parents' higher formal education. A multiple regression showed that these five factors accounted for 22.9% of the variance ($R^2 = .229$). Four of these factors (all but sibling group placement) were significant predictors of a need for clinical services.

Health services

This service cluster consisted of two items: the need for medical services beyond routine care and handicap aids. On average, .32 of these items was selected as having been needed since 1996. Slightly more than three-fifths (62%) of the parents selected one or both of the items, and this group of parents needed one of the services in this cluster, on average. A higher cluster score was associated with only one factor, a higher number of child problems. This factor accounted for only 6.5% of the variance but was a significant predictor of a need for medical services.

Housing assistance

This item was selected as needed by 35% of the parents. Kin, currently unmarried parents, and parents who adopted more children were more apt to feel they needed housing assistance than nonkin, married parents, and parents who had adopted fewer children. These factors accounted for only 5.9% of the variance. Kinship status and current nonmarried status were significantly related to a need for assistance with housing. Income information was available on a 50% random selection of cases, but because of this lower number of cases, income was not included in the regression analysis just reported. Income, however, was inversely related to the need for housing assistance ($r = -.23$). Parents with lower income were more likely to say they needed housing assistance than those with higher incomes.

Vocational or employment training

Nearly 29% of the parents endorsed this item as a need. Parents who were younger, identified themselves as black or Latino as opposed to Caucasian, and who stated that their children had emotional problems were more likely to endorse a need for vocational or employment training. Two of these factors—parent's age and parent's ethnicity–were significant predictors of a need for vocation or employment training, but these factors only accounted for 5.4% of the variance.

Legal assistance

Slightly less than one-fourth (23.1%) of the parents endorsed the need for this service. Legal assistance was more apt to be selected if children had more moderate or severe problems, if children were older at the time of adoption, and if parents identified themselves as black rather than Latino. These three factors together, however, only accounted for 7.6% of the variance, but all were significant predictors of parents' needs for legal services.

Summary of Factors Related to Needs

As these findings make clear, many characteristics of the parents and the children were not associated with particular needs or were associated with only with one cluster of needs. For example, kinship and nonkinship status, the type of agency that arranged the adoption (ACS or a contract agency), the ages of children at various points in time along the road to adoption, and children's gender were essentially unrelated to the various groupings of need. In fact, most of the associations with various need clusters concerned only a few factors: the number of perceived child problems in general or a particular child's problem, such as a learning disability; the ethnicity and age of the parent; the parent's educational level; and whether the adoption was of a sibling group. Two factors, essentially, stand out: ethnicity and parents' assessment of children's problems.

With respect to ethnicity, Latino parents, when compared to black parents, voiced fewer needs overall, and they especially voiced fewer unmet needs. This difference in number of needs between Latino and black families was considerable and appeared again and again within the various needs clusters. The Caucasian group was small, and on the whole, their average needs either hovered between, or were lower than, the average needs of black and Latino parents. There were no significant differences between Caucasian parents and parents of other ethnicities, except in the one instance of vocational or employment service needs, where both black and Latino parents voiced more needs than Caucasian parents.

The observed difference in needs between black and Latino parents with respect to their adopted children could have been a function of the backgrounds of the interviewers. Spanish-speaking interviewers conducted about one-half of the interviews with Latino parents. These parents, more than one-half of whom had eight years or less of formal schooling, spoke about fewer unmet needs than Latino parents who chose to be interviewed in English. Both groups, however, whether interviewed in Spanish or English, differed from black adoptive parents in that they endorsed a lower number of total or unmet needs. Because the difference between black and Latino parents regarding their children's needs is evident across the board, it seems clear that the difference is not a function of particular interviewers.

Another possible explanation for Latino parents' voicing of fewer service needs is that they had significantly less formal education than black parents. Alternatively, Latino parents may have had fewer needs because they had adopted fewer children in 1996 than black parents. Nonetheless, in many other aspects related to the need clusters, the two groups of parents were alike. Black and Latino parents were, on average, the same age at the time of the interviews and voiced the same number of child problems. Their adoptive children were, on average, similar in age at the time of adoption and the interviews. Furthermore, roughly the same proportion of black and Latino parents spoke about experiencing barriers to obtaining services. A lower proportion of Latino parents, however, were kin, and their average income was lower when compared to black parents. Neither of these factors, however, was related to the number of needs that the parents identified.

It seems unlikely that the service needs of Latino parents and children were fewer than the needs of black parents and their children. Either Latino parents were more reticent about expressing themselves, or they did not always recognize or acknowledge service needs because of a diminished sense that services were important or useful. Alternatively, Latino parents may have been more apt to feel that taking care of things themselves was important, or they may have placed greater reliance on alternative, nonformal help providers. Finally, Latino parents may have feared that voicing needs would cause them to be judged as less than adequate parents. In any event, the observed difference is in line with the observations of others who have identified a tendency among Latinos to underutilize some services (Burnette, 1999; Rodriguez, 1987; Rogler, Cooney, Costantino, Earley, Grossman, Gurak, Malgady, & Rodriguez, 1983).

With respect to the number of children's problems, parents rated almost 70% of the children as having one or more. Parents reached out for services in seven out of the nine service clusters. Only the areas of housing assistance and vocational or employment training were found to be unrelated to children's problems.

In each of the service clusters, as well as in the overall number of needs, a majority of the variance remains unexplained. Clearly, many factors determining these parents' needs were not tapped by this study.

Unmet Needs

In addition to asking adoptive parents whether each of 26 services or supports was provided since they adopted, the survey asked if a service was not provided, whether the service was needed, and, if so, whether the service was needed "a little," "some," or "a lot." Table 2-7 presents the services within each cluster according to how many of the sample of 450 (or occasionally 449 if a parent could not remember) had not been provided a particular service. It then shows the proportion of who said that each service was "not needed," "needed a little," "needed some," or "needed a lot." The parents of 305 of the 450 children, for example, said that information about after-school activities was not provided, and 63.6% of these parents felt they needed such information "some" or "a lot." In all instances, the combination of "not needed" and "needed a little" consisted mostly of parents who stated that they did not need that service, whereas in the "some" and "a lot" combination, most parents endorsed "a lot" of need.

The highest unmet needs concerned information about after-school and summer activities, tutoring help, information about available services, and a telephone hotline that provides information. More than 50% of the parents who said these services had not

TABLE 2-7

Areas of Expressed Unmet Needs

Interview Items*	Not Provided N	Amount Needed	
		Not or a Little %	Some or a Lot %
After-School Services			
h. Information about after school activities	305	36.4	63.6
i. Information about summer activities	310	33.6	66.4
u. A mentoring program	424	63.7	36.3
x. Day care or after-school care	358	63.4	36.6
Educational Services			
w. Special education programs	304	79.9	20.0
y. Tutoring for child	381	46.7	53.3
Informational Services			
a. Information about services available	312	45.8	54.2
b. Assistance connecting to services	353	55.8	44.2
j. Parenting education or training	344	82.3	17.7
o. Names of other adoptive parents to call about issues	396	74.5	25.5
p. Information about adoptive parent group to meet with	364	66.8	33.2
q. Information about a group of adopted children	420	69.8	30.2
z. Telephone hotline for information about services, etc.	385	48.6	51.4
Home Assistance			
c. Help with transportation to services	391	62.2	37.8
k. Homemaker assistance	440	76.9	23.1
r. Parent aides at home now and then	439	62.7	37.3
s. Someone/place to leave child now and then—respite	419	65.4	34.6
Clinical Services			
d. Individual or family counseling	349	70.2	29.8
f. Child guidance and mental health services	333	70.0	30.0
g. Help for alcohol or drug use exposure	430	95.3	4.7
t. Someone to help with crises	393	71.0	29.0
Health Services			
e. Medical services (beyond ordinary well-child care)	228	81.6	18.4
v. Handicap aids (hearing, wheelchair, etc.)	444	98.4	1.6
Housing Assistance			
m. Housing assistance	421	73.4	26.6
Vocational Services			
l. Vocational/employment training	435	78.6	21.4
Legal Assistance			
n. Legal assistance (excluding adoption)	421	87.4	12.6

* Not always exact wording in order to conserve space.

been provided reported that each of the services was needed "some" or "a lot." Assistance in connecting to services was mentioned by 44%, various home aides and respite arrangements were endorsed by roughly 36%, and counseling services were needed by roughly 30% of parents who had not been provided these services since they adopted.

Continuing Services Following Adoption

Adoptive parents were asked to recall a time before they adopted the child in 1996 (a time when the majority were the children's foster parents), and state whether there were any services they received at that time that they continued to receive after they adopted the child. Parents for 39 of the children (8.7%) said that after they adopted, they continued to receive some services. The primary services that they listed were counseling or therapy. Some parents, however, also listed medical services, supplemental income, some educational services, and help with transportation.

Adoptive parents also were asked whether there were services they had received prior to adoption that they no longer received after they adopted. Parents for over one-fourth (27.1 %) of the children chose to comment and identified many such services. The most frequently mentioned services were counseling and psychotherapy, tutoring services, funds to help with babysitters and daycare, money for food and clothing, summer camp and trips, caseworker visits that provided support and information, parenting training and support groups, and agency medical services and visiting nurses. When asked whether, at the time of adoption, they were given information about available services in the community that they might wish to use, only 16% recalled having been given such information.

Barriers to Obtaining Services

Parents were asked whether they encountered any problems or barriers to obtaining services that they needed for the child that they adopted in 1996. The parents of over one-fourth (26.7%) of the children identified barriers to obtaining services. These parents had many more unmet needs (mean = 12.4) than parents who did not identify service barriers (mean = 7.4). When asked to specify the main barriers, parents most frequently mentioned lack of information about where to find needed services and the cost of services. These two factors also were among the most frequently mentioned barriers in a survey of 121 parents of children and youth with emotional and behavioral disorders (Soderland, Epstein, Quinn, Cumblad, & Petersen, 1995), and informational barriers were highly ranked in a study of service use by 101 parents after they received intensive family preservation services (Staudt, 1999).

In speaking about the lack of information, parents often stated, "I didn't know where to go" and "I didn't know how to get information about where to go." With respect to cost, they referenced the costs of tutoring, the charges for summer camp, and their own lack of funds to pay for these services. In this regard, a number of parents also mentioned Medicaid limits that interfered with their child's continued counseling.

The Parents Speak

At the end of the interview, parents were invited to add anything they wished. Roughly one-third chose to comment, some quite extensively. A number of parents focused on their need for information. The most common request was for information on parent support groups, mentoring for the children, and counseling services. There also were requests for information on subsidy rates and Medicaid, and a few parents requested assistance regarding financial aid for dental care and school-related costs (tutoring, tuition, books, various after-school programs, and college aid). Other parents sought information on how to locate a larger place to live or a home in a different neighborhood. There also were diverse requests for adoption-related information. Many parents sought information on books that provide parents with guidance on how to discuss adoption with their children. Others needed help in understanding how to gain access to medical history in birthfamily files, how to reach a child's birthfamily, how to obtain replacements for lost or destroyed adoption documents, the legal steps that are required to return a child to his or her birthmother, and how to ensure that children remain in the adoptive family if the adoptive parent becomes incapacitated or passes away.

A number of themes emerged again and again. Many parents spoke about needing much better preparation regarding "the difficulties we may encounter as the children grow up," the problems associated with "not getting the full story" about the children, and the import of being "provided more information about the child's background…the biological family's physical and mental health, and incidents of abuse by the birthparents or foster parents." With regard to their children's problems, parents made comments such as, "what are the possible outcomes from the drugs in his system…no one prepared us for this," and "I knew there were no guarantees but didn't know the potential for so many problems." Some parents spoke philosophically: "one can't erase what's already there, so one just tries to better their lives however one can." Other parents, however, expressed far more frustration, as evidenced by statements that "agencies hide some information" and "I feel that I was lied to… that I didn't get the truth about the children's backgrounds."

Some parents spoke of feeling quite cut off and helpless once they adopted, stating "after adopting, it's like having your medicine taken away overnight," "once we adopted, nobody cared anymore and we felt somewhat abandoned," and "after you adopt you hear nothing from the agency…I know the children are my responsibility but I would just like somebody to talk to." Other parents lamented, "it would be nice if someone cared and it would be nice if there was someone to call just to get information," "it would be nice if they followed up with the children after adoption," and "it's hard to be an adoptive parent…we need moral support." On the positive side, a few parents stated, "I'd love it if the agency contacted me because I'd like to show how well the boys are doing."

A few parents felt that assistance was not needed, stating that they preferred "to do these things on my own" and asked "why should an adopted child get something because he's adopted when a nonadopted child does not?" Other parents were concerned about their children being singled out, noting that teachers may label children who are adopted, that there is a stigma associated with being adopted, and that children may be labeled as having "special needs."

There were concerns about subsidy. Parents commented, for example, that "it should be increased since it has stayed the same for five years" and "as kids get older, the subsidy should increase" because the expenses are higher. With regard to financial concerns, several suggested that because "school lunches are very expensive," a reduction in cost should be considered. There also were concerns about Medicaid coverage for children with multiple physical problems. One mother noted, "my child has very bad asthma, a hole in his heart, and eczema...and I've received a letter that [says] I've taken him to the doctor too many times and they won't cover it all."

Parents also complained about difficulties in reaching their assigned caseworkers in the ACS Auxiliary Department, which handles subsidy records. Parents stated, "I wish it was easier to get in touch with someone at ACS...you don't get to talk to a person, so you have to trust someone to call you back," "no one ever returns my messages," and "I have six phone numbers, but no one answers the phone."

A handful of remarks addressed miscellaneous topics. Some parents, for example, felt "the adoption process took too long." With respect to kinship adoption, one parent noted that it was difficult to know how "to cope with situations that arise when the biological parent whose rights were terminated is still around" and that support would have been helpful. Another parent stated, "It's hard for me to be the mother, father, and grandmother." Finally, there were comments about parents' strong attachment to their adopted children. As one parent summarized, "we love them like there's no tomorrow."

Study Limitations

This study has an obvious geographic limitation because it is based on the experiences of adoptive families and children who had been adopted in New York City. At the time of the interviews, most of the parents were still living in New York City or its immediate environs. The study, however, has a number of additional limitations. Telephone interviews are inherently limited because they must be relatively short and, therefore, many areas of interest must be omitted. At the same time, however, telephone interviews made a very high response rate (90.5%) possible—a rate that otherwise would have been very difficult and costly to attain. Furthermore, much of the data consist of self-reports, which can be both a limitation and an advantage. The project staff wanted to hear the perspective of adoptive parents; what service providers might have said about the needs of these same children and families is not known. With regard to the parents' assessments, it is possible, for instance, that parents overassessed the problems of their children, possibly reflecting a labeling bias (Barth & Miller, 2000) or a heightened alertness that led them to identify problems. Yet, children's problems clearly existed. These children received subsidies based on documented special needs, many of which involved medical, emotional, behavioral, and other problems. Even if some bias existed, adoptive parents perceived that a majority of the children had one or more problems, and that reality for adoptive parents created distress for them as they watched their children develop.

Another problem concerns the possible stimulation of need; that is, the number of services needed may be somewhat exaggerated and it will not be clear by how much. Exposing families to 26 services is a bit like placing individuals in front of a candy counter and asking them what they have had and what they would like to have. At the same time, the parents in this study did not select all 26 services as needed. In fact, more than 20% stated that they needed two or fewer services, and some chose none. The stimulation factor, nonetheless, is a potential limitation, and for that reason, it makes particular sense to focus more heavily on areas or clusters of need than on 26 individual services.

In addition, to capture total need in a specific service area (e.g., a child's need for tutoring), the study assumed that if a parent stated a service was used or provided since finalization, there was a need for that service. Of course, parents possibly reported that they used or were provided a service in one area when the service need was elsewhere. If, however, the project staff had not counted the services provided as needed, other problems would have arisen. The result may have been a serious undercount of needed services.

A further limitation concerns what parents were asked. Parents were questioned about children's needs since the parents adopted, but needs clearly vary over time. As a result, the responses to the questions that were posed to parents resulted in an amalgam—a mixture of needs across time. These data cannot portray the nuances of changing needs with the passage of time since the day of adoption.

Conclusions

The postadoption period confronted many families with challenges, struggles, and many unmet needs. Some parents managed to access various services, but other parents did not. Because the conclusions of the study are provided throughout the preceding pages, they will not be repeated here in detail. Rather, the focus will be on more general ideas, stemming from the data that lend support to frequent statements by parents and professionals that postadoption supports and services are critically needed in the United States (Ashton, 2000; Freundlich, 2000).

Many families who adopt children from foster care clearly feel abandoned and do not know where to turn for information and support. Most parents had been the children's foster parents for quite some time and were accustomed to a range of agency supports, until the day they adopted. Their expressed unmet needs were many and concerned an urgent need for informational assistance in general, as well as substantial needs in numerous substantive areas: after-school services, educational services, home assistance, clinical services, health services, housing assistance, vocational services, and legal assistance.

These needs require concerted attention. For one, whatever prefinalization preparation may be offered by agencies, a thorough review is needed of its ingredients. As an integral part of discharge planning, practitioners must help adoptive parents to locate and establish connections to community supports. At a minimum, all families must have written information in the form of a resource guide that assists in finding information about services and supports that address potential needs. As an additional aspect of discharge planning, the development of telephone groups and buddy systems should be explored as a way of fostering connections among adoptive parents.

With respect to the development of postadoption services, services have to address the variety of needs expressed by families. In this regard, adoption professionals should be keenly aware of the danger of defining postadoption service needs according to the services that agencies have available rather than in terms of the broad array of family needs. To meet the needs of these families, it may at times be necessary to retool services provided by social workers or to contract for services (e.g., tutoring) that many families need, but social workers are not specifically trained to provide.

The data presented in this study underscore the importance of culturally sensitive efforts to reach out to all adoptive parents with information about various supports in the community. In this regard, the development of foster or "resource" parent cluster groups appears to be an important model to consider (Goodman, Goodhand, Bonk, & Omang, 1998). This model involves neighborhood-based support groups facilitated by adoptive parents working in partnership with postadoption service providers. Because this model is family-centered and neighborhood-based and includes regularly scheduled meetings and special activities, it can be a major source of information and ongoing mutual support for adoptive parents.

The issue may arise that many of the needs identified in this study pertain to children and parents in general, and that adopted children and their parents should not be the recipients of special efforts. An argument can be made that these parents chose to adopt, and that indeed is the case. At the same time, one can argue that there is a societal obligation, a social debt, to support families who have stepped forward to provide permanent homes for children who might otherwise not have found such security.

In addition to a social obligation or debt, a fiscal reason can be advanced. In fact, the provision of postadoption services has been described as cost efficient (Avery, 1998). If these children had not been adopted in 1996, most of them would have remained in foster care at great expense. Instead, they were adopted by individuals and couples, many in their middle years, largely people of very modest means, who too often did not have the wherewithal to pay for needed services and supports that subsequently might be needed. Their decisions to adopt have resulted in fiscal savings for taxpayers. Although adoption subsidies are paid to families in most instances, a considerable saving is built into every adoption in that administrative costs no longer are paid to supervising agencies once children are adopted. At least some of these administrative savings can be used to provide postadoption service subsidies for adoptive families.

There is another fiscal reason that supports the development of postadoption services. The children in this study were the lucky ones—they were adopted. There are other children who were returned to foster care from adoptive homes before finalization. These children are waiting, along with children who never have been placed with adoptive families, to find a permanent home. All too many children throughout the United States are waiting to be placed for adoption or have their relationships with their adoptive families legally finalized. One cannot help but wonder how many of these children in foster care would be adopted, or adopted more quickly, if potential families felt assured of ongoing services and supports. If those supports were more readily at hand and more waiting children were adopted from foster care, society would ultimately give those children a better chance in life.

References

Ashton, J. (2000). *Why are post adoption services needed in NYS?* Ithaca, NY: New York State Citizens' Coalition for Children, Inc.

Avery, R. J. (1995). *Special needs adoption in New York State: Final report on adoptive parent survey.* Ithaca, NY: Cornell University.

Avery, R. J. (1998). Adoption assistance under P.L 96-272: A policy analysis. *Children and Youth Services Review, 20*(1/2), 29–55.

Barth, R. P., Berry, M., Goodfield, R. K., & Carson, M. L. (1987). *Older child adoption and disruption.* Berkeley, CA: University of California, School of Social Welfare.

Barth, R. P., & Miller, J. M. (2000). Building effective postadoption services: What is the empirical foundation? *Family Relations, 49*(4), 447–455.

Berry, M. (1997). Adoption disruption. In R. J. Avery (Ed.), *Adoption policy and special needs children* (pp. 77–106). Westport, CT: Auburn House Press.

Brooks, D., Allen, J., & Barth, R. P. (2000). Adoption services use, helpfulness, and need: A comparison of public and private agency and independent adoptive families. *Children and Youth Services Review.*

Burnette, D. (1999). Custodial grandparents in Latino families: Patterns of service use and predictors of unmet needs. *Social Work, 44*(1), 22–34.

Commonwealth of Kentucky. (1993). *Strategic plan for postlegal adoption services in Kentucky.* Frankfort, KY: Department of Social Services.

Daly, K. J., & Sobol, M. P. (1994). Public and private adoption: a comparison of service and accessibility. *Family Relations, 43*(1), 86–93.

Epstein, M. H., Quinn, K., & Cumblad, C. (1993). *Needs assessment procedures and measures.* DeKalb, IL: Educational Research and Services Center.

Festinger, T. (1996). *New York City adoptions 1995.* New York: New York University, Ehrenkranz School of Social Work.

Festinger, T. (1999). *New York City adoptions 1998.* New York: New York University, Ehrenkranz School of Social Work.

Fine, D. N. (2000). *Adoptive family needs assessment: Final report.* Salem, OE: Oregon Post Adoption Resource Center, Oregon Department of Human Resources.

Freundlich, M. (2000). *Adoption and ethics, vol.2: The market forces in adoption.* Washington, DC: Child Welfare League of America, Inc.

Goodman, D., Goodhand, J., Bonk, K., & Omang, J. (1998). *Recruitment, training, & support: The essential tools of foster care.* Baltimore: The Annie E. Casey Foundation.

Hairston, C. F., & Williams, V. G. (1989). Black adoptive parents: How they view agency adoption practices. *Social Casework: The Journal of Contemporary Social Work,* (November), 534–538.

Marcenko, M. O., & Smith, L. K. (1991). Postadoption needs of families adopting children with developmental disabilities. *Children and Youth Services Review, 13,* 413–424.

Maza, P. (2000). Using administrative data to reward agency performance: The case of the federal adoption incentive program. *Child Welfare, 79*(5), 444–456.

McDonald, T. P., Propp, J. R., & Murphy, K. C. (2001). The postadoption experience: Child, parent, and family predictors of family adjustment to adoption. *Child Welfare, 80*(1), 71–94.

Michigan Federation of Private Child & Family Agencies. (1999). *Survey of adoptive parents regarding postadoption services. Final report.* Lansing, MI: Michigan Federation of Private Child and Family Agencies.

New York State Department of Social Services. (1991). *Final annual summary of characteristics of children in foster care.* New York: New York Department of Social Services.

Rodriguez, O. (1987). *Hispanics and human services: Help-seeking in the inner city.* Bronx, NY: Fordham University Hispanic Research Center.

Rogler, L. H., Cooney, R. S., Costantino, G., Earley, B. F., Grossman, B., Gurak, D. T., Malgady, R., & Rodriguez, O. (1983). *A conceptual framework for mental health research on Hispanic populations.* Bronx, NY: Fordham University Hispanic Research Center.

Rosenthal, J. A., Groze, V., & Morgan, J. (1996). Services for families adopting children via public child welfare agencies: Use, helpfulness, and need. *Children and Youth Services Review, 18*(1/2), 163–182.

Smith, S. L. & Howard, J. A. (1999). *Promoting successful adoptions. Practice with troubled families.* Thousand Oaks, CA: Sage Publications.

Soderland, J., Epstein, M. H., Quinn, K. P., Cumblad, C., & Petersen, S. (1995). Parental perspectives on comprehensive services for children and youth with emotional and behavioral disorders. *Behavioral Disorders, 20*(3), 157–170.

Spencer, M. (1985). Meeting the need for comprehensive postlegal adoption services. *Permanency Report, 3*(4), 5.

Stroul, B. A., & Friedman, R. M (1986). *A system of care for children and youth with severe emotional disturbances* (Rev. Ed.). Washington, DC: Georgetown University Child Development Center, CASSP Technical Assistance Center.

Staudt, M. (1999). Barriers and facilitators to use of services following intensive family preservation services. *The Journal of Behavioral Health Services & Research, 26*(1), 39–49.

Staudt, M. (2000). Correlates of recommended aftercare service use after intensive family preservation services. *Social Work Research, 24*(1), 40–50.

U.S. Children's Bureau. (2000). *AFCARS Report, Preliminary Data, April 2001.* Washington, DC: U.S. Department of Health and Human Services, Administration of Children and Youth.

Walsh, J. A. (1991). *Assessing postadoption services.* Chicago: Illinois Department of Children and Family Services.

Watson, K. W. (1992). Providing services after adoption. *Public Welfare, 50*(1), 5–13.

Zill, N. (1996). *Adopted children in the United States. A profile based on a national survey of child health.* Hearing before the Subcommittee on Human Resources of the Committee on Ways and Means, House of Representatives, 104th Cong., 1st Sess. Serial 104-33, May 10, 1995. Washington, DC: Government Printing Office.

Adoption
THROUGH A
Retrospective Lens

Michael P. Grand

T he creation of narrative plays a very prominent role among the many things that characterize the experience of adoption. Adoptive parents offer renditions of their journeys from infertility to adoptive parenthood. Birthparents are challenged to find a storied theme to describe their lives without the physical presence of the children they had brought into the world. Adoptees construct their narrative in the service of describing who they are, in spite of the fact that for many adoptees, the details of the first chapter of their lives remain elusive.

Individuals construct past events and actions in personal narratives to claim particular kinds of identities and to construct an understanding of specific life courses (Rosenwald & Ochberg, 1992). In telling stories, they emphasize some things and omit others. They take particular stances as protagonists or victims. They use the story to establish a relationship between themselves as narrators and the audiences they encounter. Their stories help in establishing common ground with others. They use stories to elicit social support. If self-stories are out of sync with other people, individuals quickly find themselves under the influence of revisionist attempts to reshape them in line with current, dominant narratives (Gergen, 1985). Because personal stories utilize the self as the central character in the plot line, individuals become, in a sense, the autobiographical narratives that they tell to themselves and to others. Thus, we are our own stories.

Our sense of self—that is, who we are as individuals and as members of the adoption constellation—can be found in the stories we tell about ourselves. The way we talk about ourselves and about ourselves in relation to others reflects what we mean when we use the terms personal and social identity.

One last point needs to be made about our identity and the stories we tell. Narratives create an historical sense of self. Our stories have beginnings, middles, and ends. We cast ourselves into narrative time. We tell stories that provide meaning as to how we change over the course of our lives. We offer reasons embedded within our stories for why we have acted the way we have. We try to make our stories appear to follow a rational course. When the stories of our lives appear incomplete, we fill the gaps with strong emotions that cover over the missing parts. Thus, our stories are designed to give meaning to all of the various experiences of our lives (Riessman, 1993).

Factors That Influence the Shape and Content of An Adoption Narrative

Cultural definitions, the law, expert theory, and the systemic foundation for adoption influence the shape and content of an adoption narrative.

Cultural Definitions

Definitions of cultural institutions, such as what constitutes a family (Bartholet, 1993, Liss & McKinley-Pace, 1999), influence the way we think and talk about a family narrative such as adoption. Does "family" require two parents? Does membership in particular ethnocultural groups preclude the possibility of being included in a family narrative? What role does our cultural understanding of biology play in the definition? Does a person's sexual orientation change the inclusion rules in a family narrative? Can one have more than one family without making qualifications in the definition? What definitions of family are available to people from different socioeconomic backgrounds? Does the definition change with different historical times? Clearly, narrative is grounded in wide spheres of cultural understanding. Adoption narratives are no exception to this rule.

Law

Law, as a cultural artifact, also plays a role in the development of a family narrative (Bussiere, 1998; Connolly, 1998; Hollinger, 1993). Legislation presents a limited set of relationships to constitute how a family is defined (Owen, 1994). Law sets boundaries around the concept of legitimacy. It makes concrete the notion of relinquishment. It restricts the range of relationships that are permitted within a legitimate family. As an example, under the law of many jurisdictions, two unrelated people may not be included in a legal narrative that incorporates the roles of adoptive parents.

Expert Theory

Another cultural factor that helps to shape personal narratives emerges from the influence of individuals assigned the societal role of expert. Through writing books, publishing in scholarly journals, presenting at conferences, and providing service to communities, individuals attain some status in society to offer what might be called meta-narratives. Meta-narratives are the theories that a society's professionals advance about the form and structure of personal stories. Narratives about narratives place boundaries around themes. They make salient some features and ignore others. They restrict explanations to a prescribed set of principles. One needs only to look at the role of Freudian theory over the course of the 20th Century to make the case. Not only was Freud's thinking grounded within the cultural milieu of his time, but it, in turn, helped to shape the development of future understandings.

Interestingly, within the writings in adoption, there has been little independent theoretical development (Brodzinsky, Smith, & Brodzinsky, 1998). In place of theory restricted to adoption alone, theoretical positions are used that have gained prominence in the wider exploration of family life. Of particular interest are perspectives that borrow heavily from social role (Kirk, 1964; 1981), psychoanalysis (Brinich, 1990), attachment (Barth & Berry, 1988), family systems (Reitz & Watson, 1992), and stress and coping theory (Brodzinsky, 1990). Each theory presents a developmental perspective, recognizing that the phenomena under scrutiny change over time. For the most part, they can be construed as continuity theories (Lewis, 1997), in which development follows a predictable trajectory toward an idealized end point. When individuals encounter obstacles during the course of their development, such experiences are usually thought to retard growth, not deflect it in new directions.

Counter to continuity theories, Lewis (1997) stressed the importance of recognizing the discontinuities of development. Thus, knowing the form of early development does not necessarily allow one to predict future development. For Lewis, the vicissitudes of life preclude the possibility of smoothly developing and lawfully determining trajectories. Where an individual ultimately finds oneself is a function of an interplay of several factors: genetic endowment; life circumstances; genetic-environmental interactions; and the personal, volitional shaping of a developmental course. Thus, less emphasis is placed on the launching of a trajectory than on the various and sundry deviations from a continuous path. This distinction between continuous and discontinuous perspectives has important ramifications for intervention strategies and postadoptive services and will be discussed more fully later.

During the past two decades, work in the area of developmental psychopathology (Cummings, Davies, & Campbell, 2000) brought another important idea to the fore. Recognizing the limitations of previous notions that over emphasized a single pathway to psychological well being, Cicchetti and Rogosch (1996, p. 597) argued that "there are multiple contributors to the adaptive or maladaptive outcomes in any individual, that these factors and their relative contributions vary among individuals, and that there are myriad pathways to any particular manifestation of adaptive or disordered behavior...[Thus,] in any open system, a diversity of pathways, including chance events or what biologists refer to as nonlinear epigenesis may lead to the same outcome." On the other hand, "multifinality suggests that any one component may function differently depending on the organization of the system in which it operates" (p.597). Therefore, any given event or variable in and of itself would not necessarily lead to the same outcome in all individuals. These two principles of equifinality and multifinality have important implications when considering postadoptive services, a point that will be discussed further in a subsequent section of this study.

Systemic Foundation for Adoption

Finally, developing adoption theory to recognize the role of systemic relationships is important. For the most part, clinicians and researchers alike have placed emphasis on the dyadic relationship between adoptees and their adoptive parents (Reitz & Watson, 1992). In some cases, consideration is given to the role of service providers. Birthparents also have added their voices, resulting in the concept of the adoption triad becoming a metaphorical descriptor of adoption relationships. The triad is typically drawn as an equilateral triangle with birthparents, adoptees, and adoptive parents each occupying one corner. A limitation of this representation is that it makes the assumption of equal power among the three parties to the adoption, a position that is hardly tenable. Furthermore, it assumes a rigidity of form based on the idea that the three parties remain in a static equilibrium across time.

Clearly, what is needed is a systemic understanding broader in scope and more reflective of the changing shape of relationships in adoption. To this end, Kerry Daly (personal communication, 1998) and the author have proposed the concept of the adoption constellation. This metaphor not only allows for the consideration of adoptees, birthparents and adoptive parents, but also incorporates birth and adoptive families, service providers, teachers, physicians, the courts, social service workers, legislators and the clergy. In fact, anyone whose life is entwined with adoption is a member of the constellation.

The adoption constellation is seen as changing shape across development as different relationships assume heightened or reduced emotional valence. In the beginning of the adoption, birthparents, adoptive parents, the child, and the facilitator play the most prominent roles. Whether the adoption is open will alter the shape of the constellation. Closed adoptions diminish the luminance of birth mother. Open adoptions may give her pride of place (Sobol, Daly, & Kelloway, 2000). Private adoptions move the facilitator to the foreground (Daly & Sobol, 1994). During the early life of the adoption, extended family and friends play an important role in the constellation in terms of welcoming the new member and conferring social credibility on the nuclear family (Kirk, 1964). As the child enters the school system, teachers join the constellation. One need only think about how teachers manage the notion of family inclusion to observe their direct effect on adoptive parent–child relationships. Friends of the adoptee also become important at this point because they may challenge the legitimacy of the family's definition. As the adoptee grows older, the peer group gains prominence, potentially pulling the adoptee in the direction of behaviors that will generate strong emotional responses on the part of the adoptive parents. Themes around risk taking, sexuality, and fertility will have profound effects upon the shape of the adoptive family. If the adoptee or birthparent searches for a reunion and succeeds, the elements of the constellation that have previously provided background luminescence become more salient. And when the adoptee becomes a parent, the new addition also will help to form other emotional connections between members of the constellation.

Thus, the metaphor of the adoption constellation allows for the changing shape of relationships. It recognizes that with development, power relations take on new forms. It encompasses the full range of individuals who have any connection to adoption. Emotional valences between members of the constellation are shaped by the "black holes" of silence, restricted communication, and closed records. The constellation metaphor is able to incorporate the changing shape of adoptive relationships marked by open adoption, single parent adoption, and same-sex couple adoption. This metaphor allows for the recognition that elements in the constellation may play differing roles over time. Finally, it allows for the consideration of dynamic, interactive influences among the various elements of the constellation, thus yielding a more systemic view of adoption.

The remainder of this analysis is devoted to reflections on the role that adoptee narratives and the constellation metaphor play in developing targets for postadoption services. Two studies are described, detailing adult adoptees' views of what factors are related to the success or failure of an adoption. Based on these observations, the author offers recommendations for postadoption services in support of the adoptive family.

Voices in the Construction of an Adoptive Narrative

For the most part, researchers have framed adoption through the judicious choice of theoretical constructs and accompanying data-gathering tools. Based on the theoretical positions available to the field, attempts have been made to build a systematic collection of findings that may be used to shape decisions about intervention to maximize the best interests of the adoptive family (Groze, 1996; Pinderhughes, 1996; Rosenthal, Groze, & Morgan, 1996). These studies use the basic approach of the researcher choosing the measures and either using adoptive parents as respondents or gathering data from archival sources that concern rates of placement, disruption, dissolution, and the use of services such as mental health and educational remediation.

Although such an approach has had a successful history, there is one voice that is only faintly heard in this body of work: the adoptee's. Rarely are adoptees given an opportunity to provide a personal evaluation of their adoption experience. It could be argued that they have been left out of the evaluation process because they lack the social and emotional maturity to be able to provide meaningful data that informs service provision decisions. This argument may be sound in the case of younger adoptees, but without appropriate data to test this assumption, it remains an open question. One alternative approach is to ask adult adoptees to reflect on their adoptive experience. Such a retrospective approach has been criticized (Brodzinsky et al., 1998; Groze, 1996) for providing weak data on causal relationships because variables reflecting temporal relations are all gathered at the time of data collection. This criticism of retrospective designs is clearly valid. Retrospective approaches, however, provide unique data missing from longitudinal designs. As Freeman, Csikzentmihalyi, and Larson (1986) demonstrated, asking a respondent to provide information about current experiences yields proximal explanations that are typically emotional in content. On the other hand, retrospective accounts, with the perspective of time, yield distal explanations that are marked by a contextual grounding. Mechanisms of cause and effect are placed within wider spheres of interest than the immediate situation and its emotional accompaniments. To say that one approach holds more credence is to miss the point. Instead, the two perspectives yield differing accounts that have meaning grounded in the context in which they are collected.

Successful Adoption: The View from Adulthood

The study reported in this section (Grand, 2003), involved an assessment of the influence of factors that have been thought to be associated with adult adoptees' personal evaluation of the success of their adoptions. Most of the variables (self-esteem, similarity to adoptive parents, valence of adoption communication, and age at entrance into the adoptive family) had been assessed in previous research on various aspects of adoption (e.g. Berry, 1992; Howe, Shemmings, & Feast, 2001; Levy-Shiff, 2001; Watson, 1996; Wrobel, Ayers-Lopez, Grotevant, & McRoy, 1996). In addition, this study considered the role of a sense of worth as an adoptee, feelings about birthparents, and life experiences across the lifespan as contributors to the adoptee's perception of the outcome of the adoption. This study was carried out with the expectation that such an analysis would reveal foci for later intervention for supporting the well being of the adoptive family.

Participants came to the study in one of two ways. Advertisements were placed in newspapers in six urban settings in southwestern Ontario, Canada. Of the 116 respondents, 17 men and 66 women completed the questionnaires, yielding a return rate of 74%. An additional six men and 29 women came from local search and reunion groups throughout the province. Participants ranged in age between 18 and 65.

The Adoptive Experience Questionnaire (AEQ) was made up of a series of open-ended and fixed alternative questions. The factual data and some evaluative ratings were presented in check off form. This style was intended to make it as easy as possible for the respondents to complete the questionnaire in a timely fashion and to facilitate a more standardized comparison of their responses. Not all of the items, however, were so structured. To convey sensitivity to the individual nature and importance of the adoptee's perceptions and emotional reactions, questions of a less structured nature also were included. Participants were given the choice of how much they wished to write in response to the open-ended questions.

The AEQ was designed to provide information about demographics, socioeconomic and health status, characteristics of the adoptive family, knowledge of and emotional reactions to the adoptive experience, and revelation of the adoptive status. Feelings and fantasies about the birthparents also were assessed. In addition, questions about adoptees' attempts to reunite with birthparents and their experience when it occurred were asked. Composite scores were generated for each of the main variables considered for this study:

- *Adoption Outcome* was made up of ratings of nine positive and nine negative descriptors of relationships with the adoptive parents. In addition, an overall rating of the adoption was included.

- *Feelings About the Birthparents* comprised of 12 ratings of emotional reactions toward birthparents.

- *Sense of Self as an Adoptee* was made up of three evaluative ratings of the emotional valence felt after first being told about adoptive status, as a child and then as a teenager.

- *Emotional Valence of Communications* derived from several sources: the general atmosphere during the first remembered telling of the adoption story by the adoptive parents, the sense of freedom to discuss the adoption on subsequent occasions, whether the adoption was ever discussed in an angry or embarrassing fashion by the adoptive parents, and the degree of comfort that the adoptee felt about asking subsequent questions about any aspect of the adoption.

- *Similarity to the Adoptive Parents* was a composite of ratings of personality, appearance, and interests.

- *Preplacement Experience* comprised of questions pertaining to number of months spent with birth family, number of months spent in foster care, age at adoptive placement, and age at finalization of the adoption.

For the purposes of the data analyses, composite scores were generated for each of the variables. If the measures within a variable were on different scales, they were converted to standard scores and then added together. Because different formats for the ratings of many of the variables were used, the composite scores also were converted to standardized z-scores.

In addition, the questionnaire package contained the Self-Concept Inventory (Sherwood, 1973), which is comprised of 15 bipolar dimensions and an 11-point rating scale for each dimension. Each respondent also was asked to rate his or her overall sense of self-worth on an 11-point scale with end points being "high" and "low." Total scores combined the two sources of data.

The final measure used was the Social Readjustment Rating Scale (SRRS) developed by Holmes and Rahe (1967). This scale is a standard measure of stressful life events (Cochrane & Sobol, 1980). Two measures were obtained. Participants first were asked whether each of the life events had ever happened to them. They then were asked whether the event had occurred over the past year. The scale also was modified to allow for the rating of the degree of stress for each event.

The proposed model was made operational as an observed variable path model and tested using maximum likelihood estimation as implemented in the Linear Structural Relations computer program, LISREL VIII (Joreskog & Sorbom, 1992). Assessment of the model fit was based on the ^{2} test with a nonsignificant value indicating a good fit to the data. In addition, we calculated the Goodness of Fit Index (GFI), the Adjusted Goodness of Fit Index (AGFI), the Normed Fit Index (NFI), and the Comparative Fit Index (CFI). All indices ranged between 0 and 1.00 with values approaching unity indicating a good fit to the data. The CFI is thought to be particularly appropriate for small samples (Kelloway, 1996; 1998).

Descriptive statistics and intercorrelations for all variables are presented in Table 3-1. The model provided an acceptable fit to the data (^{2} (18) = 18.30, n.s.; GFI = .96; AGFI = .92; NFI = .91; and CFI = 1.00).

Standardized parameter estimates for the model are in Figure 3-1. As shown, the earlier the child came into the adoptive home (Preadoption Experience, ß= .37, p < .01), the more the adoptive parents were perceived to be similar to the adoptee (Similarity to Adoptive Parents, ß = -.33, p < .01). The fewer stressful life events reported (Life Events, ß = .26, p < .01), the more positive the Valence of Adoptive Communication. Three factors predicted a more positive Adoptive Sense of Self: positive Valence of Adoptive Communication (ß = .56, p < .01), shorter period of Preadoption Experience, (ß = .20, p < .01), and greater sense of Similarity to Adoptive Parents (ß = -.15, p < .01). A more positive Adoptive Sense of Self, in turn, predicted a more positive overall sense of Self Esteem (ß = .27, p < .01) and a more positive evaluation of the Adoption Out-

TABLE 3–1

Descriptive Statistics and Intercorrelations for All Study Variables

VARIABLE	1	2	3	4	5	6	7
1. Adoption outcome							
2. Self esteem	.25						
3. Sense of self as an adoptee	.48	.27					
4. Feelings about birthparent	-.34	.05	-.25				
5. Similarity to adoptive parents	.14	.21	.34	-.20			
6. Communication valence	.47	.14	.69	-.40	.33		
7. Preadoptive experience	-.24	-.11	-.43	.16	-.05	-.40	
8. Life events	-.25	-.18	-.31	.22	-.18	-.31	.13

N = 108, r > .16, p < .05

FIGURE 3–1

Path Analysis Leading to Adoption Outcome and Self Esteem

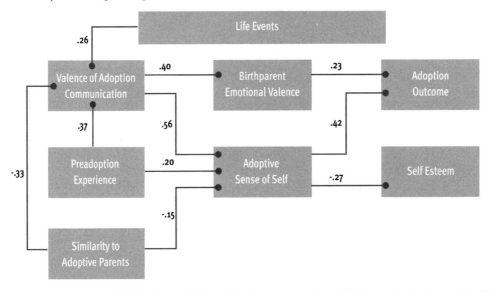

come ($ß = .42$, p < .01). In the final path in the model, the more negatively the Valence of Adoptive Communication was recalled, the more positive were the feelings about the birthparents (Birthparent Emotional Valence, $ß = .40$, p < .01). These positive feelings towards birthparents, in turn, predicted an Adoption Outcome that was rated in a more negative manner ($ß = .23$, p < .01).

Overall, the model explained 23% of the variance in Valence of Adoptive Communication; 52% of the variance in Sense of Self as an Adoptee; 16% of the variance in Birthparent Emotional Valence; 7% of the variance in Self Esteem; and 28% of the variance in Adoption Outcome.

What is immediately apparent from the results of this study is that the form and content of communication play a central role in the ultimate assessment of the outcome of the adoption. When communication is without rancor, there is no restriction on what can be discussed. When the communication is not offered in a derogatory manner, there is a more positive evaluation of self, less emotional investment in birth family, and a more positive view of the outcome of the adoption. The following examples of responses to the open-ended questions stress this point:

- "Whenever my adoption was mentioned, in the same breath I was told I should be grateful for what they had saved me from."

- "My natural mom was called every name in the book. I felt like he [adopted father] was hitting me like I was no good."

- "I was lucky. It was easy talking to my folks. They never mentioned it [adoption] much but were okay if I brought it up. We were really close."

Given the circumstances in which so many children are brought into adoption, it is easy to imagine that positive, respectful communication will become a major challenge for many adoptive families. In the past, the predominate form of adoption was the placement of young, healthy infants with unrelated families. As displayed in the path analysis, short duration between birth and placement predicted more positive adoption communication at a later point. Over the past decade, there has been a rise in the number of older children and children with special needs who are placed for adoption (Sobol & Daly, 1992). As fewer infants are being adopted, there seems to be a greater willingness to recognize adoption as a viable option in developing a permanency plan for children who are older and who have special needs (Daly & Sobol, 1993). The path analysis model would predict that one consequence of this shift to adoption of older children and children with special needs is that there will be less positive communication about adoption between children and their new adoptive parents. This hypothesis is based on two findings: (1) the more time children spend outside of the adoptive home prior to placement, the poorer their communication with adoptive parents; and (2) as children display characteristics that reflect multiple placements and developmental challenges, they will not, in all likelihood, share personality, interests, and attitudes to the same degree as would specifically chosen healthy infants. Hence, future communication between adoptive parents and their children may be strained as a result of lessened similarity between them.

Implications for Postplacement Services

Following placement, one can neither relive preadoptive history nor attempt to match child to parent. The placement is a *fait accompli*. Thus, the focus of intrafamily intervention must be directed toward communicative issues. Brodzinsky and colleagues (1998) have identified a number of situations in which communication, as reflected in the path analysis, is of clinical importance. When parents are motivated to adopt to meet their altruistic needs, for example, they often are surprised and angered when the child

and, particularly, the adolescent does not feel a sense of gratitude for having been res-
cued from negative circumstances. In some families, the child's interest in origins and
questions about birth family are viewed as evidence of the child's failure to make an
emotional connection to the adoptive parents. Parents who hold such a view clearly
are not empathetic to the reality of the child's dual family history. If the family under-
estimates the child's understanding of the adoption narrative, the discussion of the
topic could foreclose before the child is ready to move on to other matters. The child
often construes this circumstance as the parents' unwillingness to talk about adoption
related issues. Some adoptive parents profoundly fear that openness in adoption will
peak the child's interest in origins and will take the child emotionally away from the
adoptive family (paradoxically, more positive conversation seems to lessen immediate
short-term interest in the birth family).

If, as some have suggested, adoption must be understood from the perspective of loss
and its accompanying emotions (Lifton, 1994; Nickman, 1985), strains in communication come close to what Doka (1989) has called "disenfranchised grief." That is, when the
emotional valence of communication patterns is quite negative, grief in adoption may
connect with a loss that cannot be openly acknowledged, publicly mourned, or socially
supported in the family situation. The sequelae can be dramatic. Anger, depression, guilt,
hopelessness, and a weak sense of entitlement may persist for extended periods of time.
Because adoptees do not have an opportunity to experience the positive benefits of social
support and resulting opportunities to legitimize the pain of loss, adoptees may feel an
increased sense of alienation from the adoptive family (Robinson, 2000). Without social
recognition of their grief, they may hold on to these feelings tenaciously.

It is not only adoptees who experience a sense of personal isolation and social rejection of their grief over loss. Robinson (2000) has detailed the intense sense of loss and
disenfranchised grief that some birth mothers experience and has argued strongly for the
need to recognize these feelings and to cast them into a normative framework. Adoptive
parents who have felt the pain of infertility may experience similar feelings of isolation
and social rejection when their social network and adoption professionals deny their
grief. These feelings on the part of adoptive parents contradict the widespread but erro-
neous belief in clinical practice that entrance of a child into an adoptive family will lead
to the resolution of the grief of infertility (Daly, 1989). At each stage of development,
some adoptive parents are painfully reminded of the child who was never born to them.

Clearly, the emotional intensity that may underlie strained adoption communications
and the consequences of such discourse on subsequent development cry out for intervention. Before specific suggestions are offered, however, certain ground rules must be stated.
First, adoption is more a process than a status. Hence, do not assume that all families in
adoption will be in need of assistance, nor that everyone who seeks intervention does so at
the same point in the development of adoptive family life. The principles of equifinality
and multifinality are at work here. Second, there are many routes to a common end, just as
from a common beginning, and there are many possible endings. There should be no
expectation, therefore, that a prescriptive approach to intervention will meet the needs of
all adoptive families seeking assistance in improving communication patterns. For some

families, communication difficulties will emerge with the child's growing cognitive under-standing of adoption. For others, adolescents' identity challenges will herald new tensions in the family. A lucky few will find a way to remain in communicative contact throughout each developmental transition.

How are practitioners to respond to the challenge of assisting adoptive families who are experiencing strains in communicative patterns? There must first be a return to basics. With the growing trend toward the adoption of children who in earlier times were as-sumed to be unadoptable, the mark of success seems to be placement of the child rather than a standard of positive family relations. It remains an open question whether prepa-ration of preadoptive parents includes enough focus on the value of supportive adoption conversation. In the interests of not discouraging potential adoptive parents, has a discus-sion about the many psychological needs that children bring to adoption been forgotten? Is time still being taken to explore the applicants' motivations for adoption? How have they dealt with their own grief over infertility? Are they told that seeking out assistance in the future is not a mark of failure but represents good parenting? When photo listings are used to advertise the availability of children, are applicants encouraged to concentrate on the attractive features of the child and ignore the child's special needs? Finally, no adop-tion should be pursued without arrangements for needed medical, educational, and psy-chological services being in place. Clearly, if the goal is to develop effective support ser-vices for adoptive families who will grapple with difficult interpersonal situations, there must be a strong foundation for the development of adoptive family life.

The next challenge is to develop a cadre of highly trained professionals who can offer therapeutic interventions at the individual, dyadic, and family level, and who are sensi-tive and knowledgeable about the issues of loss and grief in adoption. North America does not suffer from a dearth of mental health workers, but a combination of expertise in mental health and adoption is a rare commodity. Faculties of social work, psychology, and medical schools must put adoption on the curriculum and not consider it solely as an option in the development of a permanency plan for children. Without therapists who understand interpersonal and adoption issues, most adoptive families who seek assistance in modifying their communication patterns will receive only half an intervention.

What form should interventions that target strained communication take? First, therapy must recognize the importance of narrative construction, particularly those features that reflect meaning, value, and a sense of self. The notion of cure must be dispelled and replaced with the idea of specific adaptations. Families face new chal-lenges with the approach of each new developmental milestone. Because discontinuity is the norm for development, there will be families who display competence at one moment and difficulties at another. Intervention should be offered as needed and not as a cure-all for future crises. Therapy should be historical, exploring a rendition of the self and grounded in a history that is ultimately framed in the present (Efran, Lukens, & Lukens, 1988). Therapists must ask how the past is being used in the moment to make sense out of struggles in the lives of the adoptive family. The therapeutic encoun-ter also must provide opportunities for the unspoken to be verbalized. Disenfranchised grief is rarely resolved (Doka, 1989), but with its exposure and the addition of social support and validation of the grief, opportunities become available to find ways to live with loss without being personally or interpersonally destructive.

There are many therapies that fit with this analysis. The primary ones come from narrative family therapy (Coyne, 1985; Madanes, 1990; Watzlawick, Weakland, & Fisch, 1974; White & Epston, 1990). The closest fit, however, was represented by Eron and Lund (1996) in their book, *Narrative Solutions in Brief Psychotherapy.* As a basic principle, these authors argued that individual and social constructions, embedded in dialogue between people, are linked to problems within the family. The challenge is to generate alternative constructions, embedded in conversations that are linked to solutions. Because ways of framing current experience are said to be embedded in more historical stories, the goal of therapy is to "restory" experiences of past events in a way that will lead to the reframing of present circumstances.

For Eron and Lund (1996), guiding people to rethink their assumptions about problems and reconsider the actions of others is an important component of therapy. Individuals are assumed to have preferred views of how they would like to behave, how they see themselves, and how they would like others to see them. Eron and Lund (1996), like White & Epston, 1990, suggested that this view is not readily apparent because it is often buried under the problem-saturated accounts of self. Strong negative emotions emerge when family members act in ways that are outside their preferred style, evaluate themselves outside of their preferred parameters, and believe that others see them in ways that deviate negatively from how they would like to be seen. In essence, these patterns are what strained communication represents within the adoptive family.

The distance between how family members see themselves and how they believe other family members see them is greatest at transition points in the life of the adoptive family. When an adoptee expresses a desire to search for a birthparent to complete a sense of self, for example, adoptive parents may perceive this desire as an act of personal and familial rejection. If the disjunctive attributions are too wide, a problem cycle emerges in which views become entrenched and negative emotions escalate. Problems are no longer regarded as something between people but are thought to reside within self and the other. In an attempt to restore balance, combatants typically engage in a "more of the same" strategy (Watzlawick, Weakland, & Fisch, 1974).

Eron and Lund stressed that the most important aspect of their approach is that the therapist "introduce and cultivate an alternative story for parents of who their children are and want to be" (p. 139). To accomplish this goal, the therapist must draw out key stories from the past and alter how people see self and other in the present. The "mystery question" posed by Eron and Lund—"Given your preferred attributes, how did you wind up in such a situation and viewed by others in a non-preferred way?" (p. 69)—is a key device is bringing forth new narrative positions. Therapeutically helpful conversations invite people to take clear positions about their intentions, consider the effects on their behaviors and on others, and indicate whether these effects are preferred or not.

In summary, there are three key strategies in working toward change: find and shape stories that are consistent with a preferred view of self, circulate the stories among members of the family, and develop alternative explanations for the evolution of the problem, thus permitting the realigning of problem behaviors with how the individual prefers to be seen by others. This approach provides a medium for dealing with strained communication. It recognizes and finds ground for the expression and modification of feelings of guilt that have been disenfranchised. It allows for the exploration of alternative understandings among members of the adoption constellation. Perhaps of most importance, this approach yields the possibility of developing greater empathy for the personal narratives of each family member.

Professionally delivered therapy is not the only approach for helping families cope with strained adoptive communication. Support groups and peer mentoring, for example, may be of real value, particularly when assistance is sought before the problem has escalated to an extreme level. When families cannot find their way to solutions using ordinary means, however, narrative-oriented family therapy may prove to be a viable and positive option.

The Step Adoption Perspective

To see a phenomenon in a new light, it sometimes is necessary to consider adjacent situations that bear partial similarity. A recently completed qualitative, clinical interview study of 26 step adoptees yielded some interesting suggestions for expanding the list of interventions that might prove helpful in full adoption (Grand, 2002).

Step adoptions comprise approximately four times as many adoptions as do full, nonrelative adoptions (Daly & Sobol, 1993). In the study reported in this section, a consanguineous mother and a stepfather who adopted the child had raised all but one of the adult step adoptees who participated. This high ratio of stepfathers to stepmothers adopting a child is consistent with the wider demographics of step adoption (Daly & Sobol, 1993). Nine men and 17 women from three major metropolitan areas answered a newspaper request for participation in this study of step adoption family life. The adult adoptee participants were between the ages of 19 and 59.

The analysis of the interview transcripts was based on the contrasts that were found between the step adoptees who evaluated their adoptions in a positive manner and the step adoptees who viewed their adoptions negatively. Although the data provided a rich source of information on the dynamics of step adoption families, only those findings that have a direct bearing on intervention services in full adoption are reported here.

Consent to the Adoption

In the adoptions adult step adoptees rated as successful, they recalled either that their consent was informed and freely given or that they were too young to offer informed consent. In the vast majority of the adoptions that were rated as unsuccessful, the adoptees viewed consent as imposed on them. There was little or no communication about the topic, and the child simply was asked to sign papers. In some cases, the child felt a sense of resignation, as there was nothing that could be done to stop the adoption from going forward. In all of the situations with imposed consent, the adoptees reported that resentment regarding the circumstances persisted into adulthood.

Given the current initiative toward the adoption of older children, the issue of consent becomes important. Will consent be freely given? Who will insure that children are fully informed of the consequences of providing consent? Is the child's legal representative truly independent of other interests and parties? Although these questions do not directly concern the issue of postadoption services per se, the answers will affect the demeanor of the child within the adoptive family and have some effect on future adoptee–adoptive parent relations. If potentially problematic situations are not to be exacerbated, then care must be taken in obtaining consent for adoption from older children.

Parenting Style

How quickly the adoptive stepfather took on the role of parent differentiated adoptions rated as successful from ones rated unsuccessful. In the case of successful older child adoptions, the adoptive father moved slowly toward assuming a parenting role. In unsuccessful older child adoptions, the opposite was the case. One would expect similar findings for older full adoptees placed for adoption with nonfoster families. This finding does not mean adoptive parents should abrogate their parental responsibilities, but it does mean that adoptive parents should be aware that like the adoptee, they must grow slowly into the role of family member.

A second issue relates to the delivery of discipline. All step adoptees in the study expected the adoptive parent to take disciplinary action. In successful adoptions, however, certain patterns emerged. Discipline was not imposed too early in the life of the adoptive family. Before discipline was imposed, a relationship of trust and respect was established between the stepfather and the adoptee. A balancing act, however, was required because adoptees did not psychologically view the adoptive stepfather as fully occupying the role of father until he felt comfortable imposing appropriate, although not extreme, discipline. Yet, in all of the poorly rated adoptions, disciplinary attempts were construed as coercive and extremely intrusive. Step adoptees in these adoptions stressed the harsh tone of the father. What seemed to separate the two groups was timing. Until trust and respect were established, disciplinary attempts proved futile.

A third factor that set successful and unsuccessful step adoptions apart was how well individuals fit in the family. In successful adoptions, adoptees almost always described a similarity between themselves and their adoptive parent. In some cases, the similarity was appearance, but more often, it was interests or personality. Furthermore, many participants stated that the interest the adoptive parent took in the ongoing life of the child around school, friends, hobbies, holidays, and sports played an important role in connecting the adoptee to the adoptive parent. In unsuccessful adoptions, there was almost universal rejection of the idea that the adoptee and the adoptive parent had anything in common. In these cases, there seemed to be no attempt on the part of the adoptive parent to enter into the wider life of the adoptee.

What adoptees described as markers of success should be part of parent education for all parents, not simply adoptive ones. In the context of postadoption services, however, opportunities should be made to discuss good parenting over the course of development. Parent preparation is fine as far as it goes, but it probably has less impact than on-the-ground experience and accompanying guidance. In addition, parent education courses must be adoption sensitive. Adoptees and their adoptive parents begin with differing genetic proclivities (Cadoret, 1990), and hence, enforced attempts to impose similarity of interest and ability should not be the goal. The challenge is to find means for parents to enter comfortably into and support the world of the child.

Quality of the Marital Relationship

For the step adoptees in the study, successful adoptions were highly related to perceptions of quality in the marital relationship. If the marriage was seen as good, the adoption was perceived in parallel terms. On the other hand, if the marriage was rated as poor, so was the adoption.

This finding is not unexpected. Adoption is grounded in other relationships. If there is strain in the marriage, it is hard to imagine that the adoption will be trouble free. When adoptive parents are not able to put resources into the parent–child relationship because significant time and emotional energy are focused on the management of the marriage, the child is bound to suffer. The quality of the marital relationship curiously has received little attention in full adoption. Theoretically, the focus has been on adoptive relationships without considering how these relationships are grounded in other interpersonal relationships. There may be a reluctance to consider that in some cases, children are placed with families where difficult marital relationships have been covered over to expedite the adoptive placement. If prospective adoptive families make such efforts, marital therapy and support would be welcome additions to postadoption services. Clinical lore also would suggest that when the adoptee is having an emotionally difficult time, the adoptive parents will feel a strain on their own relationship as they attempt to respond to the adoptee's needs. Professional support again would be welcome in such circumstances. Few adoptive parents, however, would avail themselves of marital therapy if seeking this service is interpreted as a sign of an inappropriate placement. Such a stigma clearly must be removed.

Relationship to the Extended Adoptive Family

The adoptee's relationship to the extended adoptive family is a key ingredient in a successful step adoption. In the study, there was not a single case in which the adoptee rated the adoption as unsuccessful when the adoptive parent's extended family (grandparents, aunts, uncles, and cousins) treated the adoptee as one of their own. On a concrete level, being treated "as one of our own" meant gifts on holidays and birthdays of an equal value to the gifts provided to consanguineous children at the same rank in the family, not referring to the step adoptee as the consanguineous parent's child but simply as the couple's child, and the step adoptee having an equal share in the inheritance. In the adoptions rated as unsuccessful by step adoptees, it was not clear whether the adoptee rejected the adoptive parent's extended family or vice versa. Based on the transcripts, rejection in both directions was likely in play.

The dynamic of extended adoptive family has not been considered extensively in developing an understanding of the adoptee's connection in full adoption. The earlier discussion of the constellation would suggest that the extended family plays a prominent role in shaping the form of the adoption. This discussion leads to two recommendations in support of the adoptive family. First, extended family should be involved in the facilitation process. Their roles should be highlighted and welcoming strategies considered. Second, extended family must be aware of the strong positive role that they can play across the life of the adoption. Because grandparents are free from disciplinary responsibilities, they can offer valuable emotional support to the child and, particularly, the adolescent adoptee at a time when parents are caught up in disciplinary battles. Knowledge of the beneficial role of extended family should be stressed in family education programs provided as part of a postadoption package of services.

Search and Reunion Issues

The findings of the step adoption study with regard to search and reunion paralleled the findings in research on these issues in the context of full adoption. Almost all step adoptees were interested in learning more about their missing consanguineous parent and his family. Most step adoptees had searched and experienced a reunion. The role played by the adoptive parent was important for many adoptees. If the adoptive parent encouraged the search and did not see it as a threat to the stability of the parent–child relationship, the search brought the adoptee closer to the adoptive parent. This dynamic was of particular importance following a reunion with the absent parent. The adoptee often returned to the adoptive home filled with excitement but also in need of emotional verification and support. If the adopted parent's reception was supportive, a lasting positive impression was created; if the adopted parent's response was negative, the adoptee turned emotionally to the absent parent for support.

This finding suggests that search and reunion need not be a threat to the stability of the adoption. Adoptive parents must learn that the search is much more a reflection of the adoptee's need to write the first chapter in his or her life than a statement about the quality of the adoption. More public education is needed on search as an important part of the journey of establishing a sense of self. Knowledgeable professionals must be available to give advice and support for parents. Similarly, competent professionals are needed to help adoptees sort through the cascading emotions that accompany search and reunion. Search and reunion are not easy moments in the life of the adoptive family, but they are important ones.

When considering postadoption services, the important role of legislation in accessing information about origins cannot be ignored. Laws in too many jurisdictions have sealed adoption files and allowed few opportunities for adoptees to obtain identifying history. Arguments in support of closed files are typically framed in terms of respecting birthparents' wishes and preserving the integrity of the adoptive family. Nothing could be more poorly thought out. If the voices of birthparents were heard, it would be obvious that a vast majority of birthparents want adoption files to be opened. For example, figures from the Vital Statistics Agency, Government of British Columbia (2005), for the period between 1996 and 2005 indicate that less than 3.3% of all birthmothers in the province filed a disclosure veto, blocking adult adoptees from accessing identifying information.

A further .03% filed a contact veto. This leaves 96.7% of birthmothers who did not use legal means to block the possibility of face-to-face reunion. Birthparents were never promised confidentiality, nor do they want confidentiality 20 years after the adoptive placement (Robinson, 2000). As genetic screening plays an ever larger role in medical practice, adoptees are at a distinct disadvantage when they do not have a complete medical history of genetic relatives. Nonadoptees have ready access to such information, and adoptees should have equal legal rights.

Opening records supports adoptive and birth families. In those jurisdictions where adoptees have free access to their adoption files when they reach the age of adulthood, there are no reports of mass crises within the adoption constellation. If there is truly a commitment to full postadoption services, then opening adoption records must be a part of the endeavor to work towards the best interests of the adoption constellation.

Conclusion

Research on postadoptive services has primarily focused on parents' and professionals' assessment of the needs of adopted children. This tends to focus the source of the difficulty on the make-up of the child. There is no denying the fact that many children, particularly those who are identified as "special needs," require access to targeted services to help them meet developmental and medical challenges. However, an exclusively, child-focused orientation detracts from addressing more systemic issues within the adopted family. By giving voice to adults, reflecting back on their adoptive experience, we are able to avoid what social psychologists refer to as the fundamental attribution error (Ross, 1977): the tendency to explain negative behavior by reference to the personality of the other. The studies presented in this analysis point toward an assessment of needs, grounded in an understanding of adoptive family process. Thus, specific developmental challenges must be considered within the context of the adoptive family and its wider circle of community, and not solely within the child.

Central to this analysis is the factor of strained adoptive communication within the family. How well children and parents can talk to each other, particularly about adoption related issues, will affect the long term success of the adoptive experience. An unwillingness to hear the other's sense of grief over loss, disrespect for and by the extended birth and adoptive family, and secrecy all place the adoptive family at risk. Too often when we think of needs, we think of services to "fix" the child. The message of the studies presented here is that we must also think of services that will support the integrity of the adoptive family. Counseling to assist the marital dyad, family therapy addressing patterns of communication, and social support of extended family and friends are all components in a more contextually based integration of services.

Almost 40 years ago, David Kirk (1964) alerted the adoption community to acknowledge the differences between adoptive and nonadoptive families. His perspective is still apt. However, we also must recognize that adoptive families face many of the same challenges as other families, particularly around issues of communication, intimacy, openness, and flexibility. Clearly, we must find a balance between treating the adoptive family as unique and recognizing that, at times, wider issues of family life are also important. When we are able to accomplish this task, an ecologically valid set of post adoption services will be realized.

References

Barth, R. P., & Berry, M. (1988). *Adoption and disruption: Rates' risks and responses.* New York: Aldine De Gruyter.

Bartholet, E. (1993). *Family bonds: Adoption and the politics of parenting.* Boston: Houghton Mifflin Company.

Berry, M. (1992). Contributors to adjustment problems of adoptees: A review of the longitudinal research. *Child and Adolescent Social Work Journal, 9,* 525–540.

Brinich, P. M. (1990). Adoption from the inside out: A psychoanalytic perspective. In D. Brodzinsky & M. Schechter (Eds.). *The psychology of adoption* (pp. 42–61). New York: Oxford University Press.

Brodzinsky, D. M. (1990). A stress and coping model of adoption adjustment. In D. Brodzinsky & M. Schechter (Eds.). *The psychology of adoption* (pp. 3–24). New York: Oxford University Press.

Brodzinsky, D. M., Smith, D. W., & Brodzinsky, A. B. (1998). *Children's adjustment to adoption: Developmental and clinical issues.* Thousand Oaks, CA: Sage Publications, Inc.

Bussiere, A. (1998). The development of adoption law. *Adoption Quarterly, 1,* 3–25.

Cadoret, R. J. (1990). Biologic perspectives of adoptee adjustment. In D. Brodzinsky & M. Schechter (Eds.). *The psychology of adoption* (pp. 25-41). New York: Oxford University Press.

Cicchetti, D., & Rogosch, F. A. (1996). Equifinality and multifinality in developmental psychopathology. *Development and Psychopathology, 8,* 597–600.

Cochrane, R., & Sobol, M. P. (1980). Personal distress and mental disorder. In M. P. Feldman & J. Orford (Eds.), *The social psychology of psychological problems.* (pp. 151–182). London: Wiley.

Connolly, C. (1998). The description of gay and lesbian families in second-parent adoption cases. *Behavioral Sciences and the Law, 16,* 225–236.

Daly, K. J., & Sobol, M. P. (1993). *Adoption in Canada.* Ottawa, Canada: National Welfare Grants, Health and Welfare.

Daly, K., & Sobol, M. P. (1994). Public and private adoption: A comparison of service and accessibility. *Family Relations, 43,* 86–93.

Doka, K. (Ed). (1989). *Disenfranchised grief: Recognizing hidden sorrows.* Lexington, Mass: Lexington Books.

Efran, J. S., Lukens, R. J., & Lukens, M. D. (1988). Constructivism: What's in it for you? *Family Therapy Networker, 12,* 27–35.

Freeman, M., Csikzentmihalyi, M., & Larson, R. (1986). Adolescence and its recollection: Toward an interpretive model of development. *Merril-Palmer Quarterly, 32,* 167–185.

Gergen, K. J. (1985). The social constructionist movement in modern psychology. *American Psychologist, 40,* 266–273.

Grand, M. P. (2002, August). *A comparison of outcomes in step and full adoption: The adult adoptee's perspective.* Paper presented at the meeting of the North American Council on Adoptable Children, Chicago, IL.

Grand, M. P. (2003). Adult adoptees' evaluations of the outcome of their adoptions: Routes to positive and negative outcomes. Unpublished manuscript, University of Guelph, Guelph, Ontario, Canada.

Groze, V. (1996). A 1 and 2 year follow-up study of adoptive families and special need children. *Children and Youth Services Review, 18*, 57–82.

Hollinger, J. H. (1993). Adoption law. *Future of Children, 3*, 43–61.

Holmes, T. H. & Rahe, R. H. (1967). The social readjustment scale. *Journal of Psychosomatic Research, 11*, 213–218.

Howe, D., Shemmings, D., & Feast, J. (2001). Age at placement and adult adopted people's experience of being adopted. *Child and Family Social Work, 6*, 337–349.

Joreskog, K., & Sorbom, D. (1992). *LISREL VIII: Analysis of linear structural relations*. Mooresville, IN: Scientific Software.

Kelloway, E. K. (1996). Common practices in structural equation modeling. In C. L. Cooper & I. Robertson (Eds.). *International Review of Industrial and Organizational Psychology* (pp. 141–180). Chichester, England: John Wiley and Sons.

Kelloway, E. K. (1998). *Using LISREL for structural equation modeling: A researcher's guide*. Thousand Oaks, CA: Sage Publications.

Kirk, H. D. (1964). *Shared fate*. New York: Free Press.

Kirk, H. D. (1985). *Adoptive kinship: A modern institution in need of reform*. Brentwood Bay, BC: Ben-Simon Publications.

Levy-Shiff, R. (2001). Psychological adjustment of adoptees in adulthood: Family environment and adoption-related correlates. *International Journal of Behavioural Development, 25*, 97–104.

Lewis, M. M. (1997). *Altering fate: Why the past does not predict the future*. New York: Guilford Press.

Lifton, B. J. (1979). *Journey of the adopted self: A quest for wholeness*. New York: Basic Books.

Liss, M. B., & McKinley-Pace, M. J. (1999). Best interests of the child: New twists on an old theme. In R. Roesch, & S. D. Hart (Eds.), *Psychology and the law: The state of the discipline* (Vol. 10, pp. 339–372). New York: Kluwer Academic/Plenum Publishers.

Nickman, S. L. (1985). Losses in adoption: The need for dialogue. *Psychoanalytic Study of the Child, 40*, 365–398.

Owen, M. (1994). Single-person adoption: For and against. *Children and Society, 8*, 151–163.

Pinderhughes, E. E. (1996). Toward understanding family readjustment following older child adoptions: The interplay between theory generation and empirical research. *Children and Youth Services Review, 18*, 115–138.

Province of British Columbia, Ministry of Health (2005). *Adoption disclosure and contact vetoes*. (Vital Statistics Agency, Knowledge Management and Technology Division). Victoria, BC: Author.

Reitz, M., & Watson, K. W. (1992). *Adoption and the family system*. New York: Guilford.

Riessman, C. K. (1993). *Narrative analysis*. Newberry Park, CA: Sage Publications.

Robinson, E. B. (2000). *Adoption and loss: The hidden grief*. Christies Beach, Australia: Clova Publications.

Rosenthal, J. A., Groze, V., & Morgan, J. (1996). Services for families adopting children via public child welfare agencies: Use, helpfulness, and need. *Children and Youth Services Review, 18*, 163–182.

Rosenwald, C. G., & Ochberg, R. (Eds.). (1992). *Storied lives: The cultural politics of self-understanding*. New Haven, CT: Yale University Press.

Ross, L.D. (1977). The intuitive psychologist and his shortcomings: Distortions in the attribution process. In L. Berkowitz (Ed.), *Advances in experimental social psychology* (Vol. 10, pp. 174–221). New York: Academic Press.

Sobol, M. P., & Daly, K. J. (1994). Canadian adoption statistics: 1981–1990. *Journal of Marriage and the Family, 56,* 494–499.

Sobol, M. P., Daly, K., & Kelloway, K. (2000). Paths to the facilitation of open adoption. *Family Relations, 49,* 419–424.

Sherwood, J. J. (1973). Self-concept inventory. In J. P. Robinson & P.R. Shaver (Eds.), *Measures of social psychological attitudes* (pp.123–125). Ann Arbor, MI: Institute for Social Research.

Watson, K.W. (1996). Family centered adoption practice. *Families in Society, 77,* 523–534

Watzlawick, P., Weakland, J., & Fisch, R. (1974). *Change: Principles of problem formation and problem resolution.* New York: Norton.

White, M., & Epston, D. (1990). *Narrative means to therapeutic ends.* New York: Norton.

Wrobel, G. M., Ayers-Lopez, S., Grotevant, H. D., & McRoy, R. G. (1996). Openness in adoption and the level of child communication. *Child Development, 67,* 2358–2374.

SECTION TWO

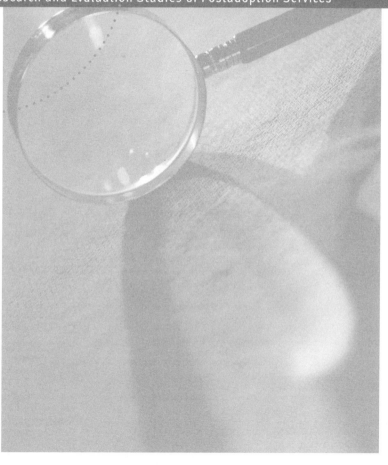

Research and Evaluation Studies of Postadoption Services

A STUDY OF THE
Illinois Adoption/Guardianship Preservation Program

Susan Livingston Smith

By the summer of 2001, the Illinois Adoption/Guardianship Preservation Program had been in place for 10 years. Adoption preservation services (APS) in Illinois started in 1991, after the state's Family Preservation Act of 1988 explicitly included adoptive families among those the state should strengthen and preserve. The legal mandate specifies that services be provided to adoptive families who are at risk of child placement or adoption dissolution. The preservation program understands that children who are adopted after stays in foster care often have a range of problems (such as prenatal substance exposure, maltreatment, and interrupted attachments) that place them at risk for later challenges. In Illinois, adoption preservation services also are available for families who have adopted infants domestically and adopted children internationally. In 1996, Illinois received a federal waiver to offer subsidized guardianship as a permanency option. Since that time, guardianship families also are eligible for program services.

As of 2005, APS operates through nine contracts with private agencies with programs in 20 sites. The service components include in-depth assessment, intensive therapeutic services, support groups for children and parents, 24-hour crisis intervention response, case management and advocacy services, and limited cash assistance. An extensive evaluation of the program was completed in June 1995 (Howard & Smith, 1995; Smith & Howard, 1999). Since 1995, the number of families served has substantially increased. At the time of this study, APS served approximately 600 families each year— more than in the first four years of the program combined.

In addition to the growth in the number of families served and the expansion of the program, the service delivery model of APS has changed significantly since its inception. The original model resembled the design of the intensive short-term, home-based, family preservation services called the Homebuilders program, with a focus on intensive crisis intervention for 10–12 weeks the program and links to community services. When it became apparent in the first year of that this model did not fit the needs of families, the length of intensive services was extended twice. In addition, group services were lengthened to allow some families to participate after the termination of intensive services. It also was recognized that most families who sought APS services had tried traditional counseling and found that their problems were inadequately resolved. Families needed in-depth, adoption-knowledgeable assessment—which is provided through APS.

This descriptive study analyzed the operations of APS, focusing on several research questions related to the characteristics of adopted and guardianship children and families served by APS; the problems and needs for which families sought services; the characteristics of the services; the factors associated with the severity of child problems and the risk of adoption dissolution for these families; the outcomes for children and families served; and families' evaluation of the services they received. Data collection began in April 1999 and the analysis for this report was conducted in April 2001. Data were included from cases opened and closed during that period. The sources of data included an intake form on all referred families completed by adoption preservation workers, a case summary form completed by the workers at the conclusion of services, and feedback forms that were distributed by the program to families and returned to the researchers. Most of the statistics reported in this study were based on data from the case closing summaries. Unless otherwise indicated, the percentages reported are valid percents that exclude missing data in their calculation.

The Findings of the Study: The Children and the Families

Description of Children and Families Served

Among the 912 families referred to APS over the two-year study period, 1,162 children were identified as having difficulties. Data were collected on children with identified problems who received APS; however these numbers do not constitute all of the adopted children in these families. Of the 912 referred cases, 16% had been served previously by APS, but in only 3 cases were families served twice during the study period. Of the 509 cases that were closed during the study, 582 adopted children were having difficulties.

Child and family demographics

The gender of these children was fairly even: 48% were female and 52% were male. The race and ethnicity of the children was predominantly Caucasian (51%), followed by African American (33.5%), Hispanic (6%), Asian (2.5%) and "other" (7%). Close to one-fifth of the children (19%) were transracially placed (i.e., placed with a family in which both parents were of a different race or ethnicity than the child). The mean age of children at the time of referral was 11.4 years. Figure 4-1 provides data on children's ages at time of referral.

Type of permanency arrangement

Of the children referred, 78% were previously wards of the Illinois public child welfare agency—the Department of Child and Family Services (DCFS)—and 3% were current DCFS wards. Of the current wards, only 3 children had not previously been wards of DCFS. Another 2% of children were wards of another state child welfare agency when they were

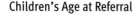

Children's Age at Referral

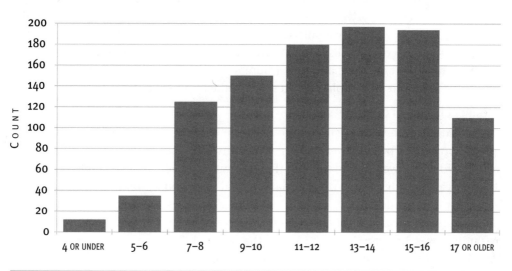

adopted. Sixty-nine percent of the children were receiving an adoption subsidy from Illinois at the time of the study. Ten percent of the children (involving 9% of the families) were in subsidized guardianship arrangements. In addition to children who had been involved with DCFS or another public child welfare agency, 10% had been adopted as infants from a private adoption agency, 3.5% had been adopted independently, and 6.5% had been adopted internationally. In summary, for the 1,047 children for whom this information was available, 80% had been involved with a public child welfare agency prior to the adoption and guardianship, and 20% were other types of adoptions.

The most common family type was a matched adoption (35%); that is, the adoptive parents and the child generally were unknown to one another prior to the adoptive placement. Adoptions by foster parents were reported for 33% of children, and relative adoptions for 29%. In the case of families whose children previously had been DCFS wards, the percentages were somewhat different: 21% were with matched families, 45% were adopted by foster parents, 24% were adopted by relatives, and 9% were in subsidized guardianship arrangements. Most children (69%) were in two-parent families, and 31% were in single-parent families. A noteworthy proportion of parents were of older age: 12% of mothers were 60 or older, and 21% of mothers were age 55 or older.

Children's disabilities

Data (based on information on the case closing forms) on children's diagnosed disabilities were available for 529 children. As Table 4-1 shows, 55% of these children were reported as having one or more disabilities. The percentages reported on this variable are actual rather than valid percents because blank items were interpreted as meaning that the child did not have the disability.

The disabilities specified as "other" in Table 4-1 were primarily learning disabilities. When asked whether the child was diagnosed as described by Diagnostic and Statistical Manual of Mental Disorders (DSM-IV) (published by the American Psychiatric Association), social workers reported that 43% of the children had such a diagnosis. The DSM-IV diagnoses most commonly reported were major depression, bipolar disorders, oppositional defiant or conduct disorder, attention deficit hyperactivity disorder (ADHD), reactive attachment disorder, and post-traumatic stress disorder. A significant percentage (41 %) of children were placed in a special education setting.

Placement history of children

Most children were young when removed from their birth families (mean age = 1.9 years). Forty-three percent were under 6 months old, and of these infants, approximately two-thirds were removed from their parents' custody at birth. Table 4-2 reports children's ages at the time of their initial removal in the public child welfare system as well as for other children.

Overall, the mean age for children at the time of their placement with their adoptee families was 3.6 years. Table 4-3 shows that most children were age 3 or older when placed with their adoptive families. Given that the mean age at referral was 11.4, children had been with their adoptive families for an average of 7.8 years at the time they received services through APS. The mean age of children at the time of adoption finalization was 5.7 years. The mean length of time between children's initial removal from their birth families and adoption finalization was 3.8 years.

Many children (43%) went directly from their birth families to the family who eventually adopted them. For children who had interim placements, the most common number reported was one, the case for 30% of children. Twenty-six percent of children had experienced two or more interim placements, and 6% had experienced four or more such placements. Three percent had experienced an adoption disruption prior to placement with their current adoptive families. When only those children previously involved with public child welfare agencies were considered, 63% had experienced other placements prior to placement with their current adoptive families.

Slightly more than a fourth of the children (27%) had been placed outside their adoptive families since their adoptions (30% of children previously involved with public child welfare and 16% of other adoptees). Most commonly, children had been placed in psychiatric hospital settings (19% of the children). Six percent had been in residential treatment placements, and families had arranged informal placements (defined as lasting more than 2 weeks) for 7% of children.

Maltreatment history of children

Based on data reported by social workers on the case closing form, most children had experienced some form of maltreatment. As shown in Table 4-4, 71% of children were reported as having experienced some level of neglect, with 45% having a history of severe neglect. Physical abuse was reported for 43% of the children and sexual abuse for 27%.

Many children were reported as having experienced multiple types of maltreatment. Table 4-5 reports the percentage of children who experienced no maltreatment

TABLE 4–1

Percentages of Children with Disabilities

Type of Disability	Percent
Mental retardation	5%
ADD/ADHD	40%
Mental illness	10%
Serious emotional problems	12%
FAE/FAS	9%
Physical disability	1%
Other	21%

TABLE 4–2

Age at Time of Initial Removal from Birthfamily

Age at Initial Removal	Public Child Welfare	Other Adoptees
Less than 6 months	32%	71%
6–12 months	10%	4%
1–3 years	35%	14%
4–6 years	15%	6%
7–9 years	5%	3%
10 years or older	3%	2%
Mean	2.2 years	1.1 years

TABLE 4–3

Age at Placement with Adoptive Family

Age Placed with Family	Child Welfare	Other Adoptees
Less than 1 year	22%	57%
1–2 years	18%	20%
3–4 years	21%	7%
5–6 years	15%	8%
7–8 years	11%	5%
9–10 years	6%	1%
11–12 years	5%	1%
13–14 years	3%	1%
Mean	4.3 years	1.9 years

Note: Due to rounding, percents may not add up to 100%.

TABLE 4–4

Types of Maltreatment Experienced by Children

TYPE OF MALTREATMENT	NONE KNOWN	YES, MODERATE	YES, SEVERE
Neglect	28%	26%	45%
Physical Abuse	57%	25%	18%
Sexual Abuse	73%	12%	15%

TABLE 4–5

Multiple Types of Maltreatment Experienced by Children

EXTENT OF MALTREATMENT	PUBLIC CHILD WELFARE	OTHER ADOPTEES
No maltreatment	14%	61%
One type	36%	17%
Two types	24%	11%
Three types	26%	11%

and who experienced one to three different types of maltreatment. As expected, children from the public child welfare system were more likely to have more extensive histories of maltreatment. Eighty-six percent of children from the public child welfare system were reported as having experienced one or more forms of maltreatment compared to 39% of other adoptees.

In summary, over the two-year period of data collection, 912 families with 1,162 children with problems were referred to APS, and services were completed with over 500 of these families. Eighty percent of the children served had previously been in the foster care system. For children adopted from the child welfare system, approximately 40% had been removed from their birth parents' custody by the age of 1 and had been placed with their current families by the age of 2. A little over a quarter of these children were age 7 or older when placed with their adoptive or guardianship families. The children who did not have histories of foster care placement were much younger when placed with their current families: 84% were 2 years old or younger at time of placement. The majority of children were reported to have one or more disabilities, with ADHD the most commonly reported disability (Table 4-1). Most children had experienced some form of maltreatment. Among children who had been in foster care, over a quarter had experienced all three types of child maltreatment (neglect, physical abuse, and sexual abuse).

Families' Problems and Needs

Range of presenting problems in families

Social workers assessed the presence of 25 possible problems in those families served by APS. The most frequently identified problems related to child behavior (88%) and emotional problems (74%). Child behavior or emotional problems were identified in 93% of cases. Table 4-6 provides the percentages of families identified as having each of the listed problems. Social workers also were asked to identify which was the primary problem in the parents' view. The primary problem according to parents almost always was framed in relation to the child: behavior and emotional problems, sibling conflicts, child attachment problems, or inability to control child. In 84% of the cases, parents presented one of these four problems as primary. Other problems on the list were reported as primary in fewer than 3% of cases.

Social workers also assessed the severity and duration of the primary problem. Problem severity was assessed as minor in 6% of the cases, moderate in 37%, and major in 57%. A review of problem statements in the cases in which problem severity was rated as minor indicated that in some cases, children had significant adjustment difficulties but the service request was limited. For example, a child with multiple disabilities was receiving services from several sources, but the adoptive mother wanted to talk with an AP worker to determine if there were other resources that might help their situation. In some other cases rated as minor on problem severity, the child was expressing grief or other concerns related to adoption but did not have significant problems in overall functioning.

Social workers also were asked to rate the duration of the primary problem. In 16% of the cases, the problem was rated as existing for less than a year; in 47%, for 1 to 3 years; and in 37%, for more than 3 years.

Reports of child maltreatment

In 21% of the closed cases, parents had been reported for abuse or neglect either prior to or during services. The majority (62%) of these cases were unfounded; 28% were indicated; and 10% were still pending.

Level of placement risk at referral

In some cases, DCFS or another source referred families to APS because the family requested an out-of-home placement for their child. It is the policy of DCFS to refer a family to APS for assessment and exploration of other avenues even when a child's therapist has recommended residential treatment for the child. If placement is clearly indicated, APS may assist the family, networking with other providers and supporting the family through the process.

The study used several measures to evaluate the risk that a child would be placed out-of-home. The stability of the child's adoption or guardianship arrangement was evaluated on a five-point scale at referral. Table 4-7 shows the status of 1,127 children as assessed by social workers. Nine percent of children were assessed as either needing or already in a long- or short-term placement.

Analysis revealed that the instability of children's current status at home was greater than social workers assessed at the time of referral. Among the closed cases, social workers assessed 11% as needing some type of placement at the time of referral. Thirteen percent of children were in placement at the close of services. The closing form on 19% of

TABLE 4-6

Families' Problems

Problem Type	Percent	Problem Type	Percent
Child behavior problems	88%	Criminal involvement of child	10%
Child emotional problems	73%	Marital relationship problem	10%
Major school problems	47%	Inadequate school placement	9%
Child attachment problem	42%	Substance abuse-child	8%
Parent unable to control child	33%	Physical illness of parent	8%
Child concerned about adoption	27%	Death-immediate family member	6%
Parent concerned about adoption	21%	Mental health problem-parent	6%
Major sibling conflicts	21%	Divorce/separation	5%
Parental attachment problems	14%	Job loss	4%
Other family problem	12%	Parental neglect of child	3%
Lack of needed resources	11%	Parental abuse of child	2%
Lack of social support	11%	Substance abuse-parent	2%

TABLE 4-7

Assessment of Children's Needs for Out-of-Home Placement

Type of Placement	Percent
Child needs (or is in) long-term placement	5%
Child needs (or is in) temporary placement	4%
No placement needed, major difficulties exist	34%
No placement needed, some difficulties exist	50%
Child and family coping adequately	8%

the cases indicated that parents were seeking out-of-home placements for their children at the time the case was closed. These data indicate that a sizeable minority of children was in or at imminent risk of out-of-home placement. At the same time, 30% of parents discussed the possibility of ending the adoption or guardianship at some point during their receipt of services.

Social workers also evaluated parents' level of commitment to their child at referral. The frequencies were very similar for mothers and fathers. Because more children had mothers than fathers, Table 4-8 presents the evaluations of mothers' level of commitment. The largest percentage of mothers (43%) were assessed as having an ongoing strong commitment to the child, as opposed to 10% who either were actively or more informally seeking to end their relationship with their children.

TABLE 4–8

Assessment of Mothers' Commitment to their Children

MOTHERS' COMMITMENT	PERCENT
Actively seeking dissolution	4%
Informally trying to disengage from child	6%
Inconsistent in commitment	7%
Committed to child, but struggling	41%
Ongoing strong commitment to child	43%

These data may appear to conflict. In reality, many families referred to APS were very stressed and felt discouraged about their ability to parent. Although they might have been very committed to their children, they may have doubted their ability to handle their problems successfully. As a result, workers reported that 30% of parents raised the possibility of adoption dissolution at some point during services but only 16% were perceived as not fully committed to their child at referral.

Children's Problems

Behavioral problems

Families participating in APS most frequently identified their children's behavior problems as the primary problem. Table 4-9 provides the percentages of children reported on the case closing form as having each of 23 specific problems. The first seven problems were present in half of the children served. The total number of behavior problems for each child was computed, yielding a mean number of problems per child of 7.6.

Emotional issues

Based on a list of emotional issues commonly reported in adopted children, social workers assessed those issues present in the experiences of the children served. As Table 4-10 shows, more than 50% of the children were evaluated as struggling with grief, attachment, or identity issues.

In summary, children's emotional and behavioral problems were the most frequently identified problems, although other commonly identified problems included school problems, attachment difficulties, inability to control the child, and children's concerns about adoption. The majority of children demonstrated acting-out behaviors such as defiance (88%), lying (76%), verbal aggression (75%), tantrums (59%), or physical aggression (56%). In addition, most children struggled with emotional issues such as grief, attachment problems, and identity. There had been a report of child maltreatment in approximately 20% of the cases, and of these cases, 28% were indicated for abuse or neglect. At referral, 17% of parents were rated by social workers as not committed or inconsistent in their commitment to their children. As mentioned previously, at the time of case closing, workers reported that 30% of the parents raised dissolution of the adoption or guardianship as an option at some point during services.

TABLE 4-9

Behavior Problems of Children and Rating of Severity

PROBLEM	PERCENT PRESENT	PERCENT MODERATE	PERCENT SEVERE
Defiance	88%	51%	37%
Lying	76%	49%	27%
Verbal aggression	75%	47%	28%
Peer problems	70%	47%	24%
Withdrawal	59%	44%	15%
Tantrums	59%	37%	22%
Physical aggression	56%	40%	16%
Rejects affection	49%	35%	14%
Hyperactivity	44%	28%	16%
Stealing	42%	28%	14%
Destruction of property	42%	31%	11%
Curfew violations	29%	16%	13%
Running away	26%	16%	10%
Sexual acting out	21%	15%	7%
Arrests/legal difficulties	19%	13%	6%
Wetting/soiling	16%	11%	4%
Suicidal behavior	14%	12%	1%
Self mutilation	12%	9%	3%
Cruelty to animals	9%	7%	2%
Sexual aggression	7%	4%	3%
Gang involvement	7%	4%	3%
Homicidal behavior	7%	6%	1%
Fire setting	6%	4%	2%

TABLE 4-10

Emotional Issues of Children as Identified by Social Workers

EMOTIONAL ISSUE	YES	NO	UNSURE
Grief	67%	20%	14%
Attachment problems	55%	36%	9%
Identity issues	56%	25%	19%
Depression	48%	32%	20%
Search issues	22%	67%	11%
PTSD	16%	60%	24%

Factors Associated with Problem Severity and Placement Risk

Severity of Child Problems

The study used the total number of behavior problems as a measure of the severity of child problems. The number of child behavior problems was significantly associated with age ($r = .17$; $p < .001$) and gender ($t = -2.12$; $p < .05$). Older children and boys had more behavior problems. The number of behavior problems, however, was not associated with age at placement, a child welfare history (children who had previously been DCFS wards did not have significantly more behavior problems than did the other adopted children), or adoptive family composition (children from single-parent families did not have significantly more behavior problems than children from two-parent families).

Table 4-11 shows how the severity of behavior problems varied by type of adoption or guardianship ($f = 2.83$; $p < .05$). Children's mean behavior problem score by type of adoption or guardianship ranged from 8.37 for foster parent adoptions to 6.97 for subsidized guardianships.

The primary factor related to the severity of children's behavior was a history of abuse. A history of physical or sexual abuse, but not of neglect, was associated with a higher level of behavior problems. Behavior problem scores and significance tests for types of maltreatment are reported in Table 4-12.

The association between specific types of maltreatment and children's other problems yields interesting insights. Two types of maltreatment were associated with a child's attachment problems: neglect (chi square = 14.82; $p < .001$) and physical abuse (chi square = 14.61; $p < .001$). A history of sexual abuse, however, was not associated with attachment problems. A history of multiple types of maltreatment also was associated with attachment problems (chi square = 16.97; $p < .001$). Sexual abuse had the strongest relationship with symptoms of post-tramatic stress disorder (PTSD) (chi square = 110.53; $p < .001$). There was also an association between PTSD symptoms and physical abuse (chi square = 59.40; $p < .001$) and neglect (chi square = 23.52; $p < .001$). A history of multiple types of maltreatment was strongly associated with PTSD symptoms (chi square = 104.11; $p < .001$). In addition, as shown in Table 4-13, a history of multiple types of maltreatment was strongly associated with the level of children's behavior problems ($f = 7.42$; $p < .0001$).

It is important to reiterate that the associations among the variables tested for this population of children referred to APS because of significant problems may differ from those that would be found in a study of a general population of adopted children. Adopted children in the general population who have not experienced maltreatment, for example, may have a lower level of behavior problems than children with no history of maltreatment who are referred to APS.

Certain disabilities were associated with more behavior problems. Children whom social workers assessed as mentally ill were likely to have significantly more behavior problems ($t = -5.51$; $p < .001$). Children identified as mentally ill had a mean of 11.2 behavior problems compared to 7.8 for children who had not been so identified. Likewise, ADHD was associated with a higher number of behavior problems ($t = -3.67$; $p < .001$). Surprisingly, however, children identified as affected by fetal alcohol syndrome/

TABLE 4–11

Children's Mean Behavior Score by Type of Family

TYPE OF FAMILY	MEAN BEHAVIOR SCORE
Matched Adoption	7.34
Foster Parent Adoption	8.37
Relative Adoption	7.16
Subsidized Guardianship	6.97

TABLE 4–12

Association of Behavior Problems and Maltreatment Types

TYPE OF MALTREATMENT	NEGLECT	PHYSICAL ABUSE	SEXUAL ABUSE
Not identified	7.11	7.01	7.25
Present	7.91	8.68	8.64
T-test	-1.82	4.09	-2.99
Significance	.070	.001	.005

TABLE 4–13

Number of Maltreatment Types and Behavior Problem Scores

NUMBER OF MALTREATMENTS	BPI SCORE	PERCENTAGE OF CHILDREN
No known maltreatment	7.16	(28%)
One type of maltreatment	6.67	(33%)
Two types of maltreatment	8.89	(20%)
Three types of maltreatment	8.82	(19%)

TABLE 4–14

Association of Emotional Issues and Outcome Measures

ISSUE	# BEH. PROBLEMS	PARENTS SEEKING PLACEMENT	PARENTS RAISING DISSOLUTION AS OPTION
Identity issues	**		
Grief issues	*	**	**
Attachment problems	***	***	***
Depression	***	***	***
Search issues			
PTSD symptoms	***	**	**

*$p<.05$; **$p<.01$; ***$p<.001$

fetal alchol effect did not have significantly more behavior problems than children who were not so identified. As Table 4-14 shows, a higher level of child behavior problems also was associated with the presence of certain child emotional issues (as assessed by social workers), parents seeking placement for the child, and parents' consideration of dissolving the adoption.

Placement Risk and Dissolution Risk

Although parents' seeking placement was significantly related to the parent's raising the possibility of adoption dissolution (phi = .39; $p < .0001$), the two variables were, in fact, distinct. Some parents who seek placement for their children may maintain a strong, ongoing commitment to the child, but believe that the child needs to be cared for in another setting for a time period. Others seeking placement are no longer committed to their child and want them out of their home. Likewise, parents who consider the dissolution of the adoption may actively seek placement for their children or may be expressing hopelessness, frustration, and a belief that they cannot adequately parent their children. Different factors were associated with placement and with consideration of dissolution. The data in this study yielded a profile of the types of children who appeared to be at high risk of placement and of adoption dissolution.

Nineteen percent of the families with closed cases had sought an out-of-home placement of their child. Seeking placement was associated with older age of the child (chi square = 28.22; $p < .05$) and, as stated earlier, with a child's history of neglect (chi square = 6. 19; $p < .05$), but not with other forms of child maltreatment or with gender. This second finding was somewhat surprising because neglect was the only type of maltreatment not related to severity of behavior problems, although it was associated with attachment problems. As expected, children whose parents were seeking placement had more behavior (chi square = 5 1.90; $p < .001$) and attachment problems. Also, as stated earlier, parents' seeking placement was associated with certain emotional issues for the child: attachment problems, depression, PTSD symptoms, and grief issues.

The possibility of ending the adoption was raised as an issue by parents in 30% of the closed cases. Neglect (chi square = 26.14; $p < .001$) and physical abuse (chi square = 10.25; $p < .01$) were associated with parents raising the possibility of dissolution but sexual abuse was not. Parents whose children were previously DCFS wards were more likely to raise the issue of dissolution than were other adoptive parents (chi square = 10.10; $p < .001$). Dissolution risk also was associated with older age of the child (chi square = 60.16; $p < .001$), more behavior problems (chi square = 50.95; $p < .001$), older age at adoptive placement (chi square = 60.2; $p < .001$), and the child's history of multiple types of maltreatment (chi square = 21.40, $p < .001$).

Race of the child also was related to the possibility of dissolution. Thirty-nine percent of the parents of African American children raised this possibility, compared with 27% of the parents of Caucasian children and 18% of the parents of children of other minority groups (chi square = 18.53; $p < .001$). Raising the issue of dissolution was more common in single-parent families (38%) than in two-parent ones (27%, chi square = 6.75; $p < .01$), although children in two-parent families were more likely to have attachment problems (chi square = 4.03; p < .05). Relative adoptive parents (36%) and subsidized guardians (54%) were more likely to raise the possibility of dissolution than were other types of families (26%) (chi square = 16.65; p < .001).

These analyses support the development of a profile of the child who is at high risk of out-of-home placement: a teenager who has experienced severe neglect and, most likely, abuse as well; displays a high number of externalized behavior problems; has attachment problems with regard to the adoptive parent; and is struggling with issues of grief and depression.

In summary, a number of child characteristics are associated with a child's higher number of behavior problems, parents raising the possibility of dissolution, and parents seeking placement. These characteristics include the older age of the child, male gender, being African American, a history of neglect and abuse, a history of multiple types of maltreatment, a history of foster care, and older age at the time of adoptive placement. Several types of disabilities and emotional issues were associated with either parents seeking placement of the child, parents raising dissolution, or risk measures, including a diagnosis of mental illness, attachment problems, ADHD, depression, PTSD symptoms, and grief issues. Family factors associated with more negative outcomes were single-parent families, relative adoption, and guardianship arrangements.

Services to Families

Types of Services Received

APS provides a range of services, including in-depth assessment, 24-hour on-call availability, intensive therapeutic services, support groups for children and for parents, linkage and advocacy, and cash assistance. Respite services are provided on a limited basis, usually through the use of cash assistance funds. Under the policy of APS at the time of this analysis, services were provided for 180 days, with the option of extending them for another 180 days if needed. Hence families may receive up to 360 days of service in any 24-month period. If the family is still in need of significant support after two full service periods, DCFS may authorize the provision of additional services.

With regard to 24-hour on-call availability, most families did not use the service or used it rarely. Families, however, reported that knowing they could call if they felt overwhelmed contributed to their sense of well-being and their confidence in APS. Of the families whose cases had been closed, 26% had used the on-call service at some point. These families received a mean of 3.4 hours of crisis (after hours) service.

The vast majority of families (97%) received some form of counseling, including traditional casework services, such as family and individual counseling and therapeutic interventions specific to adoption issues.

Previous studies of APS revealed that parents found support groups to be very helpful to them and their children (Howard and Smith, 1995). This study found that in 31% of the cases, parents participated in groups, and in 27% of the cases, children attended support groups. Parent support group usage in specific sites ranged from a high of 42% of families served to a low of 13%.

A majority of families availed themselves of the linkage and advocacy services of APS. In 74% of the cases, social workers connected families to existing services and assisted them in obtaining the services or benefits they needed. The majority of advocacy was done with school systems. Cash assistance was provided to far fewer families. In only 14% of the cases did families obtain emergency assistance (for such purposes as preventing eviction, purchasing needed equipment, or meeting other emergencies) or requested financial help for such services as specialized camps, special lessons, or child care to enable the family to attend group meetings. Similarly, a relatively small percentage of families (13%) received respite (the provision of care for the child to provide parents with relief from the pressures of parenting).

As Table 4-15 shows, a quarter of the families who received APS services were self-referred, and approximately one-third were referred by DCFS staff.

Service Duration

Approximately 9% of the 509 families with closed APS cases did not engage in services and were reported as having received no hours of service on the case summary form. This analysis of service patterns does not include these families, and instead focuses on the 465 families who received services and whose cases were closed during the study period. Data was obtained from the case summary forms completed by social workers at the close of services. At the time of data analysis, case summary forms had not been received for all closed cases. In a few cases, families declined to participate in the research. Overall, case closing forms were received on 78% of the cases closed as listed on monthly statistical forms.

Cases were open for a mean of 9.7 months, with a modal service period of 6 months. The majority of families were served well within the allotted 360-day period. A small percent of families (9%) received 2 or fewer months of service. These families tended to be ambivalent about receiving services, failed to keep appointments, or did not return phone calls. In a small number of these cases, families sought information only. In a fifth of the cases (21%), the service period was extended beyond 12 months. Figure 4-2 depicts the duration of services for all closed cases.

Sixteen percent of cases were reopened for services. As noted earlier, only three families were served twice during the study period. Because this measure is "point in time," however, it is not possible to determine how many of the total number of cases would reopen at some future date.

Hours of Service Received

APS families typically received many hours of service. The total service hours per case reported included contact hours with family members and collateral individuals and travel time to visit families in their homes. As shown in Table 4-16, the mean number of service hours per case was 72.4, with the highest mean number of service hours for any one service being intensive therapeutic services. Two-fifths (40%) of the families received fewer than 40 hours of services. A small percentage (8%) received 175 hours or more.

TABLE 4–15

Sources of Referrals to APS

REFERRAL SOURCE	PERCENT
Self-referred	25%
DCFS— other staff	22%
DCFS — APS liaison	14%
Private agency	16%
Other	12%
Previous client/friend	5%
School	4%

FIGURE 4–2

Duration of Services

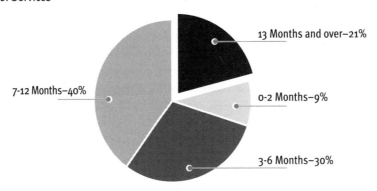

13 Months and over–21%

7-12 Months–40%

0-2 Months–9%

3-6 Months–30%

TABLE 4–16

Mean Number of Service Hours Per Case

TYPE OF SERVICE	MEAN HOURS
Intensive therapy services	37.9
Crisis response (after hours)	1.5
Parent group	3.9
Child group	3.4
Aftercare	.9
Collateral contacts/advocacy	6.4
Travel time	18.4
Mean service hours	72.4

Note: All cases did not receive all of the service activities. The total hours spent in a single type of activity were averaged for all families served.

Social workers also reported on how they met with family members during services: individual children in 81% of cases, with parents separately in 90%, and with parents and children together in 76%.

Service Techniques

Social workers identified the techniques that they used most frequently in their work with APS families. From a list of 14 possible interventions, they were asked to choose the five that they used most often with each case. The techniques used most frequently were supporting or validating the parent (86%), supporting or validating the child (60%), interpreting the child's behavior in light of his or her past (57%), teaching behavior management skills (42%), assisting parents in understanding child's losses (39%), processing loss with child (33%); de-escalating crisis (27%), and attachment building techniques (26%).

Reasons for Termination of Services

Almost a quarter (24%) of the APS families left the program before the end of six months. Social workers were asked to identify reasons for the termination of services to families. The most common reasons were that the family's goals were fully or partially met (47%) and the designated service period had come to an end (44%).

In summary, families received APS services for a mean of 9.7 months and were provided, on average, 72 service hours (an average of 7.4 hours of service a month). Approximately one-third of parents and one fourth of children received support group services.

Social Worker Evaluations of Service Outcomes

Social Workers' Evaluations of Family and Child Functioning

At the conclusion of services, APS social workers rate the changes in family functioning since the family's referral to the program. On overall functioning, 74% of families were called somewhat improved or significantly improved. Workers' ratings on other specific aspects of family functioning are presented in Table 4-17.

Social workers also rated changes in children's behavior and parents' ability to manage child behavior. In 70% of the cases, social workers rated children's behavior as somewhat or significantly improved. A similar shift was seen in parental ability to manage child behavior, as 70% of the parents were rated as somewhat or significantly better. An even greater shift was seen in parental ability to understand and tolerate problematic behavior, a variable on which 76% of families were rated as improved.

Finally, social workers assessed children's ability to discuss their feelings. They rated 71% of the children as having an improved ability to discuss feelings about emotionally laden issues. They also rated 63% as making progress in their ability to make sense of their emotions and work through them.

Social Workers' Evaluations of Child and Family Stability at Case Closing

Social workers rated the stability of the child's situation at the close of each case. At case closing, 10% of children were in a long-term placement or were assessed as needing such

TABLE 4–17

Social Workers' Evaluation of Changes Occurring in Families

Variable	Much Worse	Somewhat Worse	No Change	Somewhat Better	Much Better
Parent understanding of adoption issues	0%	0%	28%	51%	21%
Communication between parent and child	2%	2%	28%	53%	16%
Conflict among family members	2%	3%	34%	46%	14%
Parents united in approach	1%	2%	50%	34%	12%
Ability to get needed resources	0%	1%	42%	44%	14%
Level of family stress	4%	7%	18%	55%	17%
Level of social support	1%	1%	54%	36%	8%

a placement, while 6% were in or evaluated as needing a temporary placement. The majority of children (84%) were rated as not needing placement, although a fifth (20%) of children were assessed as having major difficulties requiring outside support.

Quantitative and Qualitative Evaluation of Children in Placement at the End of Services

Given the goal of APS to keep families together, a key measure of program effectiveness is whether family members are living together at the close of services. In a significant majority of families (87%), children were living at home at the conclusion of services. It is important to note, however, that families can be "together" even when the child is placed out-of-home because of extreme behavioral or emotional problems. In this study, 39% of the children who were placed outside their homes had a goal of return home. Also, most placed children maintained regular contact with their parents (based on parent reports on feedback forms, parents with placed children had weekly (77%) or monthly (14%) contact with their children). The vast majority of children (94%) were either residing at home or expected to return.

This study included a detailed analysis of the 70 children in out-of-home placement at the close of services (13% of the 544 children for whom this information was reported on the case closing form). A qualitative analysis was done of children rated as "out-of-home" at the end of services whose cases were closed between January 2000 and April 2001. In addition, telephone interviews were conducted with the social workers assigned to recently closed placement cases in order to assess the factors leading to placement, the workers' assessment of the clinical advisability of placement, and their judgment as to which services, if any, may have prevented placement.

Children who previously had been wards of DCFS were not more likely to be placed out-of-home at the end of services than were other children. The percentage of placed children who were previously wards of DCFS and of children still residing at home who were previously wards of DCFS was the same (73%). As shown in Figure 4-3, children placed out-of-home at the close of services resided in a range of placement types with the largest percentages of children in foster care (39%) and residential care (34%).

FIGURE 4-3

Out-of-Home Placements of Children at Termination of Services

(Based on n = 70)

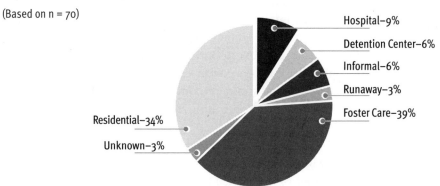

Hospital–9%

Detention Center–6%

Informal–6%

Runaway–3%

Foster Care–39%

Residential–34%

Unknown–3%

For placed children adopted by relatives or with relatives in guardianship arrange-ments, approximately 20% were with another relative (including many cases involving a foster care placement with a relative through DCFS). A higher percentage of subsi-dized guardianship arrangements than adoptions were represented among placement cases. More than a fifth (22.5%) of children in subsidized guardianship arrangements whose APS cases were closed were in placement compared to 12% of children in adop-tive families. The numbers of cases in subgroups, however, were not large enough to test for statistically significant differences.

Placed children were older (a mean of 14.2 years compared to 11.3 years for unplaced children). A higher percentage of African American children (16%) were in placement at the end of services than Caucasian children (11%). As expected, children who were placed had more severe problems. Placed children had a mean behavior problem score of 11.3, compared to 7.1 for unplaced children. A far higher percentage (63%) of parents of placed children raised dissolution as an option than parents of unplaced children (25%).

Case Reviews of Placed Children

In-depth case reviews were conducted for the 32 placed children whose cases were closed between January 1, 2000, and April 30, 2001. In 27 of the cases, there was suffi-cient information to assess the circumstances leading to placement. Attempts also were made to contact the social workers of the 18 placed children whose cases had been closed in the past year. Interviews were completed with the social workers for 11 chil-dren. These interviews, combined with in-depth case reviews, revealed that the fami-lies had received a variety of postadoption services prior to their children's placements. These services ranged from a few individual meetings with the parents to such services as school support services involvement, individual child counseling, intensive in-home family counseling, respite services, child psychologist or psychiatrist services, support through the court system, and services from Local Area Networks (a community-based service system that provides services for children with emotional problems).

A variety of factors were associated with children's out-of-home placements at the termination of services through APS. Child-related factors included severe psychological or psychiatric needs, legal problems (running away, breaking and entering, and drug and alcohol abuse), suicidal or homicidal ideation, refusal to return home after release from another facility, self-endangerment, and threats to the family, including physical and sexual aggression. Parent-related factors included a desire to have the child removed from the home (which, in some cases, involved lockouts and seeking dissolution of the adoption), harsh and inappropriate parental discipline, and high parental stress and lack of coping abilities. Approximately two-thirds of the placements were the result of severe child behaviors, and approximately one-third were the result of parental inability to cope and difficulty controlling the child. In a few cases, a judge ordered removal of the child from their home.

Approximately a third of the children were runaways, nearly one-half were diagnosed with ADHD, and a third were diagnosed with oppositional defiant disorder and conduct disorder. Severe child behaviors that were reported frequently included physical and verbal aggression, rejection of affection, peer problems, defiance, destruction of property, arrests and other legal difficulties, lying, withdrawal, curfew violations, and running away.

The majority of social workers believed that children's current placements met the children's needs, but they often did not have information on how well the child was responding to the placement. Social workers generally were not able to comment on the extent of communication between parents and children following placement because they did not maintain regular contact with parents after services through APS ended. Several workers, however, reported that the parents had called them to remain in touch. These social workers reported a variety of parent–child circumstances: some parents visited their child regularly; some children called their parents, begging to return home; some parents and children only saw one another at court; for some families, the individual family service plan specified contact; and in some cases, there had been no contact because the adoption had been or was being dissolved. The extent of communication appeared to be highly dependent on whether the goal was to return the child home.

Several social workers believed that in some cases, a goal of return home was not appropriate. In those cases, social workers cited such factors as the parent's desire to dissolve the adoption, the child's refusal to return home, and court involvement. Social workers commented that many children displayed behaviors too severe to allow them to return home, and many parents simply did not want the children back in their homes.

When questioned as to whether any steps might have been taken to prevent children's out-of-home placements, social workers typically reported that nothing could have been done. They described situations in which children's conditions and behaviors were far too severe for them to remain in the home, including serious medical conditions and behaviors such as sexual assaults against other children, self-harmful behaviors, and threatening and destructive conduct directed toward the family and others. The social workers noted that although several of the families were highly committed to their children, out-of-home care was the most appropriate placement for many children.

Social workers rated close to half (45%) of the parents of children placed at case closing as displaying ongoing commitment to their children. One social worker described the case of a 10-year-old boy who had multiple brain tumors (a terminal medical condition), a history of severe abuse and neglect, an IQ that had dropped into the lower 30s, and severe attachment problems. His behaviors involved severe verbal and physical aggression that included killing family pets and starting fires. Despite the severity of the child's behaviors and the psychological and physical harm that the child had caused the family, his parents maintained a strong ongoing commitment to him and continued to regularly communicate with him while he was placed outside the home. Such a high level of parental commitment was found to be representative of the cases in which nothing more could have been done to prevent the out-of-home placement.

Some of the placement cases involved older adolescents with extremely severe psychological and behavioral problems. In one reported case, a 17-year-old girl had experienced maltreatment in her birth family and foster care, including severe neglect and sexual and physical abuse, and had been diagnosed with bipolar disorder (indicative of a genetic predisposition to psychological disturbance). She attempted to poison members of her adoptive family and had asked gang members to kill them. The family chose to place the child in a locked residential facility and move without notifying their daughter. They also planned to dissolve the adoption. At the time of the interview with the social worker, the girl had been discharged to foster care and was participating in an independent living program.

Social workers reported that some parents of difficult adolescents remained committed to parenting their children despite severe problems. In one situation, the social worker reported that the child's parents continued to attend an APS support group after their daughter had spent two years in a residential treatment facility, had run away and remained out of state for a year, had spent time in a detention center and a residential substance abuse program, and, at the time of the interview, had once again run away. The teen's younger adopted sister, who had struggled emotionally with this situation, also continued to participate in services provided through APS.

In approximately one-third of the placement cases, social workers assessed the situation as one in which the parent was not open to change. In one case, the social worker reported that "if the mom could have taken a step back to understand the basis of why her child was excessively lying, she could have dealt with it, but the mom just couldn't depersonalize it and objectively look at this child's behavior and background…the mom had severe health and marital problems because of this." In another case, the parents adopted a sibling group of two boys and one girl. During participation in APS, the parents told the social worker that they were forced to take the boys when they really only wanted to adopt the girl. They were adamant that they no longer wanted the boys in their home, although the boys had no serious behavior problems. The social worker stated that "the parents tried to sabotage all services, and it almost seemed as if the parents were making things up."

Several of the social workers stated that in many of the placement cases, the appropriate step was either to dissolve the adoption or place the child in an out-of-home setting because of the parents' inability to cope. Some of the families had been reported to the child abuse and neglect hotline because they used inappropriate and harsh discipline. In addition, many of the families had been assessed as "lockout risks" because they "just want[ed] to get rid of the child." The social workers stated that in a few cases in which children were placed in foster care, the parents wanted to "get rid of" children when the children displayed no significant behavioral or psychological problems. One social worker reported that one child ran away from his mother five times because of her harshness and her wanting him out of the home. The child was a good student with no significant behavior problems and even attended summer school while he was "on the run," not missing a single day of school.

According to the social workers, many families reported that although adoption preservation services may not always prevent out-of-home placement or the dissolution of the adoption, one of the great benefits was that the social workers spent significantly more time with them than did other therapists.

Families' Evaluations of Services

After parents complete the APS program, they are given feedback forms to evaluate the services they received along with a postage-paid envelope addressed to the researchers. Questions relate to receipt of and satisfaction with services. At the time of this study, 293 families had returned feedback forms, reflecting a return rate of 58%.

The majority of families (57%) reported that they had received services for more than 6 months. Twenty-seven percent had received between four and six months of service, while16% received services for three months or less. Most (82%) reported that the service period was "somewhat" or "very" adequate. Only 18.5% of the 275 respondents felt that the service period was "very" or "somewhat" inadequate.

Services Offered and Received

Parents were asked which of the core APS services (described in common terms such as "counseling," "support group," and "getting needed resources") were offered to them and whether they used each service. As Table 4-18 shows, the majority of parents reported that they were offered the core services but, in most instances, far lower percentages actually used the services (the exception being counseling).

Parents also were asked to rate statements about the quality of services on a continuum of level of agreement ranging from "not at all" to "definitely." In the vast majority of cases, parents "definitely agreed" with statements that described services in terms of high quality (Table 4-19).

Satisfaction with Services

A significant majority of parents reported satisfaction with APS services (92%), with 68% stating that they were "very satisfied" (Figure 4-4). Parents also provided comments about adoption preservation services and their role in helping families with problems and needs:

> Our worker was the best thing that ever happened to us! We adopted our child three years ago. It would have been helpful if someone like our worker was there to help us in the early adjustment

TABLE 4–18

Parents' Reports Regarding Core Services Offered and Used

Service	Offered	Used
Counseling	96%	91%
Support Group—Parent	82%	45%
Support Group—Child	75%	45%
Crisis Intervention	71%	30%
Getting Needed Resources	80%	69%

TABLE 4–19

Parents' Satisfaction with Services

Service Characteristic	Level of Agreement		
	Not at All	*Somewhat*	*Definitely*
My counselor was easy to talk to	.3%	3%	96%
The agency called me back within 24 hours	1%	7%	91%
My counselor treated my family with respect	.3%	2%	97%
My counselor involved me in setting goals	2%	12%	86%
My counselor had a good understanding of adoption	1%	9%	90%
My counselor followed through on commitments	1%	11%	88%
My counselor was sensitive to my family's culture	.3%	6%	94%
My counselor was skilled and capable	2%	13%	85%

FIGURE 4–4

Overall Satisfaction

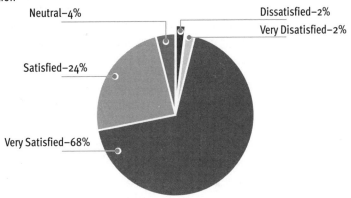

Neutral–4%
Dissatisfied–2%
Very Disatisfied–2%
Satisfied–24%
Very Satisfied–68%

stages...from the start our worker understood our situation exactly. Her guidance and advice was right on target and helped us so much. Theraplay is a great tool that we will definitely use. After talking with teachers, day care instructors, doctors, therapists, family members, and friends about our child, finally someone understood. Learning and understanding ADHD came easier for us because of our worker.

I can't begin to describe how helpful the agency has been to us! We were going through crisis after crisis, and I was near the point of despair. I felt so alone and so helpless. We were running out of options. I was driving one day and saw a truck with a slogan painted on the side: "Help is on the way!" I took that as a literal promise from God. Shortly after that we got involved at the agency. What a lifeline that has been! My worker has worked with my younger daughter and myself. Her insights and wisdom have been invaluable! My daughter is extremely adept at presenting a very charming "all together" exterior. The worker saw through it. She has been compassionate, caring, and committed. She truly has been God's gift to our family during a very difficult time I have also been involved with a mother's support group that meets on a weekly basis. There were times when that group literally sustained me. You feel so lonely and isolated when you go through experiences like this. Most people can't begin to understand. The group was a place where we could pour everything out—and know there would be no judgment. The insights of the two workers and the other moms were invaluable. Some of the situations can be so bizarre that you lose your point of reference. I don't know what I would have done without them!

Some parents also expressed concerns or made recommendations:

It would be much better if Adoption Preservation Services were not approached from an "open" or "closed" case perspective. It would work better if Adoption Preservation Services were in place from the time of adoption. We never know, as parents to these children, when we are going to need respite or immediate help.

[We received] better ways of discipline. Better understanding of the norm of children with brain trauma. We are persons who have adopted a young child. He has a number of problems that we deal with daily, and most of them we will for years to come. He will not mind anything we say (ADD + ODD). He is very strong at 6 years old. As time passes he will grow stronger and more aggressive—we (66 and 70 years old) will grow weaker and less agile to deal with him. It is imperative that we find an answer while he is younger. We have had him since he was 4.5 months (foster care) and had him 23 months when we adopted him. We love him dearly but do not want him to grow up aggressive and socially unacceptable.

By the time I found out about Adoption Preservation, my son was too involved in too many systems to be helped by Adoption Preservation. If I had known about the program earlier, I think the groups could have benefited both my children.

Parents also were asked on the feedback form to rate changes in their knowledge or functioning as a result of APS. As Table 4-20 shows, the results were very favorable, with the majority of parents reporting positive changes on a number of dimensions. A few parents, however, consistently reported a lack of positive changes. Parents reported a somewhat higher level of positive outcomes than did social workers. Parents reported

TABLE 4–20

Outcomes of Service as Reported by Parents

Outcome	Much Worse	Somewhat Worse	No Change	Somewhat Better	Much Better
Feel supported	1%	1%	7%	23%	69%
Know where to get help	0%	1%	10%	28%	61%
Understanding of my child	.4%	0%	12%	38%	49%
Confidence as a parent	0%	2%	13%	38%	48%
Specific parenting skills	0%	1%	14%	46%	39%
Level of stress in my family	3%	2%	16%	41%	38%
Child's behavior	4%	4%	18%	40%	34%
Understanding of adoption	.4%	0%	32%	26%	42%
Closeness to child	2%	4%	27%	36%	31%
Agreement between parents	.5%	1%	33%	37%	29%

the most positive results in the area of feeling supported, but social workers perceived that improvements in social support were the least frequent outcome for families.

Services Needed

Parents were asked what, if any, services were needed that they did not receive. Most parents (78%) reported they did not need services other than what they received through or with the help of APS. Among the 22% who identified an unmet service need, the most commonly cited service need was respite (14 families). Although other service needs were identified, no single service received more than four responses. These services included residential treatment, psychiatric evaluation, therapeutic counseling for attachment disorder, extended services, more help with ADHD, earlier intervention, counseling (both group and individual), private tutoring, suburban resources, and greater variety in the times or locations of groups (such as ongoing groups and groups offered closer to parents' homes).

Parents' Assessment of Out-of-Home Placements

Fifteen percent of the parents who returned feedback forms reported that their children were placed outside of the home at the time they completed the feedback form, and another 3% stated that their children had been placed out-of-home but had returned home. The most common placement type was residential treatment. In the majority of cases, the child remained connected to the family. Seventy-seven percent of parents with placed children reported that they had weekly contact with their children, and another 14% had at least monthly contact. Although parents' comments on the feedback forms did not represent the feelings of all parents served through APS, the comments were very positive. The very low number of negative comments was encouraging as was the high degree of satisfaction that the majority of parents expressed.

Conclusion

This analysis of a statewide adoption preservation program yields several insights into the nature of problems that these families confront and some of the factors associated with the severity of those problems. Families typically framed their problems in relation to the behavioral and emotional needs of their adopted children, although a range of family needs also were identified. A sizeable minority (21%) of the families served through APS had been reported for maltreatment to child protective services.

The population of families who sought services from this voluntary program was comprised primarily of those who had adopted children from the child welfare system (80% of the families served). These children, however, did not have a higher number of behavior problems nor were they more likely to be placed outside their homes at the end of services than other adopted children served by APS. Parents of children who previously had been DCFS wards, however, were more likely to raise dissolution of the adoption as a possibility.

Children's behavior and emotional problems were identified problems in 93% of the cases. The majority of children engaged in acting-out behaviors such as defiance, lying, and verbal and physical aggression, and most children struggled with internalized emotional issues such as grief, attachment problems, and identity issues. The majority of children had been diagnosed with some type of disability, with ADD/ADHD being the most commonly reported.

Many of the children (27%) had lived outside their homes since their adoptions, and 19% had had psychiatric hospitalizations. Most of the children served (87%) had experienced maltreatment, with severe neglect the most common type. Among children adopted from the child welfare system, 25% had experienced all three types of maltreatment (neglect, physical abuse, and sexual abuse).

A number of child-related factors were found to pose higher risk for children, including a history of maltreatment, particularly one with multiple forms of maltreatment; a high level of behavior problems; and attachment problems. Children at greater risk also included children placed at older ages; children who had been diagnosed with a mental illness, such as depression; and children with PTSD symptoms.

Among adoptive families who were struggling with child and family problems, certain types of families seemed to be at higher risk of breaking apart. Single parents, relative adopters, and subsidized guardians were more likely to raise the possibility of dissolving the adoption or guardianship. Parents of African American children also were found to be at greater risk of dissolution.

The factors associated with problem severity among a population of adoptive families receiving clinical services differ somewhat from the factors associated with problem severity in the general population of adoptive families. In a recent survey of families receiving adoption assistance in Illinois (Howard & Smith, 2001), several factors (relative and single parent adoptions and adoption of an African American child) were associated with fewer behavior problems of children—factors found to be associated with greater severity of problems in the clinical population studied here. In a study that compared children adopted from the child welfare system with domestic infant and internationally adopted children, the children adopted from the child welfare system were found to have higher behavior problem scores and a higher frequency of other types of problems, including special education placements and the need to take medication for behavior problems (Smith & Howard, 2001). Among the clinical population of adopted children studied here, however, the problems of children adopted from the child welfare system did not appear any more severe than the problems of children adopted through other avenues. Thus, it appears that although a lower percentage of other types of adopted children may receive clinical services, those who do so have problems as severe as children adopted from the child welfare system.

Adoption preservation services have been in place in Illinois for about 15 years. Service evaluations indicate that families who are struggling with complex, long-standing challenges value APS. Adoption preservation services go beyond the type of service provided by most mental health practitioners. This study found that approximately one-third of the service hours provided to each family through APS were comprised of travel time, after-hours crisis response, and advocacy services. These service capacities, typically not offered by private practitioners, are essential aspects of effective responses to the needs of many adoptive families. Some of these struggling families are single-parent, low-income families with a large number of children who generally cannot access traditional office-based services. Other families are coping with children with very severe behavioral and emotional problems. Support for these families must incorporate access to a social worker at any hour to help them "hang-in" as they parent their children.

Families need a range of postadoption services to sustain them from the time of adoption forward. APS in Illinois served only 2%–3% of the children on adoption assistance (a total of approximately 35,000) during the two-year period of this study. Clearly, most adoptive families do not need the level of intensive services provided by APS. Intensive services, however, are extremely important for preserving and strengthening adoptive families who need this level of support.

Research on postadoption services and clinical services for adoptive families is very sparse (Barth & Miller, 2000). Most research on clinical services for adoptive families involves very small samples of 50 or less (Groze, Young, & Corcran-Rumppe, 1991; Prew, Suter, & Carrington, 1990). To design more effective programs of post adoption services, more research is required on the needs of adoptive families and the services that respond to those needs. It also is time to move to a more sophisticated understanding of family needs and, in particular, the interventions that lead to positive outcomes for different families—the "what works and with whom" question. Systematic and comprehensive measures of child and family functioning, pre- and postmeasures, and more detailed examination of the intervention process are part of the next phase of understanding adoption preservation services.

References

Barth, R. P., & Miller, J. M. (2000). Building effective post-adoption services: What is the empirical foundation. *Family Relations. 49*(4), 447–455.

Groze, V., Young, J., & Corcran-Rumppe, K. (1991). *Postadoption resources for training, networking, and evaluation services (PARTNERS): Working with special needs adoptive families in stress.* Cedar Rapids, IO, and Washington, DC: Four Oaks, Inc., and the Department of Health and Human Services, Adoption Opportunities.

Howard, J. A., & Smith, S. L. (1995). *Adoption preservation in Illinois: Results of a four-year study.* Springfield, IL: Illinois Department of Children and Family Services.

Howard, J. A., & Smith, S. L. (2001). *The needs of adopted youth: A study of Illinois adoption assistance families.* Springfield, IL: Illinois Department of Children and Family Services.

Prew, C., Suter, S., & Carrington, J. (1990). *Postadoption family therapy: A practice manual.* Salem, OR: Children's Services Division.

Smith, S. L., & Howard, J. A. (1999). *Promoting successful adoptions: Practice with troubled families.* Thousand Oaks, CA: Sage Publications.

Smith, S. L., & Howard, J. A. (2001). *A comparative study of adopted and birth children.* Springfield, IL: Illinois Department of Children and Family Services.

Postadoption Services:
A STUDY OF Program Participants, Services, AND Outcomes

Kathleen Lenerz, Deborah Gibbs, and Richard P. Barth

A s a result of simultaneous trends over recent years, there has been an increase in the number of adoptions in the United States. Over the past decade, the number of adoptions from other countries has increased substantially (American Adoptions, 2000; National Adoption Information Clearinghouse, 2001). The opening of Eastern Europe in the early 1990s led to a surge in the adoption of children from orphanages from that region (U.S. Immigration and Naturalization Service [INS], 2000; INS, 1999; INS, 1998).

At the same time, federal and state policy initiatives have been implemented that supported increases in the rates of domestic adoption, particularly adoptions of older children with special needs. Congress passed legislation in 1992, 1993, and 1996 that provided tax incentives for adoption. In 1996, President William Clinton announced the Adoption 2002 Initiative (U.S. Department of Health and Human Services [DHHS], 2001a), which provided additional incentives for the adoption of children in foster care. The initiative's goal was to double the number of children in foster care who are adopted or placed in other permanent homes by the year 2002. In 1997, the Adoption and Safe Families Act (ASFA) increased pressures on states to find adoptive homes for children in foster care. Substantial incentive payments when states increased the number of adoptions were also made available through this act. Of the approximately 581,000 children in foster care, 127,000 are estimated to be eligible for adoption, with 97% of these children over the age of 1 year (DHHS, 2001b). DHHS also reported a substantial growth in adoptions of foster children: from 36,000 in 1998 to 46,000 in 1999 (DHHS, 2000; DHHS, 2001b). State initiatives throughout the country also appear to have boosted adoption rates. Efforts in Connecticut, for example, have quadrupled the adoption rate for children in foster care over the past five years (Hamilton, 2000).

Most adoptions are successful, as reflected by relatively low rates of termination of adoptive placements (either pre- or postlegalization). Findings from four studies con-

The authors wish to acknowledge the significant contribution of Sharon Napoli Pitman and Diane Griffith for data entry and management. We also wish to thank the families and social workers in the Casey Postadoption Services Program for their help with conceptualization and data collection.

ducted in the 1980s and 1990s show that 10% to 16% of adoptions terminate between 3 and 14 years following the adoptive placement (Barth & Berry, 1988; Goerge, Howard, & Yu, 1996; Partridge, Hornby, & McDonald, 1986; Urban Systems Research and Engineering, Inc. [USR&E], 1985). This rate is lower than the disruption rates for guardianship and long-term foster care placements (Berrick, Barth, Needell, & Jonson-Reid as cited in Barth, Gibbs, & Siebenaler, 2001). Groza and Rosenberg (1998) found that the rates of both adoption disruption (the return of a child to out-of-home care prior to the legalization of an adoption) and adoption dissolution (adoption termination after finalization) are relatively low, with 80% of adoptions remaining intact prior to finalization and 98% remaining intact after finalization.

At the same time, adoptions can be challenging. Multiple studies have found that adopted children have higher rates of conduct disorders and externalizing problems than do children in the general population (see Barth & Miller, 2000, for a review). Although there are multiple explanations for these findings, they reflect adoptive parents' perceptions of the challenges posed by their children's behavior. These findings, along with the increase in the number of adoptions of children who are older and have special needs, suggest that increased support and services for adoptive families may be appropriate.

Recognition of the importance of providing postadoption services to promote adoption stability has been reflected in the growth in postadoption services throughout the country. Funding for these programs became available when ASFA reauthorized funds for the federal Promoting Safe and Stable Families Program (SSF) and expanded that program to include postadoption services. Many states are dedicating portions of their SSF funds for adoption support and preservation, although the extent to which these funds are used specifically for postadoption services is unknown (James Bell Associates as cited in Barth, Gibbs, & Siebenaler, 2001).

Barth, Gibbs, and Siebenaler (2001) reviewed models of existing postadoption services programs. They described four types of services encompassed by these models: (1) educational and informational services, such as the provision of information through literature, workshops, or other materials; (2) clinical services, including counseling; (3) material services, such as subsidies or other financial benefits, respite care, and temporary out-of-home placement; and (4) support networks, which may be either self-help or professionally facilitated.

Little is known about the effectiveness of these types of services or the appropriate mix of services to best meet families' needs. When program outcomes have been examined, they often have focused on child behavior and adoption disruption or dissolution. The Illinois Adoption Preservation Project, which provided a variety of services to families at risk of adoption dissolution, found significant improvements in child behavior (see Chapter 4). In addition, social workers reported improvements in parents' understanding of adoption issues, communication within the family, level of family stress, and conflict among family members. Further, 87% of children remained in the home at the end of the Illinois service program (see Chapter 4). Oregon's Postadoption Family Therapy Project, which served at-risk adoptive families both before and after legalization, found a combined disruption and dissolution rate of 16% (Prew, 1990).

One multifaceted program, the Iowa Postadoption Resources for Training, Networking, and Evaluation Services (PARTNERS) provided a continuum of services to pre- and postadoptive families, including support groups, adoption counseling, and intensive services. Although 29% of the children in this program were in out-of-home placements at the end of services, these placements may not represent complete termination of the adoptive placement. (Groze, Young, & Corcoran-Rumppe, 1991).

Although there is some agreement as to which post-adoption services are most effective, there is little empirical evidence as to what families find to be most useful. Program elements that families consider helpful include self-help or other support groups for adoptive parents and respite (Barth, Gibbs, & Siebenaler, 2001). Meanwhile, evaluations of brief, time-limited adoption preservation services have shown disappointing results. Barth, Gibbs, and Siebenaler (2001) suggest that this is because such brief service models do not meet the needs of adoptive families and that "a less time-limited and more family-focused approach appears more suitable" (p. 11). Certainly more work needs to be done to understand the best approaches and services for meeting adoptive families' needs.

With the likelihood that adoption rates will continue to increase substantially, particularly for children with troubled placement histories, it is important to focus on services that can support adoptive families in maintaining stable homes for children. Recognizing the limited research regarding which families seek services after adoption and the nature of the services most likely to meet their needs (Barth & Miller, 2000), the present study was conducted as an initial examination of a large post-adoption services program. This study examines the characteristics of the families and children served, their reasons for seeking services, and the types of services provided. Most importantly, it provides evidence on multiple outcomes of the services and information on some of the factors related to positive outcomes.

This study was not of all adoptive families, but only adoptive families who sought services. Thus, it does not address the overall need for postadoption services. Because the study offers no comparison of children in adoptive families and children in other family configurations, it similarly does not shed light on the prevalence of mental health problems or dissolution rates among adopted children relative to those in other types of families. Still, the findings from this study have valuable implications for policy and practice with adoptive families. Because it focused on families who have sought and received services, this study can enrich understanding of the characteristics and needs of adoptive families experiencing difficulties, the services that appear to be most helpful, and the optimum mix of services. Thus, this study provides valuable information about the design and development of postadoption services programs, and it suggests guidelines for states and agencies when they plan services for adoptive families.

The Casey Family Services Postadoption Services Program

The Casey Family Services Postadoption Services (PAS) program was established in 1991. It currently operates in five New England states: Connecticut, Maine, New Hampshire, Rhode Island, and Vermont. The overall aims of the program are to support, strengthen, and preserve adoptive families. Additionally, this program strives to increase awareness of adoption-related issues within the communities in which it operates and to enhance the capacity of service providers to meet the needs of adoptive families.

Although the program operates somewhat differently in each site (largely in response to local needs), each location offers four major types of services: (1) counseling, both individual and family; (2) support groups for parents and children; (3) educational workshops for parents and professionals; and (4) case advocacy. Thus, it provides three of the four types of services identified by Barth, Gibbs, and Siegenaler (2001) and adds another service type—case advocacy. Service provision is grounded in a family strengths perspective, while emphasizing flexibility in addressing adoption-related issues. All services are voluntary and family-initiated. There are no fees for services nor are there any limits on the extent of services a family may receive. Families may enter services at any point in the adoption process, from the preadoption period through the adopted child's late adolescence. The Casey PAS program has been actively publicizing its services to both professional and lay audiences. Consequently, families come to the program from a variety of avenues: referral from other professionals in the community, word of mouth from other adoptive families, or as a result of outreach advertising.

Method

Data Collection

To better understand the characteristics of families seeking postadoption services, data were gathered from families at the opening of their cases. Parents completed forms that recorded demographic and adoption information; the family's history of service use; the concerns for which the family was seeking services; and information on parent–child relationships, family strengths, and child attachment. The forms from which data were gathered also were used for program administrative purposes and did not specify which parent should complete the form. Thus, mothers or fathers individually or collaboratively may have completed the forms that were used in the study. In addition to the family's report of their concerns, social workers also reported on the family's needs based on their initial assessment. Finally, social workers summarized service provision at the closing of the cases and provided their assessments of family progress in the areas in which services were provided.

Data were gathered on all families who entered services from 1997 through 2000 in five of the six program sites. The Maine site was not included because it was participating in a separate grant-related evaluation. Because there was no limit on the extent of services that families could receive or their timing of service receipt, families could terminate services and later re-enter the program. When families re-entered during the four-year study period, basic demographic and service information was gathered on the families' earlier round of services. Thus, the following descriptive information includes some pre-1997 data.

A total of 589 case openings or reopenings are represented in the data, along with 453 case closings. Only limited assessment information was obtained again from families when their cases were reopened. These reopened cases also created duplication of family data. In response to these issues, the study's information on families includes only the 400 families entering services for the first time. Of these 400 families, services to 293 families had been completed (and their cases closed) at the time of this analysis. There were 385 adopted children in these first-time families on whom data were available.

As a result of the variations in data availability as well as missing data, sample sizes in the analyses vary and are indicated for each group. An attrition analysis was done to determine if there were any differences in family or child characteristics or outcomes between families receiving services for the first time and families re-entering services. No differences were found, suggesting that the subset of families included in the following analyses were representative of all families served by this program.

Measures

The study used measures that gathered information on demographics, prior service use, adoption information, family needs, family concerns, family relationships, family strengths, attachment, service use, and family and child gains. All measures were constructed specifically for the study.

Demographic

Families provided demographic information on each member of the family, including age, gender, race, relationship, and living situation.

Prior service use

Parents completed a checklist in which they indicated whether they previously had used a given service and the extent of their use of that service. They also rated the helpfulness of each service based on a scale from 1 ("Not helpful") to 3 ("Very helpful").

Adoption information

For each adopted or preadoptive child in the family, parents provided information on the type of adoption (e.g., public or private, domestic or international. open or closed); the date the child was placed with the family; the date the adoption was finalized; whether the child was a relative, a child in foster care placed in the home, or a child who was otherwise known to the family; the child's placement history; the child's history of maltreatment; and the extent of birth family and sibling contact.

Family needs

Social workers completed a checklist of family and child needs based on their initial assessment of the family. The checklist contained 18 of the most common needs of adoptive families and other typical family concerns, including areas such as birth family issues, relationship issues, child identity issues, financial problems, and child behavior problems. Each checklist item produced a dichotomous variable indicating presence or absence of that particular need.

Family concerns

Parents completed a 27-item checklist and rating scale of family concerns (Cronbach alpha = .79). This scale contained a list of concerns common to many families, as well as those specific to adoptive families. Examples included availability of childcare, financial concerns, accessibility of mental health services, child behavior problems, and lack of adoption-sensitive community resources. On this scale, parents first indicated whether an item was not a concern. If the item was a concern, they then rated their effectiveness in coping with the concern on a scale from 1("Coping not at all well") to 4 ("Coping well"). Responses on this scale were summarized in terms of both the number of concerns a family had and their overall ability to cope. The number of items for which families indicated a concern was summed to produce an overall number of family concerns. The effectiveness of the family's coping was expressed as the mean rating of items for which a concern was endorsed, with higher scores indicating more effective coping.

Family relationships

Parents completed an 11-item family relationships scale for each adopted child in the family (Cronbach alpha = .90). The items in the scale reflected general parent–child relations, as well as parenting experiences with the particular child. Examples of items included statements such as, "I feel that this child has become a part of this family," and "I feel that things with my child are under control." Parents responded on a scale from 1 ("Rarely") to 4 ("All of the time"). A principal components factor analysis of this scale revealed two factors. The first reflected a combination of the parent's commitment to and confidence in raising this child (parenting confidence, Cronbach alpha = .87). The second showed the stress of dealing with the child's emotional and behavioral challenges (parenting stress, Cronbach alpha = .82). Scores on these two factors were coded so that higher scores indicate better functioning.

Family strengths

To assess the extent of family strengths, parents completed a 19-item family strengths scale that incorporated a variety of strengths that clinicians believe to be important factors in treatment (Cronbach alpha = .80). Examples included statements such as, "Family members are optimistic," and "Our family has supportive relationships outside the family." Parents reported the extent to which they believed each item described a strength in their family on a scale from 1("Not at all a strength") to 4 ("A super strength"). Because of the limited variability in parents' responses, it was not used in any of the analyses examining factors relating to positive outcomes.

Attachment

For each adopted child, parents completed an 8-item scale assessing their perceptions of the attachments between the child and other family members (Cronbach alpha = .88). Each relationship was rated on a scale from 1 ("Very weak") to 5 ("Very strong"). A principal components factor analysis of this scale produced three factors that represented attachment between the adopted child and parents, the child and siblings, and the child and extended family members (Cronbach alphas = .86, .90, .92, respectively).

Service use

At the closing of each case, social workers reported on the services that each family received, using a checklist that included the major program components: family system counseling, support groups, case advocacy, and educational workshops. For families who received counseling, they further recorded the approximate number of sessions and whether children and adults were seen individually or together. For families participating in groups, social workers also recorded the type of group attended (adult time-limited, child time-limited, whole family time-limited, and open-ended). Because the program practice was to record case opening and closing information only when families received counseling, service use was not recorded for families who participated in groups only. Thus, the extent of families' use of groups and workshops reported must be seen as an underestimation of the actual use of these services.

Family and child gains

Data on outcomes were available from the social workers' assessments at the closing of each case. Social workers rated the family's performance on eight outcome indicators at intake and at case closing. These indicators included family communications, understanding of adoption issues, parents' ability to help children resolve adoption issues, child behavior, child's family identity, child's individual identity, child–family attachment, and family–child attachment. Social workers completed ratings only for areas of functioning that were considered to be issues for the family and that were addressed in the course of services. Pre- and post-PAS functioning were both assessed on 5-point scales. Thus, the gain a family could exhibit depended on the level of functioning at which the family started, with the maximum being a 4-point gain.

Results

Families and Children Served

Most of the families (79%, N = 257) served by the PAS program were two-parent families. The majority of parents in these families were Caucasian (89% of 421 individuals), although this percentage varied by program site, reflecting local demographics. About half (51%, N = 321) were ages 40–49, with the remainder equally divided between younger and older parents. A small number of cases (N = 36) were opened for families who reported having no adopted children, presumably families who were contemplating or in the process of adoption. Among the 335 families with adopted children, more than half (51%) had more than one adopted child, and 36% had other children as well.

Adopted children were evenly divided by gender (52% male). Far more racial diversity existed among adopted children than parents, with only about half of the adopted children (48%) being Caucasian. Thirteen percent were African American; 13% were Hispanic; and 9% were Asian. Eighteen percent were classified as "other," which is largely an indication of mixed race. A substantial proportion (40%) of children were from a different racial or ethnic background than both adoptive parents. At the time of initial case opening, adopted children in these families ranged from infancy to 23 years, with a median age of 10 years. Adolescents represented a significant proportion of the population, with 32% over the age of 12. (Sample sizes for these analyses ranged from 340 to 376.)

The children served by this program were likely to have been adopted at young ages. Nearly third (32%) had adoptions finalized before the age of 2, and an additional third (34%) had been adopted before the age of 6. Nearly all of the adoptions (96%)

were finalized before parents sought services from the PAS program. The median time from adoption finalization to initial case opening was 4.5 years, although as shown in Figure 5-1, a substantial proportion of cases opened within two years of the adoptive placement (27%) or more than 10 years after placement (15%). (Sample sizes for these analyses range from 209 to 271.)

Exactly half (50%, N = 244) of the adopted children had a known history of maltreatment, as reported by parents. Parents' use of this term, however, may not correspond to child welfare agencies' use and may be an overestimate of maltreatment. Among the children with a history of maltreatment, nearly all had experienced neglect (92%), with physical abuse and sexual abuse less commonly reported (53% and 30%, respectively, N = 122). Most children (73%, N = 247) had been in foster care at some time prior to placement with their adoptive families. There were indications that parents used the term "placement" to refer to forms of substitute care other than foster care for children in public agency custody. Among the children reported as having been in foster care, 34% (N = 179) had more than one placement, with a mean of 1.62 placements. This finding suggests that most of the children served by the program did not have extensive placement histories.

Characteristics of adoption

Adoptions occurred more often under public (62%) than under private agency auspices. As Figure 5-2 shows, a substantial proportion (33%) involved the adoption of children from other countries. More than one-quarter of adopted children (27%, N = 385) had been with the family as a result of a foster care placement before adoption. Although contact with the child's birth parents was relatively uncommon (reported for 22% of children), 41% of children had some contact with birth siblings. When such contact occurred, it was more likely to be regular (29%) than occasional (23%, N = 97). It is unknown how many children were living with birth siblings in the adoptive home. (Sample sizes for these analyses ranged from 207 to 254, except where specified.)

Service history

Nearly all of the adoptive families served by the Casey PAS program were seen after using other services. Beyond wide use of adoption education and information (70% of families), the services that families most commonly used before coming to this program were individual child counseling (60%), parent education (58%), and informal help from extended family (51%). Least used services were psychiatric hospitalization of the child (14%), marital counseling (17%), and overnight respite (17%). More than 90% had used a mix of services, with a median of four different types. (Sample sizes for these analyses ranged from 123 to 151.)

Parents were generally satisfied with the services they had received elsewhere, as reported on the checklist they completed at intake. For all types of services except child psychiatric hospitalization, the mean satisfaction rating was at least 2.0 ("Somewhat satisfied"). (Sample sizes varied from 10 to 102, depending on how many families had previously used each service.) Help from extended family members, individual counseling for parents, and overnight respite for children were the types of services that received the

FIGURE 5–1

Time Elapsed from Adoption Finalization to Initial PAS Case Opening

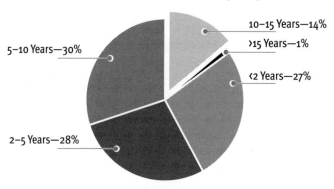

- 10–15 Years—14%
- >15 Years—1%
- <2 Years—27%
- 2–5 Years—28%
- 5–10 Years—30%

FIGURE 5–2

Types of Adoption: Domestic verses International and Public verses Private

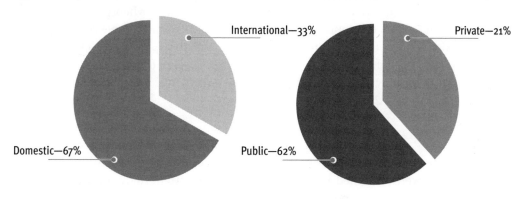

- International—33%
- Domestic—67%
- Private—21%
- Public—62%

highest satisfaction ratings. In addition to psychiatric hospitalization, families rated marital counseling, psychological evaluation, individual counseling for children, and child placement as least helpful. Thus, it appeared that parents placed greater value on the more "normalized" types of support than on more formalized therapeutic interventions.

Clinical Issues

Reasons for seeking services

At intake, social workers recorded the issues for which families indicated they were seeking help. Relationship issues (36%) were the area of greatest need. Other reasons included children's self-image (32%), children's relationships with peers and adults (32%), and grief or loss related to birth families (37%). School-related issues (30%) and child behavior (28%) were slightly less likely to be identified as needs. Decisions regarding dissolution (2%) and out-of-home placement (6%) were infrequently cited as needs, as were legal questions (3%) and financial concerns (4%). Most families identified multiple needs at case opening, with a median of 2 identified needs. (The sample size for each of these analyses was 400.)

Family concerns

Family concerns can be measured by the frequency with which a specific issue is identified as a concern and how well families cope. Figure 5-3 shows the issues most likely to be identified as concerns related to family dynamics: problematic child behavior (identified by 96% of families), balancing the needs of adults and children (96%), the demands of caring for children (91%), and emotional upsets by either adults or children (91%). Least frequently cited as concerns were lack of familiarity with a child's cultural background (26%), racism in the community (25%), significant parental losses (29%), and stressors in dealing with the service system (30%). (Sample sizes in these analyses ranged from 153 to 167.)

Areas with which the family had the greatest difficulty coping most often related to child behavior or the lack of the service system's responsiveness. Behavior-related concerns included the child's problem behavior itself—for which parents rated their coping ability as 2.22, with 4.0 being the best coping possible—and emotional upset in the family (2.51). Lack of service system responsiveness appeared when parents reported concerns about the lack of adoption-sensitive resources (2.66) and trouble getting needed mental health services (2.68). Families seemed best able to cope with the challenges of combining different cultural backgrounds (3.22), past losses of the parents (3.22), physical illness in the family (3.21), and financial concerns (3.18). (Sample sizes for family concerns ranged from 242 to 351).

Strengths

Data on families' self-assessed strengths suggested that adoptive parents had a substantial degree of confidence in their abilities and resources as parents. Nearly all items on the instrument were identified as a "medium" or "super" strength by at least two-thirds of families, although some positive bias may have affected these responses. Areas of greatest strength were comfort with adoption (3.66), open communication with children (3.43), a stable and structured family environment (3.47), and flexibility in interacting with children (3.26). Strengths rated lowest included contact with other adoptive families (2.33), previous parenting experience (2.74), and having knowledge of and comfort with the child's preadoptive history (2.85). (Sample sizes for strengths means ranged from 220 to 231.)

Family relationships

Families' commitment to adoption was demonstrated by parents' responses on the family relationships form (completed for each adopted child). Their strongest responses on this scale included belief that the child would remain part of the family (rated 3.86 out of 4.0), commitment to working through problems (3.76), belief that the child had become part of the family (3.63), and not reaching the last straw with the child (3.54). At the same time, however, parents expressed concerns about raising children with behavioral and emotional problems, reporting that they were least confident in feeling that things with the child

FIGURE 5–3

Most and Least Frequntly Expressed Concerns by Parents

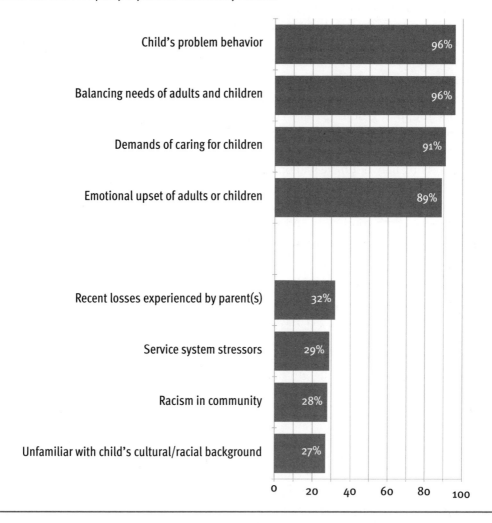

were under control (2.40), the behavior or emotional problems of the child (2.48), pleasure in parenting (2.86), and getting the child to respond to limits (2.87). Scores on the parenting confidence subscale were somewhat higher (3.31) than scores on the parenting stress subscale (2.82). (Sample sizes for these figures ranged from 115 to 189.)

Attachment

The relationship within the family that had the strongest attachments was between parents and adopted children, where the attachment score was 4.10 out of a possible 5.0. Not surprisingly, parents reported that attachments between adopted children and their siblings (3.78) and between adopted children and extended family members (3.72) were not as strong as their attachments with their parents. (Sample sizes for these scores ranged from 179 to 208, depending on the presence of these members in the family.)

Services Received

Social workers reported on families' receipt of services in the areas of advocacy, family systems counseling, support groups, and workshops. Among these services, family systems counseling was the most commonly used (71% of closed cases, N = 293). Of the families who received counseling, slightly more than half (54%) had one to three counseling sessions, and 18% had more than 10 sessions (N = 209).

Thirty-two percent of the families received case advocacy. One quarter (25%) of families participated in groups, of which child time-limited groups (47%) and adult open-ended support groups (39%) were the types most commonly used (N = 72). Parents were less likely to report having attended PAS workshops than having participated in other services. Families who attended support groups or workshops but did not receive counseling may not have had open cases, and as a result, use of groups and workshops was probably underestimated.

Many families (34%, N = 261) participated in more than one type of service. Sixteen percent received both counseling and advocacy; 7% participated in counseling and support groups; and 10% were involved in counseling, advocacy, and support group services.

Case flow

Although the length of time that cases remained open varied substantially, the PAS program generally seemed to adhere to a model of time-limited service. The median length of service overall was 141 days, or just under 5 months (N = 291). One-third (33%) of cases closed within 3 months, and 18% remained open longer than 12 months (N = 292). The data on length of services, however, represented only closed cases, and thus, may underestimate the length of service if currently open cases remain open for longer lengths of time than the closed ones examined in this study.

Outcomes

Improvements rated by social workers

Social workers rated most areas of child and family functioning as showing modest improvements. As Table 5-1 shows, the greatest gains were reported in child behavior, parents' understanding of the effect of adoption on child behavior, and effective communication (with mean gains of 1.19, 1.19, and 1.01, respectively, out of a maximum of 4.0). Gains in all areas of functioning were unlikely to have occurred by chance (p < .001). (Sample sizes ranged from 155 to 197 because social workers rated only those areas of functioning that were addressed during the course of services.)

Factors related to outcomes

There were considerable data whose relationship to program outcomes could be examined, including family and child characteristics, family functioning, and various measures of service provision. Because the relationship between the elements of service provision and outcomes is of greatest interest to service providers and program designers, only those analyses are presented here. Future analyses will include a more in-depth examination of the relationships among family characteristics, service provision, and outcomes.

TABLE 5-1			

Family and Child Gains

FAMILY-CHILD GAIN	MEAN AT INTAKE	MEAN AT CLOSING	MEAN GAIN
Effective communication	2.24	3.26	1.01*
Parents' understanding of adoptive issues	2.66	3.85	1.19*
Parents' ability to help children resolve adoptive issues	2.45	3.22	0.79*
Child's behavior	2.07	3.27	1.19*
Adopted child's family identity	2.65	3.39	0.76*
Adopted child's self identity	2.28	3.04	0.78*
Child-family attachment	2.85	3.42	0.58*
Family-child attachment	3.40	3.77	0.35*

Note: Possible gain varies, depending on level at which families started, with a maximum of 4.0.

* $p < .001$

The types, amount, and variety of services that families received were examined in relation to families' gains. Overall gain was calculated by taking the mean gain across the eight areas in which social workers rated families' functioning pre- and post-PAS. ANOVAs (analysis of variance) were used to examine the relationship between categorical variables and family gain.

Types of services received

Whether families received counseling, participated in support groups, or received case advocacy were each coded as a dichotomous variable indicating receipt or lack of receipt of each type of service. Results of the ANOVAs showed that families who received counseling or case advocacy or who participated in support groups did not show more gain than families who did not.

Amount of services

Amount of services was examined in terms of length of services and the number of counseling sessions attended. Length of service was divided into four categories: less than 3 months, 3–6 months, 6–12 months, and more then 12 months. An ANOVA revealed a significant relationship between length of service and mean family gain— $F(3,267) = 4.40$, $p = .005$. Follow-up tests showed that families who received more than 12 months of services exhibited greater gains than families who received less than three months of services ($p = .002$).

To examine whether the amount of counseling received was helpful, an ANOVA categorized the number of family counseling sessions as: one to three sessions, four to nine sessions, and more than nine sessions. A significant overall difference was found— $F(2,148) = 9.83$, $p = .0001$. Tukey follow-up tests revealed that families who received more than three counseling sessions (four to nine and more than nine sessions) showed greater gain than families who received one to three sessions ($p = .001$). The gains of families who received more than nine sessions, however, were not different than those receiving four to nine sessions. Because case advocacy is not a discrete activity that can be quantified in units (as opposed to number of counseling sessions, for example), the amount of case advocacy was not examined in relation to outcomes.

Variety of services

An ANOVA tested whether families who received a greater variety of services improved more than those receiving fewer types. An independent variable representing the types of received services was constructed with categories representing each single service, each possible pair of services, and all three types of services—counseling, groups, and advocacy. There was no statistically significant difference in family gains as a function of the variety of the used services.

Discussion

This study provides a clearer picture of the families who seek postadoption services, the types of gains they make, and some of the factors related to improved functioning. Although the data in this study came from a single postadoption services program, the fact that families came from a multistate catchment area enhances the generalizability of the results. Although some of the findings are exploratory and descriptive, they have a number of implications for policy and program planning for adoptive families.

Given the expectation of large increases in the number of adoptions of children from foster care, states and agencies may focus on that population in planning for services for adoptive families. It is worth noting that a substantial portion of the families served through this program had adopted children from private agencies or other countries. Thus, programs or policies that focus exclusively on the needs of children adopted from foster care may overlook the needs of many other adoptive families.

Families in this program also sought services long after their adoptions were finalized, and they returned to the program one or more times for further services. This finding suggests that adoption is a significant experience with lifelong effects for the family. The need for adopted children to resolve identity issues relating to the adoption, for example, may be a prominent feature of adolescent development that may not be resolved during the initial phase of adjustment. Services to adoptive families, then, may be most effective when they are available beyond the immediate postadoption period and can be flexible in response to families' and children's changing needs.

The families who participated in this program often had adopted multiple children and were likely to have other children in the family as well. The dynamics in such families can be quite complex and may vary over time as new children join the family. Programs that focus on the adopted child's adaptation but exclude the dynamics in the whole family system may not effectively address the multiple challenges these families face.

Although families came to the Casey PAS program with many different issues, child behavior was a prominent focus. In spite of the fact that parents reported great commitment to working through problems and strong confidence in their ability to maintain their adopted children in the family, they felt unprepared to deal with the psychological and behavioral problems of their children. Given that the children in this sample often were adopted at an early age and did not appear to have extensive placement histories, older children adopted from the foster care system could pose even greater challenges for parents. Future programming aimed at that population should provide even more extensive services and treatment for behavior and psychological problems.

At the same time, families benefited from services that addressed other needs. Chief among the areas of family improvement were child behavior, understanding the effect of adoption on the child's behavior, and communication within the family. The area of least change was child–family attachment. The implications for programming are that services must be multidimensional to address the variety of areas where parents seek help. Moreover, in a relatively short-term program such as this one, the more instrumental areas of functioning (such as parenting and behavior) probably are more amenable to change than more complex and enduring areas of functioning, such as attachment.

Based on their ratings of the helpfulness of the services they received prior to this program, families seemed appreciative of any services they received. At the same time, families tended to give lower ratings of helpfulness to more traditional and structured services, particularly mental health-oriented services. Social workers in the PAS program have commented that many families do not feel that community services, particularly in the mental health and educational arenas, understand the needs of adoptive families. These families may find educational and supportive approaches to be more helpful than services that take a more pathological or treatment-oriented view of their family situation.

One highlight of this study is the examination of program outcomes and the relationship between service provision and outcomes. Based on social workers' ratings of family gains, families showed improvement in all eight areas examined in the study. Thus, a program with a relatively short length of service seems capable of providing the assistance adoptive families seek.

More important from the program planners' perspective, the study provided indications about the most beneficial forms of service provision for families. Participation in support groups and receipt of case advocacy were not related to the level of family gain. Although the receipt of counseling also was not related to family gain, the amount of counseling mattered. Families who received more than a few sessions showed significantly greater gains. Family gain possibly was not associated with receipt of group and advocacy services because the present data focused on families whose primary service was counseling. Because the other services did not intend to be the primary treatment agent, they did not carry as great a weight in affecting outcomes. Both a greater intensity of counseling and a greater length of services seemed beneficial, however. Based on this finding, one might expect that programs designed to address child adjustment and family functioning through short, time-limited services may not be as effective as programs that allow families the time and support they need to progress.

All in all, these findings show that adoptive families are likely to have multiple needs, which seem most responsive to multidimensional, flexible programming that allows families to return for services as needed and does not limit the amount of services they receive. Families involved in all types of adoptions seek services at varying times during a child's life. Policies that benefit all adoptive families and allow them the flexibility to receive services when needed may go a long way toward supporting families and their adopted children.

References

American Adoptions. (2000). *Adoption statistics: A brief overview.* Accessed September 2005 at http://www.americanadoptions.com/dastatistics.htm.

Barth, R. P., & Berry, M. (1988). *Adoption and disruption: Rates, risks and resources.* New York: Aldine.

Barth, R. P., Gibbs, D. A., & Siebenaler, K. (2001). *Assessing the field of post-adoption service: Family needs, program models, and evaluation issues.* Accessed September 2005 at http://aspe.hhs.gov/hsp/PASS/lit-rev-01.htm.

Barth, R. P., & Miller, J. M. (2000). Building effective post-adoption services: What is the empirical foundation? *Family Relations, 49,* 447–455.

Goerge, R. M., Howard, E. C., & Yu, D. (1996). *Adoption, disruption, and dissolution in the Illinois child welfare system, 1976–94.* Chicago: University of Chicago Chapin Hall Center for Children.

Groza, V., & Rosenberg, K. (1998). *Clinical and practice issues in adoption: Bridging the gap between adoptees placed as infants and as older children.* Westport, CT: Praeger.

Groze, V., Young, J., & Corcran-Rumppe, K. (1991). *Post Adoption Resources for Training, Networking and Evaluation Services (PARTNERS): Working with special needs adoptive families in stress.* Cedar Rapids, IA: Four Oaks.

Hamilton, E. (2000, July 17). Adoption rate quadruples: Many children still need permanent placement. *Hartford Courant,* p. A3.

Partridge, S., Hornby, H., & McDonald, T. (1986). *Learning from adoption disruption: Insights for practice.* Portland, ME: University of Southern Maine.

Prew, C. (1990). Therapy with adoptive families: An innovative approach. *The Prevention Report. Fall,* 8.

Smith, S. L., & Howard, J. A. (1994). *The adoption preservation project.* Normal, IL: Illinois State University.

U.S. Department of Health and Human Services, Administration for Children and Families (DHHS). (2001a). *Adoption 2002: Executive summary.* Accessed September 2005 at http://www.acf.dhhs.gov/programs/cb/initiatives/adopt2002/2002body.htm

U.S. Department of Health and Human Services, Administration for Children and Families (DHHS). (2000). Current estimates as of January 2000 (2). *The AFCARS Report,* 2. Available at: http://www.acf.dhhs.gov/programs/cb/publications/afcars/rpt0100/ar0100.htm

U.S. Department of Health and Human Services, Administration for Children and Families (DHHS). (2001b). Interim FY99 estimates as of June 2001 (6). *The AFCARS Report,* 6. Available at: http://www.acf.dhhs.gov/programs/cb/publications/afcars/june2001.htm

U.S. Immigration and Naturalization Service (INS). (1997). *Statistical yearbook of the immigration and naturalization service. 1996.* Washington, DC: United States Government Printing Office.

U.S. Immigration and Naturalization Service (INS). (1999). *Statistical yearbook of the immigration and naturalization service. 1997.* Washington, DC: United States Government Printing Office.

U.S. Immigration and Naturalization Service (INS). (2000). *Statistical yearbook of the immigration and naturalization service. 1998.* Washington, DC: United States Government Printing Office.

Urban Systems Research and Engineering, Inc. (1985). *Evaluation of state activities with regard to adoption disruption.* Washington, D.C.: Office of Human Development Services.

Maine Adoption Guides:
A STUDY OF Postlegalization Services

Michel F. Lahti

Policymakers, program managers, and families are giving increased attention to the costs and effectiveness of postlegalization adoption services. The passage of the federal Adoption and Safe Families Act (ASFA) of 1997 (P.L. 105-89) was intended to move children more quickly through the foster care system and into permanent, safe, and stable families. Among the changes made by ASFA was the requirement that states initiate proceedings to terminate parental rights based on a child's length of stay in foster care. As a general rule, states must file petitions to terminate parental rights when children have been in foster care for 15 out of the most recent 22 months. The face and timing of adoption are changing.

In Maine, the Department of Human Services (DHS) has developed and implemented a Title IV-E Child Welfare Demonstration Project supported through a waiver granted by the U.S. Department of Health and Human Services (DHHS). This project, titled Maine Adoption Guides (MAGS), is a collaborative effort among the Maine DHS; Casey Family Services, Portland, Maine Division; and the University of Southern Maine. The four-year project runs from April 2000 through March 2004. The Maine DHS has overall responsibility for the waiver project and manages the state Title IV-E subsidy program. Casey Family Services is responsible for the design and implementation of the Guided Services (MAGS) model, a family-centered case management and therapeutic model that is being implemented statewide. The University of Southern Maine serves as program evaluator, conducting a randomized evaluation of the effect of the MAGS model over a four-year period. MAGS is designed to provide support to families who have adopted a child from the Maine DHS foster care system and to evaluate the effect of the case management and therapeutic components of the program through a longitudinal, randomized study.

This study describes initial evaluation results from the first year of MAGS. It first provides a brief literature review related to postlegalization services and outcomes for children and families. It then provides a description of the case management type of model that is implemented and the initial baseline results from the evaluation.

Literature Review

Erich and Leung (1998), in their review of the literature regarding the functioning of families who adopt children with special needs, noted that there is scant research into the long-term outcomes of these families and their children. The majority of the research has focused on factors affecting disruption as well as those associated with adoptions remaining intact (Barth & Berry, 1988; Barth & Berry, 1991; Boyne, Denby, Kettenring, & Wheeler, 1984; Festinger, 1986; Goerge, 1990; Groze, 1986; McDonald, Lieberman, Partridge, & Hornby, 1991; Rosenthal, 1993; Rosenthal & Groze, 1992; Rosenthal, Schmidt, & Conner, 1988; Smith & Howard, 1991; Westhues & Cohen, 1990; Zwimpher, 1983). These studies identified several factors that appear to lead to adoption disruption or dissolution: age of child at time of adoption; level of behavioral or psychological problems; nonfoster parent adoptions; multiple previous placements for children; no other children in foster care in the home; parent educational status; and younger parents. Smith and Howard (1999) found that rates of disruption reported in the literature are around 9% to 15%. They also said fewer statistics are available on dissolution (the termination of an adoption after legalization), citing only one study done in Illinois, which reported a 13% dissolution rate. In Maine, the rate of dissolution for special needs adoptions is estimated at slightly below 6% (Maine Department of Human Services, 2000/2001).

MAGS is focused on the outcomes of children with special needs and their adoptive families. This caseworker service delivery model is intended to be family centered and support family functioning over the long-term through therapeutic and other types of interventions. The definition for family centered is a model that emphasizes that children—and adults—grow and develop within family systems (Allen, Petr, & Brown, 1995). The family as a whole and its individual members are interdependent; they influence each other in numerous ways. Children's resources and needs seldom, if ever, can be viewed as theirs alone. The characteristics, resources, and behavior of the child affect the other family members, and vice versa. Because of this intimate connection, family members are experts about each other and the family unit. Child-centered models focus on the individual child who is in need of services, and the family's role is often minimized. Professional-centered models have the staff member viewed or positioned as an expert who directs care; thus, the role of the family and child is to cooperate with the actions taken by the professional. Those involved with designing this program wanted to be sure that the program design philosophically supported families in a natural and positive manner. The choice of family-centered service delivery is very purposeful.

Previous research has indicated that families who adopt children with special needs experience difficulties long after legalization of the adoption (Glidden, 1991; Rosenthal, 1993). According to Erich and Leung (1998), there is strong evidence that adopted children with special needs experience behavioral problems with a greater frequency, intensity, and duration than is the case with adopted children who do not have special needs. Studies on postlegalization child outcomes have shown that families tend to feel positive about the adoption even though the adopted children demonstrate significant needs (Rosenthal & Groze, 1992; Nelson, 1985). Erich and Leung (1998) found that well-functioning families are composed of parents who spend time addressing familial issues, effectively solve problems, exhibit a positive future orientation, and use available forms of support.

These findings, along with the experiences of the clinicians and program managers involved in designing the MAGS model, justify a family-centered approach to case management for adoptive families. With effective support, parents who adopt children with special needs can effectively guide their children and feel empowered in their family functioning.

Maine Adoption Guides Model

As a result of a planning process that the Maine DHS began in the mid-1990s, statewide implementation of the MAGS model started on April 1, 2000. Meetings involving DHS and parents, adoption agency staff, and other stakeholders led the agency to develop a specific focus on postlegalization services. Two pressures, in particular, drove the adoption policy and program development focus: the increasing numbers of children requiring adoption services and the pending implementation of ASFA. In light of these pressures, DHS managers, parents, and nongovernmental adoption agencies joined together to develop MAGS. Three principles shaped the program: adoption as a lifelong process with unique opportunities and challenges for families and communities, the normal developmental crises that most adoptive families experience—crises that differ from the dynamics of families created by birth—and the needs of adoptive families for more supports and services postlegalization. Based on a view of adoption as mutually beneficial to parents, child and society, the program recognized the responsibilities of society related to the support and preservation of adoptive families.

MAGS differs from standard practice in the provision of post legalization services in several ways. As Table 6-1 indicates, the purposes of the MAGS model are broader than provision of adoption subsidy. MAGS includes a trained clinical social worker assigned to the family for support, the standard practice for families postlegalization is no assignment of clinical support. The MAGS models array of services are more extensive, reflecting the supportive and therapeutic capacity provided through the social worker assigned to the family.

Table 6-2 presents the initial program logic model for the MAGS intervention. The immediate, intermediate, and long-term outcomes for families are similar for each point in time. The logic model is presented to assist with the development and evaluation of the intervention. As the intervention is implemented and develops, adjustments and further specification will be made to the program logic model.

Table 6-3 presents the outcome indicators for the MAGS model. Through reviewing the literature and discussions with program designers, these outcomes were agreed to as most important for this model of intervention. Model designers believe that as a result of receiving the MAGS intervention:

TABLE 6–1

Postlegalization Program Model Differences

PROGRAM ATTRIBUTE	STANDARD SERVICES	GUIDED SUPPORTIVE SERVICES
Target population	Children with special needs and their families	Children with special needs and their families
Program goals	Provision of adoption assistance funds	1. Decrease number of dissolutions 2. Increase family strengths 3. Maintain and/or increase child and family functioning 4. Provide adoption assistance funds
Staffing	DHS adoption caseworker	DHS adoption caseworker and Casey adoption staff
Services provided	1. One time assessment and planning session 2. Financial support for postadoptive services as an entitlement 3. Annual financial planning for continuance of adoption assistance	1. Initial and ongoing support based on family needs as identified in "Family Permanency Assessment" 2. Scheduled check-ins with family by Casey staff at least once every 6 months 3. Permanent assignment of Casey staff to family in an empowerment role 4. Financial support for postadoptive services, not limited to services predefined in subsidy agreement 5. Annual financial planning for continuance of adoption assistance

- Family members, especially parents, will feel supported and empowered;

- Children will at least maintain, if not improve, their overall levels of functioning at home, school and in the community;

- Adoptions will be maintained with no dissolutions;

- Children will be in the home more often, needing fewer placements out of the home;

- Families can access needed services and supports; and

Maine Adoption Guides: Guided Services Intervention Program Logic Model

INPUTS	ACTIVITIES	OUTPUTS	IMMEDIATE OUTCOMES (0–6 MONTHS)	INTERMEDIATE OUTCOMES (7–18 MONTHS)	LONG-TERM OUTCOMES (19–48 MONTHS)
• Social worker staff • Financial supports for families • Formal and informal supports for families	• Initial assessment with family—strength-based, family-centered planning • Case management activities • Therapy sessions • Resource brokerage • Regular check-ins with family (at least once every 6 months)	• Social worker meets with family for initial strengths- based, family- centered assessment. with state DHS adoption social worker before legalization. • Regular check-ins occur (at least twice a year) • Social worker available on ongoing basis to family for case management, supportive services, and therapy	• Family is supported and empowered as they respond to their child's needs. • Selected children maintain or improve functioning; family, school, social and emotional domains. • Family accesses needed resources, formal and informal supports. • Family and social worker staff express satisfaction with MAGS • Adoption is maintained • Few to no displacements— child lives at home	• Family is supported and empowered as they respond to their child's needs. • Selected children maintain or improve functioning; family, school, social and emotional domains. • Family accesses needed resources, formal and informal supports. • Family and social worker staff satisfied with MAGS given normal developmental crises. • Adoption is maintained • Few to no displacements— child lives at home.	• Family is supported and empowered as they respond to their child's needs. • Selected children maintain or improve functioning; school, social and emotional domains. • Family accesses needed resources, formal and informal supports. • Family and social worker staff satisfied with MAGS given normal developmental crises. • Adoption is maintained • Few to no displacements— child lives at home.

- Families and social workers providing services are satisfied with the implementation of this model.

MAGS is a statewide project, and services are provided through a partnership between DHS and Casey Family Services. Casey Family Services also has subcontracted out with other service providers to meet statewide needs. Families who have adopted children with special needs from the DHS foster care system are invited to volunteer to participate in the program approximately three months before their adoptions are legalized. DHS adoption staff meet with families and describe the program (assisted by a video presentation describing the service model and research component). Families

TABLE 6–3

Program Logic Model: Outcome Indicators

OUTCOME STATEMENT: *Family is supported and empowered as they respond to their child's needs.*	OUTCOME STATEMENT: *Selected children maintain or improve functioning in family, school, social, and emotional domains.*	OUTCOME STATEMENT: *Family accesses needed resources, as well as formal and informal supports.*	OUTCOME STATEMENT: *Adoption is maintained.*	OUTCOME STATEMENT: *There are few to no displacements, and child lives at home.*
INDICATORS:	INDICATORS:	INDICATORS TO BE DEVELOPED:	DEFINITION AND INDICATOR:	DEFINITION AND INDICATOR:
• Rating of levels of parent–child communication • Ratings on dimensions of parent–child relationship • Level of attachment of child-to-family and family-to-child • Level of satisfaction with adoption • Quality of caregiver health (stress) • Quality of home life • Scale scores on family cohesion, adaptability, and satisfaction	• Juvenile justice involvement—number of children arrested and/or on probation • Rating of physical status • Rating of emotional and intellectual status • Rating of relations with peers • Score and rating of competencies and problems related to child's level of functioning • Rating of level of school functioning	• Tracking on formal supports such as case management, respite, advocacy support by case manager, counseling and therapy, family therapy, marriage counseling, adoption support groups, special education services, residential treatment, and other institutional placement.	• Number of legalized adoptions that legally dissolve with the child returning to the state's custody and to foster care.	• The child or adolescent lives in her or his home on a permanent basis, as well as the number of days the child is at home. A displacement occurs when a child or adolescent is hospitalized or otherwise removed from the home to receive treatment. The child is considered to be "not at home" when he or she runs away, is incarcerated, lives elsewhere against parents' will, or is hospitalized for other than medical necessity.

who agree to participate are randomly assigned to one of two groups: Standard Services or the Guided Services provided through MAGS. Families assigned to Standard Services program receive support currently available to adoptive families through the Maine DHS, including Title IV-E adoption subsidies and health coverage through Medicaid. Families assigned to Standard Services do not receive MAGS postlegalization adoption services, but no family receives fewer services than are presently provided to all adoptive families.

Families in MAGS are assigned a social worker from Casey Family Services and provided a 15-minute video produced to explain the project and nature of the study. The Casey

Family Services social worker and the DHS adoption caseworker meet with the family just before or at the time of legalization to explain the program in more detail and complete an assessment of the family's present and projected needs. Families who participate in MAGS must agree to one face-to-face meeting with their assigned social worker every six months, although contact is expected to be much more frequent, depending on the needs of the family. Services for families in MAGS vary, but may include respite care, special camps, counseling for a child or another family member, family counseling, adoptive family support groups, and advocacy with schools. Services are provided in response to families' current needs. The Casey social worker guides the adoptive family through the expected crises for adoptive families and empowers the family, especially the parents, to be successful in the adoption process. Services are reimbursed at the Targeted Case Management rate set by the Maine Medicaid office. It is the intent, based on the outcomes reported in this study, to expand these services to the general population of adoptive families in Maine.

Research Design and Methodology

The research component of MAGS was initially implemented from November 1999 through March 2000 in conjunction with the pilot implementation of the program. This pilot period was crucial for the evaluation because it provided an opportunity to design, test, and implement the necessary procedures for random assignment, data collection, data entry, and reporting. As a result of the work done during the pilot period, the Maine DHS and Casey Family Services were able to integrate the evaluation process into the program. The following discussion describes the number of children in need of postadoption services in Maine, the process and outcome evaluation methods, and the data collection and analysis.

Population Characteristics

Maine's criteria for "special needs" results in virtually all children in foster care being classified as having "special needs." In April 1999 (the start of the implementation of MAGS), 3,100 children were in foster care in Maine. According to DHS administrative adoption data, 641 children required adoption services or were freed for adoption in January 1999. As of January 2000, the most recent information available just before the start of the project, 806 children required adoption services or were freed for adoption. In 2000, 422 adoptions of children in foster care were legalized, an 89% increase over the number of finalized adoptions in 1999 (when 223 adoptions were finalized). This increase reflects a continuing upswing in the number of adoptions of children in foster care after a four-year decrease in the number of such adoptions between 1990 and 1994.

The Elements of the Process and Outcome Evaluations

Process evaluation plays a critical role in identifying a program's strengths and weaknesses, guiding implementation, and understanding outcome data. The process evaluation of MAGS, which was implemented at approximately six months into the project, monitors the following:

- Aspects of the organizational structure of DHS and Casey Family Program
- MAGS staffing structures

- Financial commitments to implement the MAGS model

- Level of acceptance of implementation by field staff of both DHS and Casey Family Services

- Methods of project implementation and fidelity of implementation to the Guided Services Model

- Contextual factors such as DHS organizational issues, Casey Family Service organizational issues, and political support of postadoption

- Demographic profiles of families and children served

- Use of services and unmet needs

- Client satisfaction with services

- Differences in experimental and standard groups assess fidelity of randomization process

- Tracking on access to and utilization of services for both experimental and standard service groups

The outcome evaluation began in April 2000 (the second year of the program) and was completed in March 2004. During the first year of the program (April 1999 through March 2000), a pilot process was used to develop measures and data collection strategies. That process included review and approval of all outcome measures by an advisory group comprised of parents who had adopted children with special needs. The outcome evaluation is designed to assess the extent to which the children and families in the experimental group (those enrolled in MAGS and receiving services through the Guided Services Model) differ from the children and families in the control group (those who received Standard Services) with regard to a number of outcome measures. The outcome measures include the following:

- Rates of adoption dissolutions

- Displacement (the number of days the child is out of the home due to a problem)

- Family functioning

- Child functioning and well-being

- Access to and use of services

- Levels of satisfaction with services

The Research Design of the Outcome Evaluation

The outcome evaluation makes use of a randomized design. As Figure 6-3 shows, the project uses a two-group randomized experimental design so that any family or child who meets the participation criteria will have an equal chance of assignment to either the experimental or control group.

Sample size

Under this design, at least 60 children are assigned to the Guided Services (E) group and 60 children assigned to the Standard Services (C) group each year. Because of possible attrition, actual recruitment is 70 children for each group. The following sample sizes are estimated for each the four years of the project:

- Year 1 (2000–2001): 120 children (60E, 60C)

- Year 2 (2001–2002): 240 children (120E, 120C)

- Year 3 (2003–2004): 360 children (180E, 180C)

- Year 4 (2004–2005): 480 children (240E, 240C)

Data collection and analyses

Outcome data is collected through self-administered questionnaires and telephone interviews with the self-selected primary caregiver in the participating adoptive families. Some of the instruments are nationally recognized, such as the Child Behavior Checklist (CBCL) (Achenbach & Edelbrock, 1983), FACES II Family Adaptability and Cohesion Scale II (Olson, McCubbin, Barnes, Larsen, Muxen, & Wilson, 1992) and the Child Rearing Practices Report (Block, 1965). Additional questionnaires and telephone interview protocols are adapted from a national study on postadoption services conducted for the U.S. Department of Health and Human Services (Sedlak & Broadhurst, 1993). Parents are interviewed at baseline—approximately three months before legalization and once every six months for the duration of the study.

The same type of data collection occurs in the process evaluation with the addition of focus groups. Those implementing the model are interviewed by telephone, in person, and in focus groups. The data collection schedule also is approximately once every six months.

The estimated sample size for the children is sufficient for both descriptive and inferential statistical analyses. Descriptive statistics, such as percentages, rates, frequency distributions, and means, are employed to describe the experimental and control groups. Descriptive statistics are produced to answer each of the evaluation questions. Inferential statistics are used to test the statistical significance of any differences detected in the descriptive statistics. In addition, qualitative analyses are performed on responses to open-ended questions and focus group data.

The Results

The following discussion addresses the characteristics of the population of children and families served through MAGS, the results of the assessment of program implementation, child outcomes, parents' child-rearing attitudes and practices, family systems characteristics, parent and caregiver characteristics, attachment, and services to children and families.

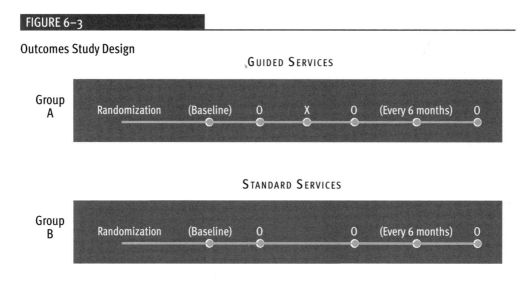

FIGURE 6–3

Outcomes Study Design

Key: O = Observation, Period of Data Collection; X = Commencement of Intervention, Ongoing

Characteristics of the Population of Children and Families

Tables 6-4 and 6-5 describe the populations of children and families enrolled in the project at the end of the first year—April 2001. There are 46% males (n = 63) with 29 in Guided Services and 34 in Standard Services, while there are 54% females (n = 74) with 42 in Guided Services and 32 in Standard Services. There are slightly more female children than male. The majority (83%) of children are between 1 month and 10 years. The majority of the adoptions are foster parent adoptions, accounting for 91% of all adoptions in the study. There are currently 137 children and 74 families in the study. In the first year of the program, 29 families representing 40 children chose not to participate in MAGS. These 29 families represented approximately 28% of adoptive families who were invited to participate.

Eight families (with 15 children) were enrolled and then left the study during the first year. Of these families, three families were receiving Guided Services and five were in the Standard Services group. Reasons for the attrition included a decision by DHS not to go forward with the family's adoption, the family's view that they had sufficient supports in place, the family's view that they had too much going on in their lives, and parents' disappointment with the services. Additional families were recruited to fill the openings.

Table 6-6 shows children were in the foster family for at least three years before entry to the study. The data provided by the state DHS indicates that these children had at least six previous placements before being placed in this adoptive home. Approximately half of all the children in the study have a clinically diagnosed disability and approximately half of those in school receive special education services. In addition, the majority of these children have some type of contact with their birth families. There were no statistically significant differences between the groups on these items.

TABLE 6–4

Participation Status: Final Totals for Year One

Guided Services (n = 71)

	AGES 0–5	AGES 6–10	AGES 11–17	TOTALS
Male	16	11	2	29
Female	14	18	10	42
Type of Adoption	Nonfoster		Foster	
No. of Children	6		65	71
Type of Adoption	Nonfoster		Foster	
No. of Families	5		32	37

TABLE 6–5

Participation Status: Final Totals for Year One

Standard Services (n = 66)

	AGES 0–5	AGES 6–10	AGES 11–17	TOTALS
Male	12	17	5	34
Female	13	13	6	32
Type of Adoption	Nonfoster		Foster	
No. of Children	7		59	66
Type of Adoption	Nonfoster		Foster	
No. of Families	7		30	37

TABLE 6–6

Child Level Information

	Assigned Group	
	GUIDED SERVICES	STANDARD SERVICES
Time in Adoptive Home at Entry to Study (Mean)	38 Months	42 Months
Number of Previous Placements in foster Care (Mean)	7	6
Percent of Children with Clinically Diagnosed Disability	54%	47%
Percent of School-Aged Children with and Individualized Education Plan	47%	53%
Percent of Children with Contact with Birthfamily	56%	45%

Results of the Assessment of Program Implementation

The implementation of MAGS was assessed through telephone interviews with professionals and a preadoption background information survey completed by adoptive parents.

Telephone interviews

In January 2001, the researchers conducted telephone surveys with the following individuals, all of whom had been involved with the program since its inception: 23 Maine DHS adoption caseworkers, three Casey Family Services staff, four state agency adoption supervisors, and one state agency program administrator.

Eighty-three percent of these respondents agreed that the Guided Services model was implemented as intended, and few offered suggestions for improvement. Ninety percent stated that they felt well informed about the project and had receiving sufficient information about MAGS. The majority of respondents (81%) stated that they were "very supportive" of the project, and the remaining respondents stated that they were "supportive." There was agreement that postadoption services were needed and that the project was "a great idea."

The professionals reported that, on average, caseworkers took 58.5 minutes to introduce MAGS to families and complete the participation and nonparticipation paperwork. Most respondents (58%) stated that this time requirement did not adversely affect their other work responsibilities, and the 23% who reported an adverse effect stated that the extra effort was worthwhile because of the benefits to families. Most all of the respondents stated that the project materials, video, forms, and other information were helpful in describing the project to families.

Most respondents (73%) stated that they had encountered no difficulties in inviting families to participate. Professionals who encountered difficulties most often reported problems telling families that they had not been selected for Guided Services. Some respondents said that the invitation process would be facilitated if materials were sent to families in advance. The majority of respondents (77%) did not believe that the invitation process in any way caused families to decide that they did not wish to participate.

Respondents also were asked about the transition process, in which participating families meet with the DHS adoption caseworker and the Casey Family Services social worker two weeks after they agree to participate. Respondents generally perceived the DHS–Casey Family Services partnership as positive. Some professionals, however, mentioned difficulties in prioritizing MAGS and coordinating schedules to meet the two-week time frame for the transition. Respondents mentioned that DHS workers do not always know the court system's timeframe, which makes it difficult to estimate when to transfer a family from DHS caseworker to the MAGS social worker. In addition, difficulties were identified in one county where, because there was no Casey Family Services staff, the program could not be implemented.

Respondents identified the following factors as most helpful in the implementation process: clear paperwork, regular management meetings, involvement of Casey Family Services, team flexibility, understanding supervisors, and willingness of staff to commit extra time. The major factors perceived as working against effective implementation were the time frames and difficulty coordinating the schedules of all the involved parties. Some respondents stated that heavy workloads prevented them from devoting adequate time to the project.

Surveys of adoptive parents

As part of the preadoption background information survey, adoptive parents were asked about their satisfaction with DHS adoption caseworkers. The majority (81%) of adoptive parents reported that they were "very satisfied" or "somewhat satisfied," but close to one-fifth (19%) were "somewhat dissatisfied" or "very dissatisfied" (Table 6-7). Satisfied respondents said their caseworkers were helpful, supportive, and caring; returned calls quickly; and were available when parents needed them. Parents also made the following:

- "Everything was great."

- "She was very attentive and responsive to our needs."

- "She answered all our questions and was available when needed."

- "She was very sympathetic to the child's needs. Returned phone calls immediately. Answered any questions we had or found the answers if she did not know."

- "They were informative, respectful, non-judgmental, encouraging, and excited about our way of life."

- "Adoption worker has been very helpful with needs of children and of us as parents."

- "She has been supportive but not overpowering."

- "Both caseworkers were very good, very thorough and very caring."

- "She was nice and helpful."

Adoptive parents who expressed dissatisfaction with their DHS caseworkers made the following comments:

- "Procedure is very slow."

- "It took over 6 months to get an adoption worker. When we did, it was months before we saw her."

- "Didn't receive much information on adoption."

- "Sometimes I felt like I kept more in-touch with them (updating) than them with me."

- "I asked many questions regarding adoption and they could not supply the answers. I had to search out the information on my own."

- "I feel that the adoption caseworker was inconsistent in her commitment to the children."

- "It took her a long time to call me back each time I called. "

Adoptive parents also were asked how well their DHS adoption caseworkers knew them, their families, and their child or children. Table 6-8 shows that parents appear to believe that the DHS caseworkers know them (the parent) the best, the family second, and the child the least.

Child Outcomes

The evaluation of child functioning was done with a telephone survey conducted with the self-selected primary caregiver for each participating child and the use of the Child Behavior Checklist (Achenbach & Edelbrock, 1983). The sample size for child outcome baseline results was 110 or greater. Children continually entered the study, and, as a result, the sample size changed with each period of data analyses. Some of the key results from the telephone interview with primary caregivers included the following:

- Children served through MAGS were primarily white (96%) with only 2% of the children Native American and 0.7% "other."

- Sixty percent of the children's caregivers rated their children's health as "excellent," 32% as "good," and 8% as "fair."

- Twenty-nine percent of the caregivers reported that their children had a clinically diagnosed disability.

- Forty percent reported that their children were taking medication for a behavioral health care problem.

- Sixty-one percent of the children were enrolled in a public school (K–12), and 17% were enrolled in a regular day care setting.

- Of the children enrolled in a public school setting, 67% had an Individualized Education Plan and received special education services.

- Seventy-six percent of the caregivers report that children were "very attached" to family members, 11% said their children were "moderately attached," and 10% stated their children were "slightly attached."

- Eighty-seven percent of caregivers reported that family members were "very attached" to their adopted children, and 11% stated that family members were "moderately attached."

- Seventy-seven percent of the caregivers believed that their adopted children were "very strongly" satisfied with their adoptions; 8% believed that their children were "moderately" satisfied; and 3% believed that their children were "slightly" satisfied.

The key findings from the CBCL (Table 6-9) are that close to half of these children score within the clinical range on the three scale scores. This means that these children would qualify for receipt of mental health services according to this measure (Achenbach & Edelbrock, 1983).

TABLE 6–7

Adoptive Parents' Satisfaction with DHS Adoption Caseworkers (n = 57)

SATISFACTION LEVEL	NUMBER OF RESPONSES	PERCENT OF RESPONSES
Very satisfied	37	65%
Somewhat satisfied	9	16%
Somewhat dissatisfied	9	16%
Very dissatisfied	2	3%

TABLE 6–8

Adoptive Parents' Relationship with DHS Caseworkers

How Well Does Your DHS Adoption Caseworker Know You? (n = 55)

PARENTS' RESPONSE	NUMBER OF RESPONSES	PERCENT OF RESPONSES
Very well	28	51%
Somewhat well	22	40%
Not very well	5	9%
Don't know	0	0%

How Well Does Your DHS Adoption Caseworker Know Your Family? (n = 54)

PARENTS' RESPONSE	NUMBER OF RESPONSES	PERCENT OF RESPONSES
Very well	24	44%
Somewhat well	20	37%
Not very well	10	19%
Don't know	0	0%

How Well Does Your DHS Adoption Caseworker Know Your Children? (n = 53)

PARENTS' RESPONSE	NUMBER OF RESPONSES	PERCENT OF RESPONSES
Very well	22	41%
Somewhat well	20	38%
Not very well	11	21%
Don't know	0	0%

TABLE 6–9

Child Behavior Checklist Scores

Percent of Child Study Population Indicated for Mental Health Services Referral (Clinical Range) (N=105)

ASSIGNED GROUP	INTERNALIZING CLINICAL RANGE	EXTERNALIZING CLINICAL RANGE	TOTAL PROBLEMS CLINICAL RANGE
Guided Services (E)	53%	48%	49%
Standard Services (C)	47%	52%	51%

Parents' Child-Rearing Attitudes and Practices

Adoptive parents were asked to complete the Child Rearing Practices Report (CRPR) (Block, 1965), a 91-item questionnaire that assesses a parent's child-rearing attitudes, values, behaviors, and goals. The CRPR covers four general domains: (1) how parents express, handle, and regulate positive and negative emotions; (2) how parents convey their authority and the specific forms of discipline that they use; (3) parents' ideals and goals with respect to their child's accomplishments and aspirations; and (4) parents' values about their child's development of autonomy, independence, and self-identity. According to Sedlak and Broadhurst (1993), the CRPR has been used fruitfully in other research addressing parents' child-rearing orientations as they relate to adolescents' personality characteristics (Block, Block, & Morrison, 1981); systematic differences between parents who are abusive or depressed and parents who are not (Susman, Trickett, Iannotti, Hollenbeck, & Zahn-Waxler, 1985); continuity in childrearing orientations over time (Roberts, Block, & Block, 1984); and the elements of creativity-fostering environments (Harrington, Block, & Block, 1987). In addition, the CRPR was used in a federally funded research project on postadoption issues (Sedlak & Broadhurst, 1993).

Previous research with CRPR identified 21 child-rearing scales that reflect different aspects of attitudes and orientations (Susman et al., 1985). Table 6-10 (which lists the 21 scales) provides the adoptive parents' mean answer score on each scale, which ranged from 1 ("strongly agree") to 5 ("strongly disagree"). This group of adoptive parents appears to agree most strongly with those behaviors that are more authoritative in nature, such as "Encourage Child's Openness to Experiences," "Parent or Child Open Expression of Affect," and "Nonpunitive Punishment."

Family Systems Characteristics

The evaluation utilizes the FACES II questionnaire developed by Olson et al. (1992) to assess levels of family functioning. This measure provides information about family cohesion and adaptability—two characteristics of family systems functioning thought to be important in adoptive families. Family cohesion is defined as the degree to which family members are separated from or connected to their family (i.e., the emotional bonding that family members have with one another). In this study, the mean family cohesion score for families (n = 67) was 68.6, with a standard deviation of 5.1. This moderate mean score means that the family is functioning normally in terms of how emotionally bonded members are to one another. Family adaptability has to do with the extent to which the family system is flexible and able to change its power structure, role relationships, and relationship rules in response to situational and developmental stress. In this study, the family adaptability mean score for families (n = 67) was 50.1, with a standard deviation of 4.7. This moderate mean score means a normal type of functioning in terms of how the family adapts to change. These balanced or moderate levels are hypothesized to be most viable for healthy family functioning, while the extreme areas are generally seen as more problematic for couples and families over time (Olson et al., 1992).

TABLE 6–10

Mean Scores for the 21 Child-Rearing Scales (n=71)

CHILD-REARING ORIENTATION SCALES	MEAN SCORE*	MINIMUM	MAXIMUM	STANDARD DEVIATION
1. Encourage child's openness to experience	1.59	1.00	3.50	.51
2. Provide rational guidance	1.61	1.00	3.00	.49
3. Parent/child open expression of affect	1.70	1.00	3.33	.40
4. Supervision of child	1.99	1.00	4.00	.72
5. Health orientation	2.07	1.00	3.33	.55
6. Enjoyment of parental role	2.30	1.00	4.00	.66
7. Parental maintenance of separate lives	2.31	1.33	4.00	.62
8. Nonpunitive punishment	2.46	1.33	4.00	.67
9. Parental worry	2.56	1.00	5.00	.92
10. Value independence	2.66	1.57	3.57	.40
11. Suppression of aggression	2.67	1.50	4.00	.54
12. Achievement	2.80	2.17	3.83	.39
13. Overinvestment in child	3.28	2.00	4.33	.50
14. Protectiveness	3.35	2.00	4.50	.53
15. Anxiety induction	3.65	1.00	5.00	.93
16. Inconsistent punishment	3.75	1.50	5.00	.86
17. Authoritarian punishment	3.79	3.00	4.50	.32
18. Guilt induction	3.82	2.00	5.00	.67
19. Suppression of sex	3.92	2.75	5.00	.55
20. Early training	4.17	2.33	5.00	.62
21. Negative affect	4.19	2.50	5.00	.67

*Strongly Agree (1) to Strongly Disagree (5)

Parent and Caregiver Characteristics

Through telephone interviews (n = 71 or greater because of continual-entry to the study), the following data regarding parent and caregiver characteristics were obtained:

- Ninety percent of the adoptive families are or were foster parents of the adopted child.

- In 92% of the families, the adopted child had other siblings in home.

- With regard to family income, 61% of the respondents reported earning less than $65,000 annually, and 39% reported earning more than $65,000 annually. One quarter (26%) reported earning less than $35,000 annually.

- Close to one-half of the families (49%) rated the quality of their home life as "excellent." Close to another half (47%) rated it as "good." A small percentage (4%) rated the quality of home life as "fair."

- Most of the families (92%) consisted of a married couple.

- In the majority of families (80%), the primary caregivers were of the same race as the adopted child.

- Sixty-two percent of the parents rated their satisfaction with their marriages as "very high," 29% rated their satisfaction level as "high," and 9% reported their level of satisfaction as neither high nor low.

- When asked how often they had enjoyed being with their child over the past month, 44% stated that they enjoyed being with their child "everyday," 48% stated "often," and 5% stated "seldom."

- Close to one-third of respondents (32%) rated their level of communication with their child over the past six months as "excellent," 49% described it as "good," and 17% rated it as "fair."

- When asked when they felt their child was "permanently theirs," 33% stated it was when their child came to live with them; 15% said it was when adoption was finalized; and almost half (48%) indicated it was at some other point in time. Most respondents who chose "other" indicated some type of family event or celebration as notable.

- Close to one-third of the respondents (32%) felt that adoption had affected their marriage or relationship with their significant other, but the majority (62%) reported no effect.

- Almost all of the respondents (97%) stated that other children in household perceived the adopted child as their sibling and that the adopted child (94%) perceived the other children as his or her siblings.

- Sixty-one of respondents reported that family life was better currently than before their adopted child came to live with them, 27% described family life as "about the same," and 12% described family life as "not as good."

- The majority of respondents (86%) stated that they felt "very strongly satisfied" with adoption, 11% stated that they were "moderately satisfied," and 3% stated that they were "slightly satisfied."

- The majority of respondents (84%) reported that they had some type of contact with their child's birth family. Almost three quarters (72%) said they discussed the child's birth family on a regular basis with their adopted child.

- Twenty-eight percent of the primary caregivers rated their health as "excellent," 51% rated it as "very good," and 21% rated their health as "good."

Attachment

The concept of attachment is prevalent in adoption research and therapeutic interventions (Brodzinsky, Smith, & Brodzinsky, 1998). Attachment issues were central in the development of MAGS because of clinicians' observations that over half of the adopted children in the study had attachment-related disorders. To explore issues related to attachment, adoptive parents were posed this question in telephone interviews: "One common way of thinking about how family members get along is by how attached they are to each other. Please define what the term 'attachment' means in your family."

The analysis grouped common words and ideas that emerged from parents' responses. The most common terms that parents used in describing attachment were "loving," "depending," and "caring." Of the 58 parents who responded, 36% described attachment as "loving." Specific comments included:

- "Love exchanged between all parties."

- "Unconditional love."

- "Loving each other even when we don't like each other."

Almost one-third of the parents (31%) used the word "depending" in the sense of "depending on someone." Comments included:

- "Being able to rely on each other in good times and bad."

- "Knowing that the person will always be there for you."

- "Being there for each other."

- "Inability to live without."

Sixteen respondents (28%) used the word "caring." Specific comments included:

- "How we show caring concern to each other."

- "Caring about each other."

- "Caring about one another's needs."

Other common terms used to describe attachment were "bonding" (16%), "doing things for each other" (16%), "being close" (12%), "trust" (12%), "enjoying things together" (12%), and "a sense of belonging" (12%). One theme that appeared in comments was "constancy" (10%), in the sense of loving or caring for someone "through good times and bad" or "no matter what." A few parents described attachment by what it did not include:

- "No harm."

- "Wouldn't hurt each other."

- "Not to manipulate and get what you want."

Some parents' comments were distinctive in their descriptions of attachment:

- "Compromising."

- "Our ability to love each other but also gives each other space. Allowing each other to do things on our own."

- "Should think alike."

- "Brother came to visit and they would physically fight. We wanted the brother moved and they were all very sad. Adoption agency was going to move the child and it felt like a death to the family."

Parents also were asked close-ended questions concerning attachment. The generally positive responses indicated that parents felt their family and their adopted child were close. Parents were asked how attached the child was to family members. Of the 97 respondents, 76% said "very attached," 11% said "moderately attached," 10% said "slightly attached," and 2% stated that they did not know. Parents also were asked how attached family members were to the child. The majority (86%) stated that family member were "very attached" to the child, 11% said "moderately attached," 1% said "slightly attached," and 1% stated that they did not know.

Interestingly, parents who answered that their child was "slightly attached" to the family gave very similar descriptions of attachment as parents who indicated that their child was "very attached" or "moderately attached" to the family. Only one respondent answered "slightly attached" to both quantitative questions.

Services Provided to Children and Families

The study also tracked families' service utilization and attempts to identify the services families prefer and use most often. The categories of monitored services are adapted from the general Targeted Case Management categories used by the Maine Medicaid department. The service categories (Table 6-11) are initial assessment, case plan (initial development and subsequent reviews), case supervision (which includes parent education and support, crisis stabilization, referral to mental health services, referral to community resources, financial assistance, and collateral contacts), advocacy, preparation and placement, and therapeutic services (for the individual child, individual parent, and family, and group services for children and adults).

Data about families' need for and use of these services were collected from parents during telephone interviews and from staff assigned to families in the Guided Services (E) group. Preliminary findings (based only on staff reports) indicate that, with services provided to approximately 30 families over a 10-month period, adopted children were recipients of 41% of the services, adoptive parents received 37%, and adoptive families received 22%. The services most often provided were parent education and support (45%), initial assessment planning (15%), collateral contacts (13%), case planning activities (6%), adult group therapy (4%), family and child therapy (4% each), advocacy (3%), individual parent therapy (2%), and mental health referrals (2%). All other services represented less than 1% of the total number of services provided. Because the service model is evolving, program evaluators need to meet regularly with program staff to establish the reliability of their services reporting over time. As experience is

TABLE 6-11

Definitions of Types of Services Provided (MAGS)

01 INITIAL ASSESSMENT: The collection and assessment of information regarding the child, family, and other relevant persons to determine the nature of individual and family issues and the services needed to foster strengths and provide supportive services to a family. Activities consist of interviewing, reviewing written materials, making an assessment of need, assessing the availability and accessibility of services, preparing reports, making case recommendations and setting objectives. This activity includes conducting family assessment at time of referral to MAGS.

02 CASE PLAN (INITIAL AND SUBSEQUENT REVIEWS): Case plans are developed in accordance with overall MAGS program philosophy of family strengthening and empowerment. A case plan is developed in conjunction with the family and in consultation with a supervisor and other professionals as needed. The case plan identifies the client's needs and delineates the objectives designed to meet those needs. The case plan is developed at completion of the intake process and is reviewed every six months or as needed.

03 CASE SUPERVISION: Consists of activities related to the implementation and monitoring of the case plan. Monitoring consists of purposeful contacts designed to assess progress and needs.

   03a. Parent Education and Support: Provide information to parents to educate and support, including contacts such as home visits and check-ins to maintain rapport, assist with parenting skills, and provide information about topics like birth family, normative development stages, or attachment.

   03b. Crisis Stabilization: Activities in response to a situation when a specific and urgent issue requires immediate attention from the MAGS social worker or on-call staff member. Subsequent contacts may also be included to assess any additional services needed to insure ongoing stability.

   03c. Referral to Mental Health Services, Including Substance Abuse Services: Coordinating information that results in a referral to an outpatient community-based mental health or substance abuse service agency. Referral can be for the child or any member of the family.

   03d. Referral to Community Resources (Other than Mental Health, Include Type): Coordinating information that results in a referral to a community-based resource or support. Referral can be for the child or any member of the family.

   03e. Financial Assistance: Activities that result in the purchase of concrete goods or services for the child and family. Financial assistance that is provided in addition to the adoption subsidy paid to the family through DHS IV-E funding.

   03f. Collateral Contacts: Sharing with and gathering information from other parties associated with the child or family.

04 ADVOCACY: Contacts with others who have influence or power in the client's life with the goal of insuring that their needs are met. Negotiating and coordinating services on behalf of children and families to assist them to obtain otherwise inaccessible or unavailable services. Negotiating the development of new resources or services.

05 PREPARATION AND PLACEMENT: Providing support to family and child when the child requires placement out of the home.

06 THERAPEUTIC SERVICES: Goal-directed, therapy sessions.

   06a. Individual Child, may include therapeutic *Life Book* work.

   06b. Individual Parent

   06c. Family, may include therapeutic *Life Book* work.

   06d. Group—Children

   06e. Group—Adult

gained as the program is implemented, service categories may be added and current definitions of service categories may be revised.

Conclusion

The results reported in this study provide important information about various aspects of MAGS. First, the implementation of the model appears to have gone fairly well across Maine, with the exception of one county where services were not provided because of staffing shortages. DHS case workers were found to have a good working knowledge of the project, to comply with data collection and reporting requirements, and to engage families in a timely manner. Data indicated that the project was being implemented as intended with few major problems. Finally, it also was found that sample sizes for the study and analysis were appropriate because families entered and remained in the study in requisite numbers.

Second, with regard to services, the results from the CBCL indicated that approximately one-half of the children in the study had a mix of problems severe enough to warrant referral to mental health providers. Very preliminary data (which will be further analyzed as the project moves forward) indicated that families primarily needed services in line with an educational and supportive model as opposed to a therapeutic model. Data also indicated that families were satisfied overall with the services they were receiving from DHS adoption caseworkers. Third, results indicated that the majority of families were functioning well and satisfied with their experiences of adopting their children. Most caregivers reported that children and family members were attached to one another.

The development and implementation of a completely new statewide program is challenging, particularly when a major focus of the program is research. This project moved forward successfully in its first year as a result of the dedication of many individuals committed to supporting adoptive families in Maine. Their dedication has been inspiring and rewarding. It is with confidence that this study enters its second year and much more will be learned about how best to serve adopted children with special needs and their families.

References

Achenbach, T. M., & Edelbrock, C. (1983). *Manual for the child behavior checklist and revised child behavior profile*. Burlington, VT: University of Vermont, Department of Psychiatry.

Allen, R. I., Petr, C. G., and Cay Brown, B. F. (1995). *Family-centered behavior scale and user's manual*. Lawrence, KS: The Beach Center on Families and Disabilities, University of Kansas.

Barth, R. P., & Berry, M. (1988). Predicting adoption disruption. *Social Work. 33*(3), 227–233.

Barth, R. P. & Berry, M. (1991). Preventing adoption disruption. *Prevention in Human Services, 9*(1), 205–222.

Berry, M. & Barth, R. P. (1990). A study of disrupted adoptive placements of adolescents. *Child Welfare, 69*, 209–255.

Block, J. H. (1965). *The child rearing practices report.* Berkeley, CA: Institute of Human Development, University of California.

Block, J. H., Block, J., & Morrison, A. (1981). Parental agreement-disagreement on child rearing orientations and gender-related personality correlates in children. *Child Development, 52*(3), 965–974.

Boyne, J., Denby, L., Kettenring, J., & Wheeler, W. (1984). *The shadow of success: A statistical analysis of outcomes of adoptions of hard to place children.* Westfield, NJ: Spaulding for Children.

Brodzinsky, D. M., Smith, D. W., & Brodzinsky, A. B. (1998). *Children's adjustment to adoption: Developmental and clinical issues.* Thousand Oaks, CA: Sage Publications.

Erich, S., & Leung, P. (1998). Factors contributing to family functioning of adoptive children with special needs: A long-term outcome analysis. *Children and Youth Services Review, 20,* 135–150.

Festinger, T. (1986). *Necessary risk: A study of adoptions and disrupted adoptive placements.* Washington, DC: Child Welfare League of America.

Glidden, L. (1991). Adopted children with developmental disabilities: Post-placement family functioning. *Children and Youth Services Review, 13,* 363–377.

Goerge, R. M. (1990). The reunification process in substitute care. *Social Service Review (September),* 422–457.

Groze, V. (1986). Special needs adoptions. *Children and Youth Services Review, 8,* 363–373.

Harrington, D. M., Block, J. H., & Block, J. (1987). Testing aspects of Carl Roger's theory of creative environments: Child-rearing antecedents of creative potential in young adolescents. *Journal of Personality and Social Psychology, 52,* 851–856.

Maine Department of Human Services. (2000/2001). *Adoption unit statistical reports.* Augusta, ME: Author.

McDonald, T., Lieberman, A., Partridge, S., & Hornby, H., (1991). Assessing the role of agency services in reducing adoption disruptions. *Children and Youth Services Review, 13,* 425–438.

Nelson, K A. (1985). *On the frontier of adoption: A study of special needs adoptive families.* New York: Child Welfare League of America.

Olson, D. H., McCubbin, H. I., Barnes, H., Larsen, A., Muxen, M., & Wilson, M. (1992). *Family inventories.* Minneapolis, MN: Life Innovations, Inc.

Roberts, G. C., Block, J. H., & Block, J. (1984). Continuity and change in parents' childrearing practices. *Child Development, 55*(2), 586–597.

Rosenthal, J. (1993). Outcomes of adoption of children with special needs. *Adoption: The Future of Children, 3*(1), 77–88.

Rosenthal, J., & Groze, V. (1992). *Special needs adoptions: A study of intact families.* Westport, CT: Praeger.

Rosenthal, J. A., Schmidt, D., & Conner, J. (1988). Predictors of special needs adoption disruption: An exploratory study. *Children and Youth Services Review, 10,* 101–117.

Sedlak, A. J., & Broadhurst, D. D. (1993). *Study of adoption assistance impact and outcomes: A final report.* Rockville, MD: Westat, Inc.

Smith, S. L., & Howard, J. A. (1991). A comparative study of successful and disrupted adoptions. *Social Service Review 65,* 248–265.

Smith, S. L., & Howard, J. A. (1999). *Promoting successful adoptions: Practice with troubled families.* Thousand Oaks, CA: Sage Publications.

Susman, E. J., Trickett, P. K., Iannotti, R. J., Hollenbeck, B. E., & Zahn-Waxler, C. (1985). Child rearing patterns in depressed, abusive, and normal mothers. *American Journal of Orthopsychiatry, 55*(2), 237–251.

Westhues, A., & Cohen, J. S. (1990). Preventing disruption of special needs adoptions. *Child Welfare, 69*(2), 141–155

THE DEVELOPMENT OF Postadoption Services IN Massachusetts

Christopher G. Hudson, Patricia Cedeño-Zamor, Cheryl Springer, Marguerite Rosenthal, Sharon C. Silvia, Steve Alexander, and Loretta Kowal

In October 1997, the Commonwealth of Massachusetts, in response to the advocacy of families and social workers, embarked on developing a system of social services for adoptive families. The Massachusetts Department of Social Services (DSS) contracted with Child and Family Services, Inc., New Bedford, Massachusetts, to develop the Adoption Crosswords program, a statewide network of information and referral, counseling, respite, family support, training, and advocacy services (Leo Farley, e-mail, 2005).

This program represented an active collaboration among families with adopted children, state legislators, DSS officials, professionals at Child and Family Services (the lead agency for the program and its six affiliated agencies), and professionals at the Salem State College School of Social Work, which was charged with the program's evaluation. As Adoption Crossroads was implemented, a number of issues arose, including challenges in balancing the needs of families for preventative, normalizing interventions with the needs of some families for intensive, ongoing clinical services; the need for flexibility for each of the participating agencies with programmatic consistency and equity across the state; and an evaluation focus on formative process issues (including consumer satisfaction and service utilization) with the need to obtain reliable information on the accomplishment of key outcomes.

Like the program itself, this study represents a collaborative review of the program by the key professionals involved in its implementation and evaluation. After reviewing the history of the program, specifically the advocacy efforts that made the program possible, this study describes the program with special attention to the problems encountered during its first three years and how they were resolved. The study then reviews the evaluation of Adoption Crossroads, including its methodology and initial findings. It concludes with a discussion of the implications of these findings and some general observations about the program.

The Development of Postadoption Services in Massachusetts

A system of postadoption services in Massachusetts was the result of the joint efforts of professionals, state agencies, and articulate adoptive parents. Together, they forged an alliance that generated new funding for services needed by a growing number of children and families. Before 1993, approximately 500 children in DSS custody were placed for adoption. Following the appointment of Linda K. Carlisle as the commissioner of DSS in 1994 and her focus on adoption, the number of adoptions of children in foster care rose significantly. In 1995, more than 1,000 children in DSS custody were placed with adoptive families, a trend that continued until her departure from her position in 1999. Since then, the absolute number of adoptions has slightly declined, reportedly because of a speeding up of the adoption process and reduction of the backlog of cases.

In addition, DSS was aware of the significant needs of many adopted children, revealed most dramatically in the disproportionate number of adopted children in psychiatric hospitals and residential treatment centers. Recognizing that adoptive families needed more extensive services (particularly for adolescents) if adoptions were to remain intact, DSS convened an Adoption Task Force in 1995 to address postadoption service issues. The task force recorded anecdotal information from social workers and mental health providers about the unique challenges that adoptive families faced but often were unanticipated or ignored. The task force also took note that few clinical programs offered adoption-competent services, and many programs with adoption expertise lacked adequate funding to provide the needed services. Through the course of monthly meetings, the task force recognized that fuller attention needed to be brought to such issues as attachment, bonding, and the problems of adolescents—issues that both adoptive parents and professionals identified. In 1996, the task force, with the sponsorship of DSS, held a conference that was well attended by professionals, mental health providers, teachers, and child protective service workers—some of whom also were adoptive parents. Among the issues addressed at the conference were the need for further understanding of attachment issues and the lack of adoption-competent therapists and social workers. The conference, which was widely considered a success, strengthened the role of adoptive parents in advocating for postadoption services. Although adoptive parents were not officially invited, the adoptive parents present nonetheless were reported to have strongly supported the provision of such services.

Subsequently, a breakfast was held at the Massachusetts State House to which legislators were invited to learn more about the need for postadoption services. Articulate parents presented compelling stories about the need for services, criticized existing services as inadequate and inappropriate, and described how existing providers often lacked specialized expertise in adoption issues. Later, adoptive parents testified at legislative hearings, where their stories caught the attention of legislators who, in the past, repeatedly had denied the requests of DSS for postadoption services funding. The personal stories were supported by DSS data detailing the number of adopted children in crisis. In response, the legislature provided new funding to DSS to establish a statewide network of adoption competent services. Former Commissioner Carlisle recently noted that the parents' advocacy was an example of the possibilities of citizen action, as well as the limitations of governmental intervention.

Implementation

Implementation of the Adoption Crossroads program was initiated in early August 1997, when DSS released a request for proposals that responded to the needs the professionals and parents identified.* Five agencies or collaborations of agencies submitted proposals which were due by the beginning of September 1997. The request for proposals (RFP) specified that a lead agency must be a "private adoption-competent child welfare organization" that would develop a "new statewide network of postadoption support services." Prospecitve lead agencies needed to document their adoption competency, including the expertise of staff in adoptions procedures, and more generally, familiarity with human behavior theories relevant to adoptive family systems. They also need to demonstrate their capacity to effectively organize and administer a statewide network of resources and services.

A review committee comprised of adoptive parents and DSS staff evaluated each proposal on the following criteria:

1. Adoption competence and expertise

2. Service elements

3. Organizational capacity

4. Budget and financing

5. Program evaluation (ability to serve linguistically and ethnically diverse populations)

By the end of September, New Bedford Child and Family Service was awarded the contract and Adoption Crossroads was open for services on October 1. Three families requested services on the first day.

As the lead agency, Child and Family Services subcontracted with five other agencies (referred to as "affiliates" in this study) throughout Massachusetts to provide the core components of the Adoption Crossroads program: information and referral, advocacy and coordination of services, an adoptive family support network, regional response teams, respite services, and training to enhance the adoption-competency of professionals. All subcontractors had a history of working with other service providers (both public and private) and in advocating for and delivering adoption-competent services for the children and families. Their adoption-competency was reflected in their understanding of the unique adjustment challenges experienced by all adoptive families and their ability to assist those families in dealing with the consequences of prior trauma and loss issues.

The services provided through Adoption Crossroads were regionally delivered, corresponding to the six regions of DSS. Child and Family Services provided services in the

---

* The first year (fiscal year 1998) of the program was not a complete year, encompassing the nine months from October 1, 1997, to June 30, 1998, whereas the subsequent years cover the July 1 to June 30 period of fiscal year 1999 or 2000.

southeast region of the state, and the five affiliates provided services in the remaining regions. In addition, each affiliate arranged for the assistance of other professionals within their communities for some program components. Several of the regional agencies have entered into subcontracts with community-based resources as a means of implementing the intended wraparound service model. Wraparound services intend to reduce fragmentation and assist families in gaining access to the resources in the community to meet their needs. Such services include consumer advocacy and interagency coordination and consultation.

As the lead agency, Child and Family Services was responsible for general oversight and management of the statewide program and with providing a single point of access for all postadoption services. To fulfill its oversight function, Child & Family Services created a statewide advisory board comprised of adoptive families. The advisory board guides the provision of services and makes recommendations for change. To meet its management responsibilities, Child and Family Services designed, established, and maintained a statewide management information system for both monitoring and evaluation purposes. Its management responsibilities also include marketing, training, establishing collaborations, troubleshooting, and monthly billing and reporting to DSS. To fulfill its responsibility for program evaluation, Child and Family Service contracted with the Salem State School of Social Work to conduct an ongoing assessment of the program. To meet the mandate of a single point of entry for adoptive services and supports, Child and Family Services maintained and staffed an 800 number 24 hours a day, seven days a week. Through this telephone service, adoptive families and professionals were provided general information, consultation, and referrals. The telephone service also functioned as the first step in the program's intake process.

As previously noted, the regional affiliates managed the local system of wraparound services and provide direct services. Each affiliate agency is regionally based to better establish a community network of wraparound services. This arrangement also allowed for better efficiency and familiarity for second stage—information and referral services.

With regard to direct service provision, each affiliate was required under its contract with Child and Family Services to

- Provide 208 hours of support group services each year,

- Develop a team of adoptive parents to act as liaisons or mentors with other adoptive families in need of support,

- Develop six to eight respite resources within the region,

- Develop a regional response team to provide services ranging from brief preventive to intensive stabilization services for families,

- Provide advocacy and coordination services to assist families in gaining access to long term supports and services, and

- Train a minimum of 50 professionals annually to enhance their adoption competency.

Each affiliate also was required to meet regularly with Child and Family Services and the other affiliates to ensure uniform delivery of services throughout the state and the coordination of such administrative functions as marketing and submission of monthly reports.

Strengths and weaknesses in this design are inherent. The strengths include the wealth of knowledge and experience that six recognized adoption-competent agencies bring to the program and the agencies' connections with their own communities. Both factors helped to streamline and facilitate the implementation of the program. A weakness results from the fact that six different administrations had to find a comfortable, acceptable, and efficient protocol to effectively implement the program. Frequent and open communication between Child and Family Services and the affiliates was, and continues to be, essential to the success of the program. Monthly meetings held by Adoption Crossroads' managers and staff on a regional and statewide basis facilitate communication and strengthen the program, a process further enhanced by team building exercises with direct line staff and with management.

Although the initial implementation of Adoption Crossroads was not always as efficient as planned, the goal consistently focused on the development of a consumer-driven, consumer-friendly, easily accessed program committed to empowering families. The importance of adoptive families and respect for families' values and expertise in making decisions for themselves have been central aspects of the program's philosophy.

The Evaluation Design and Its Development

From the outset, the evaluation of Adoption Crossroads has been viewed an integral aspect of the program. Organized by the service component, the evaluation involved the routine collection of a balanced mix of process and outcome data, including consumer satisfaction with both the delivery and effectiveness of services. A specially designed, computerized client-tracking system for the program supported the collection of data. The initial plan put forth a quasi-experimental design comparing outcomes for children and families who received various levels of services—including those who declined services—after controlling for family characteristics. Because randomized assignment to a no-service control group clearly would not be feasible, families who received minimal services (such as telephone contact only) served as a control group, with various statistical controls taking into account group differences. In addition, the evaluation plan called for before-and-after comparisons on some program components (such as response teams), using standardized measures of family functioning and other outcomes. The evaluation primarily relied on recipients' and case workers' responses to fixed-choice questions, although qualitative comments also had been sought to enhance the understanding of respondents' views.

The principal investigator, Christopher G. Hudson, took responsibility for the evaluation of the information and referral service and the response team service. Marguerite Rosenthal evaluated the coordination and advocacy component. Cheryl Springer took responsibility for the evaluation of the respite and family support components, and

Patricia Cedeño-Zamor, the evaluation of the training program. Hudson also had over-seen the analysis of the general data from the program's information system as it per-tained to the client population and overall service utilization. None of the mentioned evaluation tean members had any involvement in service provision, but rather were exclusively involved with the evaluation and its design, the data collection and analy-sis, and the dissemination of the findings.

As the evaluation has evolved, it primarily has focused on an analysis of process data, consumer satisfaction with service delivery, and the extent and types of services delivered. Data were generated through an extensive annual telephone survey of all service recipients, interviews with staff (particularly with regard to the advocacy and coordination component), analysis of information system data and review of adminis-trative reports (particularly with regard to respite and family support services), minutes of advisory board meetings (with regard to the advocacy and coordination compo-nent), and analysis of feedback from participants in training sessions.

The 15-minute telephone survey incorporated two consumer satisfaction scales developed for the program. One scale involved satisfaction with the information and referral service contact; the other scale assesses satisfaction with the agency to which the family was referred. The two scales were found to have reliabilities of .88 or higher (Crombach's Alpha). There also were several open-ended queries about the family's specific experience with the services used. Although the main focus of the evaluation had been on the service delivery process, data has been collected and analyzed with regard to the attainment of agreed upon service goals for families receiving response team, respite, and family support group services.

Throughout the development of the evaluation, numerous discussions occurred between the evaluation team and the program staff concerning outcome assessment. Although it has not been feasible to use standardized instruments in the assessment of key outcomes, program staff have continued to support the evaluation and advocate for the inclusion of additional qualitative methodologies such as focus groups. Through-out the development and implementation of the evaluation, the evaluation team and the program staff met regularly to review plans, discuss procedures for implementa-tion, and review findings and reports. Although they have not always agreed on mat-ters of evaluation design and interpretation, lead agency staff have regularly sought to implement the evaluators' recommendations.

Results from the First Three Years

The following discussion provides a brief overview of some of the major findings of the evaluation involving each of the major program components: information and refer-ral, response teams, respite care, family support, training, and advocacy and coordina-tion. These findings are drawn from the evaluations for the first three years of the program—fiscal year 1998, 1999, and 2000—with particular attention paid to the third year (Hudson, Cedeño-Zamor, Rosenthal, Springs, Hudson, Ford, Kowal, & Riley, 2001).

Information and Referral Services

Annually, the evaluation team conducts a telephone survey of 400 to 500 individuals who called the Adoption Crossroads information and referral telephone line. This survey is designed to determine callers' level of satisfaction with the service and their satisfaction with any services to which they were referred. Respondents primarily have been families, although some respondents have been professionals and concerned relatives. The telephone interview is based on a structured two-page, fixed-choice instrument. The first section, consisting of 12 items, focuses on the caller's impressions of the information and referral line. The second section focuses on services to which the caller was referred, if any. Callers also are invited to provide comments and suggestions based on their experience.

Figure 7-1 illustrates the distribution of the calls to Adoption Crossroads over the first 33 months of the program.** There were significant dips during the December holiday seasons and peaks during the summer and early fall months. The calls averaged 37 a month during the first year of service operation, 36 during the second year of operation, and 55 during the six-month period of January to July 2000. The significant increase in activity during the first half of 2000 may have been due, in part, to additional monies made available to families for summer camp expenses, a form of respite.

During each telephone survey, the interviewer elicited detailed information about the respondent's satisfaction with various aspects of the telephone contact with the information and referral service. This was then followed by a summary question: "Overall, how would you rate the quality of the information and referral service?" The results are presented in Figure 7-2. In fiscal year 2000, more than half (53.9%) of the respondents rated the service as "Excellent" (compared to 48.0% in fiscal year 1998), and 28.2% stated that it was "Very Good" (compared to 31.0% in fiscal 1998). Very few respondents rated the service as "Fair" (4.5%) or "Poor" (1.9%). For the total scale, which ranges from 1 (Poor) to 5 (Excellent), the mean score in fiscal year 2000 was 4.3 (compared to 4.1 in FY 1998). The mean score ranged from 4.0 to 4.5 each month.

Another area evaluated with regard to information and referral services relates to the number of referrals made and the level of success that clients experienced in obtaining needed services. In fiscal year 2000, staff on the service line recorded 265 referrals to the affiliates, an average of 22.0 referrals per month, which was lower than the 25.1 referral per month averaged during fiscal year 1998. These referrals did not include individuals who directly contacted the affiliates. In fiscal year 2000, 84.5% of respondents who were referred to a service stated that the service line had sent them to an affiliate agency, and 46.0% of these individuals stated that they had received services from these agencies. In addition, the remainder of the callers contacted the affiliates directly and were subsequently referred to various other agencies. Thus, for the purpose of obtaining an estimate of the overall success the referral linkages, it was assumed that the affiliates would have

---

** After the evaluation's completion in July 2004, the name of the program was changed to Adoption Journeys in Massachusetts.

FIGURE 7–1

Number of Callers, by Quarter, 1997–2000

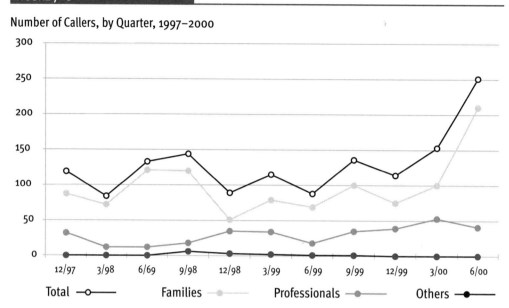

Total —○—   Families —●—   Professionals —●—   Others —●—

FIGURE 7–2

Overall Rating of Quality of Information and Referral Service

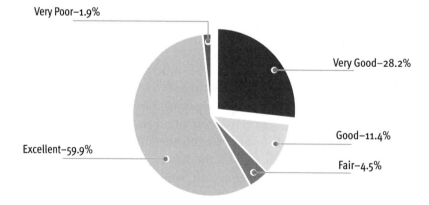

Very Poor–1.9%

Very Good–28.2%

Good–11.4%

Fair–4.5%

Excellent–59.9%

had a similar level of success in their referrals. When this 46.0% figure (or 38.5% of the total) is applied to all 892 callers, an estimate of 344 is computed, virtually the same as the 355 figure that is based on staff entries into the online progress notes. Utilization figures obtained from different recording and estimation methods will usually be somewhat different; the fact that they are as close as they are in this instance suggests that the actual number of families who received services is approximately 350. This represents the families who received services in fiscal year 2000, including families who were referred by the lead agency to affiliates and families who contacted the affiliates directly. Although

FIGURE 7–3

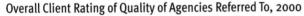

Overall Client Rating of Quality of Agencies Referred To, 2000

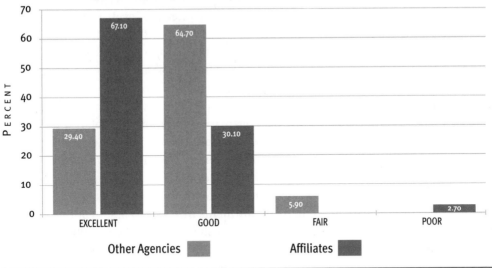

the majority of these clients were engaged directly by the affiliates, the lead agency information and referral service successfully referred 145. Of these, 78 were linked successfully with the various response teams.

When respondents were asked about the services to which they were referred, they reported a high level of satisfaction (Figure 7-3). They were particularly satisfied with services provided by the affiliate regional agencies, with two-thirds (67.1%) rating the services as "Excellent" and 30% rating these services as "Good." Services provided by nonaffiliate providers were not rated as highly. Only 29.4% of the respondents rated services provided by nonaffiliates as "Excellent," with 64.7% indicating that nonaffiliate services were "Good." Only very small numbers of respondents, from none to 5.9%, gave the ratings of "Fair" or "Poor" to either affiliates or nonaffiliates.

When clients reported that they successfully linked to a referred service, they were asked several questions about the number of sessions they received and the type of service involved. A key question, thus, concerned the amount of service—measured in appointments or visits—that they received. The data reveals that the typical (median) number of sessions is 5.3, both for affiliate and nonaffiliate agencies. This figure includes open and closed cases. While this figure may appear low, it is within the range found in many agencies across the nation, which traditionally, before the era of managed care, have had median lengths of treatment of around six appointments. Caution should be used in interpreting the figure; it is based on the sample of 67 clients of affiliated agencies and 16 from nonaffiliates who could name an agency from which they were receiving services *and* remember approximately how many sessions they had attended.

With regard to the types of services that families received as a result of the information and referral process, evaluators interviewed a sample of 77 families. Close to one-half

(45.5%) of these families were received response team services; 14.3%, support services; 10.4%, respite care; 10.4%, advocacy services; and 11.7%, some combination of services. Although a small number of clients were successfully engaged in services, when families received services, they participated at an increasingly intensive level, as indicated by an increase in median appointments from 3.9 in fiscal 1998 to 5.3 in fiscal year 2000.

Overall, the program has done well to maintain and even increase the level of satisfaction of its information and referral callers from program inception through fiscal year 2000. In total, a third of the survey respondents (36.3%, or 128) in FY 2000 reported that they received some kind of service. While many clients were engaged in services directly by the affiliates, the lead agency information and referral service referred 265 families to its affiliates, 145 of whom staff listed as receiving services. In the case of referrals to response teams, 101 new referrals were made, with 78 or 77.2% receiving documented services. Despite the smaller numbers of successfully engaged clients, when clients did receive services, the service became somewhat more intensive, as indicated by an increase in median appointments from 3.9 to 5.3. In addition, overall satisfaction among those successfully linked also rose in fiscal year 2000, with only small numbers voicing frustration over particular aspects of service delivery.

Response Teams

Central to the Adoption Crossroads program are the regional, affiliate-based response teams that provide families with home-based services. The response teams are designed to provide timely intervention in averting crises, to assess children and families, and to offer adoption-competent services. These teams typically consist of an MSW social worker, a paraprofessional, and a volunteer parent advocate and, whenever, possible interview their clients in their homes. Children and families who have long-term clinical needs or chronic conditions that require attention may be referred to other providers for additional wraparound services.

The response teams saw 195 families during fiscal year 2000, up from 119 in FY 1999. Response teams were evaluated based on two primary sources of data: (1) a telephone survey of the primary contact person for each family, and (2) information supplied by Adoption Crossroads' statewide information system. Through the annual telephone survey of all persons who called the information and referral service, data were collected on the number of families referred to a response team and those who received response team services, counseling (or therapy), respite, or family support services from an affiliate. In fiscal year 2000, the survey identified 100 people who had received services through Adoption Crossroads, 77 of whom received assistance from an Adoption Crossroads regional affiliate. Clients who received response team services were asked questions about the problems that the response team addressed, the methods used, and their assessments of the process and the outcomes of service delivery.

Each respondent was asked, "What issues, concerns, or problems did these meetings [with the response team] focus on?" The most common problem that respondents identified was their child's aggressive, destructive, or out-of-control behavior (identified by 42.4% of the respondents). Other common concerns were problems with attachment (34.6% of the families), obsessive-compulsive disorders (21.2%), adjustment problems (16%), family relationships difficulties (16%), and postplacement stabilization (16%).

In fiscal year 2000, Adoption Crossroads staff documented 1,643 response team contacts and related activities, as well as 1,547 hours of staff time for the 195 families who were seen one or more times. This level of activity represents a 57% increase in contacts and a 105% increase in response team hours compared to fiscal year 1999. There were 253 office interviews and 487 home visits, with a mean of 3.8 visits per family during 2000. This figure, which is based on staff reports, is less than the median of 5.3 reported earlier, which was calculated from interviews with a sample of families.

The typical family who was provided response team services received 7.9 hours of service (1.2 hours of office interviews, 4.4 hours of home visits, 1.5 hours of telephone calls, .6 hour of meetings or case conferences, and .2 hour of social activities, preparation of mail, and other unspecified activities). Almost four-fifths (78.5%) of all direct contact time was in the clients' homes.

Each family who received response team services also was asked, "What did the workers do to help with these concerns?" In fiscal year 2000, the most common interventions were the provision of advice (32%), referrals (24%), discussion (20%), and the provision of information (16%). Mentioned less frequently were listening (12%), help in problem solving (12%), help in insight development (8%), training (8%), and mediation (4%). The interventions most frequently received in fiscal year 1999 (advice, information giving, empathy, listening, ventilation, and training) were mentioned considerably less frequently than in fiscal year 2000, but discussion, help with problem solving, and the provision of referrals were mentioned more frequently.

Each family also was asked, "Overall, how would you rate the quality of the service you received?"—a question designed to elicit information about families' perceptions of the process of service delivery and the professionalism of response team services. In FY 2000, the 30 families who answered this question expressed a high level of satisfaction: 68.7% gave the response team service an "Excellent" rating, while the remaining respondents rated the service as either "Very Good" (21.8%) or "Good" (10.0%). None rated it "Fair" or "Poor."

Families also were asked to assess the progress that they had made on the problems that were the focus of response team services. They were asked to list each concern, issue, or problem, and to rate their progress according to the following scale:

- None—(0) No apparent progress or situation worsened

- Minimal—(1) Beginning evidence of movement and work on concern or problem

- Moderate—(2) Problem or concern clearly reduced

- Substantial—(3) Issue or concern almost resolved, but recurs sometimes

- Achieved–(4) Issue or concern resolved, at least no longer requiring professional help

These ratings were analyzed on both a case and problem basis. When analyzed on a case basis, the ratings were averaged for each case, irrespective of the number of problems that were identified, to obtain a global rating of progress for that case. The average for each case, stated as a decimal value (such as 1.72), was then recategorized, using the following ranges that corresponded to the original ratings:

- None—0 to .5

- Minimal—6 to 1.5

- Moderate—1.6 to 2.5

- Substantial—2.6 to 3.5

- Achieved—3 .5 to 4.0

In this way, a global rating of progress was determined for each case based on the arithmetic average of the problem ratings.

The distribution of these ratings, presented in Figure 7-4, shows that in 2000, 14.3% of the clients said their goals were "achieved" (up from 8.7% in 1999); 14.3% rated their progress as "substantial" (21.7% in 1999); 25.0%, "moderate" (21.5% in 1999); 28.6%, "minimal" (34.7% in 1999); and 17.9% (13.0% in 1999) stated that there was no apparent progress or the situation had worsened.

Given the seriousness of the difficulties clients bring to the response teams and the modest number of sessions attended, mean ratings of 1.8 (just under 2.0 or moderate) are certainly to be expected (n = 28). Although clients gave high ratings to the professional services, they were somewhat more sparing in their assessments of their own or their family member's progress. Given the high levels of satisfaction reported by the families, they apparently do not hold their workers responsible for their minimal or modest progress.

When the analysis for fiscal year 2000 examined progress ratings based on the number of sessions received, client assessments of progress increased from the minimal–moderate level for those seen one to six times (n = 16), to the moderate and moderate–substantial for those seen more than seven times (n = 11). This analysis suggests that the response team intervention addressed client concerns more successfully when clients were seen for relatively longer periods of time.

Finally, progress on presenting problems was identified according to type of problem. The problems were coded, and average ratings were computed for each problem. Only those problems identified by three or more clients were included. The greatest success was achieved with the following problems: attachment issues (2.5; n = 6), mental health issues (2.5; n = 10), and adoption specific issues (2.3; n = 9). The median progress ratings for each of these three issues were in the moderate–substantial range. A minimal–moderate level of progress was achieved with family relationship issues (1.6; n = 7) and problems with behavior or anger (1.6; n = 15). The least success was achieved with "other unspecified problems" (0.6; n = 5). The data indicate that children's acting out behavior is one of the problems that families most frequently encounter, but that the progress ratings have remained relatively modest since the program's first year of operation.

FIGURE 7–4

Respondents' Rating of Progress

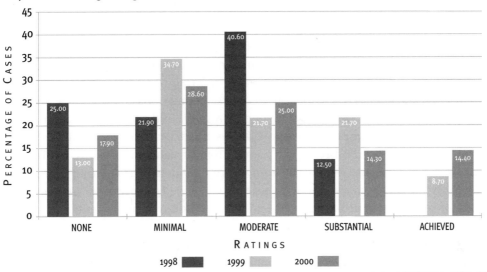

Respondents reported a high level of satisfaction with the quality of the response team service. In fiscal 2000, 85.9% of the respondents rated the service as either "Excellent" or "Very Good," compared with 80% in fiscal year 1999. Clients reported that what they found most helpful were the support and empathy of the social workers. Few identified features of the service they liked least. Of the clients who did express concerns, about half mentioned factors beyond the control of Adoption Crossroads program (e.g., a worker leaving an agency). Clients who had discontinued response team services were asked their reasons for terminating services. They most often listed session limits, the unavailability of their child, and their child's lack of need for services.

Respite Care

Because healthy parent–child relationships are strengthened by temporary relief from day to day concerns, stressors, and responsibilities, Adoption Crossroads includes respite care (that is, services designed to give families an interval of rest or relief) as one of its core services. Respite care is designed as a positive experience for the parent and child, one that promotes the child's development and enhances the appreciation of familial bonds. Respite care is particularly important when families adopt children with special needs (particularly medical and emotional problems) either from foster care or from abroad. The evaluation of Adoptions Crossroads respite care services focused on services provided during a one-year period: July 1999 through June 2000. Evaluation data were collected from staff interviews, monthly reports, respite care subcommittee meetings, and telephone interviews with 22 families who used respite care services provided by Adoption Crossroads. Although the program provided three broad categories of respite care— respite child care, recreational and social events for children and parents, and total and partial funding of camperships (which consist of scholarships or payments for adoptive children who attend designated summer camps)—the evaluation focused only on respite child care and recreational and social events. To date, appropriate mechanisms are not in place to formally evaluate the campership program.

Respite child care

In most instances, Adoption Crossroads affiliates provide respite child care through coordinating contact between the family and an agency-based respite care provider or reimbursing families who secure their own private respite care provider. Most of the affiliates cover large geographic areas with diverse populations and resources, and, as a result, there is variation across the state in how respite child care is provided. In 1999–2000, the number of respite child care providers associated with regional affiliates ranged from 4 to 10 per region. All regions reported ongoing concerns about recruiting and maintaining an adequate number of respite care providers, particularly given the increased demand for respite care services that each region had experienced. "Camperships" consist of scholarships or payments for adoptive children or adolescents who attend designated summer camps.

Telephone interviews with parents indicated that most respite care was provided in a home other than the family's, most respite child care was provided overnight or on weekends, and most families used respite child care one or two times over the one-year period. Monthly staff reports indicated that there had been a steady increase in requests for and use of respite child care during the three years of the program. During 1999–2000, 338 children received respite child care, compared to 185 in 1998–1999. An increase was also observed in the number of respite care episodes, from 262 in 1998–1999 to 374 in 1999–2000.

The telephone interviews with parents who used respite child care services in 1999–2000 sought information about the value of the services, particularly for parents who lacked a personal support network. The 22 parents were asked, "What about respite care was helpful?" Eighteen parents described "getting a break" from parenting as most helpful, and three parents replied that "being able to attend a meeting" was most helpful. In addition, parents were asked, "Who else has provided you and your family with respite services? How often have you used them?" With this question, parents also were asked whether possible sources of social support family, friends, coworkers, or community groups had assisted them with respite care "never," "sometimes," or "often." Of the 22 respondents, 11 reported "never" using any social supports for respite childcare. Parents most frequently named "agency-based groups" as the source of respite care, but only six parents listed them. Five parents reported that "other relatives" had assisted with respite childcare. In the course of the telephone interviews, several parents stated that their child's emotional, behavioral, or physical problems made it very difficult to ask for respite services from ordinary sources of help.

Although the 22 parents may not be statistically representative of the total Adoption Crossroads population, important data emerged about the ages of the children for whom parents needed respite childcare. The 22 parents had 30 adopted children who had received respite care services in 1999–2000. The children ranged in age from 2 to 17, with

13 of the 30 children falling between ages 10 to 14. The parent of a teen with a history of running away recalled, "The provider was not prepared to deal with a 16-year-old and his problems and wasn't able to supervise him properly. "

Adoption Crossroads has recognized that one of the most challenging aspects of respite child care is the ongoing need to recruit specially trained respite care providers who are skilled in caring for children with serious emotional, physical, and behavioral problems. Staff and administrators refer to such individuals as "behaviorally skilled providers." During telephone interviews, the 22 parents were asked, "What could have improved your respite care experience?" This open-ended question most often elicited responses regarding respite for parents with "special needs children." Six parents identified the need for "more providers for children with special needs" or "more money to reimburse specially skilled private providers."

Recreational and social events

The second type of respite care provided by the Adoption Crossroads program involves recreational and social events. Interviews with staff regarding social and recreational events revealed two important aspects of this nontraditional form of respite care. One, the planning of social and recreational events requires considerable staff time and energy. Two, there are inherent difficulties in measuring the short- and long-term benefits of recreational and social events for adoptive families. Staff observations revealed that recreational and social events may do far more than provide an interval of rest or relief. Staff commented that recreational and social events provide families with several opportunities. The parents may develop personal networks within which they may arrange informal respite for one another without using the formal assistance of Adoption Crossroads, and thus normalizing some stressors. The parents and children may find a unique space to both "be and not be together," thus reducing family-based stressors. Finally, parents, children, kinship systems, and others may appreciate the strengths of adoptive families, taking pleasure in extrafamilial and interfamilial relationships.

Family Support

The family support services provided by Adoption Crossroads support children and their parents in attaining and sustaining a sense of entitlement regarding their full status as family members. Family support services are designed to achieve permanence, promote healthy parent–child relationships, and reduce the social isolation of adoptive families, who often regard their circumstances as overwhelming and their feelings as unacceptable (Smith & Howard, 1999).

Adoption Crossroads offers two types of family support services: (1) agency-based parent and young adult liaisons who meet with family members individually, and (2) agency-based support groups for children, adolescents, parents, and kinship systems. The evaluation of family support services focused on parent and young adult liaison services and support group services provided during a one-year period: July 1999 through June 2000. Evaluation data on family support services were obtained from staff interviews, monthly agency reports, and telephone interviews with 22 parents (not included in the respite care interviews) who used support group services. In each region, individual parent liaisons (i.e., adoptive parents who agency staff select and train to serve as members of an adoptive family support network) are matched with adoptive parents and are available to them on an as-needed basis. Special attention is given to matching parent liaisons with families based on similar language, ethnicity, culture, and specific adoption circumstances. Parent liaisons provide immediate telephone support to a family if requested or recommended by the agency's on-call worker and they often refer families for support groups and respite care. In some regions, parent liaisons function as leaders or coleaders of agency-based support groups. Most parent liaisons participate in adoption competency training, and in some regions, they attend monthly or bimonthly supervision groups. The number of parent liaisons in each region ranges from 3 to 12.

At the time of the 1999–2000 evaluation, there were six young adult liaisons throughout the state. Young adult liaisons are adopted individuals who are matched with an adopted adolescent for whom they serve in a role similar to that of a "Big Brother" or "Big Sister." The young adult liaison acts as a role model. The relationship, which becomes meaningful for both parties, reinforces the interpersonal dynamics of social support and enhanced self-esteem. A focus of Adoption Crossroads has been to locate, engage, and train young adult liaisons.

In each region, there are family support groups. All regions have parent support groups, and many regions have developed groups for children, adolescents, and kin (i.e., grandparents and other relatives who have adopted). The support groups are designed to recognize the considerable variability in family structure—families involve single and married parents and different groupings of adopted and biological children—and family circumstances, incorporating both adoption and guardianships and national and international kinships systems. Table 7-1 summarizes the average number and type of support group available per month statewide.

The number and types of groups offered by region varied, depending on staff resources and client requests. Some regions regularly offered parent, child, adolescent, and kinship support groups, but other regions served only certain populations. Support groups differed by length of sessions and number of meetings per month. Parent groups often met for an hour or more, and school-based children's groups often lasted 40–45 minutes. Most groups met twice a month, although some groups met weekly or monthly. In 1999–2000, Adoption Crossroads served 2,485 clients through family support groups, an average of 207 clients per month.

Data obtained from telephone interviews suggested that families attended family support groups between six and 15 times. Ten of the 22 telephone respondents said that they were continuing or planning to continue attending support groups in the future. These data were consistent with staff impressions that most families remain connected to open-ended support groups. Respondents most often stated that they or their children ended their involvement in support groups because the groups themselves ended, a finding that was consistent with the short-term nature (six to 12 sessions) of many of the support groups, particularly for children and teens.

TABLE 7-1

Average Number of Support Groups per Month Statewide

Parent groups	34
Teen groups	8
Children's groups	4
Kinship groups	5
Adult adoptee/birthparent	2
TOTAL	53

Data obtained from telephone interviews have assisted the program in identifying some of the characteristics of families who used support groups. Although only a small subgroup of 22 individuals participated in the telephone interviews, the preliminary data provide information about the families themselves and various aspects of the service that can inform the future development of support groups. Telephone respondents were asked, "What issues, concerns, or problems were discussed in support groups?" Of te 35 "often" responses, 20 indicated a family member as the source of soupport. However, 32 of the 35 "never" responses specifically noted a family member as "never" used as a source of support. Telephone respondents also were asked three questions about their social support networks. Two asked parents to describe how different individuals or organization-based groups had been helpful in supporting their parenting, and the third asked about types of support that had been most important to them. The fact that only 13 of the 22 parents answered these questions may indicate a perceived lack of support from family, kinship, and community systems.

The 13 respondents rated a range of individuals as "often," "seldom" or "never" used as sources of support. All of the respondents rated the use of support as "often" or "never" for each individual choice (friend, sibling, parent, coworker, etc.). There were a total of 35 "often" responses and 35 "never" responses. Of the 35 "often" responses, 20 indicated a family member as the source of support. However, 32 of the 35 "never" responses noted a family member as a source of support. Nine of the 35 "often" responses noted "friends," whereas 4 of the 35 "never" responses noted the use of friends. Three respondents specifically indicated that friends who were "often" used as sources of support were also adoptive parents. Nonetheless, the number of respondents who described their social support network as "seldom or never helpful" was far greater than all other responses. When asked about the importance of a range of individuals and organizations, the most frequently noted "extremely important" source (10 out of 13) was a counselor.

When asked what they found most helpful about support groups, the 22 parents gave 24 responses. The most common responses were "not being alone—knowing that others have similar problems—getting peer support and input" (45%). Of the 16 parents whose children or teens participated in support groups, six noted "being with other kids" as most helpful (25%). Based on the telephone interviews, overall satisfaction with Adoption Crossroads support groups was quite positive. Seventeen of the 22 respondents rated the support group services as either "excellent" (41%) or "very good" (36%).

Training

During the first three years of the Adoption Crossroads program, Child and Family Services and the regional affiliates provided adoption-related training. The training was designed to provide opportunities for adoptive parents, adoptees, professionals, and adopted children and youth to gain adoption-related information and communicate with one another about sensitive topics. The project hypothesized that training on adoption issues, when added to clinical interventions, would increase participants' knowledge about adoption and enhance positive parent and child behaviors.

Evaluations were conducted in each of the three years. At the end of each training session, participants completed a written evaluation. These participants gave high ratings to trainers with regard to their knowledge of the subjects, the quality of their presentations, and their responsiveness to participants. Moreover, respondents consistently highly rated their overall satisfaction with the training. They valued both the topics covered and the opportunity to role-play and learn what "works" from experiential exercises and concrete examples.

The evaluations demonstrated that participants benefited from workshops that focused on normalizing adjustment (for both children and parents, pre- and postadoption), dealing with emotions, understanding behavior, effective interventions for problems, and culture-specific adoption issues (both domestically and internationally). The evaluations also indicated that parents wished to obtain additional training on how to talk to children about adoption, and how to work with older adoptees. The respondents also requested workshops on mediation and burnout prevention.

Advocacy and Coordination

Case-specific advocacy and service coordination are fundamental components of the Adoption Crossroads strengths-based model, which incorporates traditional social casework services for families who request help with postadoption problems and the core social work values of client self-determination and family empowerment. These components of Adoption Crossroads' model are designed to assist families to move towards their desired level of family functioning. At the same time, Child and Family Services, as lead agency, engages in advocacy and coordination activities at the systems and policy levels.

Four activities comprise the advocacy and coordination component of the Adoption Crossroads program: case specific advocacy and service coordination, organizational culture change, wraparound services, and systemic and policy-oriented efforts by the lead agency. Case specific advocacy and coordination are designed to meet the diverse social casework needs of families; they include assisting families to develop clear goals (with specific outcomes) as they negotiate various service systems, and (2) modeling and empowering families to be assertive advocates for themselves. Organizational culture change addresses the challenges of larger social systems. This service area recognizes the efforts of families to develop and nurture working relationships with staff in agencies to which they turn repeatedly over time. Adoption Crossroads staff attempt to facilitate consistent relationships between families and the many gatekeepers and providers of services whose assistance they need. Wraparound services refer to the array of services that families need. To support families in accessing the array of needed services, Adoption Crossroads assists families in identifying the services they need and developing strategies for maximizing their access to those services, provides families with information regarding obtaining needed services, and facilitates service delivery by developing professional contacts with key agencies and professionals within the regional affiliate's geographical area. The lead agency's role in advocacy and coordination is to gather information about service needs, emerging trends, and obstacles to service acquisition in the six regions and provide that information to larger social service systems. Specific activities have included tracking advocacy and coordination needs across the six regions, developing working relationships with key staffing major state agencies and at private insurance companies to facilitate better service provision for families, and bringing systemic problems to the attention of policymakers and advocating for policy changes.

Since the beginning of Adoption Crossroads, regional and lead agency staff annually have completed questionnaires designed to elicit information about their advocacy and coordination activities and their assessment of successes and challenges in this program component. Based on the most recent evaluation of this work in fiscal year 2000, some progress apparently has been made in facilitating clients' access to needed services. At the same time, several serious systemic problems (most of which are related to rules and regulations of other agencies and insurance companies) continue to impede clients' ability to obtain the services they need. Adoption Crossroads staff, particularly those associated with the program for a period of time, reported that they had some successes with individual families in service coordination and advocacy. Success has been associated with the staff's increased familiarity with other agencies and the key personnel in their regions who share case responsibilities. Case advocacy activities, however, vary. Some staff focus primarily on assisting clients to learn to advocate for themselves, and others directly advocate with agencies for the services clients need.

Staff responses to questionnaires indicate that they experience considerable frustration with the eligibility rules and time frames (time limits and waiting lists) of both public and private agencies that could provide assistance to the families Adoption Crossroads serves. Among the issues bearing on clients' access to services, which staff consistently names as the principal concern, are rules restricting access to services and inconsistent interpretations of the rules and regulations of other agencies. The types of organizations that staff routinely cite as posing problems for adoptive families are the state's child welfare agency; the state mental health department, which has limited services to seriously mentally ill children and adolescents; private and publicly contracted health insurers who deny children certain mental health services, particularly long-term psychotherapeutic care and in-patient hospitalization; and the public schools, which frequently misunderstand the developmental challenges of adopted children and are resistive to providing appropriate special education programs. Staff view budgetary constraints, legal requirements, and managed care approaches as factors increasing the difficulties they encounter in putting wraparound services in place. Adoption Crossroads respondents noted, on their written questionnaires and in group interviews conducted in the spring of 2001, that high turnover among state agency staff compound problems related to lack of sophistication about adoption-specific needs.

The evaluation of the advocacy and coordination component also focused on the lead agency's responsibility for negotiating changes in external systems' rules and regulations that affect the population served by Adoption Crossroads. Staff of Child and Family Services meet monthly with the regional coordinators to gather information about systemic difficulties, develop monthly reports that describe policy matters that have arisen in individual cases and on an ongoing basis, and hold meetings with key personnel in other state agencies in order to clarify criteria for services. Administrative personnel reported some modest successes in addressing some systemic problems, but the evaluation did not address the effectiveness of these efforts.

Discussion

The Adoption Crossroads program, in many respects, has exemplified the challenges and opportunities inherent in a state's contracting with a private agency for management and service provision under a lead agency model. The lead agency, Child and Family Services, recognized the varied needs of diverse communities and has built considerable flexibility into the Adoption Crossroads program, supporting a range of models of respite and family support offered by its affiliates. This flexibility has been particularly valuable in resolving the potentially contradictory pressures to simultaneously increase normalizing and supportive interventions for families (through family support groups, recreational activities, and financial aid for camperships) while providing access to more intensive, clinically oriented services. Although the program increasingly has sponsored recreational activities and provided camperships, it also has incrementally increased the numbers of families receiving clinical response team services and the average length of these services.

During the three years of the program, funding largely remained level. Increases in the range and intensity of services have been possible because of staff creativity and the unused service capacity inherent in the start-up phase of any new program. Nonetheless, Child and Family Services was faced periodically with the need to assure that any new funding, such as that obtained for camperships, was invested in new service development and that consumers had consistent access to services throughout the state.

Social isolation is one of the central difficulties facing adoptive families who are troubled (Smith & Howard, 1999). While social isolation is not a difficulty for all adoptive families, our findings suggest that it may well be the case for families as well as children who have extraordinary "special needs." Children's special needs may contribute to social isolation as well as to real obstacles in procuring respite childcare. The obstacle most commonly cited by parents and staff is the lack of respite providers trained to manage difficult behavioral or emotional problems. Moreover, the telephone interviews indicated that the age range of children for whom parents are seeking respite care extended well into adolescence. It is difficult to find adequate and appropriate childcare for adolescents under the best of circumstances. Adding the possibility that many of these preadolescents and adolescents suffer from emotional, behavioral, and physical problems, the parents' need for respite childcare is impressive. Practitioners need further information about the possibility of an increasing use of respite childcare services for adolescents. If this need is present among adoptive families, they need to know why this is the case and how to address it.

Other obstacles to respite childcare were identified by staff as well as by respite care providers. Adoptive parents may be hesitant to ask for respite childcare services because they fear being seen as inadequate or identified as "at-risk." Adoptive parents also are acutely aware of the normative separation anxiety that exists for many adopted children, and they are especially reluctant to leave their children. Finally, parents with limited financial resources are unable to pay a private provider and wait for reimbursement. The fact that respite child care is not usually occurring in the adoptive family's home also might be an obstacle to using respite child care. Out-of-home respite childcare that involves an unfamiliar environment combined with multiple separations or transitions might be especially stressful for adopted children and their parents, thereby undermining some of its benefits.

Respite childcare clearly is both needed and appreciated by Adoption Crossroads families. As community-based prevention, respite childcare provides a "break" that both children and parents need. At the same time, however, families and staff are articulating serious mental health needs as they discuss the simple need for the service. Adoptive families who are coping with serious emotional and mental health issues need respite childcare from skilled providers. Yet even skilled providers may not be able to fully address the mental health needs of children, adolescents, and families with complex physical and psychological trauma.

While all families in contemporary society benefit from all forms of respite care, adoptive families represent an increasing family population for whom respite care is essential for family permanence and stability. Loss, separation, abandonment, and attachment are some of the most deeply challenging human events. The realities as well as the fear of such human events are part of the everyday lives of adoptive families, thus both heighten the need for respite care and complicate its achievement. The full range of respite care services comprises a central preventive intervention that addresses familial needs and bolsters the personal and social strengths of children and parents.

These findings regarding the family support component suggest that parents who use Adoption Crossroads support groups are isolated from family and community-based resources, yet they are capable of reaching out to individuals who might be especially sensitive to their needs. Positive emphasis is being placed on professionals who are perceived as primary social supports. For this reason, liaisons and group leaders may need additional training and their own structured sources of support, such as peer supervision or process groups. The findings also suggest that practitioners need to know more about why parents may not use their own families of origin as sources of support. Families whose kinship systems reject adoption are wise to seek alternative sources of support, such as Adoption Crossroads. At the same time, practitioners may need to increase efforts to educate kinship systems and other social networks (the workplace, churches, schools) to destigmatize adoption. Kinship support groups may need to target extended family members of adoptive families, rather than focusing primarily on kinship systems that are involved in adoption.

Staff and administrators know that the success of the support groups depends on the skills of the leaders. Group leaders vary in their knowledge and skills. In some regions, leaders are professionals trained in adoption work. In others, the leaders are adoptive parents who have been trained by the agency as liaisons and group leaders. Although no consistent patterns associate the leaders' background with the success of the groups, this is an area of ongoing attention. There is a need for continuing high quality adoption-specific training for both professionals and parent liaisons, especially with regard to children's and teen groups.

Adoption is both an event and a process that is deeply personal and broadly social. Adoptive families are formed in the context of loss for children as well as parents, all of whom often need to grieve the loss of an idealized or imagined family. This grieving may be complicated by misconceptions associated with adoption in society at large. In some important ways, adoptive families are different from other families but they are not, by definition, more troubled or dysfunctional (Smith & Howard, 1999). Adoption Crossroads family support services recognize this difference and the need for support as well as validation for parents, children, adolescents, and kinship systems coping with the challenges of adoption.

The activities associated with case coordination and advocacy have become more refined over the life of Adoptions Crossroads, and they have improved as the program has become better known in the regions and as personnel have developed expertise about the services and protocols of the various agencies and programs. Some progress has been made in resolving systemic issues, but inconsistencies in interpreting and implementing policies by some state agencies and resource scarcity continue to thwart optimal service provision to children and families served by Adoption Crossroads. In addition, staff turnover in some agencies makes it necessary to repeat processes related to service coordination and policy change.

The flexibility of Child and Family Services has been a significant strength of the program, but it also poses challenges related to consistency in standards related to social service practice and service utilization targets throughout the Adoption Crossroads program. Implementation of the wraparound model through the advocacy and coordination component, for example, has required discussion of the priority that case and policy advocacy (both of which were part of the initial program plan) should be given. Because many affiliates have chosen to focus their efforts primarily on case-specific advocacy and coordination, Child and Family Services has assumed primary responsibility for policy advocacy that focuses on the access of families with adopted children to the state's various human service programs.

Flexibility in Child and Family Service's oversight of the system of affiliated agencies also posed challenges for program evaluation. Initially, the evaluation plan required a significant investment of time on the part of direct service staff in administering instruments related program outcomes, a plan that has not proven to be feasible. As an alternative, Child and Family Services has supported an evaluation focus on consumer satisfaction and on other efforts to assess the implementation and utilization of program services. Even the task of assessing seemingly concrete features of the program (e.g., numbers of clients served or number of referrals that result in service engagement), however, has posed challenges. These challenges have included the need to obtain affiliate agency compliance with the lead agency's data reporting protocols and the achievement of some consensus as to what truly constitutes service engagement.

Conclusion

One of the most significant strengths of the Adoption Crossroads program has been the collaborative sharing of responsibilities, not only between agencies, but also between families and professionals as well as among direct service workers, administrative staff, and evaluators. The collective efforts of the various constituencies have resulted in significant satisfaction on the part of the families served and clear evidence of progress toward the diverse goals that Adoption Crossroads has sought to achieve.

References

Hudson, C. G., Cedeño-Zamor, P., Rosenthal, M., Springer, C., Hudson, B., Ford, D. A., Kowal, L. W., Riley, D. (Feb. 5, 2001). *Adoption Crossroads: The third year evaluation.* Salem, MA: School of Social Work, Salem State College.

Smith, S. L., & Howard, J. A. (1999). *Promoting successful adoptions.* Thousand Oaks, CA: Sage Publications.

THE NATURE OF Effective Adoption Preservation Services:
A QUALITATIVE STUDY

Susan Livingston Smith

Adopted children are overrepresented among children with emotional and behavioral problems (Brodzinsky, Schecter, Braff, & Singer, 1984; Howard, Smith, & Ryan, 2004; Miller, Fan, Christensen, Grotevant, & van Dulmen, 2000; Rosenthal & Groze, 1994; Smith & Howard, 1999, Smith, Howard, & Monroe, 1998; Wierzbicki, 1993; Zill, 1996). Children adopted at older ages and children who had damaging experiences prior to placement with their adoptive families are particularly overrepresented among this population of children (Simmel, Brooks, Barth, & Hinshaw, 2001; Rosenthal & Groze, 1994; Howe, 1997; Zill, 1996). Yet, little is known about the services that adoptive families need to assist them in effectively parenting these children to adulthood (Barth & Miller, 2000).

Adoption in the United States has changed dramatically over the past 30 years. As the number of newborns surrendered by unwed parents has declined, the proportion of children who are adopted through other situations has increased. Children adopted by nonrelatives in the U.S. today are predominately adopted from the child welfare system. Many of these children are adopted after experiencing poor prenatal care (including, for many children, prenatal alcohol or drug exposure) and other damaging experiences, such as neglect, abuse, or extended periods of institutionalization. Likewise, children adopted from other countries may experience such damaging experiences before adoption.

Prior to the marked increase in the adoption of children with special needs beginning in the 1980s, it was assumed that the existing array of community services for all children and families could meet the therapeutic needs of adoptive families. As adoptive parents unsuccessfully sought help for their children, however, the need for specialized services became more apparent. The development of postadoption services is largely a response to the advocacy efforts of adoptive families. Postadoption services assume that adoption is different in significant ways from parenting birthchildren and that service providers must understand these differences. Services also assume that service providers must understand the developmental impact of neglect, abuse, and interrupted attachments on children to effectively serve these children and their families.

A number of states have developed and are developing a range of services tailored to meet the specific needs of adoptive families. These services include information and referral, education and training, support groups, mentoring, respite care, advocacy, crisis intervention, search and reunion services, and therapeutic counseling (Howard & Smith, 1997). Efforts to improve mental health services for adopted children and their families have resulted in services designed to educate large numbers of community mental health professionals about adoption-related issues and the development of programs exclusively designed for adoptive families. One such program is the Illinois Adoption Preservation Program on which the research reported in this chapter focuses.

The Illinois Adoption Preservation Program is one of the most well established therapeutic programs for adoptive families in the nation, particularly noteworthy because of the scope of its services and the numbers of families served. The program is primarily aimed at adoptive families who are experiencing difficulties significant enough to threaten the family's stability. It is not intended to serve the broad spectrum of families with postadoption needs. Several evaluations of this program have documented that both social workers and adoptive parents report a variety of positive outcomes of these services. In the initial evaluation of the program during the first four years of its development, for example, children showed significant improvement overall on pre- and post-measures of the Achenbach Child Behavior Checklist (Howard & Smith, 1995).

An earlier evaluation indicated that two-thirds of the adoptive families served by the Adoption Preservation Services (APS) program had received counseling prior to contacting APS but felt that their problems had not been sufficiently resolved (Howard, & Smith, 1995). Many of the comments that families made on their evaluation forms attested to their perception that the specialized adoption services offered by APS were different from other services that they had received and had made a big difference in their families' functioning. The following response from a mother served by APS is an example of these comments:

> I had gone everywhere I could think of for help. No one had proper help for us until the adoption support services. Our whole family had become dysfunctional. Our marriage was coming apart. We did not know how to cope with our daughter. No one had ever told us about any of what she was going through. We had this fantasy that adoption was the same as forming a family biologically. We were not prepared to help our children, especially our daughter, with the grieving process, the guilt, the anger.
>
> We have all grown to understand adoption and ourselves better. We've learned it's okay that we can't always take away our children's pain—but we can help them cope with it. We have become more open with our inner thoughts. We've learned to share as a family—to be supportive. It saved our family from totally splitting up.

The Need for Research on Adoption Preservation Services

Adoption preservation services are intensive therapeutic services for troubled adoptive families. To advance the development of these services, two types of research are needed.

First, there is a need for efficacy research that demonstrates the outcomes of these services. Only a few reported studies on therapeutic services to this population of families exist, and most of the programs that have been studied served 50 or fewer families (Groze, Young, & Corcran-Rumppe, 1991; Prew, Suter, & Carrington, 1990). Previous evaluations of the Illinois Adoption Preservation Program have yielded insights into the nature of problems for which families seek services and the factors associated with problem severity (Howard & Smith, 1995; Smith & Howard, 1998). A current study of this program employing a battery of pre- and postmeasures should yield greater understanding of the types of changes occurring over the course of the treatment program and the characteristics of children and families who seem to be helped or not helped by this program.

Second, the field requires an in-depth understanding of the intervention itself—what specifically is the nature of the adoption preservation services provided and the various methods and interventive strategies which comprise this body of services? The nine private agencies that provide, by contract, adoption preservation services in 20 sites across Illinois specify a core body of services in their program plans, but the specific nature of these interventions—and the characteristics that account for their effectiveness in cases where other interventions have failed—are unclear. A clear delineation of this model of intervention would make it possible to replicate this model in other locales.

To further the development of postadoption services for troubled adoptive families, there must be an understanding of the model of therapeutic intervention that effectively addresses the needs of these families. The purpose of this study is to develop a deeper understanding of the nature of effective adoption preservation services. In other words, in situations where these services are perceived by workers and families to be successful, what is the nature of the service that was provided? This study is an initial effort to examine the intrinsic nature of the services that the Illinois Adoption/ Guardianship Preservation Program provides.

Method

This study uses triangulation among data sources, data collection strategies, and time periods in order to provide a rich body of data for this analysis of adoption preservation services. It is based on three sources of data, briefly described in the next section: interviews with eight families served by APS, the open-ended responses of 193 families to evaluation forms, and responses of 36 APS social workers to a survey related to the nature of APS. The responses of these families and social workers provide a foundation for delineating the professional parameters of adoption preservation work and offer a skeletal framework on which to build future qualitative studies of APS.

Data Sources

Families interviewed for the study

Telephone interviews with five families (four interviews with mothers only and one with both parents) and in-person interviews with three other families (two interviews with mothers only and one with both parents) form the basis for the case studies. The three in-person interviews were conducted in 1992 in an early evaluation of APS and were included in this study to expand the richness of available data. In addition to the content analysis of the interview responses, the researcher reviewed forms completed by social workers regarding the services provided to the interviewed families. This review was designed to increase the researcher's understanding of the context of the families' problems and the services they received. The families represented all types of adoptive families—those who adopted through the child welfare system, attorney and private agency domestic infant adoptions of non-state wards, and international adoptions.

The interview protocol used during these interviews was comprised of open-ended questions to explore each family's reasons for seeking adoption preservation services, the family's experience in receiving services, and the benefits of the services for the family. Parents also were asked about how adoption preservation services differed from services they had received previously and the specific interventions that most helped their families.

Families' open-ended responses on feedback forms

At the conclusion of services, adoption preservation workers provide families with feedback forms and a self-addressed stamped envelope so that they may mail the forms to the Center for Adoption Studies, a research center at Illinois State University. Families rate the quality of the services and impact of the services they received. Families also are invited to write additional comments on the back of the forms, and many families add comments about the services that they received. For this study, the comments of 193 families (extracted from approximately 400 forms returned by families from 1998 to 2001) were analyzed.

Surveys of adoption preservation workers

Finally, surveys of APS social workers were analyzed. These surveys contained nine open-ended questions designed to elicit the social workers' insights about specific aspects of their work, particularly the knowledge and expertise which they use most extensively in their work and their philosophy of APS. The surveys were distributed in the spring of 2001. Of the approximately 50 social workers in the AP program, 36 returned surveys.

Data Analysis

The researcher performed content analysis on transcriptions and notes from interviews as well as a compilation of all the open-ended written responses from families, identifying and organizing specific themes into categories of meaning. Interviews were ordered first, as these provided the most comprehensive view of the range of problems for which families seek assistance through APS. Families' open-ended responses on the feedback forms then added to the breadth of this analysis by providing a wider continuum of themes on a number of categories, particularly dimensions of services and conditions limiting the success of services. Finally, the researcher compiled and analyzed the responses to each question on the social worker survey in a manner similar to the analysis of the parent feedback form. The social worker surveys were the primary source of data for understanding the professional knowledge and expertise that underlie effective adoption preservation services as well as guiding principles of APS. Through the course of these analyses, a conceptual map of effective adoption preservation services evolved, which the researcher used to organize key themes.

Findings

The experiences of many families receiving adoption preservation services and the understanding and experience of social workers delivering these services provide an overall picture of the nature of effective adoption preservation services. The findings are summarized in relation to categories of meaning in a conceptual map of effective adoption preservation services, as presented in Figure 8-1. The following discussion includes a number of quotes from families and social workers that provide poignant documentation of these themes.

This section describes four families who were interviewed (using a pseudonym for their child), and the contextual factors associated with the problems that brought them to APS. This chapter will discuss the situations of these four families, which illustrate the myriad factors that are relevant to an understanding of the problems that adoptive families face, beginning with the section on the families' presenting problems.

Elizabeth was adopted from an Asian country shortly before her fifth birthday. Her mother described her as having a "whole host of problems" from the very beginning. She had been found abandoned on the street at age 1 and had resided in an orphanage for nearly four years. In this very large institution, three caregivers supervised 60 children in each room. It was thought that Elizabeth had been physically abused as she was covered with bruises when her adoptive family met her. Elizabeth was a combative child with very primitive language skills at the age of 5. She had hysterical, extended tantrums for at least two years after her adoption. She had great difficulty dealing with any new situation and could not be in public for any period of time without becoming afraid and hysterical. Her mother stated that Elizabeth was creating chaos in the family. She had extreme developmental delays and emotional difficulties that necessitated constant supervision and many expensive therapies. There were conflicts between Elizabeth and her sister. Her mother described the differences between her children: "It got to the point [where] we had the two. The one was the good one and the other, the bad one. It was always good and bad. The one would bring home a note saying how wonderful she was and such a good listener. And the other would be sent home from school."

Lisa was placed in her first week of life with a family who had one biological child and who could no longer have children. The family had an open adoption in that they had met Lisa's birthfamily and had some ongoing contact with birthfamily members. The adoptive family was aware of the birthmother's legal problems and viewed her as a bad influence on Lisa. Lisa developed behavioral and emotional problems, including lying, stealing, and hoarding items. These problems intensified when she began middle school. According to her mother, Lisa was "always just a very angry child." Lisa also

FIGURE 8–1

Map of Effective Adoption Preservation Services

FAMILY CONTEXT
- Adoption story
- Child's history
- Martial issues
- Sibling issues
- Parenting dynamics

ENVIRONMENTAL CONTEXT
- Previous helping experiences
- Extended support network
- School system response
- Availability of needed services
- Connnection to adoptive families

PRRESENTING PROBLEMS
- Child behaviors
- Child emotional issues
- Parenting difficulties
- Child's special needs
- School difficulties
- Sibling conflict

GUIDING PRINCIPLES OF ADOPTION PRESERVATION WORK
- Be accepting, nonblaming
- Provide empathic listening/understanding
- Start where client is
- Join with and empower parents
- Educate parents, re: child
- Teach new parenting strategies
- Address adoption dynamics
- Be accessible and reliable
- Link with services/advocacy
- Intervene on multiple levels
- Carefully terminate services

EFFECTIVE ADOPTION PRESERVATION SERVICES

WORKER KNOWLEDGE/EXPERTISE
- Adoption knowledge
- Impact of deprivation/maltreatment
- Impact of prenatatal substance exposure
- Sensory integration problems
- Learning disabilities
- Range of mental health problems of children
- Attachment therapies
- Family systems therapy
- Therapeutic parenting
- Varied child therapeutic techniques
- Group work
- Handling own emotional reactions

CONDITIONS LIMITING SUCESS
- Limited knowledge development
- Social worker inadequacies
- Insufficient parental commitment
- Parental incapacity
- Child severe/irremediable problems
- Time limits on services

OUTCOME OF SERVICES
- New perspective/understanding
- Improvements in child
- Increased parenting abilities
- Improved family climate
- Linkage with needed resources

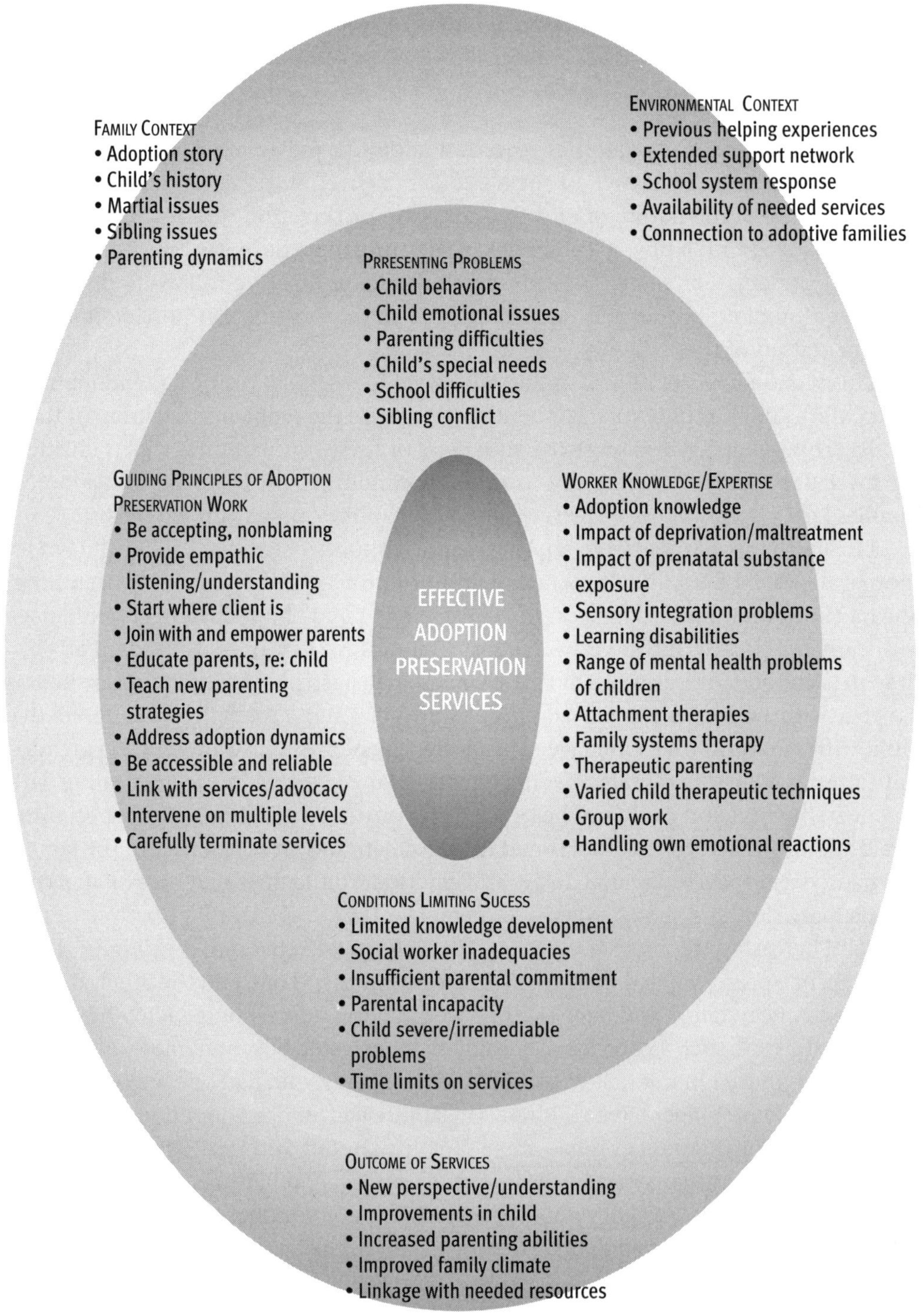

was identified as having learning disabilities. Throughout her childhood, Lisa had socialization problems and difficulties getting along with other children. There was ongoing conflict between Lisa and her sister, who was considered by the family to be "the good kid." Behaviors and emotions indicative of attachment problems were also present—mistrust of adults, withdrawal, and feelings that she did not "fit in" with her family. Lisa's father viewed the adoption as a complete mistake and wanted out of the adoption. He and his wife fought about how to handle the situation and were "on the brink of divorce" when they finally sought assistance through APS.

Jeffrey, age 12 at referral, had been removed from his birthfamily at age 4, along with his younger sister. He had been found foraging in a garbage can for food for himself and his sister. From the time of their adoptive placement with an infertile couple who had never parented, Jeffrey resisted attaching and demonstrated a host of acting-out behavior problems, including rage and aggression toward his adoptive mother. While his adoptive mother was recuperating at home following knee surgery, Jeffrey pushed her down the stairs and she had to have additional surgery. At the time of referral, he had begun demonstrating PTSD symptoms. While taking a shower one night, he began screaming hysterically, "I'm locked in the closet and I can't get out." The counselors whom his parents consulted felt he was too disturbed to be treated as an outpatient and recommended residential treatment. Securing payment for this treatment had been an obstacle. The family no longer lived in the state where they had adopted Jeffrey, and although the family had a Medicaid card from this state, the child welfare department had refused to acknowledge for a long period of time that Jeffrey was known to them. The adoptive parents also worried about the impact of Jeffrey's problems on his younger sister who was much more attached and well adjusted.

Karen was the only child of a couple who had been older at the time of their marriage, although her father had adult children from a previous marriage. Karen was placed with her adoptive parents when she was four, when her previous foster-adoptive placement ended (Karen's adoptive parents found out years later that Karen had no idea that the family she was leaving was not her birthfamily and she could not understand why they did not keep her with them). Karen had been removed from her birthfamily at age 2 as a result of physical abuse and neglect. In her adoptive family, her behaviors were difficult from early on. She was hyperactive, did not sleep, had tantrums, and screamed for two to three hours at a time. She would not accept or return affection. At the time of referral, Karen was a preadolescent and had falsely reported her parents for abuse a second time, an occurrence which caused her adoptive mother, a teacher, to give up and want to end the adoption. Throughout grade school, Karen's behavior problems continued at home and at school. She was destructive, full of rage, and aggressive. In fourth grade, Karen became so angry and destructive that she spent 10 weeks in a psychiatric setting, but returned, according to her family, "worse than ever." She was diagnosed as bipolar with possible borderline personality. She and her family received mental health services from a total of seven psychiatrists, psychologists, and social workers, who had given Karen "every kind of drug." Karen was placed in a variety of special classrooms, none of which adequately addressed her needs. Her parents thought that her last teacher belittled her and damaged her already low self-esteem. Karen also played her parents against one another and attempted to create conflict between them by lying to each one about the other.

Presenting Problems of Families Coming to Adoption Preservation

Almost all of the parent responses indicated that their adopted child's behavioral or emotional problems led them to seek adoption preservation services. The presenting problems were grouped as follows: child behavior problems; child emotional problems; parenting difficulties; school difficulties; special needs of the child (a range of conditions such as developmental delays, brain trauma, genetic disorders, etc.); and sibling conflict. Some of the parents who were interviewed described marital difficulties, and in this analysis, these issues are discussed under the category of family context.

Child behavioral and emotional problems

The most commonly reported difficulties related to problems with children's behavior, and, more specifically, to behaviors that parents could not control and negative behavior patterns that they could not change. In some cases, children's behaviors had worsened prior to referral, and in other cases, the behaviors had been chronically severe. Reported behaviors encompassed a range of child behavior problems, particularly defiance, aggression, tantrums, lying, stealing, and attachment problems.

The children's behavioral and emotional problems were intertwined. Behavior problems often seemed to be the manifestation of emotional problems. Elizabeth's mother, for example, stated:

> When she first came, all she did was scream when she didn't understand what was going on...And for the first year, I mean that's all she was, was mad....When she first came it was horrible...because, I mean, all you did was fight with this kid. All you did was fight! You'd say, "Okay, let's go," and she would just sit on the ground and scream. And she didn't want even to go to the park...she started first grade, and school was just horrible. I mean she would come home just screaming...just screaming...she would come home just hysterical, because I'm sure she was frustrated.

Elizabeth's behaviors of screaming, fighting, having tantrums, and defiance, and her emotions of confusion, fear, frustration, and anger seemed to be conjoined.

Parents also commonly described their children's low self-esteem and adoption/identity issues. Lisa, for example, struggled with her feelings related to adoption. She had difficulty understanding her birthmother's problems and disconnecting her own self-image and destiny from her birthmother's life. Lisa and Elizabeth's situations also reflect their struggle with being the "bad kid" in the family in juxtaposition to a "good kid," a dynamic which further exacerbates self-esteem issues.

Parents often described their children's depression and grief. In Lisa's case, the adoption preservation worker told her parents that Lisa had been "clinically depressed for a while," and the social worker helped them to understand Lisa's depression. Parents also described their children's difficulty in regulating emotions. Many of the children, including

Jeffrey and Elizabeth, had difficulty controlling anger and handling change or unstructured situations. One mother described her 16-year old son's problems controlling his anger.

> Brad had had problems throughout his childhood, but when he reached the age of 12, things just escalated. His anger was pretty much out of control. He could not handle you ever telling him "no." He would punch walls, throw things like glasses and books, or break his sister's Barbie dolls and then say he didn't do it. He wrote "bitch" on the side of my new van with a rock. It didn't matter what you did—until he got over his rage, you couldn't deal with him. After he would have those rages, he would go into a deep sleep. Sometimes he would have several upsets in one week.....Brad needed to have the same routine every day and does much better if in a controlled environment.

After several hospitalizations, Brad was placed in a facility where his psychiatrist had adopted children and his psychologist was adopted. The two professionals felt that most of Brad's problems were related to adoption. As Brad's situation illustrates, adoption/identity struggles affect the ongoing adjustment of many children. One parent wrote, "Our daughter has severe emotional problems, partially centered on her feeling that she has no family."

In some situations, the problems seemed to be more acute and were, in some cases, precipitated by a recent loss. In her interview, one parent described her daughter's struggles in understanding her adoption and dealing with her feelings about being a different race from her parents:

> Before we started the sessions, she would say to me, 'I wish I was white like you and Dad.' And I felt bad about that—I didn't want her to feel that way.....These things still come up occasionally when she's angry at me. She'll say, "Well, I want to go find my mom."

This 8-year-old was exhibiting only a few moderate behavior problems following her parents' separation and divorce, but her parents did not know how to help her with her adoption-related loss and identity issues.

Parenting difficulties

Many parents described severe difficulties in parenting that had been ongoing for many years and that seemed to intensify prior to contact with APS. Brad's mother, for example, described her family's difficulties in coping with Brad's extreme anger and his destructiveness:

> Brad had already had two hospitalizations for depression and behavior and was ready to be admitted again. We were close to divorce. I was close to a nervous breakdown. I was afraid of Brad, and his sister was scared to death of her brother when he got angry. She would sleep with her desk in front of her door at night, and her grades were falling. Bill wanted to deal with Brad the wrong way. Bill and I couldn't agree on how to handle Brad, and this was very difficult for me. I was always in the middle. Brad hated his dad, and his dad hated him because of the way he acted and the way he talked to me.

As was the case with Brad's family, parents frequently contacted APS when literally "at the end of their rope." Often, they had been to many experts for help without seeing improvement in their situations. Parenting stress was compounded by parents' feelings of failure and a sense of hopelessness about their ability to help their child. Also, as was the case with Brad's family, ongoing conflict with a spouse about how to handle the child was an additional stress for some parents. Lisa's mother described conflict with her husband who, at the time the family contacted APS, was discussing the possibility of leaving the family:

> I just really kind of thought it was my parenting. He was really struggling. He really felt that the whole adoption was just a big mistake, and he wanted out. We just had no idea. I just thought I was doing everything incorrectly. And my husband always kind of thought that there was something bad as far as Lisa was concerned.

These comments from Lisa's mother illustrate how parenting stress intensifies when parents disagree about their child's problems and their views differ on how to parent. Poor communication and the absence of agreement prevent parents from presenting a united front to the child. Some parents also experience role conflicts in relation to loyalty to one's spouse and loyalty to the child. Lisa's mother described feeling pulled between her husband and child and perceived her family as literally "splitting apart." Other conflicts may arise if the adopted child's problems cause serious problems for another child in the family, as was the case with Brad's sister. The parent may be torn between the needs of each child and may be required to defend one child against another.

Some parents recognized that their own frustration and anger had led them to respond in an unreasonably harsh way to their child. One mother, for example, wrote,

> I could have very easily slid into very destructive, abusive parenting. I became desperate and full of rage and anger myself—for lack of not knowing what was truly happening in my life, not understanding how different these kids are.

Finally, some parents described how an ongoing sense of frustration and stress in relation to excessive and unceasing parenting demands made it difficult for them to feel positively toward their child. Elizabeth's mother, for example, described her discussions with the adoption preservation worker who encouraged her and her husband to give positive messages to Elizabeth to boost her self-esteem. The adoption preservation worker frequently gave Elizabeth such messages, but Elizabeth's mother found this practice difficult to implement, because, she stated, "when you're living with someone like that, like the last thing you want to do is tell them how pretty they are. You know, it's like they're trying to cause all this chaos."

The child's special needs

As a theme, children's special needs are obviously linked with child behavioral and emotional problems. Many children had been diagnosed with ADHD (Attention Deficit Hyperactivity Disorder). In addition to learning disabilities, parents frequently listed such diagnostic labels as depression, ODD (Oppositional Defiant Disorder), FAS/FAE (Fetal Alcohol Syndrome/Fetal Alcohol Effects), PTSD (Post Traumatic Stress Disorder), and RAD (Reactive Attachment Disorder). A few children, including Elizabeth, had pronounced developmental delays as a result of severe deprivation. The developmental delays identified by parents included language, speech, and comprehension problems and an overall lack of socialization. In some cases, parents reported special needs that are rare among the general child population. As examples, parents' responses included the following:

- "He has autism and the school was not helping...we had been to our MD and also a specialist in autism";

- "He was shaken at two months old and has residual problems (brain trauma)";

- "My child was finally diagnosed as having mental-related problems same as natural mother and uncle."

In their descriptions, parents made a number of references to gaining a richer understanding of the special needs of their children through adoption preservation services.

School difficulties

Parents often indicated that their children were unable to perform acceptably either academically or behaviorally in school. As Lisa's mother stated, "Lisa had problems in school from kindergarten on," and it was not "until things got really bad at school" that the family sought help from APS.

Many parents reported that school personnel provided them with constant negative feedback about their children. Efforts to facilitate their children's adjustment at school were an ongoing source of stress for these families. One adoptive mother of four children with special needs reported that all of her children had problems at school and that it was a rare day when at least one teacher or principal did not call to complain about one of her children.

Some children, including Lisa, had not been able to obtain educational services that met their needs. Lisa's mother, for example, wrote: "Through the help we received, our adoptive daughter is now placed in a therapeutic day school getting the intensive therapy she needs so she can achieve academically."

Sibling conflicts

Several parents reported that their children had problems getting along with others, including their siblings. Elizabeth's mother, for example, stated: "She doesn't give and take...she tries to control. She just wants to be able to say, 'give it to me' and take it away." Similarly, Lisa's mother reported that there were significant conflicts between Lisa and her older sister, a dynamic that was addressed in therapy. Extreme anger on the part of adopted children may create many stresses within the family that impact other siblings. In Brad's situation, for example, his mother noted that his younger sister was afraid of him and felt she needed to protect herself.

Familial and Environmental Context of Presenting Problems

The following quote from a mother whose family was served through APS presents a vivid description of problems for families seeking help and some of the family and environmental factors that form the context for these problems. She described the impact on her family of ongoing, severe parent-child difficulties. She focused on the effect of these difficulties on her marriage, on individual family members' mental and physical health, and her concerns for other children in the family.

> I felt as if there was finally someone who understood, who could help, finally. We were lost, sinking, destroying our family rapidly before these services. We spent thousands upon thousands of dollars, not counting the time involved in seeking help. This was the only place we could find help, information, relief...an understanding of how these troubled kids work and how to try and cope with their behaviors. How to deal with the emotions these kids stir up in us. How to still love them.

> It's so hard to try to put into words the devastating effects on the family these kids could have. And even more difficult trying to write down what the Adoption Preservation Program has meant to our family. It is so difficult, because I don't want to leave out anything—the destruction, the financial drain, the breakdown of the marriage, breakdown of physical health. I could go on and on and still not cover all the physical and emotional problems of raising kids with 'attachment disorder.' At times, the fear of your life and safety of the siblings from the child you loved so dearly, the child you opened your home and heart to. From the child who can't love back.

Family context of presenting problems

As is the case with any serious family problem, the problems described by families served through APS are embedded in a multilayered context. Adoption preservation workers reported that unlike many other kinds of practice, APS serves families with severe and complex presenting problems that have multilevel contextual dynamics. The fact that the family is an adoptive family is a contextual aspect that increases the complexity of presenting problems. The following comments are examples of social workers' responses that referred to this context:

> In adoptive families, adoption adds many layers of complexity to already difficult situations....The depth of issues, behaviors, and problems our families face is much greater than in generalist practice. The issue of loss and grief for all family members is profound. We see everything, so we must have extensive knowledge of many emotional/psychiatric child issues.

> Many of the same basic issues [as in birthfamilies] are present, though they are often much more intense. Attachment issues are more prevalent, as well as relinquishment and grief issues...problems are much more severe, prominent and pervasive...families are often more disillusioned when they first see us. They are much more likely to use dissolution as an option than birthfamilies. The level of crisis when a case is opened often seems very high. Often, children have had disruptions in attachment, and the typical parenting techniques and behavioral interventions don't work.

As these comments illustrate, loss is central to adoption for both children and their parents. One social worker wrote, "At the core of an adoptive family is loss that is often not recognized or acknowledged by either the parents or the child. We often begin with the past more than the present."

Adoption connects adoptive families to other family systems. As one social worker noted, "With APS families, you are dealing with history of more than just one biological family (sometimes many families)." Adoptive parents and children often have complicated feelings about the child's connections with birthfamily, and they struggle to recognize, articulate, and resolve these feelings. In some families, as was the case with Lisa's family, the contact with the birthfamily must be managed. In other families, as was the case with Karen's family, children long to meet birthparents, and APS addresses this issue.

Adoption also poses challenges in the marital relationship. According to one social worker,

> The fact that APS families have adopted becomes a part of the couple's history—the decision of whether or not to adopt, how that decision was made, commitment to the child and one another, and many more issues. Sooner or later, everything revolves back to the fact that this family chose to adopt and the implications that decision has had and is having on their lives.

Some couples come to adoption because of infertility, which may carry with it loss, feelings of failure, blame (in some situations), and other intense feelings and couple dynamics. In some cases, parents have unequal commitments to adoption and to the child who is having difficulties. One social worker, for example, wrote,

> We have seen a growing number of families where one of the parents states that [he or she] never wanted to adopt the child in the first place and felt the need to placate the other. Much anger focuses on the adolescents when normal rebellion occurs. [It is] very difficult sometimes to get the family to 'go there' to resolve the issue.

Even when parents began the adoption process with equal levels of commitment, they may experience conflict regarding the parenting of a difficult child, and one parent may simply "give up."

Also salient in problem development is the child's history. Each child brings a unique history and constellation of needs that pose challenges with regard to both their own development and their families' parenting. The problematic early life histories of some adopted children (as was the case for Elizabeth, Jeffrey, and Karen) may result in layers of emotional and behavioral pathology that complicate problem resolution. Social workers often noted the added layer of complexity, as reflected in the comment of one social worker who said, "Due to problems of kids, different parenting skills are needed. For example, cause and effect, reward and punishment do not work with children with attachment disorders."

The family context also includes sibling relationships. Sibling issues may arise from the particular sibling configuration, the presence of birth and other adopted children in the family, the adopted child's position in the family, and the impact of one child's problems on other siblings. As was the case with Lisa and Elizabeth, there may be a good kid/bad kid split in the family that fuels the low self-esteem, anger, and frustration of the identified "problem child." In some cases, parents devote an inordinate level of energy to the resolution of one child's problems and other children in the family feel neglected. Often, a high level of conflict develops between the child who is experiencing many problems and his or her siblings.

Environmental context of problems

As revealed by the mother's comments at the beginning of this section, environment contributes to the problems that families experience. Families are often unable to find professional helpers who understand the nature of their children's problems and have the skills to help the family address those problems. Parents' responses indicated that the lack of understanding on the part of the professional community compounded their feelings of failure and hopelessness. In describing her family's many meetings with different professionals, one mother wrote, "We were told, and felt, that our parenting skills were inadequate." Many other parents reported a lack of success in previous efforts to obtain help. One parent stated, "We'd tried seeking counseling services and other supportive help with no success anywhere else." In this vein, one adoption preservation worker wrote, "Families have often worked with many programs and professionals prior to coming to AP," and in spite of "having a great number of skills and strengths," these parents have been "battered and beaten up by the clinical community." She added that parents have often "tried *everything* and stuff doesn't work for very long." They often come to APS disillusioned and distrustful of professionals.

Another adoption preservation worker described APS as a "last-straw program." Families may have many negative feelings related to practitioners' sins of omission or commission in their past experiences with agencies. One adoption preservation worker stated, "Many APS families feel they are abandoned by the agency through which they adopted." In addition to disappointing and frustrating experiences with adoption agencies, parents often unsuccessfully sought help from mental health professionals or the child welfare system prior to contacting APS. Many parents had not found professionals who understood their child's problems, adoption issues, or their parenting difficulties, or professionals who could suggest effective interventions.

Some adoptive parents reported that other family members and friends did not understand their situations and did not welcome their adopted child when the child had problems. One mother reported that members of her extended family had cut off contact because they could not accept her son's behavior problems and bad language. Another mother of several children with special needs reported that she could find no one to baby-sit her children and that she either had to stay home or take her children wherever she went. As a result, she and her husband had not been out alone in years. The only time that she had been relieved of parenting duties occurred when she had been hospitalized and her mother had cared for her children. Another parent described the lack of support from family and friends by saying, "You feel so lonely and isolated when you go through experiences like this. Most people can't begin to understand." The isolation and loneliness of many adoptive parents are reasons that they experience support groups as a lifeline.

Many parents also reported difficulty obtaining the specific services that they needed. Jeffrey's family, for example, described difficulties in securing payment for residential treatment from another state (which funded this service for families who resided in that state). Many parents reported an inadequate response to their children's needs from school systems. Social workers and families reported that some of the services that families need—particularly respite care and funding for residential treatment—were simply not available or were very difficult to obtain.

Guiding Principles of Adoption Preservation Work

Parents and social workers described a number of principles as particularly important in adoption preservation. These principles appeared to be fundamental to and implicit in any therapeutic work with families. Many families in this study, however, reported that only in the APS program did they encounter social workers who implemented such guiding principles as not judging clients and listening carefully to what clients are saying. They described these experiences as unusual and as extremely helpful to them.

An accepting, nonblaming approach

An accepting and nonblaming tone in the helping relationship is extremely important in adoption preservation work. "First do no harm" is a mantra for many helping professions, but APS social workers often must attempt to undo the harm that already has been visited on some families. Social workers may need to repeatedly tell parents, "It's not your fault."

Social workers noted that some parents not only blame themselves but feel that professionals have blamed them for their child's difficulties. As one social worker wrote, "Adoptive parents often feel like 'second-class' parents because of many issues—I try very hard to present possible interventions in a nonblaming, nonthreatening manner—as one adoptive parent to another." Social workers placed utmost importance on developing a nonblaming attitude and a perspective that recognizes the strengths of adoptive parents and children. As one social worker commented:

> We don't blame parents. Most of our parents are great parents with children who have very difficult problems....Families generally have the internal strengths to help the child deal with the many difficult issues they bring into the family....99.9% of these kids will do best in the homes they're in. These kids come with serious baggage that parents may or may not have been prepared for. These parents need a lot of support and validation....Our goal is always to help strengthen the bonds of the family. Care is always taken to listen and believe parents and trust that they know their child best.

Parents expressed their appreciation for social workers' non-blaming attitudes and, in some cases, they stated that this approach was quite different from what they previously had experienced with other professionals. Parents wrote such comments as,

- "The therapist wasn't tempted to blame the adoptive parents";

- "This was the first agency to not make us feel like it was our fault"; and

- "The therapist's first words were, 'It's not your fault. It's not something you're doing or not doing.'...Finally, there was someone who understood and didn't see me as a bad mother!"

Empathic listening and understanding

One mother, in response to a question about what the adoption preservation worker had done that truly helped her family, stated "Just to listen to us and sometimes to say,

'Oh, you're doing a great job. And we realize that this (what we're going through) really is horrible.'" Other parents also described their appreciation of their social workers' listening and understanding skills:

- "From the start, she understood our situation exactly. Her guidance and advice was right on target and helped us so much. After talking with teachers, day care instructors, doctors, therapists, family members and friends about our son, finally someone understood and sympathized."

- "We were desperate to find a therapist who would take the time to listen, to see all the facets of our family life and do it with respect and kindness.

- Our counselor truly understood the problems and struggles we were facing—really cared."

Social workers emphasized that they must "create a base of empathy and understanding on which to build a stronger relationship." Focusing on the importance of listening skills and active expressions of understanding the family's experience, one social worker stated, "Empathetic listening is most helpful in the beginning when the families need someone to vent to," and accepting what they say as "normal, not crazy" is validating to parents. Another social worker stated that "good engaging skills and a positive outlook that is contagious" are essential. Other social workers made similar comments:

- "*Listen* first and always. Many of our families have been blamed by other professionals or family members for their child's behavior. I give parents lots of permission, and children too, to be angry, tired, confused—whatever it is they are feeling and validate that this is hard work."

- "Validating feelings and reactions, instilling hope, allowing the telling of individual and family stories. Sharing of photographs as part of the storytelling process."

- "Listen. Believe the parents. Hear their story. Hear the child's story. Join the family where they are so that we can help them feel heard. Lots of validation and praise of what they have been doing well."

Some social workers reported that at the beginning of services, many parents needed to vent in an almost uninterrupted way for an extended period of time. They needed to describe all that they have been through and all that they have tried, without being redirected by the social worker. In some cases, particularly when parents are very angry, social workers see the parents and the child separately in early sessions. When seen separately, parents have the freedom to vent without inflicting their anger on the child.

Start where the client is

Although a basic counseling principle, "starting where the client is" is extremely important in adoption preservation work, this principle may require that the social worker go out of her way to meet with clients on their own terms (such as meeting them in their homes). This principle requires the social worker to listen to the family's story for as long as the family needs to talk and gauge what needs to be done initially based on the level of distress and crisis in the family. As one social worker wrote, "Assess the level of distress in adoptive families and work with each family at the appropriate level: de-escalate crisis situations, work with the family to find appropriate referrals for treatment, set therapy goals that meet the family's needs." When families have concrete needs, social workers focus on those needs first. As one social worker stated, "I start with a basic plan that starts with making sure the family's basic needs are met, i.e. heat, food, medical needs. As this is going on, a relationship is being built and trust developing."

"Starting where the client is" also applies to the focus of counseling interventions. One social worker observed, "Initial interventions focus on what the family is stating it needs, i.e. advocacy in the school or community, therapy or case management services. This supports the idea that adoptive parents know what they and their child need. Parents feel they are being heard and supported by the process."

One family's written response described a social worker's failure to adhere to this principle. The parent wrote, "We feel issues regarding the reason we call[ed] [adoption] preservation was not dealt with. Everything regarding his past with family and issues that were unrelated to why we called for help. He did a sexual acting out and we needed help with this. In the time we used your services, the issue of his act never was addressed."

Join with, support, and empower parents

In some cases, mental health clinicians spend most of their time in therapy with the child, and parents may feel uncertain about what is happening and feel confused about how they can best help their child. Successful adoption preservation requires that the therapist first "form an alliance with the parents" in order to work with and through them to help their child. Individual work with the child may be necessary, but in such cases, the parents should be kept abreast of the child's progress in therapy and, in most cases, parents should participate in the therapy. One social worker's response described the spirit of this ideal:"Involve parents in their children's treatment. Let parents know that they know their child better than anyone, including the worker. I see parents with the child frequently." A second social worker echoed this sentiment, saying,"Care is always taken to listen and believe parents and trust that they know their child best."

Some parents reported that their children often presented themselves well to and were manipulative of other adults. They found that when therapists primarily saw their children on an individual basis, the therapists seemed to overidentify with their children's view of reality. One parent wrote about the impact of involving parents in the child's treatment, "Our worker has worked with my youngest daughter and myself. Her insights and wisdom have been invaluable! My child is extremely adept at presenting a very charming 'all together' exterior. Our worker saw through it."

Another aspect of making an alliance with and empowering parents to help their child is collaboration, both with the parents and, when possible, with children, in goal setting. In response to a question on the survey about how goals were determined, almost every social worker stated that goals were established collaboratively with family members. Some social workers mentioned other factors that impact goal setting, for example, one social worker stated, "Goals often depend on the amount of community services available to the family and if the family has already exhausted these services."

"Joining with" parents also means recognizing their strengths, validating them by praising what they're doing well, and helping them to see the positives in their child. Social workers made the following comments:

- "I try to reassure them of their many strengths and let them know that the problems they are experiencing are rooted in early trauma and loss that occurred way before they adopted."

- "I take the approach, 'This kid is a handful, how have you managed so long?'"

- "An APS therapist must also get to know the interest, strengths, and uniqueness of each family member in order to understand ways to best approach each family member."

These statements reflect the importance of identifying strengths in parents and children alike for relationship building, normalizing perceptions, and strengthening family members' hope and motivation.

Finally, this principle embodies a philosophical view of human nature that is important to adoption preservation—that there is good in all people. One social worker stated, "Look at the strengths in the family and in the child and draw from these. Even the most difficult child is a survivor who has shown enormous strengths."

Educate parents to understand their child

Adoption preservation differs from other forms of intervention because of its educational focus. As one social worker wrote, "There is a lot more of an educational component [in APS versus other programs]. Families must learn why kids behave as they do. We move from that to strategies involving how to treat the kids." As one adoption preservation social worker noted, the educational role of APS social workers includes helping parents to "understand the dynamics of adoption from the child's point of view, understand the child's feelings and behaviors in order to parent to the child's needs, clean up any misconceptions about any and all adoption issues, and understand the impact of genetics and negative early life experiences on their children."

As these comments indicate, the foundation of APS is its focus on helping parents to understand the nature of their child's problems, how the child's history has influenced his or her current feelings and behaviors, and the implications of their child's particular special needs. Social workers must have specialized knowledge to assess and understand the nature of children's problems. Family dynamics enter into the problem situation, but social workers must be able to make sense of children's behavioral and emotional problems in order to help the family address these problems. At the same time, adoption preservation assists parents to normalize their views of their children. Introducing families to other families with similar problems (for example, through support group experiences) can facilitate this process. Finally, parent education includes helping parents to have realistic expectations of their child. In some cases, progress for children is very slow, and social workers must help parents to understand and accept the implications of their child's special needs.

Parents' comments about the importance and impact of the education they received about their children's problems illustrate the central significance of the educational component of APS. Parents, for example, wrote:

- "Educating us about our options, available resources, and family interaction was ongoing throughout."

- "The counselor who led the group gave us the first-ever insight into the problems and functioning of a drug-exposed child."

- "[APS] has been excellent for helping me...and in educating me about adopted kids and how they feel about themselves, setting boundaries, and consequences, dealing with past abuse—physical, sexual, emotional. I've learned a lot about ADHD, fetal alcohol/drug abuse, and helpful medications. The list is endless."

Address adoption-related dynamics

Loss, grief, attachment, and identity: An intrinsic part of education is the facilitation of parents' and children's understanding of adoption-related issues and the impact that adoption has on the child and the family. One social worker articulately described the importance of the family's understanding of adoption issues:

> Adoption is a life process, not an event, [and it] impacts each developmental stage of the child as well as the life cycle of the entire family. Assisting the family in understanding adoption issues— what they are, how they impact current behavior and functioning—is the key to assisting families in working through these issues. Workers must be sensitive to the fact that adopted children struggle with attachment issues... Workers also understand the importance of early childhood attachments, the impact of trauma, and the importance of loss as it relates to the adoptive triad.

Social workers reported that they used many techniques to assist families in understanding adoption dynamics. They used family loss history graphs not only to gather information about family members' losses but also to help family members communicate with one another about their experiences and feelings and assist one another with these issues. They used Lifebooks and a wide range of attachment building strategies (discussed later in the section about adoption preservation expertise).

Many parents cited the role of adoption in contributing to their family's problems and stated that it was important to understand the impact of adoption when working to resolve these problems. One parent stated:

> Issues of adoption are ongoing throughout the development of a child and as each of these developmental stages occurs it is important to have a support system in place to carry the family through... These problems don't 'go away' or get cured as these children grow....There are also the issues of loss both for the children and the adults. Most adoption agencies do not

prepare families for these issues and often lie to prospective parents about the true conditions the children are coming from. Adoptive children have lots of issues birthchildren do not.

Teach new parenting strategies

Social workers recognized that traditional parenting techniques often do not work with children with special needs. They stated that a primary aspect of adoption preservation services was helping parents to learn how best to respond to their child, both in managing behavior problems and helping children with adoption issues. Parents expressed the benefits from such strategies. One parent wrote, "We found someone who finally understood our children's problems and gave us a plan on how to help solve them." Another parent stated, "We learned how to deal with the children concerning their real mother. It helped us understand things about being [an] adoptive parent that we did not understand."

Karen's mother, for example, described how she benefited from her social worker's assistance in developing new parenting strategies, including the development of different communication patterns within the family and new approaches in her interactions with Karen. Karen's mother described herself as a "control freak" and, through the APS program, she learned to pick her battles carefully with Karen. She learned that she could not back her daughter into a corner but had to give her choices and allow her to save face. She stated, "Now when I'm considering what to fight over I'll ask myself—will this matter in five years?"

Be an accessible and dependable support to the family

One parent described her adoption preservation social worker as "available like no one else:"

> When something would happen, I'd call and she would talk me through it. Often in the past, we'd made mistakes because there was no one available to help. We'd hear, 'Do you have an appointment?' or 'The doctor is with someone and will call you back,' but he never would.

Families in crisis particularly need social workers who are available to them and keep their promises. Social workers commented on the importance of such basics as being a reliable source of support for families. One social worker wrote, "I let parents know I'm available if they need to talk to me, and I honor this." Another social worker emphasized, "Earn the trust of the family by extending a sincere, genuine feeling that our goal is to help maintain the family intact, and that my service/contribution to that goal is to be as available as time constraints allow."

Many parents praised their social workers for making extra efforts to be available to them. They described social workers as "very generous with their time and availability," "always was there whenever we needed her," and "willing to be available at any time in an emergency situation." Many parents expressed their appreciation for their social workers' availability in times of crisis. One parent stated:

> I've had to call several times after hours or on weekends. They always respond to me promptly and make sure I'm okay with our situation before they let me go. On one occasion, we had a crisis and the on-call worker came to our home and spent about three hours working it through with us. I've also had other workers volunteer to come out when our worker wasn't available.

Link with services and advocate as needed

Two basic components of adoption preservation services are helping families to access needed resources in the community and advocating with and for them for just treatment in other service systems. When they compared adoption preservation services with other types of interventions, some social workers mentioned the extensive collateral work involved in adoption preservation and described the difficulties of finding appropriate resources for children whom the child welfare system no longer serves.

Parents expressed their appreciation for their social workers' assistance in finding needed services and, in some cases, advocating for services that were difficult to obtain. One parent described this assistance as a source of "great relief and helpfulness regarding questions about the system...[in] trying to get assistance from either the State of Illinois ICG (Individual Care Grant) system or from the school district support system." Another parent whom APS helped to obtain residential treatment wrote, "My son has been placed with Interventions to get the help he so desperately needs."

Often, adoption preservation social workers helped link families with specialists who could accurately diagnose their child's special needs or problems. One parent wrote that the social worker had connected them with "medical treatments and evaluations that we were not aware of their existence." Another parent stated, "Our son's substance abuse problem was recognized by our worker, and help was gotten by us." In some situations, assisting families to obtain appropriate evaluations of children is a preliminary step to further advocacy. As one parent noted,

> We were able to secure support from local agencies [that] previously would not assist our family. He is in court-ordered residential placement paid by the state. Without the assistance to get a psychological [evaluation], education [evaluation], and to obtain support from local agencies, this may not have been possible.

The most common arena in which linkage and advocacy took place appeared to be the school system. Many parents reported receiving help in obtaining school-related services. One parent commented that she had received "great support to help us with the school's ideas of 'normal.' The adoption preservation workers come to IEP [Individual Education Plan] and teacher meetings. They help the teachers understand the behaviors and learning style of the kids."

For some families, respite services were enormously helpful. One parent wrote, "Camp Take-a-Break has been one of the most powerful interventions for us. Options for parents to get a break are so often extremely limited or totally unavailable because of the child's behaviors."

Intervene on multiple levels

Parents praised the comprehensive nature of the services they received. One parent, for example, reported, "We have had counseling in the past with other agencies, but they weren't as thorough and efficient as the AP worker." Another parent wrote, "They have been with us every step of the way—helped with other children and problems, went to school with us—just great. We enjoy the support group and all the material they have."

Lisa's mother stated that the comprehensive nature of the services she received was the main reason why the APS program succeeded in helping her family when other interventions had failed. She described how APS had focused on different aspects of her family's situation and had comprehensively targeted the dynamics of her family's problems. She stated:

> I think what was most helpful for us was the fact that the services were very comprehensive. I mean, she just said from day one that whatever it was that we needed, that they would be there to provide that for us. And so they helped with individual counseling for Lisa, they helped with family counseling for our whole family. She did private work with my husband and I individually as well as marital counseling between my husband and I. [She] had a session with my younger daughter, Sarah, and I individually, because she could see that there were some things that Sarah and I needed to address. And then, she worked with Sarah and Lisa because their relationship was really pretty conflictual. And I really do believe it was the comprehensive nature of the whole aspect of the program that helped us the most. She went with us when we had IEP meetings…brought my daughter to the school…she did a lot. She worked very closely with us for quite a long time.

Elizabeth's mother also talked about how coordination of services in multiple settings helped Elizabeth internalize new messages. Through this approach, she heard the same message at school, at home, and from the social worker. This repetition and reinforcement made an impact. Similarly, other parents reported that they benefited from interventions on multiple levels and in collaboration with other professionals involved with the family. One parent stated:

> We had a counselor briefly while our son was in foster care. We used placement [stability] prior to adoption. We also began private counseling about the same time as adoption preservation. Our AP worker and counselor work together. Our AP worker comes to our home and has come to court, detention, etc. Moral support is tops. Our worker has spent time in the police station with us, gone to detention to visit my son, we've had on-call workers come to our house at night to work through a crisis situation.

> [We received] help and support planning services appropriate for my son. Other counseling, drug screening, psych. evaluation, dealing with the legal system.

Careful termination

Although not a topic on which many families commented, a few parents raised the issue that the worker had failed to carefully terminate their cases. In interviews with parents, most families reported that their social workers had given them the maximum amount of time possible (or more) and that they knew they could contact the social worker by phone, if needed. The few parents who reported inadequate termination of services underscored the importance of social workers' planning for termination and preparation of clients. Because loss and abandonment are fundamental issues for adopted children, careful termination of services is particularly important with them. One parent, for example, stated,

My worker was great with my son, but she missed several appointments with us and was hard to catch and reschedule with. When she left, she attempted but did not follow through on saying goodbye to him. So there was not good closure there—which is why he doesn't want to continue with the new worker.

Essential Knowledge and Expertise for Adoption Preservation Work

Four themes were identified in this category: knowledge and intervention approaches; assessment techniques and tools; group work; and the social workers' own emotional reactions.

Knowledge and intervention approaches

Adoption preservation work requires a wide range of professional knowledge and expertise in many specialized areas. Social workers most frequently cited the need for knowledge about adoption, attachment, separation and loss, grief, and the impact of maltreatment on children. Parents often reported their appreciation for their social workers' understanding of adoption. Lisa's mother, for example, stated, "This was the first agency that informed us of the kinds of challenges that many adoptive children and families face. We just had no idea. I just thought I was doing everything incorrectly."

Knowledge about children's behavior disorders and mental health problems also is essential in adoption preservation work. This knowledge base must include an understanding of problems resulting from children's prenatal exposure to alcohol and other drugs; sensory integration problems; ADD, ADHD, and other learning disabilities; attachment disorders; depression; PTSD; and other types of emotional difficulties that children have.

With regard to intervention approaches, many social workers stated that adoption preservation professionals must be grounded in family systems theory and family systems therapy. Although these two areas were mentioned most consistently, almost every psychological theory or methodology was identified by one or more social workers. Some social workers also emphasized the need to draw on an eclectic knowledge and skill base in this work. Social workers also stated that they utilized a range of therapeutic techniques with families. Foremost among these techniques was Theraplay, an attachment therapy on which adoption preservation social workers had received training from The Theraplay Institute in Chicago. Some social workers also incorporated techniques from Hughes's (1999) Dyadic Developmental Psychotherapy approach, on which workers had been offered training. Finally, social workers listed a range of child therapy techniques, including play therapy, art therapy, Lifebook work focusing on adoption identity issues, storytelling, therapeutic board games, feelings and anger management workbooks, sand tray work, and reading therapeutic books. Some social workers also mentioned revisiting as a technique for helping children integrate their histories. In this technique, the social worker or adoptive parent and the child visit the child's birthplace and previous homes, talk with previous foster parents, and take pictures.

Social workers mentioned a number of strategies for working on parenting skills, including teaching therapeutic parenting skills; behavioral techniques, such as behavior modification, modeling, communication skills training, role-playing, contracting, and parent coaching; and cognitive-behavioral techniques. Other techniques included journaling, stress management, EMDR (eye movement desensitization reprocessing), and narrative therapy. Social workers stated that they used search and reunion mediation in some cases.

Assessment techniques and tools

Social workers reported that they commonly used a variety of assessment methods. An in-depth history of the child and the family's integration of the child always form a part of the initial adoption preservation work. Social workers explore the parents' view of problems, the severity of the child's problem behaviors, and the dynamics of the family system. Social workers also assess, as one social worker stated, "the developmental/emotional stage of the child and the family; parenting skills, the couple relationship; the extended family support, and community resources." Finally, workers also explore family cohesiveness and the parents' level of commitment and motivation for seeking help.

Social workers reported that the standardized instruments most often utilized in these assessments were the Parent Feelings Form, the Achenbach Child Behavior Checklist (CBC), and the Parenting Stress Index, although they also used other instruments. One social worker stated that the Youth Self-Report Form of the CBC was a helpful tool for assessing how an adolescent compares himself or herself to others of the same age. Some social workers utilized the Risk Assessment protocols from the Department of Child and Family Services or a crisis triage sheet to assist them in prioritizing the family's problems. Social workers also reported utilizing a wide range of assessment strategies to understand families' needs and to assist families in recognizing the important issues they face, including attachment, loss, and grief issues. These strategies included a review of the losses of each family member andfor some, use of the Randolf Attachment Disorder Questionaire (RADQ), a standardized inventory of attachment-related difficulties.

Group work

In addition to the intensive services provided by adoption preservation social workers, parents praised the support groups for parents and children offered by APS. Connecting with other adoptive families in a group setting often enables parents to move forward very quickly, gain a new perspective on their situation, and feel supported. One parent stated the following about her experiences with her support group:

> When I first came to the parents' support group, I remember feeling so overwhelmingly grateful that I had finally found others who know exactly what I was thinking and feeling. These parents could actually finish my sentences—they were so [attuned] to where I was at in my life. I can't imagine life without having met them. It was a safe place to work out my problems. They gave me hope, and a possible thought of actually getting through this. We laughed and cried. We searched our souls together.

Another parent said,

> There were times when that group literally sustained me. You feel so lonely and isolated when you go through experiences like this. Most people can't begin to understand. The group was a place where we could pour everything out—and know there would be no judgment. The

insights of the two AP workers—and the other moms—were invaluable. Some of the situations can be so bizarre that you lose your point of reference. You begin to wonder if you're not the one who is troubled! They would bring me back to reality over and over again. I don't know what I would have done without them!

Likewise, adopted children benefit from being with other children who are struggling with adoption, particularly with feelings of "not fitting in." All parents reported positive results from their children's participation m support groups. Parents noted that their children's views of themselves became normalized in much the same manner that their parents' perceptions of the children became normalized.

Handling emotional reactions

The final question on the social worker survey simply asked whether the social worker had any other observations about adoption preservation work. Their responses overwhelmingly focused on their personal reactions, namely, the difficulty they experienced in doing this type of work and the fact that they found it challenging and sometimes rewarding. Social workers' comments included:

- "This is the most difficult work I have ever done because it involves innocent children who have been victimized by their earliest experiences. So many are so damaged. It is hard for parents who have so much love to realize that love is not enough. They too experience deep loss—the loss of their dream of the idealized child."

- "This is very, very hard work. Staff need much supervision, debriefing time. Staff have to work hard to not get burned out. The needs of our families exceed our resources just like the needs of their children exceed the adoptive parents' resources."

- "The work is very challenging but very satisfying."

Conditions Limiting Success

Even when families receive optimal services through APS, not every family will find solutions to its problems. Some parents' responses relayed their sadness and frustration that their family situation seemed very bleak. Their responses reflected a number of factors that can impede the achievement of positive outcomes. The study identified seven key themes: limited knowledge development; social worker inadequacies; insufficient parental commitment; severe, irremediable difficulties with the child; parental incapacity; time limits on services; and inadequate community resources.

Limited knowledge development

A key factor that limits the success of adoption preservation services is that little is known about the effective treatment of many of the conditions which children and families face. Knowledge is very limited about treatment of severe attachment problems, the effects of chronic trauma in early childhood, and developmental disorders stemming from severe deprivation. In addition, because of the severity of some of the problems that children experience, social workers and families must accept very slow and, in some cases, limited change. One social worker described her approach in relation to this reality by saying, "The clinician must feel comfortable with the idea that we cannot *fix* the child or the situation (this is not short-term, solution-focused therapy), but we can walk with the family, support them, believe them, teach them, and things do get better."

Social worker inadequacies

In some cases, professional inadequacy can limit the achievement of successful outcomes. Social workers may violate some of the guiding principles of adoption preservation services by failing to be reliable, not starting where the client is, or not involving the family adequately in setting service goals. A few parents complained that their social workers seemed new or inexperienced. One parent, for example, commented that her social worker was not sufficiently savvy to avoid being manipulated by the parent's teenage daughter.

Insufficient parental commitment

One parent wrote, "My child needs help to stop him from taking things. It's getting so bad that I can and will not live with it. He have gotten so he will not mind...throws fits now. I am thinking of undoing his subsidized guardianship on him." In this situation, the parent was not able to sustain her commitment to the child, and APS was not successful in ameliorating her son's behavior problems. Although additional services might have resulted in some improvement, their effectiveness would have been limited by the mother's absence of sustained commitment. Social workers reported other situations in which the parents' inability to sustain their commitment to parenting was a major obstacle to positive family adjustment.

Severe, irremediable difficulties with the child

Some parents stated that had they known about APS sooner, they could have avoided the compounding of family problems and the resulting pain. Other parents indicated that their problems were too serious or their children too old to benefit from services at this point, but that they believed that APS could have helped their families if only they had received these services sooner. One parent, for example, stated:

> By the time I found out about AP, my son was too involved in too many systems to be helped by adoption preservation. Although if I had known about the program earlier, I think the parent/ adolescent group could have benefited both my 21-year-old daughter and my 15-year-old son.

Some parents stated that they had benefited from the APS program, although their child's problems were not "fixed." In these cases, parents had been helped to understand their child better, and, in some cases, had located resources to address the child's extreme needs. Most importantly, parents' ongoing commitment to their children usually was reinforced in spite of their recognition that their children would have chronic difficulties. One parent, for example, observed:

> [Before coming to APS], we were unable to secure accurate diagnosis and treatment for our child. Numerous therapists were unable to help remediate our child's behavior, [which] grew

> more unmanageable. First of all, our counselor understood aspects of our situation that others did not....We were helped to accept the fact that we were in a situation that we could not fix...that we weren't to blame for this, that what our child needed was more than we could provide. Arrangements were made for residential treatment, but we retain full parental rights.

Another wrote,

> There have been many times that I have had serious struggles with this adoption, many surprises, many regrets. Without this program, I highly doubt we would have succeeded. Undoubtedly, I have a very difficult child, and life would be easier without him. Yet, I am committed to making this work.

In some situations, parents reported that their child's special needs were irreversible and predictive of ongoing problems. One parent, for example, described the brain trauma that her child had experienced as a result of maltreatment. She stated:

> We are persons who have adopted a young child. He has a number of problems that we deal with daily and most of them, we will for years to come. He will not mind anything we say. (ADD + ODD). He is very strong at six years old. As time passes, he will grow stronger and more aggressive—we (66 and 70 years) will grow weaker and less agile to deal with him. It is imperative that we find an answer while he is younger. We have had him since he was 4.5 months (foster care) and had him 23 months when we adopted him. We love him dearly, but do not want him to grow up aggressive and socially unacceptable. He was shaken at two months old and has residual problems...brain trauma.

Parental incapacity

Improvement in the family situation is unlikely when the child's severe problems combine with serious incapacities on the part of parents that compromise their ability to continue parenting. At times, parents have serious mental or physical difficulties. Some parents are elderly and have chronic or even terminal health conditions. For example, one adoptive mother wrote on her feedback form: "Since he got into his teens he have been very hard to obey my rules—won't talk to the counselors. Want to have his way in everything. I just can't handle him any longer. I am in difficulty right now...I am taking care of my husband. He has Alzheimer's."

Another parent described her situation in which her own physical incapacity limited her ability to parent a very difficult child:

> My daughter was unable to accept us as her family (after 4 $\frac{1}{2}$ years). She blamed us for her foster family's unwillingness to adopt her. She was defiant to the extreme. We were concerned about our safety....Since I have recurrent metastatic cancer, one of the foster families who did respite care on several weekends and then again while I was undergoing chemo and radiation for several months adopted her. That family is one in a million and I am grateful to...[the] support group who brought us together.

In some cases, families are not able to develop and sustain effective strategies for parenting a child with special needs because of very poor health, the death of a spouse and their subsequent inability to cope with difficult adolescents, or extreme rigidity.

Time limits on services

At the time of this study, families served through APS may receive up to a year of services within a 24-month period. To continue services beyond 12 months, approval must be obtained from a state-level Adoption Preservation Program administrator. Families may return to the program at a later date, if needed. If families require ongoing services and are no longer eligible for APS, social workers seek to link them with other services in the community. The rationale for the time limit is that the specialized service must be made available to all the families who need them.

Clearly, the most common and critical comment from parents (and their most common recommendation for changes in the APS program) related to the time limit on APS services. Many families reported that APS was the first resource they had found that truly met their needs, and they felt that they needed longer or ongoing access to their social worker. Some parents had arranged to work with another counselor, but they stated that it was hard to begin again with another professional or that it had been difficult to find a professional who understood adoption issues. Other comments included:

> I did not feel ready to end the services. Our family has ongoing situations that sometimes are okay, but a lot of times, we need the support of a counselor that could help the kids. I realize there are many families to be served, and you can't possibly keep them open forever, but my family and I certainly could benefit from longer contact with our counselor.

> The one problem I see in this program is that it has to end when the process is lifelong. Some of these kids may never be able to live on their own and may always be dependent on their parents.

For some families, the termination of group service was most traumatic because the service had served as a major source of support in their lives. Although the APS programs at some of the sites have ongoing support group services, other sites have time-limited groups which meet for a designated number of weeks. Several parents recommended that support groups be made available on an ongoing basis as a source of support and safety net. One parent who attended a time-limited support group, for example, stated:

> Some of us were ready to move on without the support of the group—but some of us were not and that's the biggest tragedy. Some of us in the group had nowhere and no one else for support. And yet, we had to disband because we were already past the time limit of time allowed for services... Our only outlet was the support group, and now that's gone too.

By contrast, a parent who attended an open-ended support group wrote, "The monthly support meetings are great. They are my lifeline to sanity. I hope they will always continue."

Inadequate community resources

One of the primary goals of APS is to link families to services that will enable them to cope with the stresses of parenting a child with special needs. In some cases, families in difficult situations are able to continue to "hang in there" if they know supports are available to assist them. For some families, however, the services that they need are not available or are extremely difficult to obtain. Parents, for example, reported:

- "I wished we had had a plan to take him in an emergency. During times he was especially disruptive to the family, I had hoped for a place that would have kept him for a while. We all needed a break from him. He is now in residential treatment. I don't know what we would have done without Adoption Preservation."

- "It is very difficult to get a respite worker. One of the most necessary services was someone to provide supervision for this child when parents were at work and this could not be accomplished at all."

- "Our caseworker was very friendly, but no services are available for help for our son and our lives."

In each of these situations, parents reported that they believed that more could have been accomplished if additional services had been available to them.

Outcomes of Services

Parents reported many positive outcomes in their family situations that they attributed to APS. Often, they commented on positive gains in multiple areas. For example, one parent wrote,

> Our counselor was a gentle, caring professional. She not only helped my daughter to go through some scary times but also helped us to go on. We now (not always, but often) listen to one another before losing our cool. Our daughter still receives consequences but not out of anger. We are grateful for our worker's help and know that she's only a phone call away.

Another stated,

> Better ongoing counseling touching all parts of our lives, extremely helpful medical/[psychological] referrals, a parent support group, better and more services from school district....We were desperate to find a therapist who would take the time to listen, to see all the facets of our family life and do it with respect and kindness. Our worker has helped us to see all that, and we are so different now because of her! We are no longer in crisis mode. It literally saved us emotionally and saved our daughter in all facets of her life.

Five themes were identified in relation to positive outcomes as a result of adoption preservation services: new perspective/understanding of the situation; increased parenting abilities; improvements in the child; improved family climate; and linkage with needed resources.

New perspective and understanding of the situation

Probably the foremost benefit parents reported as a result of the APS program was a new perspective on their situation, including an understanding of their child's special needs. One parent reported that she was better able to cope with her child's behavioral problems because "understanding the root cause helped [me] to understand what is really going on inside the child's mind." In some cases, parents recognized that their child would continue to have problems, but they expressed confidence that they would be able to cope with the situation.

Often, parents who had sought help from many professionals prior to seeking adoption preservation services stated that APS differed from other mental health services because it helped them understand their adopted child and the reasons for the problems they were experiencing. One parent, for example, wrote:

> Why these kids (with attachment problems) don't respond to traditional child rearing was never a question, because no one had ever said these kids were different before getting involved with this program. We went from doctors, top hospitals, spent thousands of dollars and never found any help. We lived with everyone telling us we need to do this, do that, and nothing worked....The social workers of the AP Program taught me how to try and love my daughter again, how not to take her actions so personally. To this day, I can draw on our past sessions to try and deal with something that might be going on. I can hear advice given in the past, and apply it. I've been given the tools to try and piece my life back together. They gave me strength to continue parenting our special-needs daughter.

Parents reported many aspects to the change in their perspective, including moving from a sense of extreme stress to an orientation of acceptance and the development of an "I can cope" attitude. One parent stated:

> Sometimes I've felt that the world was falling in and what's going to happen... this is such a bad situation. I learned that it really wasn't. It gave me a perspective that, in fact, other people are dealing with situations far more trying than what we have to deal with. It kind of helps us to know that there are other people having similar difficulties.

Parents found the support group experience to be one of the most powerful interventions for bringing about a new perspective. Jeffrey's mother, for example, described her feelings prior to receiving services through APS and again after her first support group meeting:

> We were to the point that we thought that there was something wrong with us, that we were somehow bad parents....I couldn't understand what kind of mother I must be to have this child attacking me, and [be] that angry. After being here the very first time, I went home crying realizing that it wasn't all my fault. The people here told us why they were here and I was hearing the same kinds of stories from most of them. It helped me accept the fact that it's a problem my son's got that he can't deal with and that his anger, even though it's directed at me, it's not because of anything I've done.

Parents also reported that an aspect of their new perspective was a more normalized view of their adopted child. They began to see their child not as a "bad kid," but as a child who was not all that atypical. One of the parents who was interviewed about his experience in a support group described the shift in perspective by saying, "That's been kind of amazing when people describe behaviors like exactly what we see. We found that the behaviors that drive us crazy with our kids are real typical of all these children." As one parent stated, after hearing about very serious problems from other parents, "We'd come home saying, 'I'm so happy, our kids are great!'"

Another aspect of parents' new perspective was a strengthening of both their hope for the future and their commitment to their children. One parent attributed these gains to her support group experience, saying, "So, then you don't feel like the problem is so unusual that there's no help for it. No matter how bad things are, they survive. We found out that if they can survive, we can survive. No matter how bad problems get, we can survive too! There are ways to deal with it."

Increased parenting abilities

Parents credited APS with helping them to understand how to better parent their children based on a broader understanding of their children's needs and capacities. Lisa's mother, for example, described how her social worker had helped the family understand what the label "oppositional defiant disorder" meant in relation to parenting a child. Lisa's mother stated:

> She [the social worker] just told us [that] you just can't negotiate with a child like this and also gave us ways to have Lisa obey without getting into piles of trouble (power struggles)....[Through APS], we were able to see things that we were doing that were inconsistent with parenting....The worker was very helpful in terms of confronting some things...as far as parenting, especially in areas that my husband and I might disagree. We see the things that Lisa was doing as being much more typical of the kinds of things that some adoptive kids go through, as opposed to just being a bad kid. We tend to talk more about issues now, and we tend to come to an agreement before we do anything.

Many parents reported that they had grown in their ability to help their children with their struggles with adoption and other emotional issues. Parents also reported learning better strategies for handling problem behaviors. Some parents very simply stated that they had learned "how to handle [their] children better." Other parents were more impassioned in describing these changes, such as the parent who stated:

> Peter was our social worker [through] this turbulent experience....he made a very definite difference in our lives—all positive. He guided us towards positive ways of doing things. He was a very calming influence on our day-to-day living, and we will miss him very much....He entered our life when there was chaos and left when there was calm.

Improvements in the child

Parents reported improvements in their adopted children that they credited to APS. Some parents described total remediation of the child's difficulties:

- "During the first year after adoption, my then-9-year-old daughter had periodic bouts of anxiety and sadness. Our worker did an excellent job with my daughter, who is fine now."

- "My kids went from F's to A's and B's."

- "My son has a more positive image of his adoption. He doesn't seem to mind 'looking different' now. (He was having many questions about his birthmother—feelings that she did not love him.) School behavior has returned to excellent."

- "Our son's counselor was extremely caring and helpful to our son. I credit the positive experience that he is presently having in college, in a large part, due to her counseling."

Most often, parents reported ongoing progress in their child's situation. The types of reported improvements varied, but included improved behavior, school performance, and attachment as well as internal changes such as increased self-esteem and comfort related to adoption issues. Comments from parents who had observed ongoing progress included:

- "Child is learning to be more affectionate";

- "Helped to open up the lines of communication by getting our child to express some of her feelings"; and

- "Our daughter has grown, emotionally, two or three years in the 10 months she has been seeing your counselor."

In some cases, parents reported progress but recognized that their children would have ongoing needs. Karen's parents, for example, reported that their daughter felt more secure but still feared rejection. They reported that for the first time, Karen was able to express affection, call them "Mommy" and "Daddy," and be physically close to them. They stated that they were much more committed to Karen and that she was attached to them to the extent of her capability ("3/4 attached"). Karen's father reported that she was neither hospitalized nor "out of control" on her last birthday, the first such achievement in years.

Parents also reported improvement in their children's feelings about adoption. Lisa's mother, for example, stated:

> Lisa could talk with the worker about her birthmother (Sherry). I think for Lisa, that helped her an awful lot, because she found out that some of the other girls didn't even know their birthmother...a lot of these girls were struggling with just never having seen their birth mom. And so, it made Lisa look at that whole situation in a different light that she was really blocking. And one thing I think that she helped Lisa and us with was that even though Lisa is Sherry's daughter, it doesn't mean that Lisa has to become Sherry. She [the social worker] worked with Lisa to make Lisa realize that Lisa gets a chance to make her own choices. And that she doesn't have to repeat the same things that her birthmother did.

Improved family climate

Parents also noted overall family improvement. Some parents reported improved communication as a major outcome of the services they received. Examples of parents' responses that described positive changes in overall family functioning included:

> She helped us start communicating again, because it was bad. I mean we were pretty dysfunctional. We weren't having any family dinners or anything. Marital counseling helped my hus-

band and I start effectively communicating...to clear up many misunderstandings and misconceptions. In fact, had it not been for the help we received through the AP program, I don't believe our family would still be together... we tend to talk more about issues now, and we tend to come to an agreement before we do anything... We never had that before, and we are doing it now. And I think we both better appreciate each other's perspective on things right now... and I think we listen to each other better and take each other's opinion into account more, and then we come up with a plan.

Family counseling helped identify and target many of our problems as a family. The tone in our household is kinder, warmer, and more compassionate. We better understand the incredible impact adoption can have on a child, especially one who has learning disabilities.

Linkage with needed resources

A final outcome reported by parents was their ability to obtain resources to relieve their problem situations. In some cases, the linkage involved advocacy to facilitate greater responsiveness on the part of systems with which families were already linked. As discussed earlier, adoption preservations social workers commonly advocated on behalf of families with school systems to ensure that families' needs were addressed. Lisa's mother credited APS with helping facilitate a more appropriate school placement for her daughter:

Through the help we received, our adopted daughter is now placed in a therapeutic day school getting the intensive therapy she needs so she can achieve academically. Through therapy, I believe Lisa better understands herself...Her self-esteem is improved....Her anger and rage are greatly reduced, and she's even starting to smile, laugh, and make friends.

Parents also reported receiving such services as specialized evaluations for children, respite care, and funding for residential treatment. One parent described her family's outcome this way: "I adopted a FAS child. I was looking for financial help and a support system. We found a great childcare person through your services." Another parent stated,

I can't say enough about how she (the social worker) helped. My child was placed in a residential school near the end of our services. This is being paid for with I.C.G. and S.S.I. funding. I arranged the placement and funding with a lot of help and guidance from our AP worker. Things are going much better between my son and myself, and I believe that he will be able to return home within the next year.

Discussion

This study is a beginning attempt to examine, through qualitative approaches, the types of interventions that are effective with adoptive families with serious difficulties. It is important to reiterate that the definition of effective services is based on the perceptions of families and social workers and not on a standardized measure of outcome. Feedback from parents who were served effectively through the APS program demonstrates that these families can be invaluable sources of information regarding the specific interventions that best address the needs of adoptive families. Their articulate expression of their presenting problems and their poignant descriptions of the improvements they have seen as a result of the dedicated work of adoption preservation social workers vividly document the importance of this work.

Effective adoption preservation services are shaped by many influences. This study identified several categories of influences (depicted in the conceptual map) based on an analysis of workers' and parents' perspectives. First, to be effective, adoption preservation services must address the complex context of families' presenting problems at both the family and environmental levels. The multiple layers of contributing factors drive the need for potent interventions that are relevant to the dynamics of presenting problems (although some of these factors are so severe that they limit the outcomes that can be achieved). Adoption is a theme that appears throughout the identified categories because it is embedded in the problem context and the kinds of interventions that are needed.

To be effective, adoption preservation social workers must have knowledge of the broad range of families' presenting problems. These problems include adoption-related topics (such as attachment, loss and grief, and family dynamics related to adoption) and the plethora of problems confronting children with complicated histories. Children who have experienced severe deprivation, maltreatment, negative prenatal influences, multiple moves in foster care, and interrupted attachments present many challenges to the families who parent them. Social workers must understand these dynamics in order to help parents understand the nature of the problems that they face and the types of parenting strategies that best address these problems. Beyond understanding, however, social workers must possess the requisite skills and expertise to intervene effectively in these problem situations. Interventions that effectively address many of the problems of the children and families served through APS are only now being developed, and, for the most part, such interventions have not been the subjects of research. This reality poses limitations on the ability of social workers to intervene effectively and heightens the personal stress they experience in providing adoption preservation services.

Adoption preservation work is very difficult, and as one social worker stated, the demands often exceed social workers' capacities. The ability to manage the challenges and stresses of this work also will affect the effectiveness of professionals. A social worker in the field of adoption preservation must be able to convey hope to families who may have very limited capacity for change; deal with the emotional impact of working with children who have been damaged by their previous life experiences; and work with parents and children who have chronic and complex difficulties and very intense emotional reactions. In order to manage these demands, social workers need considerable support from colleagues, supervisors, collateral resources, and others.

In order to ensure the effectiveness of adoption preservation services, it is essential to understand the conditions that limit the success of these services. This study's analysis of parents' descriptions of their APS experiences adds breadth to an understanding of such factors as severe and irremediable conditions of the child and severe, chronic problems in parenting. Families with serious, chronic problems need a wide array of postadoption services to enable them to continue parenting. One powerful example was the situation described by the elderly mother who was parenting a child with brain trauma. In that case, a myriad of community supports were necessary to assist the family throughout their son's childhood. These services, which included, at minimum, respite care, also extended to locating another foster family who could provide ongoing back-up and support and possibly act as substitute parents if the adoptive parents became incapacitated.

The vast majority of parents in this study reported positive outcomes from the services they received. Most often, they reported an increased understanding of their situation, improvements in their children and their own abilities to parent them, and success in obtaining needed resources. Parents' descriptions of what they appreciated most about adoption preservation services further validate the themes identified in the social worker survey as guiding principles of adoption preservation work. These themes also surfaced in interviews with parents when they described the particular aspects of the services that were of most help to them and reflected on how APS differed from other mental health services that they had received. Of particular importance to parents in this regard were feeling understood and not being blamed; being validated and empowered as parents; learning the reasons that their adopted children were having difficulties; and receiving assistance regarding those aspects of adoption that were negatively affecting their families.

Most families reported that APS assisted them in moving from a position of not being able to cope (which carried with it many negative emotions and negative perceptions of both their children and themselves as parents) to a position of confidence in their abilities as parents, a renewed acceptance and appreciation of their adopted child, and a sense of hope for the future.

The following conclusions can be drawn from this study:

- The problem situations of families seeking adoption preservation services involve a complex set of dynamics. A constellation of factors—including the child's history, the dynamics of the family's adoption experience, the marital relationship, and the sibling relationships in the family—must be assessed to reach an adequate understanding of families' problems.

- Presenting problems are usually framed in relation to a child's behavioral and emotional problems. To effectively address these issues, a broader array of problem dynamics must be addressed, including the child's special needs, any school difficulties, parenting difficulties, sibling conflicts, and, when present, marital difficulties that impact parenting.

- Effective interventions require careful attention to the unique adoption dynamics involved in each family's problems. Interventions must be comprehensive in focus, attending to the sub-systems of the family that are involved in the problem and other systems that are pertinent to problem resolution. Helping parents develop a broader understanding of their child and family problems is fundamental to change. To achieve a new perspective, parents must develop an understanding of their child's special needs and their child's emotional issues related to adoption. Contact with other adoptive families is an effective approach in facilitating this broader understanding for parents and children.

- Parents need help in developing parenting strategies that most effectively address their child's needs and capacities. In addition, adopted children need help in expressing and addressing their own emotional needs, including specific aspects of their adoption; feelings of grief, depression, and anger; and self-esteem needs.

- Adoption preservation social workers need professional knowledge and skills in the areas of family systems therapy, attachment therapies, and a range of child therapeutic approaches. In addition, they need considerable supervisory and peer support to manage the stresses of this work.

Emerging Questions

This study examines the question of what constitutes effective adoption preservation services. This question is embedded in another implicit one: what outcomes must families achieve for services to be considered effective? In some families, children's special needs limit their ability to function in a "normal" range. The most desirable outcomes that can be achieved in these situations are parents' understanding and acceptance of their children (including their limitations) and the identification of parenting strategies that optimize children's development and families' coping abilities. In other situations, considerable improvement in child and family functioning may be realistic. The concept of "effective adoption preservation services" will vary depending on what outcomes are realistic for a family.

Adoption preservation social workers stated that they used a number of theories and interventions, but this study did not inquire into how various intervention methods were applied. To gain an understanding of how and in what situations specific methods of intervention are applied, more in-depth qualitative study of adoption preservation services would be needed. Further study also would be needed to examine outcomes of various methods of intervention. If, for example, social workers use interventions based on attachment theory (such as Theraplay) with certain families, what specific changes would need to result from these interventions to allow researchers to draw conclusions about their effectiveness?

Many questions remain with regard to the research question addressed by this study. Families felt helped by the services they received, but it is not known if other interventions may have provided greater assistance. Children with severe problems pose ongoing challenges, and it is not clear what the future holds for them. It is likely that any modification of chronic maladjustment will require potent interventions to reach families as early as possible and to assist them periodically throughout their children's development.

The primary remaining question regarding the effectiveness of adoption preservation services is the extent to which the conditions that limit the success of these services can be overcome. In those cases in which parents reported a lack of improvement in their family situations, it was unclear whether social workers with more skill or earlier intervention may have yielded more positive outcomes. In any arena of social services, barriers must be overcome in order to remedy family problems, within the family system itself and the external environment. Some interventions likely will be successful with certain types of families and not with others. It is important to expand the understanding of which services are effective for the range of adoptive families who seek help.

APS has gone one step beyond traditional mental health therapies in helping parents understand that many adopted children with chronic emotional and behavioral problems do not respond to traditional parenting strategies in the same ways as other children. Nonetheless, the field is only beginning to develop the strategies that are effective with these children. Much remains to be understood about the most effective treatments for children with neurological impairments that result from severe trauma and for children with severe attachment disorders. Such information is essential to maximizing the effectiveness of adoption preservation services.

References

Barth, R. P., & Miller, J. M. (2000). Building effective postadoption services: What is the empirical foundation? *Family Relations, 49* (4), 447–455.

Brodzinsky, D. M., Schecter, D. E., Braff, A. M., & Singer, L. M. (1984). Psychological and academic adjustment in adopted children. *Journal of Consulting and Clinical Psychology, 52* (4), 582–590.

Groze, V., Young, J., & Corcran-Rumppe, K. (1991). *Post Adoption Resources for Training, Networking and Evaluation Services (PARTNERS): Working with special needs adoptive families in stress.* Washington, DC and Cedar Rapids, IA: Four Oaks, Inc./Department of Health and Human Services, Adoption Opportunities.

Howard, J. A., & Smith, S. L. (1995). *Adoption preservation in Illinois: Results of a four-year study.* Springfield, IL: Illinois Department of Children and Family Services.

Howard, J. A., & Smith, S. L. (1997). *Strengthening adoptive families: A synthesis of post legal adoption opportunities grants.* Normal, IL: Illinois State University. Available through National Resource Center for Special Needs Adoption.

Howard, J. A., Smith, S. L. Ryan, S. D. (2004). A comparative study of child welfare adoptions with other types of adopted children and birth children. *Adoption Quarterly, 7*(3), 1–30.

Howe, D. (1997). Parent-reported problems in 211 adopted children: Some risk and protective factors. *Journal of Child Psychology and Psychiatry, 38* (4): 401–411.

Hughes, D. A. (1999). *Building the bonds of attachment: Awakening love in deeply troubled children.* Lanham, MD: Jason Aronson Publishers.

Miller, B. C., Fan, X., Christensen, M., Grotevant, H. D., & van Dulmen, M. (2000). Comparisons of adopted and nonadopted adolescents in a large, nationally representative sample. *Child Development, 71* (5), 1458–1473.

Prew, C., Suter, S., & Carrington, J. (1990). *Post adoption family therapy: A practice manual.* Salem, OR: Children's Services Division.

Rosenthal, J. A., & Groze, V. K. (1994). A longitudinal study of special-needs adoptive families. *Child Welfare, 73*(6), 689–706.

Simmel, C., Brooks, D., Barth, R. P., Hinshaw, S. P. (2001). Externalizing sympromatology among adoptive youth: Prevalence and preadoption risk factors. *Journal of Abnormal Child Psychology, 29*(1), 57-69.

Smith, S. L., & Howard, J. A. (1998). *Evaluation of adoption preservation program.* Springfield, IL: Illinois Department of Children & Family Services.

Smith, S. L., & Howard, J. A. (1999). *Promoting successful adoptions: Practice with troubled families.* Thousand Oaks, CA: Sage Publications.

Smith, S. L., Howard, J. A., & Monroe, A. D. (1998). An analysis of child behavior problems in adoptions in difficulty. *Journal of Social Service Research, 24* (1-2), 61-84.

Wierzbicki, M. (1993). Psychological adjustment of adoptees—A meta-analysis. *Journal of Clinical Child Psychology, 22,* 447–454.

Zill, N. (1996). *Adopted children in the United States: A profile based on a national survey of child health* (Serial 104-33, pp. 104-119). Washington, DC: U.S. Government Printing Office.

FACTORS AFFECTING RECENT Adoption Support Levels IN THE Washington State ADOPTION SUPPORT PROGRAM

David Fine, Lee Doran, Lucy Berliner, and Roxanne Lieb

When children are removed from their families because of severe maltreatment or neglect and later are freed for adoption, they typically enter their preadoptive families with a complex set of developmental, medical, emotional, and behavioral needs. As a result of their traumatic histories, these children may engage in hyperactive, aggressive and oppositional behavior; experience depression and anxiety; have sleeping and eating disorders; sexually act out; or exhibit the neurological effects of in-utero exposure to drugs and alcohol. At the same time, families who adopt children with special needs experience challenges and life cycle stages that are unlike those of biological families (Groze, 1996). There may be an increase in problem child behaviors and the need for services and supports over time. As a result of these factors that impact both children and families, postadoption services (including financial supports for families who adopt children with special needs) have been found to play an important role in mitigating the risk of adoption failure (Barth, 1988).

In 1971, the Washington State Legislature made a policy decision to encourage the adoption of children with special needs through a program that offers financial support for their adoptive families. The legislature recognized that parents who chose to adopt children from foster care had little, if any, financial support to assist them in meeting their children's needs and often faced significant financial risks because of their children's needs for costly medical treatment, physical or behavioral therapy, and special schooling. Created in 1971 and subsequently expanded in 1996, the Washington State Adoption Support Program responds to the financial support needs of adoptive families.

Over the past five years, Washington State has dramatically increased the number of children who are adopted from the child welfare system. As more families have adopted children with special needs from the foster care system, the number of families receiving adoption support has increased, as has the number of families who receive supplemental support payments through the program. This chapter briefly examines the federal law that established adoption assistance and more specifically describes the Washington State adoption support program. It then describes a study of the program and the findings related to the children and families served and the characteristics of children and families who have been approved for different types and levels of adoption support.

Adoption Support and Federal Law

In 1980, the federal Adoption Assistance and Child Welfare Act (Public Law 96-272), which provides the overarching legal framework for child welfare services in the United States, was enacted. Among other mandates, P.L. 96-272 required each state to implement an adoption assistance program to provide adoptive families with adoption support payments (referred to as subsidies), Medicaid coverage for their children, social services, and reimbursement for nonrecurring adoption costs when they adopted children with special needs from the foster care system. Under federal law, the amount of a child's adoption subsidy may not exceed the amount that would have been paid if the child had remained in foster care. Federal funding is provided to states as reimbursement for a certain proportion of the costs incurred in their adoption assistance programs. In Washington State, the federal participation rate is 52% of the costs incurred in the program (North American Council on Adoptable Children, Washington State Subsidy Profile Web Site, 2001).

P.L. 96-272 makes adoption assistance available to children who meet certain criteria. One criterion is that the child is eligible for the federal Aid to Families with Dependent Children (AFDC) program (based on the qualifications for that program as of July 1996) or for the Supplemental Security Income (SSI) program. Another criterion is that the child has one or more "special needs." "Special needs" refer to characteristics of children which may create barriers to their adoption. Under federal law, each state is permitted to define the special needs that will be recognized for purposes of adoption assistance eligibility in that state. Generally, special needs criteria include age; ethnic minority status; membership in a sibling group; and physical, emotional, or mental disabilities.

Children who do not qualify for the federal program may receive adoption assistance under state programs that are financed without federal reimbursement. The benefits provided under state programs are usually similar to those of the federally funded adoption assistance program.

The Washington State Adoption Support Program

Washington State's Adoption Support Program predates the federal program by almost 10 years. When the Washington State Legislature created the Adoption Support Program in 1971 (RCW 74.13.100), the specific purposes were to encourage the adoption of hard-to-place children and reduce the total cost of foster and institutional care. The Washington State legislature noted:

> It is the policy of this state to encourage, within the limits of available funds, the adoption of certain hard to place children in order to make it possible for children living in, or likely to be

placed in, foster homes or institutions to benefit from the stability and security of permanent homes in which such children can receive continuous parental care, guidance, protection, and love to reduce the number of such children who must be placed or remain in foster homes or institutions until they become adults (RCW 74.13.100).

Between 1971 and the enactment of P.L. 96-272 in 1980, the program provided state-funded adoption support to children in foster care who were considered "hard to place" for adoption. Later, P.L. 96-272 authorized federal financial support for the benefits provided to many children. In 1996, the Washington State legislature reaffirmed its commitment to adoption support by authorizing additional (supplemental) payments for families to eliminate financial barriers to adoption. From the outset, the program has provided a flexible process for obtaining adoption support based on negotiations between parents and the state. Currently, almost all of the children who are adopted from the child welfare system in Washington State have needs that qualify them for adoption assistance. Consequently, the vast majority of families who adopt children from foster care apply for adoption support.

Adoption Support Eligibility

The benefits that children and families receive in Washington State are identical regardless of the federal or state funding source. Washington State children are eligible for the federal adoption assistance program when they meet one or more of the special needs criteria; the state has determined that the child cannot or should not be returned to the parent's home; and a reasonable effort has been made to place the child without adoption assistance (except where it would be against the best interest of the child) (Section 473 [42 U.S.C. 673] [c][2] of the federal Social Security Act). The requirements involving children's financial eligibility for federal adoption assistance are quite complex, because, as stated earlier, eligibility is tied to the former Aid to Families with Dependent Children (AFDC) program or the Supplemental Security Income (SSI) program. Eligibility for Title IV-E funded adoption assistance can be established in one of four ways:

- The child is AFDC-eligible and meets the definition of a child with special needs; or

- The child is eligible for Supplemental Security Income (SSI) benefits and meets the definition of a child with special needs; or

- The child is eligible as a child of a minor parent and meets the definition of a child with special needs; or

- The child is eligible due to prior title IV-E adoption assistance eligibility and meets the definition of a child with special needs.

Special needs determinations

Adoption assistance eligibility requires a determination that the child has special needs based on *all three* of the following criteria (defined in section 473(c) of the Act):

- The State has determined that the child cannot or should not be returned to the home of his or her parents (section 473(c)(1) of the Act); and

- The State has determined that the child cannot be placed with adoptive parents without providing Title IV-E adoption assistance or Title XIX medical assistance, due to a specific factor or condition that may include (but is not limited to) ethnic background, age or membership in a minority or sibling group, the presence of a medical condition, or physical, mental or emotional disabilities; and

- The State has determined that a reasonable effort has been made to place the child with appropriate parents without providing adoption assistance. An exception is made to this requirement only when it would not be in the best interests of the child because of factors such as strong emotional ties with prospective foster adoptive parents (where the child resides in the home as a foster child).

Further, federal guidelines require that there be a judicial determination that continuation in the home was contrary to the welfare of the child or that placement in foster care was in the best interest of the child. When children meet federal eligibility criteria, they must be offered an adoption support agreement. Adoption support agreements constitute binding contracts between the department and adoptive families. The state cannot unilaterally change the terms of an adoption support agreement. Agreements must include: (1) the amount of adoption support payments and any additional assistance which is to be provided as a part of the agreement including, where appropriate, indication of eligibility for Title XIX and Title XX services, (2) a stipulation that the agreement shall remain in effect regardless of the state of residence of the adoptive family, and (3) a stipulation that the agreement must be renewed at least every five years with termination from the program resulting from the adoptive parent's failure to renew.

Adoption support agreements are completed on a standardized template (form DSHS 10-228, revision 6/96), requiring only the entry of specific child, family, adoption support program services, and nonrecurring expense information. In 1997, 79% of Washington State adoptions of children in the child welfare system met the federal criteria for the adoption support program (U.S. Department of Health and Human Services, 1999).

A child is eligible for adoption support when adoption is the most appropriate plan for the child and the child either currently resides in or is eligible for and likely to be placed in a foster home or institution; is legally free for adoption; is 17 years of age or younger at the time of the adoption support agreement; has one or more special needs; and is considered "hard-to-place" for adoption. A child's eligibility for adoption support continues until the child ceases to be the adoptive family's legal responsibility; stops receiving financial support from the adoptive family; or reaches 18 years of age. A child can continue to receive state funded adoption support until the age of 21 years if the child has not completed high school and is a full-time student.

"Special needs" and "hard-to-place" criteria

As noted earlier, "special needs" criteria for purposes of federal adoption assistance refer to children's conditions that may prevent placement with an adoptive family. Special needs criteria in Washington State are: ethnic background; age of 6 years or older; inclusion in a sibling group; emotional problems; physical and/or medical problems; and significant developmental delays. A child must meet one or more "hard-to-place" criteria to be eligible for state-funded adoption assistance. Children are defined as "hard-to-place" for adoption when they have been registered for three months with the Washington Adoption Resource Exchange (WARE) or the Northwest Adoption Exchange (NWAE) and a nonsubsidized adoptive family (that is, a family willing to adopt without an adoption support agreement) has not been identified for the child (WAC 388-70-520). A child's registration with WARE or NWAE is not necessary when a foster parent adopts a child who has lived in the foster parent's home for at least six months before becoming legally free for adoption; demonstrates close emotional ties to the current foster family and emotional damage might occur if the child is moved to a new family; and the foster family is identified as the adoptive family of choice by the agency responsible for the child. State and federal eligibility requirements for adoption assistance in Washington State are summarized in Table 9-1.

Determination of adoption support

Consistent with federal law that prohibits the use of standardized formulas to determine adoption support payments or services, Washington State law explicitly acknowledges that adoption support payments may vary from family to family and from year to year (*Children's Administration Adoption Support Program Desk Manual,*1999, RCW 13.112). Legislation and agency policy state that the following child and family factors may be considered when setting or adjusting the amount of adoption support payments: family size; family living expenses; special needs of family members; income and resources; medical needs; access to health care; and any other expenses likely to be needed by the adopted child (RCW13.112). The determination regarding the adoption support amount is to be a "realistic evaluation of the child's need to live in the particular family and the cost of the living expenses of the individual family" (WAC 388-70-560(2)). State law also specifies that adoption support payments should include amounts "sufficient to remove any reasonable financial barrier to adoption, if necessary to facilitate or support the adoption of a special needs child" (RCW 13.115).

Types of Adoption Assistance

In Washington State, children may receive monthly adoption support, a special rate maintenance under certain circumstances, supplemental maintenance under certain circumstances, and Medicaid and additional services.

Monthly adoption support

Federal and state rules limit payments for monthly adoption support to the monthly cost for basic and specialized foster care. A 1996 survey by the Adoption Policy Resource Center

TABLE 9–1

State and Federal Eligibility for Adoption Assistance in Washington State

STATE ELIGIBILITY CRITERIA	FEDERAL ELIGIBILITY CRITERIA
1. Placed or eligible to be placed in foster care	1. Cannot be returned home
2. Legally free for adoption	2. Reasonable efforts have been made
3. Under the age of 18	3. SSI or AFDC eligibility
4. One or more special needs	4. One or more special needs
5. "Hard-to-place" for adoption	

Hard to Place

- Registered with adoption exchange without a successful match; OR
- Child in the home for more than 6 months; child has close emotional ties with current family; and current family is family of choice.

Special Needs

- Ethnic background
- 6 years of age or older
- Sibling group
- Emotional problems
- Physical/medical problems
- Significant developmental delays

found that foster care rates were higher than adoption assistance rates in 18 states; 25 states had adoption assistance rates which matched foster care rates; and 7 states had adoption assistance rates that were higher than foster care rates (with matching federal funds available only up to the foster care rate). The Washington State Legislature has set the maximum adoption support rates at slightly less than the foster care rates for the same age child. The discount to the foster care maintenance rate is relatively stable across age categories at about 8% to 10%. As of July 2000, the maximum monthly adoption support rates were $317 per month for children under age 6, $390 for children ages 6 through 12, and $462 for youth 13 or older.

Special rate maintenance

In Washington State, a special rate of up to $148 may be added to adoption support monthly payments to cover costs that are associated with a child's special needs. The special rate maintenance may be made available for such needs as respite care, extra daily supervision, classroom supervision of a child, housekeeping, and the child's involvement in special activities. Requests for special rate payments require documentation of costs by the adoptive parents.

Supplemental maintenance

Under state law, supplemental maintenance payments may be provided for children adopted on or after July 1, 1996 if they would have been eligible for exceptional cost payments or additional services in foster care (RCW 13.115). Supplemental payments are designed to assist adoptive families in meeting additional expenses associated with a child's exceptional needs. These payments may be made in addition to special rate payments to reduce financial obstacles to adoption.

Medicaid and additional services

In addition to financial assistance, children who are eligible for adoption support are eligible for medical services under the state's Medicaid program. In addition, children and their families are able to access psychological counseling and evaluation, parent training, and nonrecurring costs associated with the adoption process.

Implementation of the Washington State Adoption Support Program

In 1996, the management of the state's Adoption Support Program was transferred from the Children's Administration headquarters to the regional service system. Currently, each of the six regional service delivery regions in the state has at least one adoption support program manager who negotiates adoption support agreements with the families who live in the geographical area. Adoption support agreements are approved at the regional level and are signed by both the Adoption Support Program Manager and the Regional Administrator.

Adoption Support Program Trends

Washington State adoptions have increased dramatically in recent years, as shown in Figure 9-1. The increase has occurred during a time when other statewide initiatives such as the Family For Kids Partnership (FFKP) were being implemented. The FFKP was a statewide initiative that brought together public and private agencies, the judicial system, tribal organizations, legislators, families, business leaders, and others to reform the foster/adoptive system. It was funded through the Stuart and Laurel Foundations, the Children's Administration of the Department of Social and Health Services, Casey Family Programs, Children's Home Society of Washington, and the Office of the Administrator of the Courts (Family for Kids Partnership, 2001).

As noted earlier, the enactment of state and federal legislation encouraged the adoption of children with special needs in the child welfare system.

As shown in Table 9-2, the size of the state's adoption support program also has grown dramatically. Over the past four years, the average monthly caseload has risen by 82%, growing from 3,678 children in 1996 to about 6,700 children in 2000.

Subsidy Levels and Program Costs

Children who receive adoption support in Washington State fall into three general groups: (1) children who receive no monthly adoption support payment but receive medical and preauthorized counseling benefits; (2) children who receive the basic monthly adoption support rate; and (3) children who receive adoption support at a special rate (in excess of the maximum monthly rate for the child's age for the applicable fiscal year) and/or supplemental payments (including one-time payments). Based on a snapshot of all active cases since 1982, it is estimated that of all cases in which children have received some form of adoption support, 23% received no monthly payment, 64% received monthly support at the basic rate, 12% received basic support plus special or supplemental payments, and 1% had varying levels of nonrecurring pay-

FIGURE 9–1

Washington State DSHS Adoptions of Children with Special Needs

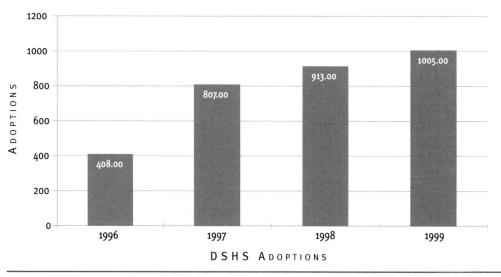

DSHS ADOPTIONS

TABLE 9–2

Growth in Washington State's Adoption Support Program, 1996–2002

FISCAL YEAR	AVERAGE MONTHLY CASELOAD	% ANNUAL INCREASE	CUMULATIVE GROWTH (BASE YEAR: 1996)
1996	3,678	—	—
1997	4,040	10%	10%
1998	4,683	16%	27%
1999	5,455	16%	48%
2000	6,714 (est.)	23%	83%
2001	7,178 (est.)	7%	95%

Sources: Data for average monthly caseloads from the Caseload Forecast Council, Human Services Caseload Forecasts—Adopted November 1999. FY2000 and 2001 estimates obtained from the Caseload Forecast Council, November 2000.

ments for some type of episodic need (personal communication, Children's Administration Adoption Support Program Manager).

Approximately 6500 children are currently in the Adoption Support Program, with about 65 children added each month. All children on Adoption Support receive Medicaid and preauthorized counseling services.

- Twenty-three percent (1,500) of all children on Adoption Support receive only Medicaid and preauthorized counseling services.

- Seventy-seven percent (5,000) of all children on Adoption Support receive monthly cash payments;

- Eighty-six percent (4,300) of these children receive monthly basic rate, or basic plus special rate, cash payments. Basic and special rate payments continue for the duration of the Adoption Support Agreement.

- About 700 (14%) of the children receiving monthly cash payments receive one-time or recurring supplemental adoption support payments for child care, extra supervision, or 'other' needs. These payments are available only for adoptions after July 1, 1996, for foster families who are unable to adopt a child without continuing to receive the extra funds provided while in foster care.

Between 1996 and 2000, the state legislature modestly increased the maximum rates for basic adoption support and special rates by 7%. As of April 2000, adoption support payments for children totaled $2.3 million (Doran & Berliner, 2000). The increase in adoption support costs is primarily a function of an increase in the number of children receiving monthly basic support as opposed to increases in payment rates, which, in reality, have been minimal.

The Study Methodology

As a result of the growth in the state's adoption support program (both in terms of size and cost) and the decentralization of its implementation, questions have arisen regarding the factors that determine adoption support payment levels. Specifically, there have been questions about the extent to which the level of financial support is a function of case and family characteristics, or, alternatively, is a function of other more exogenous measures, such as region of residence, the year the adoption occurred, or the year that the child was enrolled in the adoption support enrollment program. In this study, the dependent measures were the levels of adoption support awarded to adoptive families after regional social workers' reviews of families' applications for adoption support and other materials. This *three-category* outcome variable was used as the basis for two study questions:

- What child, case, and family measures distinguish families who are awarded basic monthly adoption support and families who are not provided this support?

- What child, case, and family characteristics distinguish families who receive basic adoption support only from families who basic support plus special rate and/or supplemental payments?

The study examined the above pair of two-group comparisons based on the original three category AS outcome classification. This was done under the assumption that the factors affecting various levels of support may be very different for the decision to offer a case basic support versus choosing to provide the highest payment level (basic and supplemental subsidies).

Program Data Systems

The study relied on two information systems maintained by the Washington State Children's Administration for monitoring adoption support cases and payments to adoptive families: the Adoption Support Case and Management Information System (CAMIS) and Social Service Payment System (SSPS). CAMIS contains demographic information on the adopted child. SSPS provides event records per case per month that document the amount and type of payment to parents for each adopted child in their care. The study obtained CAMIS and SSPS data for all children who were active in the Adoption Support Program on April 30, 2000 (n = 6,480). CAMIS records included information on the child's age, gender, ethnicity, race and adoption support program start date. SSPS payment records provided information about the type and amount of adoption support received during the month of April 2000. A supplemental SSPS data set was accessed which contained payment records for each active case as of April 2000 for the first three months after the child's enrollment in the adoption support program.

Sample

The final sample for the study was affected by the Washington State Legislature's expansion of the Adoption Support program in 1996 to include supplemental payments and the implementation of this policy change in the subsequent fiscal year (July 1, 1997–June 30, 1998). Because implementation of this policy occurred at varying rates across Washington State counties and AS program offices during this fiscal year, the researchers limited the population of interest to those adoption support applications among the active April 2000 cases that began July 1, 1998 onward (n = 1951). That is, we selected AS cases that were still receiving adoption support in April 2000 whose initial application for these funds occurred on July 1, 1998 or later. This allows an empirical test of the fully implemented policy change that was only officially initiated in mid-1997. A random sample of n = 400 cases was selected from this subpopulation of 1951 recent adoption support enrollees for further data collection.

Data Collection

The data in this study were collected primarily from two hard copy forms: (1) the Adoption Support Application, which is completed by the adoptive parents to initiate the adoption support program process; and (2) the child's registration form, completed by the social worker responsible for the adoption support application process. Regional office and adoption support program staff use these two forms to determine whether adoption support will be provided and the level of support. A listing of the sample of 400 adopted children was forwarded to the Children's Administration. These sampled records contained only three measures: (1) the Adoption Support client identifier (ID), (2) the child's CAMIS ID, and, (3) the region where the application for adoption support was initiated. The Children's Administration forwarded to each of the six AS regional offices the portion of the sample that could be accessed from their respective case files. The adoption support manager in each region examined their list of sampled client identifiers and CAMIS ID numbers and then pulled the hard copy files for these sampled records. The AS manager then made copies of the Adoption Support Application and the Child Registration Form for each sampled case; redacted any personally identifiable information (such as the child's name, the adoptive parents' names, and the city where the adoption occurred); and attached the redacted confidential records to the project's cover sheet (which contained the Adoption Support client ID and CAMIS ID). The regional staff forwarded the materials to the research staff for data entry. Of the 400 sampled cases, 384 (96%) were successfully found, copied and redacted in the regional offices and forwarded to the researchers. It was determined that the majority of the missing records involved errors in the adoption support application date (that is, the hard copy indicated a date prior to the sampling cut-off of July 1, 1998).

Measures

The Adoption Support Application contained closed- and open-ended items. Closed-ended items asked adoptive parents about the specific resources available to the family to meet the special needs of the child (such as benefits through the Social Security, Supplemental Security Income, or Division of Developmental Disabilities as well as inheritances); the family's annual gross income; and the parents' birthdates and race/ethnicity. Open-ended text fields included descriptions of the child's special needs and unusual costs and/or services required to meet those needs. The Child's Registration form also contained closed- and open-ended items. Closed-ended items included the type of adoption; the date that the child entered foster care; the child's total number of placements prior to adoption; and the child's special needs and conditions based on statutory criteria (race, age 6 or older, sibling group, and medical/physical, emotional/behavioral, and developmental disabilities). Open-ended items included a general diagnostic statement describing the child's social history and current functioning and the reasons for the adoptive family's request for adoption support.

A database was generated to capture closed-ended measures for each sampled case. The open-ended text was reviewed and qualitatively analyzed. Research staff generated constructs and indicators based on the social workers' notes. These additional quantitative summary measures were incorporated in the database. Data records from the Child's Registration form and the Adoption Support Applications then were merged with the Adoption Support CAMIS records as well as the SSPS payment records for each child's first three months in the Adoption Support Program. For each of the 384 cases, data elements were available concerning the child's demographics, placement history, special needs, and available resources as well as the adoptive parents' demographics, resources (income), and requested types of support at the time of the Adoption Support Application. In addition, data were obtained regarding the level of adoption support payments made during the three-month period under consideration and were summarized based on amount and type of funding. The summary payment measure (the outcome of interest for this study) was categorized as: (1) no monthly adoption support payment; (2) basic adoption support monthly payment; and (3) basic plus special rate/supplemental payment.

Data Management

Data management was essential because the final data set for analysis included child and family variables from several data systems and informants. Paper records were obtained from local Adoption Support case files and the statewide information system; both adoptive parents and social workers completed the case file forms; and the hard copy documents contained both quantitative and qualitative data. The various data sources, informants and measurement methods clearly had the potential to yield significant inconsistencies across comparable variables.

Three situations exemplify the study's approach to managing item inconsistencies. The first situation involved child age. Neither the Adoption Support case file forms nor the CAMIS records provided to us by Central Administration or the AS Regional Offices contained children's dates of birth. Washington State Department of Social and Health Services Human Subjects Review Committee as a condition for our undertaking the study eliminated this measure from any file transfers from the state data systems to the researchers. The CAMIS records, however, did include an integer value for the child's age as of the record extraction date (April 30, 2000). This measure, in conjunction with the date on the Adoption Support Application form, allowed an estimation of the child's age at the time the Adoption Support Application was made. An approximate check variable was the designation on the Child Registration form where the social worker marked whether the child met the special needs category of being six years of age or older. A comparison of these two measures (estimated age and special needs status of 6+ years of age) resulted in five cases with logically problematic results that is, the child was assessed as having a special need by being age 6 or older and the child's estimated age was 4 years or younger. For these records, both age and the special needs variables were recoded as missing information.

The second situation involved data inconsistency on race/ethnicity. In this instance, CAMIS child race and ethnicity codes were compared to the social worker's designation of the child's race as a special needs condition. Inconsistencies for this variable pair were not easily resolved. About 9% of children identified as white via the CAMIS data were coded by the social worker as having a special need because of race. The problem could not be resolved by setting the value on race/ethnicity in these cases as "missing" because the existing child race/ethnicity variable (based on CAMIS) would then be a more conservative test of any relationship to the outcome of interest (support payment level). The result might have been an underestimation of child minority status and other calculated measures, such as the race/ethnic match between adoptive parents and child. Therefore, each measure was maintained as originally coded.

The third data inconsistency situation related to measures of child problems by different informants. Through coding of qualitative data, for example, inconsistencies were uncovered between social workers' and adoptive parents' ratings of children as having emotional or behavioral problems. In this situation (and others), however, it was determined that "inconsistencies" did not necessarily present problems because informants may use different assessment criteria and may observe children under different conditions and settings (such as at home or at school). As a result, data values were not modified for any of the items in which adults in differing roles made different judgments about the child.

Finally, a data management issue unrelated to item consistency affected the analyses. Relatively high proportions of responses were missing on some data elements from the Adoption Support hard copy forms. High rates of missing information were found for demographic data on adoptive parents, such as their race/ethnicity and age. No effort was made to impute values for these items. A further discussion of both data inconsistencies and data quality are presented later in this chapter.

Statistical Analysis

Univariate and bivariate analyses were performed to describe the study sample. Item frequencies and measures of central tendency and dispersion (where applicable) were calculated for child demographics, adoptive family background measures, child needs and resources; and family resources. Bivariate analyses were performed consistent with item metrics. Cross-tabulations were used with categorical measures, and mean comparisons were implemented with interval variables using either t-tests or analyses of variance.

A major goal of the study was to assess whether levels of adoption support have an empirical basis, given child and family needs. To meet this goal, multivariate analyses used binomial logistic regression procedures to determine independent predictors for level of adoption support within the subsamples reflected by our two overall study questions. The first sub-sample analysis assessed predictors of receipt versus denial of basic monthly adoption support. The second analysis examined which measures, if any, distinguished families approved for basic monthly support compared to families approved for "basic plus" or supplemental adoption support funds. Measures were selected for inclusion in the step-wise multivariate analyses based on prior empirical findings. Variables in the final model were retained if $p < 0.05$. Researchers calculated goodness-of-fit (GOF) measures and, where necessary, examined diagnostic statistics (Hosmer & Lemeshow, 1989). All analyses were done using the Statistical Package for the Social Sciences (SPSS), version 10 (SPSS Inc., Chicago).

The Results

Sample Characteristics

The children

Table 9-3 summarizes the background characteristics of the children in the sample. Slightly more than half (53%) were female. The children's mean age, as of the date of the adoption support application, was 6.2 years (SD = 3.5). About 30% of the children were age 3 or younger, and only 7% were estimated to be 13 years or older. Almost two-thirds (68%) were white; 13% were black; 11% were Hispanic; 8% were American Indian; and fewer than 1% Asian.

The adoptive families

Table 9-4 provides data on the children's adoptive families. As noted earlier, there was considerable missing data on adoptive parents' race/ethnicity (19% missing for the first

TABLE 9-3

Characteristics of the Children; n = 384

CHILD CHARACTERISTICS	NUMBER	PERCENT
Gender		
Female	204	53%
Male	179	47%
Age at Adoption Support Program enrollment (n=383)		
Mean	6.2	
Median	5.5	
Standard Deviation (SD)	3.5	
Age, categorized		
3 and younger	113	30%
4–6	111	29%
7–9	89	23%
10–12	45	12%
13 and older	25	7%
Race/ethnicity (n=380)		
White	257	68%
Black or African American	51	13%
Hispanic	41	11%
American Indian or Alaska Native	30	8%
Asian/Pacific Islander	1	<1%

adoptive parent's race/ethnicity) and age (51% missing data for the second parent's age). The majority of families had at least one White parent (86%). When either adoptive parent's race/ethnicity was considered, 76% of the cases showed a match between the adoptive parent's race/ethnicity and that of the child. Mean ages for adoptive parents were 44.0 (SD = 9.16) for the first parent and 42.0 years (SD = 8.88) for the second parent. Family size averaged 4.5 individuals (SD = 2.0). Mean family annual income was almost $48,000. Fifteen percent of these families had annual incomes of less than $20,000. On the higher end of the income scale, 15% reported an income between $60,000 and $79,000, and 11% cited incomes of $80,000 or more during the past year.

Case characteristics

As Table 9-5 shows, about three-quarters (73%) of the sampled cases came from the more populous Western region of Washington State. The adopted children averaged 3.0 placements (SD = 2.1) in the foster care system prior to joining their adoptive families. Prior placements ranged from 1 to 14, with 13% of the children having 6 or more placements. Although the Adoption Support program records were sampled as of July

TABLE 9–4

Characteristics of the Adoptive Families (n = 384)

Family Characteristics	Number	Percent
Race/ethnicity, adoptive parent 1 (n=310)		
White	265	86%
Black or African American	20	7%
Hispanic	10	3%
American Indian or Alaska Native	13	4%
Asian/Pacific Islander	2	‹ 1%
Race/ethnicity, adoptive parent 2 (n=250)		
White	222	90%
Black or African American	10	4%
Hispanic	8	3%
American Indian or Alaska Native	7	3%
Asian/Pacific Islander	3	1%
Age, adoptive parent 1 (n=237)		
Mean	44	
Median	43	
Standard Deviation (SD)	9.16	
Age, adoptive parent 2 (n=187)		
Mean	42	
Median	42	
Standard Deviation (SD)	8.88	
Family size (n=384)		
Mean	4.5	
Median	4.0	
Standard Deviation (SD)	2.0	
Family annual gross income (n=357)		
$20,000 or less	52	15%
$20,000 –$39,000	113	32%
$40,000–$59,000	99	28%
$60,000–$79,000	54	15%
$80,000 or higher	39	11%
Race/ethnic match—either parent and adoptive child (n=310)		
Yes	236	76%
No	74	24%

TABLE 9–5

Case Characteristics (n=384)

Case Characteristics	Number	Percent
Region		
Eastern Washington	103	27%
Western Washington	281	73%
Prior placements (n=384)		
Mean	3.0	
Median	2.0	
Standard Deviation (SD)	2.1	
Prior placements, categorized		
1	93	24%
2	120	31%
3–5	120	31%
6 or more	51	13%
Year placed, adoptive home (n=340)		
1994 or earlier	34	10%
1995	40	12%
1996	60	18%
1997	87	26%
1998	95	28%
1999	24	7%
Quarter/year entered Adoption Support Program		
1. Q3/1998	55	14%
2. Q4/1998	35	9%
3. Q1/1999	61	16%
4. Q2/1999	58	15%
5. Q3/1999	42	11%
6. Q4/1999	44	12%
7. Q1/2000	66	17%
8. Q2/2000	22	6%
Time between adoption placement and Adoption Support Program enrollment, years (n=339)		
Mean	2.3	
Median	1.9	
Standard Deviation (SD)	1.7	
Type of adoption		
Adoptive home	44	12%
Foster parent adoption	94	25%
Foster/adopt home	143	38%
Relative adoption	100	26%
Any foster care payment at adoption support application		
No	94	25%
Yes	289	75%
Federal Title IV-E fund eligibility (n=300)		
No	63	21%
Yes	237	79%

1998 onward, many of the children had been placed with their adoptive families prior to the application for adoption support. Almost a quarter (22%) had been placed with their adoptive families in 1995 or earlier, and another 18% had joined their families in 1996. On average, the adoption support application process was implemented about 2.3 years (SD = 1.7) after children were placed with their adoptive families.

Consistent with the process used to select a representative sample of Adoption Support applications from July 1998 onward, the distribution of cases across the eight calendar quarters was relatively stable. As an example, 14% of the sample applied for adoption support during the third quarter of 1998, and 12% to 16% of the sample applied for adoption support during each of the four quarters of 1999. The fewest cases (6% or 22 cases) were filed during the last time period, the second quarter of 2000. This drop in the last quarter may be due to lags in data processing given that we selected our sample from the population of all AS cases as of April 30, 2000.

Finally, the case data included three other descriptive measures: the type of adoptive placement; whether foster care payments had been made to the adoptive parents before the Adoption Support application; and whether the child was eligible for federal Title IV-E funding. About 12% of the sample were identified as an adoptive home recruited specifically for the child. Twenty-five percent were foster parent adoptive homes, that is, the children originally were placed with foster families and during the placement, adoption became an option with those families. In 38% of the sampled cases, the homes were foster/adopt—the original foster care placement was understood as one phase of the process leading up to adoption. Over a quarter (26%) were relative adoptions (i.e., the child was adopted by kin). It is not known how many of the cases were relative placements earlier in the child's foster care experience (as either licensed or unlicensed homes) or situations in which relatives opted to adopt the child without serving as a foster parent first. Finally, in terms of fiscal responsibility, 79% of the cases were identified as eligible for Title IV-E support.

Children's problems

The study operationalized children's problems through a review of social workers' text responses on the child's registration form. The social workers' professional judgments did not include documentation from standardized assessment instruments. As Table 9-6 shows, 62% of the children were rated as having emotional or behavioral problems at the time of the Adoption Support application. In addition, children were rated by social workers as having problems related to the mother's drug or alcohol use during pregnancy (56%); medical or physical problems (46%); sensory/developmental delay issues (40%); learning problems (23%); and likelihood of having problems of some type in the future (24%).

Children's special needs conditions

The Child Registration Form also contained a checklist for special needs conditions as specified by state statute. As Table 9-7 demonstrates, emotional/behavioral problems (62%), physical problems (47%), and developmental delay (36%) were often cited as the basis of the child's special needs. In addition, in 40% of the cases, children were identified as part of a sibling group. In 40% of the cases, children were identified as

TABLE 9-6

Children's Problems (n = 384)

CHILD PROBLEMS	NUMBER	PERCENT
Emotional/behavioral problems	237	62%
Learning problems	89	23%
Problems related to mother's drug or alcohol use during pregnancy	217	56%
Sensory/developmental disability problems	155	40%
Medical/physical problems	176	46%
Likely to demonstrate problems in the future	94	24%

Note: Child problems coded from reviewing social worker text detailing social history and current functioning on the ASP Child's Registration form

TABLE 9-7

Children's Special Needs (n=384)

Special Needs Conditions	Number	Percent
Race/ethnicity	120	32%
Age 6 or older	147	40%
Part of sibling group	150	40%
Emotional/behavioral problems	235	62%
Physical problems	178	47%
Developmental delays	136	36%

Note: Special needs conditions checklist completed by social worker on ASP child's registration form

being 6 years of age or older. About a third of cases (32%) identified the child's race/ethnicity as a special-need condition. Across the six measures, almost 20% (n = 70) of the cases had four or more special needs, 31% had three, 34% had two, and 16% were identified with only one special need.

Child resources and family costs

Table 9-8 provides summary data from the Adoption Support Application completed by adoptive parents. In only 9% of cases was the child eligible for Social Security, Supplemental Security Income, or Developmental Disabilities payments. Parents, however, were very likely to have medical insurance (83%) to cover their adopted child.

In the open-ended section of the application in which adoptive parents identified unusual costs that would be incurred and/or services that their child would need, adoptive parents most often mentioned mental health services (52%) that included therapy/counseling and medication. Respite care (35%) was endorsed in a significant minority of cases. Almost a third of adoptive parents (32%) noted costs associated with medical services (31%), including treatment for conditions such as asthma, medication for medi-

TABLE 9–8

Adoption Support Application Issues (n = 384)

RESOURCES AVAILABLE TO CHILD	NUMBER	PERCENT
Child eligible for SSA, SSI, or DDD	36	9%
Parents have medical insurance	317	83%
Child—unusual costs		
Mental health services	200	52%
Special education services	91	24%
Physical therapy or related services	82	21%
Medical services	120	31%
Special accommodations	69	18%
Family needs child care/respite	136	35%
Child needs social activities	48	12%
Other family cost issues		
Family income inadequate	26	7%
Other dependent costs	43	11%
Other family expenses	61	16%

Note: Unusual costs coded from reviewing parents' text responses on Adoption Support Application

cal problems, and dental care. Close to one quarter (24%) of adoptive parents listed special education services such as developmental services and tutoring (24%), and about one-fifth (21 %) listed physical and occupational therapy for gross and fine motor delays and speech problems, special equipment, and eye care. About 18% of parents noted the need for funds to cover special accommodations, including larger cars or houses; travel to obtain services for the child; and replacement of property as a result of damage caused by the child. Only 12% cited unusual costs associated with the child's social activities such as camps, scouting, and sports.

Adoption support

The focus of the study was on the level of support obtained by adoptive parents based on their applications and the social workers' assessments. This outcome measure was operationalized via the state's monthly payment system. Researchers examined payment records for the three months following the approval of the Adoption Support Application. As Table 9-9 shows, about 18% (n = 68) of the cases were not receiving monthly adoption support, although they may have received other one-time expenses during that time period. It is not known (and it is not relevant to this study) whether these families subsequently were added to the monthly adoption support program. In 38% (n = 146) of the Adoption Support Applications, families received a basic monthly adoption support. In 44% (n = 170) of the cases, families were granted both basic monthly adoption support payments and on-going supplemental payments.

TABLE 9-9

Adoption Support (n=384)

MONTLY SUPPORT LEVEL	NUMBER	PERCENT
None	68	18%
Basic	146	38%
Basic + supplemental	170	44%

Bivariate Analyses

Using many of the variables presented in the first eight tables, researchers completed bivariate for the two outcome measures generated from the adoption support measure. The first set of bivariate analyses involved case characteristics in relation to either not receiving any adoption subsidy versus those families that had a basic monthly support payment. The second set focused on comparing case characteristics by whether the family received a basic monthly stipend or whether they got a basic support stipend plus additional payments (basic + supplemental).

Measures associated with receipt of basic adoption support

The first set of bivariate analyses focused on identifying measures that distinguished cases that did not receive any level of ongoing adoption support (n = 68) from cases that received an award of basic monthly support payments (n = 146). The most notable aspect is the relative paucity of statistically significant findings. With regard to child, case, and adoptive family characteristics, the two groups were comparable on child gender and race/ethnicity. There were no differences in the residence (by region) of the children and families, the type of adoption, history of foster care payment, or federal Title IV-E eligibility. Likewise, on interval case measures, the decision to provide basic monthly adoption support was unrelated to the number of children's prior placements, time between placement with the adoptive family and the application for adoption support, and when the application was made and approved. For adoptive family measures, the two groups did not differ on the match between parent(s) and adopted child on race/ethnicity, family size, or adoptive parent ages.

As shown in Table 9-10, only one background measure yielded significant group differences: family annual gross income. Families with fewer resources were much more likely to receive basic monthly adoption support than families earning $80,000 or more each year. The data trend in this regard was expected. About one third (35%) of families who earned $80,000 received basic adoption support; 64% of families earning between $60,000 and $79,000 annually received basic adoption support (OR = 3.33); and 80% of families earning less than $20,000 annually received basic support (OR = 7.60).

As shown in Table 9-11, results followed a similar pattern for measures of child problems, special need conditions, resource availability, and unusual costs related to the child's needs. No group differences were found among the child problem variables coded from the Child Registration Form completed by social workers.

TABLE 9–10

Case Characteristics and Provision of Basic Adoption Support (n = 214)

	Total N	% Receiving Basic AS	Odds Ratio	P Value
CHILD CHARACTERISTICS				
Gender				0.15
Female	114	73%	1.00*	
Male	99	64%	0.65	
Age at Adoption Support Program enrollment				0.61
<4	80	66%	1.00*	
4–6	54	67%	1.08	
7–9	40	78%	1.86	
10–12	22	73%	1.44	
>12	17	59%	0.77	
Race/ethnicity				0.60
White	142	65%	1.00*	
Black	29	72%	1.43	
Hispanic	19	79%	2.04	
Other	20	74%	1.63	
CASE CHARACTERISTICS				
Region				0.76
Eastern Washington	50	70%	1.11	
Western Washington	164	68%	1.00*	
Type of adoption				0.83
Adoptive home	21	67%	1.10	
Foster parent adoption	41	68%	1.18	
Foster/adopt home	88	72%	1.39	
Relative adoption	62	65%	1.00*	
Any foster care payment, at adoption support application				0.25
No	55	62%	1.00*	
Yes	158	70%	1.46	
Federal Title IV-E fund eligibility				0.60
No	44	66%	1.00*	
Yes	124	70%	1.22	
ADOPTIVE FAMILY				
Family annual gross income				<0.01
$20,000 or less	25	80%	7.60	
$20,000 –$39,000	46	76%	6.05	
$40,000 –$59,000	65	72%	4.96	
$60,000–$79,000	33	64%	3.33	
$80,000 or higher	29	35%	1.00*	
Race/ethnic match—either parent and adoptive child				0.37
Yes	124	64%	1.00*	
No	45	71%	1.40	

*Reference group indicated with an odds ratio of 1.00.

TABLE 9–11

Child Problems, Special Needs and Adoption Support (n = 214)

	TOTAL N	% RECEIVING BASIC AS	ODDS RATIO	P VALUE
CHILD PROBLEMS				
Emotion/behavior problems				0.73
No	97	67%	1.00*	
Yes	117	69%	1.11	
Learning problems				0.94
No	180	68%	1.00*	
Yes	34	68%	0.97	
Problems related to mother's drug or alcohol use during pregnancy				0.89
No	93	68%	1.00*	
Yes	121	69%	1.04	
Sensory/developmental disability problems				0.96
No	138	68%	1.00*	
Yes	76	68%	1.01	
Medical/physical problems				0.26
No	122	71%	1.00*	
Yes	92	64%	0.72	
Likely to demonstrate problems in the future				0.46
No	152	70%	1.00*	
Yes	62	65%	0.79	
SPECIAL NEEDS CONDITIONS				
Race/ethnicity				0.21
No	136	66%	1.00*	
Yes	71	75%	1.51	
Age 6 or older				0.03
No	129	64%	1.00*	
Yes	74	79%	2.08	
Part of sibling group				0.07
No	137	65%	1.00*	
Yes	70	77%	1.82	
Emotional/behavioral problems				0.90
No	86	69%	1.00*	
Yes	121	69%	1.04	
Physical problems				0.53
No	107	71%	1.00*	
Yes	100	67%	0.83	
Developmental problems				0.87
No	144	69%	1.00*	
Yes	63	68%	0.95	
RESOURCES AVAILABLE TO CHILD				
SSA, SSI or DDD				0.36
No	200	69%	1.00*	
Yes	14	57%	0.60	
Parents have medical insurance				0.24
No	38	76%	1.00*	
Yes	176	67%	0.62	

TABLE 9–11 CONTINUED

Child Problems, Special Needs and Adoption Support (n = 214)

	Total N	% Receiving Basic AS	Odds Ratio	P Value
CHILD—UNUSUAL COSTS				
Mental health services				0.40
No	120	66%	1.00*	
Yes	94	71%	1.29	
Special education services				0.52
No	174	67%	1.00*	
Yes	40	73%	1.28	
Physical therapy or related services				0.95
No	182	68%	1.00*	
Yes	32	69%	1.03	
Medical services				0.74
No	145	69%	1.00*	
Yes	69	67%	0.90	
Special accommodations				0.31
No	181	67%	1.00*	
Yes	33	76%	1.56	
Family child care/respite				0.46
No	176	69%	1.00*	
Yes	38	63%	0.76	
Child needs social activities				0.01
No	191	65%	1.00*	
Yes	23	91%	5.54	
OTHER FAMILY COST ISSUES				
Family income inadequate				0.07
No	202	67%	1.00*	
Yes	12	92%	5.46	
Other dependent costs				0.22
No	190	67%	1.00*	
Yes	24	79%	1.89	
Other family expenses				0.96
No	179	68%	1.00*	
Yes	35	69%	1.02	

*Reference group indicated with an odds ratio of 1.00.

Further, no group differences were found among most of the child variables addressing special needs, such as race/ethnicity, sibling group membership, emotional/behavioral problems, physical problems, or developmental concerns. The lone exception involved young age as a special need designation. Families that adopted children age six or older were over twice as likely to be receiving basic support relative to those with adoptive children age five or younger.

Among parent-generated measures, the two groups (families who received basic monthly adoption support and families who did not) yielded comparable levels of resource availability and perceived need in connection with unusual costs. There were no statistical differences in parents' views of unusual costs associated with their child's needs for mental health services, special education services, physical therapy, medical treatment, special accommodations, or respite care. The only significant bivariate finding involved parents' views of the need for services that addressed their children's social activities and skills. Among the 23 families who cited this need, 91% received basic adoption support compared to 65% of the families who did not express a need for such services (OR = 5.54). Finally, parents' judgments about other costs related to the adoption did not vary between the two groups. Concerns about the family's income, anticipated expenses for other dependents, and considerations related to other general household money issues were comparable for families that received and families that did not receive basic monthly adoption support.

Measures associated with receipt of supplemental adoption support

The second set of bivariate analyses identified measures that distinguished families who received basic adoption support (n = 146) and families who were awarded supplemental monthly payments along with basic adoption support (n = 170). As shown in Table 9-12, child gender, and race/ethnicity were not related to receipt of supplemental adoption support. However child age at adoption support was significantly associated with likelihood of receiving basic and supplemental payments. Relative to families that adopted very young children (under age 4) those with older children had higher rates of supplemental funding.

Among case characteristics, family residence, the type of adoption, and prior foster care payments were unrelated to group status. Federal Title IV-E eligibility was significantly associated with group status, however. Children who were Title IV-E eligible were almost twice as likely as noneligible children to receive supplemental support (57% vs. 40%; OR = 1.98). Also, a family's annual gross income was related to receiving supplemental adoption support. Compared to higher income families earning $80,000 or more per year, those making less than $40,000 were more likely to have been granted these additional dollars. There were no differences among the three higher income categories ($40,000–$59,000, $60,000–$79,000, and $80,000+) with regard to the receipt of supplemental monthly support, however.

Mean differences also were examined among child, case and family interval measures. (These data are not shown). The two groups were statistically comparable on the average number of placements; the time between placement with the adoptive family and the parents' application for support; the adoption support application period (across calendar quarters from the third quarter of 1998 through the second quarter of 2000); and adoptive parents' ages.

As shown in Table 9-13, child problems (as detailed by social workers on the Child Registration Form) often significantly distinguished families who received supplemental adoption support from families who did not. Children identified as having emotional/behavioral, learning, and sensory/developmental delay problems were more likely to receive supplemental dollars when compared to children without these problems. Interestingly, among the special needs categories, the category of emotional/behavioral problems was not related to the outcome in this sub-group comparison. The difference may reside in how emotional problems were operationalized. In the former

TABLE 9–12

Case Characteristics and Provision of Supplemental Adoption Support (n = 316)

	Total N	% Receiving Basic+ AS	Odds Ratio	p Value
CHILD CHARACTERISTICS				
Gender				0.49
Female	173	52%	1.00*	
Male	143	56%	1.17	
Age at Adoption Support Program enrollment				0.01
<4	86	38%	1.00*	
4–6	93	61%	2.31	
7–9	80	61%	2.39	
10–12	39	59%	2.18	
>12	18	44%	1.21	
Race/ethnicity				0.57
White	207	56%	1.00*	
Black	43	51%	0.84	
Hispanic	37	60%	1.17	
Other	26	44%	0.59	
CASE CHARACTERISTICS				
Region				0.15
Eastern Washington	88	60%	1.44	
Western Washington	228	51%	1.00*	
Type of adoption				0.33
Adoptive home	37	62%	1.73	
Foster parent adoption	81	65%	1.99	
Foster/adopt home	118	47%	0.92	
Relative adoption	78	49%	1.00*	
Any foster care payment, at adoption support application				0.92
No	73	53%	1.00*	
Yes	242	54%	1.03	
Federal Title IV-E fund eligibility				0.04
No	48	40%	1.00*	
Yes	200	57%	1.98	
Family annual gross income				0.03
$20,000 or less	47	57%	1.35	
$20,000–$39,000	102	66%	1.91	
$40,000–$59,000	81	42%	0.72	
$60,000–$79,000	42	50%	1.00	
$80,000 or higher	20	50%	1.00*	
Race/ethnic match—either parent and adoptive child				0.06
Yes	191	59%	1.00*	
No	58	45%	0.57	

*Reference group indicated with an odds ratio of 1.00.

TABLE 9–13

Child Problems, Special Needs, and Supplemental Adoption Support (n = 316)

	TOTAL N	% RECEIVING BASIC + ADOPTION SUPPORT	ODDS RATIO	P VALUE
CHILD PROBLEMS				
Emotional/behavior problems				<0.01
No	115	44%	1.00*	
Yes	201	60%	1.93	
Learning problems				<0.01
No	238	48%	1.00*	
Yes	78	71%	2.56	
Problems related to mother's drug or alcohol use during pregnancy			0.95	
No	137	54%	1.00*	
Yes	179	54%	0.99	
Sensory/developmental disability problems				0.05
No	185	49%	1.00*	
Yes	131	60%	1.57	
Medical/physical problems				0.11
No	173	50%	1.00*	
Yes	143	59%	1.44	
Likely to demonstrate problems in the future				0.07
No	244	57%	1.00*	
Yes	72	44%	0.61	
SPECIAL NEEDS CONDITIONS				
Race/ethnicity				0.12
No	211	57%	1.00*	
Yes	102	48%	0.69	
Age 6 or older				0.75
No	178	54%	1.00*	
Yes	131	56%	1.08	
Part of sibling group				0.07
No	179	50%	1.00*	
Yes	134	60%	1.47	
Emotional/behavioral problems				0.08
No	118	48%	1.00*	
Yes	198	58%	1.50	
Physical problems				0.86
No	168	55%	1.00*	
Yes	145	54%	0.96	
Developmental problems				0.02
No	197	49%	1.00*	
Yes	116	63%	1.75	
RESOURCES AVAILABLE TO CHILD				
SSA, SSI or DDD				<0.02
No	286	52%	1.00*	
Yes	30	73%	2.56	
Parents have medical insurance				0.52
No	58	50%	1.00*	
Yes	258	55%	1.21	

TABLE 9–13 CONTINUED

Child Problems, Special Needs, and Supplemental Adoption Support (n = 316)

	Total N	% Receiving Basic + Adoption Support	Odds Ratio	p Value
CHILD—UNUSUAL COSTS				
Mental health services				<0.01
No	143	45%	1.00*	
Yes	173	61%	1.95	
Special education services				0.04
No	236	50%	1.00*	
Yes	80	64%	1.73	
Physical therapy or related services				<0.01
No	244	49%	1.00*	
Yes	72	69%	2.35	
Medical services				0.77
No	219	54%	1.00*	
Yes	97	53%	0.93	
Special accommodations				0.36
No	255	53%	1.00*	
Yes	61	59%	1.30	
Family child care/respite				<0.01
No	194	37%	1.00*	
Yes	122	80%	6.92	
Child needs social activities				0.94
No	270	54%	1.00*	
Yes	46	54%	1.03	
OTHER FAMILY COST ISSUES				
Family income inadequate				0.82
No	291	54%	1.00*	
Yes	25	56%	1.10	
Other dependent costs				0.62
No	27	54%	1.00*	
Yes	8 38	50%	0.84	
Other family expenses				0.78
No	266	54%	1.00*	
Yes	50	52%	0.92	

*Reference group indicated with an odds ratio of 1.00.

case, it reflects a summary judgment by the authors of qualitative text written by the social worker. The second approach involved check boxes on the same document that conformed to state statute for identifying special needs—and emotional/behavioral problems was listed as one of those closed-ended items. These two items yielded consistent results in about 70% of the sample. However, there were discrepancies among the remaining 30% between our rating of social workers' clinical notes and their checking a 'special needs' box. (Interestingly, the discrepant results were almost equally balanced between the two measures.) At this point it would be foolhardy to speculate on which was more accurate. As noted earlier, the open- and closed-ended items on these forms were not completed using standardized diagnostic tools. Differences in the amount of documentation provided between social workers as well as variation in training (ours as well as state workers) could easily yield this level of discrepancy. (See later sections for suggestions about future approaches to this issue.) Finally, sibling group membership was another special needs measure associated with receipt of supplemental adoption support compared to receipt of basic monthly adoption support only. Among the special needs problem measures, only developmental concerns were related to receipt of supplemental adoption support.

Certain child resources and family costs also were associated with receipt of supplemental adoption support. Children who received Social Security benefits, Supplemental Security Income benefits, or disability payments were more than twice as likely to receive supplemental adoption support compared to children not enrolled in these programs. Parents who identified unusual costs associated with their children's needs for mental health, special education and physical therapy services and for respite care were significantly more likely to be awarded supplemental adoption support.

Multivariate Analyses

Basic adoption support

Table 9-14 provides regression coefficients, standard errors, and adjusted odds-ratios for the final multivariate model predicting provision of basic monthly adoption support relative to no such support. Only two measures were independently associated with this outcome: family gross annual income and the parent's identification of the need for social activities as an expected "unusual cost." The limited number of variables bivariately related to basic monthly adoption support was followed by even fewer variables entering the multivariate equation. Essentially, family income distinguished the households that did and did not receive basic adoption support. Although one of the expected parent cost measures also entered the equation (social activities), the number of families stating the need for these services was quite small, and thus, the relevance of this finding to program planning is limited. The goodness-of-fit (GOF) measure suggests that one cannot reject the hypothesis that the model fits the observations. (GOF is derived from calculating observed and estimated expected frequencies within each decile of risk for each outcome group. A p-value is calculated for this contingency table using the chi-square distribution.)

Supplemental adoption support

Table 9-15 summarizes multivariate logistic regression findings predicting social worker decisions to provide some families with basic and supplemental adoption support and other families with basic monthly adoption support only. The final model contained child and case characteristics and problem and cost measures. Child age was independently associated with families' receipt of supplemental adoption support. Adoption support applications were more likely to be approved for basic and supplemental support for children in each successive age group after the age group of 3 years or younger. The likelihood increased monotonically across children in age groups 4–6 years, 7–9 years, and 10—12 years (adj. OR = 2.76, 4.39 and 5.46, respectively). Families with

TABLE 9-14

Analysis for Basic Adoption Support

Multiple logistic regression analysis assessing child, case, family, and problem variables on adoption support cases obtaining basic monthly adoption support relative to cases not awarded any support (n = 198)

VARIABLE	B	SE(B)	ADJUSTED ODDS RATIO	P-VALUE
Family annual gross income				
$20,000 or less	1.97	0.64	7.14	0.005
$20,000 - $39,000	1.72	0.53	5.60	
$40,000 - $59,000	1.54	0.48	4.69	
$60,000 - $79,000	1.12	0.54	3.06	
$80,000 or higher (Ref.)	—	—	1.00	
Unusual costs				
Needs social activities, Yes	1.53	0.77	4.62	0.048

Hosmer and Lemeshow GOF test, chi-square = 0.61, p = 0.98

adolescents (age 13 or older) were more likely to receive supplemental adoption support compared to very young children (OR = 2.04), but not to the same degree found for children in the middle age ranges.

Type of adoptive home was a case characteristic that entered the final model. Nonrelative families specifically identified as adoptive placements for children, and families who fostered their adopted children while the children were in care were significantly more likely to receive supplemental adoption support than were adoptive families who were related to the child. Additionally, medical/physical problems doubled the likelihood that a family would receive supplemental adoption support (OR = 2.15). Consistent with this finding, it also was found that parents who identified physical therapy as an expected unusual cost were more likely to receive this higher level of support. In addition, family needs for childcare and respite were found to be highly associated with supplemental adoption support (OR = 11.73). Finally, payment level was affected by the quarter in which the application for adoption support was processed. Within the study timeframe from the third quarter of 1998 through the second quarter of 2000, the chances of receiving supplemental adoption support increased about 25% per quarter. As with the prior logistic regression analyses, model fit was acceptable.[*]

Discussion

Based on the findings of this study, it appears that monthly adoption support has become the norm throughout Washington State. Over 80% of the sample received either

---

[*]   The penultimate logistic regression (LR) model predicting supplemental adoption support resulted in significant lack of fit. An examination of diagnostic statistics and various scatterplots led to identifying two cases that had unduly large effects on model estimates and GOF. These were families that were predicted to be in the supplemental group, but were only receiving basic monthly support. The LR was run again without these records. Results were substantively the same in terms of odds ratios obtained and the GOF test results improved.

TABLE 9–15

Analysis for Supplemental Adoption Support

Multiple logistic regression analysis assessing child, case, family, and problem variables on adoption support cases obtaining supplemental adoption support relative to cases awarded basic monthly adoption support only (n = 307)

VARIABLE	B	SE(B)	ADJUSTED ODDS RATIO	P-VALUE
Child age at Adoption Support Program enrollment				0.002
<4 (Ref.)	—	—	1.00	
4-6	1.01	0.38	2.76	
7-9	1.48	0.43	4.39	
10-12	1.70	0.49	5.46	
>12	0.71	0.63	2.04	
Type of adoption				0.004
Adoptive home	0.39	0.34	1.48	
Foster home	1.34	0.41	3.83	
Relative adoption (Ref.)	—	—	1.00	
Medical/physical problems, Yes	0.77	0.30	2.15	0.01
Unusual costs				
Family childcare/respite, Yes	2.46	0.33	11.73	<0.001
Physical therapy, Yes	1.06	0.36	2.87	0.003
Application date, qtr./yr.	0.22	0.07	1.25	<0.001

Hosmer & Lemeshow GOF test, chi-square = 11.02, p = 0.20

basic monthly adoption support only or both basic and supplemental adoption support. Based on this, it would be easy to assume the existence of significant differences between those families approved for adoption support and families who were not approved, and that these differences would relate to case history, current child problems, and family needs. Likewise, it might be assumed that the group of families who received basic adoption support and the group of families who received basic plus supplemental adoption support also would differ in the scope of case and family issues. It should be noted that there were concerns at the inception of the study about possible problems in coding the extent or severity of certain variables (such as child problems) that might hamper the identification of differences between the two groups of families.

In fact, the results were somewhat different than common sense expectations. Virtually no differences were found between families who received no adoption support and families who received basic monthly adoption support. Analyses indicated that a family's gross income generally was the sole factor that affected the decision to award monthly adoption support, and that the income "cutoff" for approval of basic support was relatively high. This outcome is consistent with the intent of state policy to encourage the adoptions of children in foster care who often have significant, serious problems.

Because the cases in the two groups of families (no support versus basic adoption support) did not differ on substantive measures, a question arises about the reasons that the applications of a minority of families for basic support were not approved. One conjecture, which could not be assessed in this study, is simply that these families ultimately received adoption support, only at a later date. A second possibility is simply that neither we nor the AS system collect the types of information that could account for differences between receiving no support or a basic subsidy.

Analyses of families who received basic adoption support against families who received basic plus supplemental adoption support yielded more substantive differences. Parents who adopted older children were more likely to receive supplemental support, a finding that reflects an understanding of older children's needs as a result of expanded role situations (such as the child's place in school and community) and the increasing psychological problems that many children have as they grow older.

Medical issues were associated with supplemental adoption support, but emotional/mental health issues were not predictive of supplemental support. One possible explanation for this finding is that all of these issues were subsumed under the rubric of "medical" needs. Alternatively, the finding may be attributable to limited mental health service availability in some of the communities represented in the sample. This issue of mental health service availability is an issue that broadly affects the population of children in foster care for lengthy periods of time (Berliner & Fine, 2001).

Although mental health issues were not part of the final multivariate model, one factor that predicted higher adoption support levels was respite care. Families' identification of the need for respite services may be a useful indicator of self-care efforts in response to on-going challenges associated with parenting children with special needs. Finally, the adoption support application date was independently related to the receipt of supplemental support. The more recent the adoption support application, the more likely the family was to receive supplemental support. This trend is consistent with the program's growth in both caseload and cost.

In addition to what can be learned from empirically supported findings, the absence of statistically significant relationships for certain measures can inform the understanding of the adoption support program. For example, geography, the gender of the child, and child and parent race/ethnicity were not factors in the initial determination of any level of adoption support. Administratively decentralized programs can be prone to significant variation in implementation, some of which can be a positive response to local issues while other aspects can reflect serious inconsistencies with policy and statutory requirements. There were not, however, significant regional variations, and most case demographics were unrelated to adoption support levels. It was interesting that Title IV-E status also was unrelated to adoption support levels, a finding that was contrary to the expectation that federal eligibility would be associated with higher levels of adoption support. Data on this measure, however, were relatively incomplete.

Interest in identifying factors that distinguish among adoption support levels and the program's overall cost could lead to the development of an empirically based prediction or actuarial model (as has been the case in many social and health programs). One could estimate, for example, the probability of receipt of basic plus supplemental support relative to the receipt of basic support only, using the measures in the final multivariate model. Different cut points could be selected, and cases could be compared between their predicted likelihood for receipt of supplemental support versus their actual support group status. This approach has utility both for modeling costs and for monitoring the consistency of program implementation. A minority of cases could be identified at either end of a spectrum of predicted versus actual professional practice. At one end of this spectrum were adoption support cases in which it was predicted that the family would receive supplemental support (based on factors that made the family similar to families who received such support) but which, in fact, did not receive this benefit. At the other end of the spectrum are those families where the estimated likelihood of receipt of supplemental support was quite low but the families had been awarded supplemental support nevertheless. In either case, more information might be requested from the adoption support social worker. It should be noted these types of inconsistencies do not necessarily indicate program problems, as the empirical model predicting case status may be weak or flawed.

The foster care field has used efforts to assess the sensitivity and specificity of system decisions widely, primarily in modeling future risk to children, and there may be a tendency to apply such a strategy in adoption support programs to predict levels of adoption support. At this time, however, policymakers and managers should resist such an approach for two reasons. First, in both statute and policy in many states, including Washington State, the goal of adoption support programs is to assist adoptive parents in addressing their adopted children's problems, both known and unknown. This principled commitment is not intended to be fine-tuned through a risk assessment that results in either excluding some adoptive families from support or leading parents to consider more adversarial or tactical relationships with adoption support social workers. At the same time, the administrative and monitoring functions within adoption support programs are not highly developed or standardized, and therefore, the capacity to review and revise adoption support decisions generally is limited, it is a false precision to commit to reviewing false positives or false negatives. Given how the two forms are presently being used, questions about the accuracy and consistency of documentation should be explored before having too much faith in empirical risk models built on these data. A good example of this problem was presented in the results for emotional/behavioral problems in relation to receiving supplemental support. The 'problems' were operationalized via qualitative social worker notes as well as special-needs check box—and varied significantly between these approaches.

To build on the prior point, there is a major technical constraint on the use of empirical models in adoption support. In Washington State, the registration and application forms currently in use are not constructed for rigorous empirical assessment but, instead, are designed to provide social workers with a way to summarize both written and verbal data. The state is only in the early stages of developing practical, yet psychometrically, valid approaches to the measurement of constructs characterizing the very complex web of child, family, and community variables. This research project, combined with current efforts to codify adoption support forms in the state, emphasize the level of effort required to generate simple summary indicators. Although the use of standardized tools would enhance the assessment process, it nevertheless would come at a significant cost to the program, its staff, and the adoptive parents who are its intended beneficiaries.

Although there are many questions about the wisdom of incorporating empirical tools into routine adoption support decisionmaking, it is clear that the findings of this study are consistent with program goals. The adoption support program was designed to be flexible and sensitive to the needs of adoptive families and children and to local community conditions. The study results indicate an underlying and general logic to the diverse decisions made regarding different levels of adoption support—a finding consistent with the program's design. An analysis of the adoption support payments made to all families enrolled in the program might yield a different picture, but such an analysis would require additional data on the factors affecting families and children and the costs of community services. These measures are well beyond the scope of the present research on adoption support in Washington State.

Limitations of the Study

This study has several limitations. First, the research relied on routine agency documents at six regional offices across Washington State, materials that were not developed with research in mind. These documents are used administratively to make professional decisions about adoption support, and, as a result, there were limitations in capturing case variation on some measures. As an example, the Child Registration Form uses a Yes/No checklist for the child's problems and does not provide a format for social workers to rate the scope or severity of the problems. From a research perspective, the absence of such ratings constrains an assessment of case issues and the decisions related to an award of adoption support and/or the level of support. A related limitation is that the study involved a review and coding of the qualitative text in the documents that described child and family issues and resources. Researchers made every effort to conduct the review and coding in a consistent and rigorous manner, but the process is certainly open to question. Another limitation relates to the fact that parents were allowed to submit, along with the application, materials that supported their need for adoption support and that documented the problems of their child and/or family. The study did not seek copies of these materials. It is not clear to what extent this information, which might have shed additional light on each case, was reflected in the records that were reviewed (such as in medical examination records, psychological reports, children's Individual Education Plans, and developmental assessments).

A second general limitation involves the data obtained from the state's CAMIS and SSPS. The researchers enjoyed the full cooperation of the central office adoption support staff who facilitated data extractions with state programmers. As researchers learned with hard-copy forms they reviewed, however, research is not the major focus of the state's information systems. Computerized records regarding payments and case characteristics were, in some cases, inconsistent with regional office information on such vital information as the child's race/ethnicity. The study was not able to address these data problems completely. Had the study solicited information directly from adoptive parents or the adoption support social workers, it may have been possible to resolve inconsistencies across computerized and hard copy instrumentation. In addition, the matching process between the two databases, although excellent, was not perfect and, as a result, some sampled records had problematic case identifiers or dates.

The third limitation relates to the issue of data collection directly from adoptive parents. Larger and more rigorous studies could enhance the understanding achieved through the use of standardized instruments by engaging multiple respondents, such as adoptive parents and school and health personnel who are knowledgeable about the child. Such an approach has been used successfully in studies of long-term foster care (see Berliner & Fine, 2001). The collection of systematic data on child functioning and symptoms would require a much different research design and set of research questions than were used in this study, with its focus on child and family issues at the time of the adoption support application. The use of standardized tools (such as the Child and Adolescent Functional Assessment Scale or the Child Behavior Checklist) likewise would be problematic given the retrospective approach used in this study.

Fourth, there were methodological limitations regarding the number of cases that were randomly selected. It would have been ideal to obtain a sufficiently large sample to test for differences among the six regions, particularly given the decentralized implementation of the adoption support program across the state. Because of the required coding of qualitative text, the sample size needed to test for regional differences was simply too costly.

Conclusions

Permanency for children in a safe family environment is the explicitly stated goal of the child welfare system. When children cannot return to their biological families, adoption is the clearly preferred outcome. The Adoption Support Program represents a policy decision by the Washington State Legislature to encourage the adoption of children from the child welfare system. The growth in the program, particularly over the last four years, suggests that the policy has been successful. More families are adopting children with special needs; the number of families who receive basic monthly adoption support is increasing; and more families are receiving supplemental support. The findings of this study indicate that, in contrast to earlier periods in the implementation of the Adoption Support Program, the norm is now that adoptive families receive, at minimum, basic monthly adoption support.

The study also indicates that the major differences in levels of adoption support are related to selected child problems and family resources, a finding consistent with policy and legislative intent. The program in Washington State is consistent with the view that adoption support provides a reasonable incentive and support for families who adopt children from the child welfare system. The increasing costs of the program are related to the intent of state policy that financial support be provided for families who adopt children whose stays in foster care have been long term and who may have significant problems (Berliner & Fine, 2001).

This study found that the regional implementation of the adoption support program in Washington State is collaborative and non-adversarial. The flexibility of the program is both an obvious strength and a not-so-obvious weakness. Local flexibility may raise questions regarding equity among cases and may not allow for sufficient attention to the significant variations among communities in terms of service availability.

Problems exist with regard to more rigorous monitoring of adoption support. First, monitoring is costly. Second, the use of a more "mathematical" approach across the state in determining payment levels would be inconsistent with the intent and spirit of state legislation and policy. The findings of this study suggest that the program uses a rational set of distinctions, particularly in relation to the award of supplemental payments. Similarly, the program uses a reasonable rationale with regard to decisions related to the award or denial of basic adoption support, primarily relying on family income.

This research raises a number of additional questions for further study. First more work is needed regarding the technical limitations that have been identified. Specifically, more psychometrically grounded forms need to be developed, and the judicious use of standardized instruments to inform professional judgment needs to be explored further. Second, this study did not address how families were actually using adoption support nor whether the support was adequate to the tasks they confronted, both of which are important areas for further research. Third, the study focused on the initial decision regarding adoption support at the time the application was made. Change is inevitable, and field-based research is needed to assess fluctuations in the needs of families and children and family resources over time. A key component in each of these areas of additional research is the direct input of adoptive parents and their children. Although there are significant challenges in designing and implementing such studies, serious efforts are needed to find creative ways to involve families and children in future adoption support research.

References

Barth, R. P. (1988). Disruption in older child adoption: We now know enough to develop a profile of children whose placements are in greatest jeopardy. *Public Welfare. 46* (1), 23-29.

Berliner, L. & Fine, D. (2001). *Long-term foster care in Washington: Children's status and placement decision-making, final report.* Seattle, WA: Washington State Institute for Public Policy.

Children's Administration Adoption Support Program Desk Manual, rev. (1999, June). RCW 13.112. Olympia, WA: Author.

Doran, L. & Berliner, L. (2000) *Adoption Support: Program Administration, Caseload and Subsidies and Decision Making.* Seattle, WA: Washington State Institute for Public Policy.

Families for Kids Partnership, (2001). Washington Permanency Report: 1998–2003 Seattle, WA: Author.

Groze, V. (1996). A 1- and 2- Year Follow-Up Study of Adoptive Families and Special Needs Children. *Children and Youth Services Review, 18* (1-2), 57-82.

Hosmer, D.W. & Lemeshow, S. (1989). *Applied Logistic Regression.* New York: John Wiley & Sons.

North American Council on Adoptable Children (2002). Washington State Subsidy Profile: http://www.nanac.org/stateprofiles/washington.html, Accessed February 15, 2002.

U.S. Department of Health and Human Services (1999). Administration for Children and Families, Children's Bureau, November, 24, 1998; rev. June 25, 1999.

Washington State Caseload Forecast Council, (2000, November) *Human services caseload forecasts*, Olympia, WA: Author

SECTION THREE

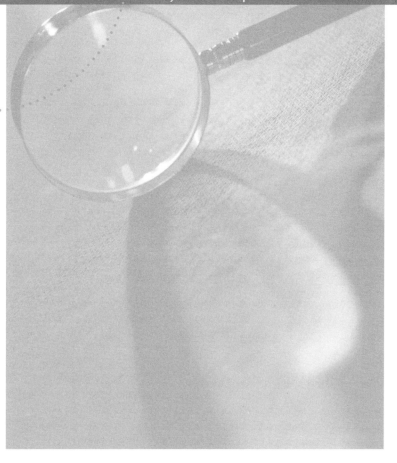

Research Methods in the Study of Postadoptive Services

Postadoption Services:
LESSONS FROM McCord

Jeffrey J. Haugaard

I n 1988, this researcher read an article by Joan McCord (1978) entitled, "A Thirty-Year Follow-Up of Treatment Effects." That article contains information that child welfare professionals must consider as we evaluate the effectiveness of postadoption services for children and families. McCord's 30-year follow-up of an extensive intervention to help boys avoid delinquency found that although almost all of the men recalled the intervention fondly and believed that it had a strong positive influence on their lives, objective measures showed that the men who received the intervention had fared no better than a nontreated control group. The McCord study suggests that empirical analysis of any service is essential to evaluating the service and that participants who receive a service are not good evaluators of that service. This chapter draws on the McCord study and describes a variety of issues that evaluators of postadoption services should consider. It also suggests some solutions to problems associated with many postadoption service evaluations.

The McCord Study

In her article, McCord (1978) started by describing the intervention for boys at risk for delinquency that she subsequently evaluated:

> In 1935, Richard Clark Cabot instigated one of the most imaginative and exciting programs ever designed in hopes of preventing delinquency. A social philosopher as well as physician, Dr. Cabot established a program that both avoided stigmatizing participants and permitted follow-up evaluation (p. 284)

Schools, community organizations, and police referred boys considered "average" and boys considered "difficult" to the program. The boys and their families were interviewed and were then paired on family, home, and personal variables, and on the extent to which they were "delinquency prone." By a toss of a coin, each pair was then split into a treatment group and a control group. McCord wrote:

The treatment program began in 1939, when the boys were between 5 and 13 years old. Their median age was 10 1/2. Except for those dropped from the program because of a counselor short-age in 1941, treatment continued for an average of five years. Counselors assigned to each family visited, on the average, twice a month. They encouraged families to call on the program for assistance. Family problems became the focus of attention for approximately one third of the treatment group. Over half of the boys were tutored in academic subjects; over 100 received medical or psychiatric attention; one fourth were sent to summer camp; and most were brought into contact with the Boy Scouts, the YMCA, and other community programs. The control group, meanwhile, participated only through providing information about themselves. Both groups, it should be remembered, contained boys referred as "average" and boys considered "difficult" (1978, p. 284).

Thirty years after the beginning of the intervention, McCord and her colleagues searched for the 506 men who had once been in the program, and located 480 (95%) of them. Forty-eight of the 480 participants had died. All others were sent questionnaires, and 113 men from the treatment group (54%) and 122 men from the control group (60%) returned them. Through the questionnaires, McCord explored the men's memories of the intervention (for the men in the treatment group) and their criminal behavior, health, and family life.

Of the men in the treatment group, 13 could not remember participating in the treatment program and 13 others said that the program had not been helpful. Two-thirds of the men, however, stated that the program had been helpful to them. They said that it had provided activities that kept them off the streets, taught them how to get along with others, helped them to have faith and trust in others, reduced their prejudices, and provided better insight into life. Many commented that their counselors had had an important influence on their lives, and a few noted that the relationship with their counselor was probably what had kept them out of jail or away from a life of crime. Many men asked for information about their counselors so that they could try to contact them.

A comparison of those in the treatment and control groups, however, did not show the same positive picture of the intervention. There were no differences in many of the mental health and physical health outcomes experienced by the men in either group, including none in whether they had died, been in a treatment program for alcoholism, or been in a treatment program for another mental disorder. There also were no differences in whether they had a juvenile delinquency record, been convicted of a "minor" crime as an adult, or been convicted of a "major" crime as an adult. The only group differences showed that the men in the control group had better outcomes than the men in the treatment group. They were less likely to have been convicted of more than one crime, less likely to have problems with alcohol, less likely to die at an early age, and more likely to be in a white collar occupation. The men in the treatment group showed no outcomes that were better than those in the control group.

One is left feeling rather deflated. Boys in the treatment group received long-term, community-based treatment directed by a counselor to whom many boys grew close and who was remembered fondly by many of the men interviewed. Yet, it seems that the intervention was not valuable to participants for its stated purpose—preventing delinquent behavior—and one could argue from McCord's findings that participating in the intervention was even harmful to some in this regard. Professionals concerned about postadoption services and other intervention programs could draw three conclusions of importance from examining the McCord study. These three possible lessons are:

- Many people do not know what is good for them, or what has been good for them.

- Interventions of the sort evaluated by McCord are ineffective.

- Careful assessments of intervention outcomes are essential to test the efficacy of specific programs and to create knowledge about interventions

A thorough examination of these three lessons, however, suggests that the intervention described by McCord may not have been as ineffective as it first appears.

The Three Lessons

Lesson 1: Many People Do Not Know What Is, or Has Been, Good for Them.

Many researchers assess the effectiveness of interventions such as the one described by McCord and postadoption services by asking participants to rate the intervention. Examples of questions that can be asked in this type of assessment are "Did you learn what you hoped to learn in this group?" and "Were the instructors knowledgeable about the course material?" The questions may be more specific: "Did participation in this group increase your confidence that you can handle problems as they arise?" or "Did your ability to respond quickly to problem situations improve after participation in the group?"

To receive accurate answers to questions like the first two examples (involving an assessment of what was learned in general) participants must have accurate assessments of their knowledge before the intervention, the type and amount of their knowledge deficits, and their knowledge at the end of the intervention. It is not clear that anyone has the capacity to know what he or she does not know. Consequently, it is doubtful that evaluations of this sort say much about the actual effectiveness of the intervention. To answer questions similar to the second two examples (involving an assessment of specific behavioral changes), participants must assess their abilities accurately, both before and after the intervention, and then successfully compare the two. If the questions are asked immediately after the program, the participants also must be able to accurately assess the extent to which changes in knowledge or attitudes will translate into changes in future behavior. It is equally doubtful that most individuals have these abilities.

McCord suggests that there may be little association between individuals' evaluations of an intervention and the actual effectiveness of that intervention. Many men returning questionnaires to McCord reported that their experiences with the program were very positive and that their counselor had had a meaningful influence on their lives. That influence, however, was difficult to detect with objective measures. Part of the disconnectedness between the men's assessment of the program and the objective assessment may have been caused by variations in the effectiveness of the intervention. This possibility is discussed in the next section. Despite this possibility, McCord's results point to the likelihood that there may be only a weak association between what participants think about a program and the influence of the program on their lives. To the extent that such an association is absent or limited, asking program participants or their instructors to assess a program may say little about the effectiveness of the program. It is true that when program providers ask participants to assess the program, the participants may feel that they and their opinions are valued, and their answers may provide useful information about the process of presenting the program. The value of these types of questions, however, may be limited to these issues.

Lesson 2: Interventions of the Sort Evaluated by McCord Are Ineffective.

McCord's analysis suggests that the intervention itself was ineffective. These data cannot simply be disregarded because they are troubling. Researchers must consider the possibility that the interventions were ineffective, even if it means that beliefs about the value of such interventions must be reassessed. It is also important, however, to consider the possibility that the intervention only appears ineffective because the data do not accurately reflect the effectiveness of the intervention.

Conflicting theory and data

First, it is possible that the efforts of the individuals who provided the intervention were misplaced. It is often difficult to consider such a possibility, because doing so may require that cherished theories supporting the interventions be discarded. Theories, of course, must not be abandoned too quickly. Seymour Sarason (1975), one of the fathers of community psychology, was fond of saying that one must be cautious not to discard existing theories because data conflict with them. Theories are often the product of extensive experience, and data can be incorrectly gathered or analyzed with the consequence that numbers, or data, do not always equal truth (Sarason, 1975). In some instances, it is wise to follow Sarason's tendency to rely on theory over data.

In the face of considerable conflicting data, however, researchers and practitioners must take care not to hold on to theories too tightly. The danger of clinging to theories is well demonstrated by examining the ways in which treatment for autistic children was hampered by early theories about autism. In the 1950s and 1960s, psychoanalytic theory dominated the thinking about autism and conceptualized autism as a child withdrawing from a hostile world (Mesibov, Adams, & Klinger, 1997). Theory held that parents, and mothers, in particular, were responsible for creating an environment in which the child felt unwanted and from which the child withdrew. As it turns out, this theory was completely wrong. We now know that autism is a brain disorder. Many therapists, however, held onto the psychoanalytically derived theory about autism in the face of mounting conflicting data. In the process, they ruined the lives of many families, and, in particular, the lives of many mothers who felt responsible for inflicting the terrible disorder on their children.

Determining that sufficient conflicting data exist to compel the abandonment of a popular theory is more of an art than a science. General guidance cannot be given about this process, and it is likely that some individuals are more prone to hold onto theories and others are more prone to abandon them quickly. The best guide is the careful, dispassionate analysis of the theories and the data that support and oppose them. Researchers and practitioners must be cautious, however, when interpreting data, even data gathered and analyzed well. Data can be organized and analyzed in a variety of ways, and some of these can lead to quite different conclusions than others. The analysis of data, like art, can be seen differently from various angles.

Differences within groups

Almost all data in the social sciences come from groups. Group results from intervention studies can obscure subgroup differences and can give misleading information about the benefits of an intervention to some subgroups. In the case of McCord's study, the data came from a large and diverse group of boys. All of the differences between the boys are not known, but certain differences are clear, including that the boys were different ages when they started the program. Some boys were as young as 5; others were as old as 13. It may be, for example, that the intervention was particularly valuable for younger boys, but not valuable to the older boys, possibly because of their longer developmental course before participation in the intervention. These possible differences in outcomes could be hidden by analyses of group data, particularly if the subgroup of younger boys was much smaller than that of older boys.

A controversial review of the consequences of child sexual abuse by Rind, Tromovitch, & Bauserman (1998) provides an example of the ways in which group data can be misleading. Using undergraduate samples, Rind and colleagues examined studies of the consequences of child sexual abuse and concluded that significant consequences of child sexual abuse did not exist. These conclusions pose several problems, and a number of papers have closely examined the data from which the conclusions were drawn. Of relevance to our consideration of the McCord study is that the group data in the Rind study obscured the wide range of consequences experienced by the students who had been sexually abused. Because these data combined the minimal effects reported by the large percentage of students who had experienced relatively noninvasive, single occurrences of abuse with the acute and long-lasting consequences reported by a small percentage of students who had experienced severe abuse, the consequences experienced by the more severely abused children were obscured. The same effect may hold for the McCord data. It may be that the intervention was very valuable for some men and not valuable for others, but it would require more fine-tuned analyses to determine whether this is true. In fact, researchers and practitioners should subject any intervention to this sort of detailed analysis to determine: for *whom* in the group the intervention was helpful, not simply whether it was helpful for the group as a whole.

Such in-group analysis is particularly important when assessing postadoption services because of the wide variation among adoptive families. Some families adopt older children who have experienced years of abuse and neglect, and other families adopt infants. Some families adopt children who resemble other children in the family, and others adopt children of different races. Older parents adopt some types of children and younger parents adopt other types. When gathering data on postadoption services, sufficient data must be gather to allow for those receiving services to be divided into theoretically-derived subgroups, with analyses conducted to see if differences in outcomes exist among the subgroups. Such an analysis, for example, could aid in determining whether a particular postadoption service is useful to families who adopt older children but not useful to families who adopt infants. It is often difficult, however, to gather a large enough sample to maintain sufficient statistical power for analyzing data from several subgroups of families who receive postadoption services. There are solutions to this problem, and they are discussed in the final sections of this paper.

Process evaluation

McCord's evaluation was an outcome evaluation; that is, it assessed the effectiveness of the intervention over time. It is not known how effectively the intervention was implemented, however. Evaluations of program implementation are often referred to as process evaluations (Gliner & Morgan, 2000; Roehl, 1996). It may be that the intervention designed by Dr. Cabot was implemented with varying degrees of effectiveness (remember that 13 of the men did not even recall receiving the intervention). It is possible that the counselors who implemented the program well and spent considerable time with the children they mentored achieved greater success than counselors who either did not understand how the program was to be implemented or who implemented it poorly. If the evaluation had been limited to those children whose counselors implemented the program as intended, they may have reported far better outcomes than the children who received no services. McCord did not report a process evaluation of the program, however.

All evaluations need to assess the extent to which services were provided as expected. If, for example, an agency wants to assess the effectiveness of a 12-week preadoption parent training program, the agency first should assess the extent to which the program was delivered as directed. If participants attended, on average, only 6 weeks of sessions, it is clear that a 12-week program was not being provided. If trainers strayed from the curriculum (either by omitting or changing material with which they disagreed), the curriculum was not taught. In either case, an outcome evaluation would say too little about the 12-week training program to be useful. If a process evaluation showed that the curriculum was delivered as expected and that almost all parents attended all sessions, however, then an outcome evaluation would be appropriate. A process evaluation is almost always a prerequisite to an outcome evaluation.

Identifying goals

A final issue suggested by McCord's analysis is that the goals of an intervention must be specified and the intervention assessed based on those goals. McCord, for example, used a set of outcome criteria to assess the intervention, but it is not clear that the designers of the intervention were striving to meet those criteria. This issue is particularly important in adoption studies because it may be hard to identify the appropriate goals for adoptive families and for the postadoption services. For example, is the goal for a child adopted at age 12 after a life of several placements in foster care and abuse by his birthparents to function behaviorally and academically like his nonadopted peers at age 15? Or should the goals for that child be quite different? A more appropriate goal may be for the child to feel that he is part of his adoptive family, with less emphasis as far as outcomes are concerned on academic performance or behavioral functioning. In postadoption services, the goal simply may be to communicate to the child and family that the agency is concerned about them and will be available to them over time.

An example of this issue can be seen in a paper written by Sandra Scarr (1985) that describes the ways in which scientists form and modify theories. Illustrating her hypothesis that people are prone to assume that proximal events have more influence than distal events, Scarr presented data correlating positive parenting practices with children's later IQ. She showed that there is a moderate positive correlation between positive parenting practices at one point in time and a child's IQ measured 18 months later. This data would suggest that improving parents' parenting practices would lead them to have children who are more intelligent. As her further analysis shows, however, the effect of positive parenting practices on the child's IQ disappears when the mother's IQ is considered. Using positive parenting, in reality, does not result in smarter children. Does this finding suggest that courses that teach positive parenting are not useful? If the child's intelligence were the sole outcome of such courses, it would be concluded that teaching positive parenting is not useful. If other outcomes were the focus (such as parent/child relationships or the child's ability to form peer friendships), however, then it may be discovered through additional analyses that teaching positive parenting is very useful.

A thorough assessment of a postadoption service should explore outcomes related to a variety of goals, including the stated goals of the intervention and other goals that may seem relevant. Such an assessment may show that some goals of the intervention are realized while others are not. The assessment may even show some unanticipated benefits.

Summary

McCord's data suggest that interventions of the sort examined are not useful and may be harmful. There are several reasons, however, to believe that such a sweeping conclusion is not warranted. It is not known whether the interventions were useful for some children but not for other children, nor is it known whether other the intervention influenced aspects of the children's lives positively. Service assessments must allow for an examination of clearly defined subgroups and must be based on clearly articulated goals for those services.

Lesson 3: Careful Assessments of Service Outcomes Are Essential To Test the Efficacy of Specific Programs and Create Knowledge About Services.

The McCord study shows the possibility that services that are designed using the best theories available may be ineffective. Examples of ineffective services can be found throughout the literature. As indicated earlier, many services designed for autistic children in the 1950s and 1960s, based on then-accepted theories, were failures (Mesibov, Adams, & Klinger, 1997). A somewhat more recent example involves efforts to reduce the incidence of child sexual abuse through programs aimed at young children. Many such programs have involved one-time presentations to young children that focus on cognitively complex issues such as "good touch" and "bad touch." Reppucci & Haugaard

(1989) found that such presentations had little or no influence on young children, and that other, more extensive programs designed to increase children's knowledge about sexual abuse were likewise ineffective. Evaluations have revealed that children's increased knowledge about sexual abuse often did not last long, and the children's behavior seldom changed (Reppucci & Haugaard, 1989).

Providing theoretically sound but ineffective services is problematic for several reasons. Obviously, such services do not meet their goals and, thus, do not mollify the problems they are designed to address. Second, ineffective services may keep individuals away from effective services. A family, for example, may participate in a program to improve their parenting, that, unbeknownst to them, is ineffective. They are unlikely to enroll in a second program that may be effective because they believe that they were helped by the first program. Finally, ineffective services can inappropriately increase a sense of personal failure. After completing an ineffective parenting program, for example, parents may blame their parenting failures following the completion of the program on their personal shortcomings, believing that they received effective and extensive help from professionals and yet still were not successful parents. This inappropriate sense of personal failure may influence the parents' self-view and consequently their ability to parent effectively (Chang, 2001).

The only way to judge services' effectiveness is to conduct methodologically sound assessments of them. Informal assessments by individuals who designed or conducted the services are likely to be problematic because they rely almost completely on subjective judgments that can be influenced by service providers' hopes that their efforts will be useful (Cone, 2001). Furthermore, as discussed earlier, informal assessments by program participants can be misleading, at least partly because participants may not be able to judge the influence that the program has had on them. Nevertheless, methodologically sound assessments do pose a number of challenges, as discussed below.

Outcome questions matched to research methods

Just as it is important to specify and assess the goals of an intervention, the assessment strategy must be matched to the goals of the assessment. If the objective of a postadoption service, for example, is to assist adoptive parents to feel connected to and supported by an agency, the assessment would properly focus on parents' assessment of the usefulness of the service and whether they felt that the professionals who provided the service were concerned about them. A self-report questionnaire would be an appropriate strategy. Alternatively, if the objective of a postadoption service is to make parents aware of the needs of certain children and provide them with skills to address those needs, the assessment should focus on the parents' knowledge and skills related to the issues presented during the program. An appropriate strategy to assess their knowledge may be a written test. An appropriate strategy to test their skills likely would include asking parents to respond to vignettes of children's behavior problems or to participate in role-play in which they respond to a troubled child. This type of assessment strategy is more complex and costly, but it may be essential to accurately assess parents' behavior. A program may have several goals, such as improving parenting skills and establishing a positive relationship between agency and family. In such cases, the evaluation should be comprised of several components, each of which is designed to assess specific aspects of the program.

Services versus rigorous assessment

A fundamental conflict that must be faced when assessing postadoption services is that methodologically sound assessments often constrain the ways in which services can be delivered. These constraints can limit the scope and/or the effectiveness of the services. The conflict between services and assessment manifests itself in two primary ways. First, the provision of services principally has a present focus, and the assessment of services principally has a future focus. Parents, for example, may need assistance with the challenges their children present or with problems they encounter with social service programs, schools, or other agencies. Although services often are provided with the intent that they will also influence future behavior, the service focus is primarily on thoughts, emotions, or behaviors in the present. Conversely, assessment focuses on current services with the goal of providing the most effective services in the future. While it is hoped that service recipients will be helped by the services they are receiving in the present, the principal focus of assessment is the accumulation of knowledge that will be useful in the future.

The second primary conflict is that the best practices for providing services often conflict with the best practices for assessing those services. The medical field is one of the best examples of a profession that has spent considerable effort assessing services. As one example, human trials are used as part of the process of testing a new drug that hypothetically will address a medical problem. Patients with a particular problem are asked if they are willing to participate in a randomly assigned study. They know that if they agree to participate, they will be randomly assigned either to receive the drug that scientists believe will be helpful or to receive a placebo that scientists know will not be helpful. Researchers in the medical field often purposefully give some patients an intervention that they know will not help them in order to assess whether other patients are helped by the intervention. (It should be noted that in many human trials, patients who receive the placebo are allowed to receive the experimental treatment if it is shown to be effective. Further, in some trials where the efficacy of a treatment is clear early in the experiment, the trial is stopped and all the participants are given the experimental treatment.) Much of the progress in developing specific, successful treatments for a wide range of physical ailments has resulted from medical researchers' willingness to engage in methodologically sound research. Certainly, most physicians are oriented toward the provision of services in the present, but almost all the services they provide have been developed through research with a future focus.

Most mental health professionals have been reluctant to follow the same path as physical medicine and use procedures primarily designed to assess the effectiveness of services. It would be difficult for many professionals to randomly assign some families to postadoption services and inform other families that they will not receive services. Even if service and no-service groups were created, many professionals would attempt to assign families who appear to most need services to the service groups and families who appear to have the least need to the no-service groups. Although this tendency may be ethically appropriate and is certainly understandable, the reluctance to implement random assignment, to a large degree, has resulted in only limited literature about service effectiveness. A primary focus on providing services to families in the present minimizes learning about service effectiveness and reduces the ability to provide services with documented effectiveness to families in the future. Researchers and practitioners may need to choose whether service delivery or service assessment is the primary goal of their work. It can be difficult to do both well. Strategies to accomplish this goal, however, are proposed in the next section.

With regard to the ethics of conducting methodologically sound research, it is reasonable to argue that a decision to withhold a service from some individuals in order to evaluate service effectiveness is ethically troubling only if it is known that the service would benefit the individuals from whom it is being withheld. The lack of clear knowledge about service effectiveness may mean that it is not unethical to withhold services from some individuals to assess service effectiveness. One could go even further and argue that the failure to pursue knowledge about service effectiveness in a methodologically sound way is unethical because researchers and practitioners have an ethical duty to provide the most effective services possible.

Toward Creating a Knowledge Base About Postadoption Services

To provide effective postadoption services, it is necessary to create a research-based literature that describes the effectiveness of different types of postadoption services for different types of adoptive families. Without this literature, postadoption services will be based only on professionals' own experiences or their judgments regarding programs developed by others without a clear indication that the programs are effective. Because extensive literature on the evaluation of postadoption services does not exist, professionals who create and deliver postadoption services currently rely on theory, their own or others' experiences, and the limited existing literature. The field requires a focus on the development of a methodologically sound postadoption services literature.

Creating a body of research literature on any topic involves the steady accumulation of research findings. No postadoption service or other intervention can be evaluated solely on the results of one or two studies. Each study of postadoption services will have limitations, and it is only through the accumulation of an array of studies, each with their own limitations, that an understanding of the effectiveness of an intervention can be created. Although individual studies may each have their own shortcomings, a series of studies must be developed in which all is done as well as possible. The development of a literature on postadoption services could be facilitated in several ways.

Shifting the Emphasis (Somewhat) from Service Provision to Service Assessment

Although decisions to assess the effectiveness of the intervention in a methodologically sound manner will enhance the body of knowledge about such interventions and their effectiveness, such an approach is likely to require changes in service delivery. This may include developing a willingness in the field to withhold or delay services to some families to assess the effectiveness of the services with other families.

Most medical research is carried out at universities or in teaching hospitals that receive funds from public or private agencies to conduct such research. As a result, many patients who agree to participate do not pay for the services they receive. Some patients may even receive inducements to participate, such as cash payments. Unfortunately, little money is available for research on postadoption services. Adoption funding tends to focus on increasing the number of adoptive families, and thus far, most public or private agencies have shown little interest in basic research on adoptive families or postadoption services. Because most research on adoption services is conducted through agencies, however, it is important to identify strategies that may make a methodologically sound assessment process more palatable to them.

Delaying services to some families

In many cases, agencies that create new postadoption services do not have the staff to provide such services to all of their clients. Random assignment of some families to a group for whom services will be delayed (by six months or one year, for example) and a subsequent comparison of the changes in the families who receive services with the families in the "services delayed" group can reveal the short-term benefits of the service. Such an approach would require program evaluators to conduct several assessments of both groups of families during the delay period, however, so that the rate of change in the two groups of families can be charted.

Cooperation between agencies

Agencies that are ready to provide a new type of postadoption service can partner with another agency that works with a similar population of families, and that also provides postadoption services. Statistical comparisons of family characteristics between the two agencies could help to determine the extent to which the families are similar. If the families are sufficiently similar so that statistical controls for any differences would be proper, families from the partner agency could be used as a no-treatment control group. Although this strategy presents several problems and is not as methodologically rigorous as one in which families from the same agency are randomly assigned to service and no-service groups, it could nevertheless be useful as an early evaluation of a postadoption intervention.

Adding or subtracting components of services

Postadoption services often include a wide range of treatment components. The effectiveness of some components can be judged by providing these services to some families and not to others. An agency, for example, that provides monthly parenting classes and on-call caseworkers for all adoptive families for one year postadoption might add monthly peer support groups for 50% (randomly chosen) of the families it serves. By comparing the functioning of the families over time, the agency could gauge whether the peer support groups enhanced the services that were provided already. Similarly, an agency that provides weekly parenting and support classes for adoptive families for one year postadoption could randomly assign some families to a group that received these classes only monthly. A comparison of the two groups could provide information regarding whether weekly classes were superior to monthly classes in terms of effectiveness.

Creating an Organization to Facilitate Research

A significant impediment to all adoption research is the difficulty of assembling a sufficiently large, homogeneous sample in a single geographic location. Adoption research that must rely on small- or moderate-sized samples of families that are quite different from each other can be problematic. As noted earlier, if families with very different characteristics who might respond quite differently to the services are included in the same sample, studies of postadoption services. Similar problems arise in other types of adoption research. In a study of adoptive families' attitudes about openness in adoption, for example, it may be that single-parent adoptive families responded to questions on openness differently than did two-parent families, or that transracial adoptive families responded to questions on openness differently than same-race families. In such a case, studying an adoption-related issue like openness with a sample that includes small numbers of many types of families is likely to be misleading. Because of problems such as this, the adoption research literature needs to be composed of a series of studies involving adoptive families with similar characteristics (such as, for example, single-parent families, families who adopt internationally, families with birth children, and families adopting medically fragile children). The difficulty, however, is that only researchers in major metropolitan areas may have access to large enough samples of families with similar characteristics. As a consequence, the formation of a comprehensive adoption-research literature has been hindered.

The solution rests on the willingness of a foundation or other organization to step forward to develop and maintain a process through which adoption researchers can work with adoption agencies from across the country to obtain large enough samples of families with the characteristics of interest. A researcher interested in the issues faced by single-parent families, for example, could use this process to find a sample of 100 or so single-parent adoptive families from across the country, a sample far larger than could be gathered in a single geographic location. This would provide opportunity for more researchers to complete methodically sound studies, thus promoting the field's ability to provide effective postadoption services.

Conclusion

Adoption experts often create postadoption services on the basis of current theories on child and family development. As shown by McCord (1978), however, these interventions can fail to meet their expected goals. It is only through methodologically rigorous assessments of postadoption services and other interventions that interventions that successfully achieve their goals can be distinguished from interventions that do not.

Because adoptive families will be aided only by effective interventions and, ethically, professionals are required to help the families with whom they are working, rigorous assessments must be integrated into postadoption services.

References

Chang, E. C. (Ed.). (2001). *Optimism & pessimism: Implications for theory, research, and practice.* Washington, DC: American Psychological Association.

Cone, J. D. (2001). *Evaluating outcomes: Empirical tools for effective practice.* Washington, DC: American Psychological Association.

Gliner, J. A., & Morgan, G. A. (2000). *Research methods in applied settings: An integrated approach to design and analysis.* Mahwah, N.J.: Lawrence Erlbaum.

McCord, J. (1978). A thirty-year follow-up of treatment effects. *American Psychologist, 33,* 284-289.

Mesibov, G. B., Adams, L. W., & Klinger, L. G. (1997). *Autism: Understanding the disorder.* New York: Plenum Press.

Reppucci, N. D., & Haugaard, J. J. (1989). Prevention of child sexual abuse: Myth or reality. *American Psychologist, 44,* 1266-1275.

Rind, B., Tromovitch, P., & Bauserman, R. (1998). A meta-analytic examination of assumed properties of child sexual abuse using college samples. *Psychological Bulletin, 124,* 22-53.

Roehl, J. A. (1996). *National process evaluation of Operation Weed and Seed.* Washington, DC: National Institute of Justice.

Sarason, S. B. (1975). Psychology to the Finland station in the heavenly city of the eighteenth-century philosophers. *American Psychologist, 30,* 1072-1080.

Scarr, S. (1985). Constructing psychology: Making facts and fables for our times. *American Psychologist, 40,* 499-512.

Conceptual Mapping THE Challenges FACED BY Adoptive Parents IN USING Postplacement Services

Scott D. Ryan, Alison Glover, and Scottye J. Cash

Approximately 46,000 children were adopted from the public child welfare system in the United States in 1999. Additionally, during that same time period, approximately 127,000 children in foster care were awaiting adoption (U.S. Department of Health and Human Services, 2001). Each year, increasing numbers of children enter the child welfare system, with a corresponding increase in the number of children who become available for adoption. As increasing numbers of children are adopted nationwide, several important areas of research clearly need to be explored further. Although research generally demonstrates that rates of adoption disruption are relatively low, disruption is concentrated among adoptions of children with special needs—the children who are overwhelmingly served by child welfare systems (McDonald, Lieberman, Partridge, & Hornby, 1991; Pinderhughes, 1998; Valdez & McNamara, 1994).

An additional concern is the provision of postadoption services to families who have adopted children. Postadoption services generally are viewed as the best preventive approach to adoption disruption. What constitutes postadoption services, however, is widely variable, and their effectiveness is generally not well researched. Nevertheless, postadoption service provision generally has minimized disruptions and ease burdens on adoptive families. As a result, public child welfare agencies have great interest in determining the mix of postadoption services that best meet the needs of adoptive families. To that end, this analysis describes a qualitative study of postadoption service needs and utilization from the perspective of adoptive parents. It explains the conceptual mapping research methodology used, presents the findings from the data that were collected, and summarizes the results. This study targets the unique challenges and experiences associated with being an adoptive parent, the barriers that adoptive parents face in pursuit of postplacement services, and their perspectives on how to overcome these barriers.

Concept Mapping

Concept mapping has been used widely in business and academia as a qualitative research and planning method. The process was developed by William Trochim (1989), who described concept mapping as a structured process that focuses on a topic or construct of interest, involves input from one or more participants, and produces an interpretable pictorial view of the participants' ideas and concepts and how they are interrelated. The process of concept mapping involves developing the focal question and selecting participants, generating statements in response to the focal question, sorting and rating the statements that are generated, analyzing the results statistically and computing concept maps, and using the maps to guide strategic planning.

Concept mapping has been used in a wide variety of settings to tackle widely varying topics and questions, including evaluation of school curriculum by teachers (Keith, 1989), the experience of depression among college students (Daughtry & Kunkel, 1993), and conceptualizations of the mental images of God (Kunkel, Cook, Meshel, Daughtry, & Hauenstein, 1999). It also has unique uses within the arenas of social services program evaluation and planning, and it has been used to evaluate various community programs such as Big Brothers/Big Sisters (Galvin, 1989) and mental health services and programs (Biegel, Johnsen & Shafran, 1997). Specifically within family and child welfare, concept mapping has been used to describe the difficulties faced by foster parents (Brown & Calder, 1999) and support the implementation of family-based, in-home services (Tracy, Biegel, & Johnsen, 1999). Finally, concept mapping has been used to evaluate the implementation and impact of community-based child welfare services (Falconer, Cash, & Ryan, 2001). No research was found, however, that used this methodology with adoptive parents to learn their views of the postplacement support needs.

Methodology

Sampling

Three districts in a U.S. southern state were selected for inclusion in the study. These districts represented the state's northern, central, and southern regions. The adoptive parents who participated in the study were systematically selected from each district's list of adoptive parents who received an adoption subsidy for their children through the state public child welfare agency. Additionally, private adoption providers in each of the three districts were offered the opportunity to contribute the names of potential adoptive families who may have been interested in participating.

For the northern district, the researchers obtained a list of 681 adopted children whose parents receive adoption subsidies on their behalf. Of those children, 504 children—representing 295 unique adoptive families—had complete contact information (including parent name, address, and telephone number). Additionally, an organizer for an adoptive support group provided the research team with a list of 16 additional families who had adopted through private agencies. Thus, 311 letters about the study were mailed to adoptive families within the northern district.

In the central district, the research team obtained a list of 1,273 children whose parents received an adoption subsidy on their behalf. Of those children, 1,116 had complete contact information. Parent information was matched to the children, yielding a total of 471 unique adoptive families. Three hundred families were randomly selected and letters about the study mailed to them.

In the southern district, researchers obtained a list of 1,355 children who were receiving adoption subsidies. Excluding duplicate listings and listings without complete contact information, there were a total of 708 unique adoptive families. From these, 300 adoptive parents were randomly selected and mailed letters informing them of the study.

Using the listing for each district, the potential participants (the adoptive parents who were sent introductory letters) were sorted by city of residence to ensure that individuals in underrepresented or outlying geographic areas were not excluded from the study. To that end, for each city of residence, research staff used a systematic sampling scheme and attempted to telephone every fourth person on the list. For cities with less than four potential participants in residence, researchers attempted to call at least one individual. If the contacted individual consented to participate, a research staff member completed the telephone interview and typed the respondent's answers into a prepared interview guide on a desktop computer. Upon completion of the interview, research staff explained the concept mapping process and invited the individual to participate in a subsequent sorting and rating session. If the individual declined to participate in the survey by telephone but stated an interest in participating in the study, the staff member offered to mail him or her the materials with a prepaid return envelope.

Using this method, staff member attempted to contact approximately 230 adoptive families from the 911 sent letters. However, because of unreturned messages, wrong numbers, and other impediments to obtaining contact, 91 ultimately were reached. Of those, 41 adoptive parents (45%) chose to participate in the first part of the study, and 12 completed the subsequent sorting and rating portion of the study. These sample groups will be discussed in depth later in this study.

Instruments and Data Collection

In addition to demographic questions, adoptive parents were asked four qualitative questions that asked them to describe three unique experiences or challenges that they faced raising their adopted child; three things that they did or supports they used to cope with the challenges they faced; three barriers or obstacles that hindered them, as adoptive parents, from accessing postplacement services and supports; and three ways that the barriers to postplacement services and supports could be overcome.

Compilation of responses

After the interviews were completed, the three-person research team compiled and reviewed the responses to each question. Each team member independently reviewed the responses and screened out duplicate statements. The research team members reviewed one another's lists and eliminated duplicate statements when the lists of all three members discarded that statement. If the count was not unanimous (such as when only two of the three team members agreed to keep or discard an item), the members further discussed the item, retaining the statement if consensus could not be reached. A conservative, inclusionary stance was taken to retain as much information as possible and to reduce any researcher bias. The number of statements for each of the four qualitative questions appears in Table 11-1.

Sorting

Twelve adoptive parents accepted the invitation to participate in the sorting process. Each was given a set of cards for each of the four qualitative questions. Each card contained an individual statement that had been generated through the response and compilation processes. Each participant was asked to sort the statements into conceptual clusters that were meaningful to him or her. Participants then were asked to place each cluster in a separate envelope. On the outside of the envelope, participants were asked to write a short name depicting the concept represented by the statements contained in the envelope.

Rating

After participants sorted the statements, they were asked to rate each statement, even if they had not personally experienced the event described. The statements were listed in a survey format, and each participant was asked to rate each statement on two separate seven-point Likert-type scales for each focal question (ranging from "1 = Not Very" to "7 = Very"). For Question 1 regarding unique experiences or challenges that parents faced raising their adopted child, adoptive parents ranked each statement on two bases:

- How common do you think this experience or challenge is for adoptive families?

- How well to you think the adoption professionals in your community have addressed this item?

For Question 2 regarding what adoptive parents did or what supports they used to cope with the challenges they faced in raising their adopted child, adoptive parents ranked each statement on two bases:

- How important do you think the item is as a way to assist adoptive families?

- How well do you think the adoption professionals in your community have supported or used this item?

For Question 3 regarding the barriers that hindered adoptive parents from accessing postplacement services and supports, adoptive parents ranked each statement on two bases:

- How important is it to address this barrier or obstacle to help adoptive families?

- How well do you think the adoption professionals in your community have addressed this item?

For Question 4 regarding the ways that the barriers to postplacement services and supports could be overcome, adoptive parents ranked each statement on two bases:

- How important do you think the item is in assisting adoptive families to access services?

TABLE 11–1

Amount of Statements Generated per Question by the Participant Groups

QUESTIONS	PARENTS
Question 1	
Total Generated	110
Duplicates	50
Final Statements	60
Question 2	
Total Generated	90
Duplicates	34
Final Statements	56
Question 3	
Total Generated	55
Duplicates	11
Final Statements	44
Question 4	
Total Generated	58
Duplicates	8
Final Statements	50

- How well do you think the adoption professionals in your community have addressed this item?

Each concept is represented by a cluster of related statements with assigned labels, such as "spirituality" or "behavioral issues." As such, each cluster will contain statements that are representative and descriptive of the underlying concept. The program will further assign layers based on the mean rating score derived from the participant scales. The number of layers for each conceptual cluster, as shown in the figures throughout this study, provides a reference regarding the importance of each concept in relation to other concepts presented in the same figure. For example, a cluster with four layers may be deemed more important or desirable than a cluster with two layers. Each cluster, therefore, can be compared conceptually to other clusters in the figures in relation to the ratings each concept received (for example, the level of importance versus the level of attention given by adoption professionals).

Analyses

Using Concept Mapping software (described more fully at http://conceptsystems.com), the researchers analyzed the collected data. The statistical technique, designed for the management and interpretation of certain types of qualitative data, uses multidimensional scaling and cluster analysis to derive a visual representation or map of the conceptual relationships among a set of qualitative statements. The concept map produced by the computer program depicts clusters of statements, each ostensibly representing an underlying concept.

In concept mapping, a multidimensional scaling analysis creates a map of points that represents the set of statements and is based on the similarity matrix that resulted from the sorting task. The output from the multidimensional scaling is a set of x-y values that can be plotted and includes some diagnostic statistical information. The plot is called the "point map" and consists of dots representing the statements, each identified by a number. A hierarchical cluster analysis is subsequently conducted to represent the conceptual domain in concept mapping. This analysis is used to group individual statements on the map into clusters of statements that presumably reflect similar concepts. The end product is the cluster map, which shows how the multidimensional scaling points were grouped.

A bridging value (ranging from zero to one) also is computed for each statement and cluster as part of the concept mapping analysis. The bridging value tells whether the statement was sorted with others that are close to it on the map or whether it was sorted with those located farther away. The bridging value helps interpret what content is associated with specific areas of the map. Statements with lower bridging values are better indicators of the meaning of the part of the map in which they are located than statements with higher bridging values. The program also computes the average bridging value for a cluster; clusters with higher average bridging values are more likely to "bridge" between other clusters on the map. Clusters with low average bridging values are usually more cohesive and easier to interpret, and they better reflect the content in that part of the map.

The software permits the researchers to specify the number of clusters desired in the solution. Starting with the default solution generated by the computer software, the statements in each cluster are reviewed. Possible solutions with greater and fewer numbers of clusters are successively reviewed. At each step, researchers decide whether splitting or combining the clusters may improve the conceptual clarity and overall bridging factors. After careful review of the various options, the researchers select the solution that provides the best fit with the data.

The researchers then assign a name to each cluster, based on the statements included in the cluster and the names given by the session participants. The individual statements in each cluster also are examined to assist in the interpretation of the underlying concept represented by the statements.

Findings: Characteristics of the Sample

The following discussion provides information on the characteristics of the telephone sample and the characteristics of the parents who participated in the sorting and rating procedures.

Characteristics of the Telephone Sample

Forty-one of the 91 adoptive parents contacted by telephone agreed to participate in the telephone interviews. As shown in Table 11-2, the participants were mostly female (85.4%), and their mean age was 49.2 years. More than half were Caucasian (58.5%),

TABLE 11-2

Characteristics of Adoptive Parents Who Generated Statements (n = 41)

GENDER	
Male	14.6%
Female	85.4%
AGE (YEARS)	
Mean (standard deviation)	49.2 (11.0)
RACE/ETHNICITY	
Caucasian	58.5%
African American	26.8%
Hispanic	4.9%
Native American	2.4%
Other	7.3%
EDUCATIONAL LEVEL	
Did not complete high school	4.9%
Completed high school/obtained GED	19.5%
Some college credit	31.7%
Bachelor's degree	14.6%
Master's degree	24.4%
Doctoral degree	4.9%
MARITAL STATUS	
Married	73.2%
Not married	26.8%
EMPLOYMENT STATUS	
Not currently employed	43.9%
Employed part time	7.3%
Employed fulltime	48.8%
FAMILY INCOME (ANNUAL)	
Mean (standard deviation)	$60,138 ($57,368)
NUMBER OF CHILDREN PER HOUSEHOLD	
Mean	2.51
NUMBER OF ADOPTED CHILDREN PER HOUSEHOLD	
Mean	1.88
SOURCE OF ADOPTION	
Public child welfare agency	80.5%
Private (domestic)	14.6%
Private (international)	4.9%
ADOPTION SUBSIDY (MONTHLY)	
Mean (standard deviation)	$311 ($148)

more than a quarter (26.8%) African American, 4.9%, Hispanic; 2.4%, Native American; and 7.3% were of another race or ethnicity. Educational levels varied widely. Slightly less than half of the participants (43.9%) had a bachelor's degree or higher (14.6% had a bachelor's degree; 24.4%, a master's; 4.9%, a doctoral). Almost 5% had not completed high school, 19.5% had completed high school or obtained a GED, and 31.7% had some college credit. Almost three-quarters of participants were married at the time of the interview. Approximately half of the participants (48.8%) were employed full-time. The mean family income was $60,138 per year, with a median income of $46,500.

Table 11-3 shows that the spouses of the participants (n = 30), who were overwhelmingly male (83.3%), had a mean age only slightly lower than the interviewees (49.1 years). Seventy percent were Caucasian; 23.3%, African American; 3.3%, Hispanic; and the remaining 3.3%, another race or ethnicity. Most spouses were employed full-time (86.7%). More than three-quarters had either some college credit or a college degree. Almost half had completed a bachelor's or higher degree (30% had a bachelor's degree; 13.3%, a master's; and 3.3%, a doctoral).

The participating parents had an average of 2.5 children (17 years old or younger) residing in the home and an average of 1.9 adopted children (Table 11-4). The gender distribution of the children was 57.3 % male and 42.7% female. The children's mean age was 9.5 years. Most children were Caucasian (42.7%) or African American (35.9%); 2.9% were Hispanic; and 18.4% were another race or ethnicity. The majority of the children in the participants' homes were adopted (74.8%), with smaller percentages being biological children (14.6%) and children in foster care (10.6%). The adoptive parents described almost 40% of the children as having behavioral needs and 30.1% having medical needs. The adopted children and children in foster care placed in the participants' homes had an average of 2.1 previous placements (with a range from no previous placements to 11 placements). On average, they had been with their current families 5.5 years. Most of the parents had adopted their oldest child from the public child welfare system (80.5%). Smaller percentages had adopted privately (14.6% domestically and 4.9% internationally). The average subsidy for children whose parents reported that they received subsidy was $311 per month.

Characteristics of the Sample: Sorting and Rating

As indicated earlier, 12 adoptive parents completed the sorting and rating process. All participants were females, and their mean age was 50.1 years (Table 11-5). Three-fourths were Caucasian, and equal percentages (8.3%) were African American, Hispanic, or "other." All had attended college: one-third had some college credit, one-quarter had a bachelor's degree, one-third had a master's degree, and 8.3% had a doctoral degree. One-third of the participants were married. One-half were employed full-time, and one-half were not currently employed. Their average annual family income was $66,313.

The participants' spouses (n = 8) were all Caucasian males who were employed full-time (Table 11-6). Their mean age was 48.9 years. More than one-third (35%) had completed some college credit, 50% had a bachelor's degree, and 2.5% had a doctoral degree.

TABLE 11–3

Characteristics of Spouses of Adoptive Parents Who Generated Statements (n= 30)

GENDER	
Male	83.3%
Female	16.7%
AGE (YEARS)	
Mean (standard deviation)	49.1 (8.7)
RACE/ETHNICITY	
Caucasian	70.0%
African American	23.3%
Hispanic	–
Native American	3.3%
Other	3.3%
EDUCATIONAL LEVEL	
Did not complete high school	3.3%
Completed high school/GED	16.7%
Completed technical school	3.3%
Some college credit	30.0%
Bachelor's degree	30.0%
Master's degree	13.3%
Doctoral degree	3.3%
EMPLOYMENT STATUS	
Not currently employed	10.0%
Employed part time	3.3%
Employed fulltime	86.7%

The children of the sorting and rating participants (N = 23) were 73.9% male and 26.1 % female (Table 11-7). Their mean age was 9.6 years. More than half were Caucasian (65.2%); 13%, African American; 8.7%, Hispanic; and 13%, another race or ethnicity. There was an average of 1.9 children in total and 1.3 adopted children per household. Almost two-thirds (65.2%) of the 23 children were adopted, 26.1 % were the biological children of the participants, and 8.7% were children in foster care. Their parents reported that nearly half of the children (47.8%) had some type of special medical need and that 43.7% had some type of special behavioral need. The adopted children and the children in foster care in this group had, on average, one placement prior to living with their current family. On average, this group of children had lived with their current families for 5.8 years. Three-fourths of the parents had adopted their oldest child from the public child welfare system, and smaller percentages had adopted privately (16.7% domestically and 8.3% internationally). For parents who reported that their children received adoption subsidies, the average subsidy was $249 per month.

TABLE 11–4

Characteristics of Children of Adoptive Parents Who Generated Statements (n = 103)

GENDER	
Male	57.3%
Female	42.7%
AGE (YEARS)	
Mean (standard deviation)	9.5 (4.9)
RACE/ETHNICITY	
Caucasian	42.7%
African American	35.9%
Hispanic	2.9%
Native American	–
Other	18.4%
RELATIONSHIP TO PARENT	
Birth child	14.6
Adopted child	74.8
Foster child	10.6
BEHAVIORAL SPECIAL NEEDS?	
Yes	39.8%
No	60.2%
MEDICAL SPECIAL NEEDS?	
Yes	30.1%
No	69.9%
NUMBER OF PREVIOUS PLACEMENTS	
Mean (adopted/foster children only)	2.1
HOW LONG CHILD HAS LIVED IN HOME (YEARS)	
Mean (adopted/foster children only)	5.5

Findings: Results of Concept Mapping

The following discussion addresses the results of concept mapping for each of the four qualitative questions. For each question, information first is presented regarding the statements made in response to the question and how the participants conceptually related these statements. Next, information is provided about the participants' ratings of the statements. Following this information, the data for each question is summarized and examined.

Question 1

The first question asked about adoptive parents about the unique experiences or challenges that parents faced in raising their adopted child.

TABLE 11–5

Characteristics of Adoptive Parents Who Sorted and Rated (n = 12)

GENDER	
Male	–
Female	100%
AGE (YEARS)	
Mean (standard deviation)	50.1 (12.2)
RACE/ETHNICITY	
Caucasian	75.0%
African American	8.3%
Hispanic	8.3%
Native American	–
Other	8.3%
EDUCATIONAL LEVEL	
Did not complete high school	–
Completed high school/obtained GED	–
Some college credit	33.3%
Bachelor's degree	25.0%
Master's degree	33.3%
Doctoral degree	8.3%
MARITAL STATUS	
Married	66.7%
Not married	33.3%
EMPLOYMENT STATUS	
Not currently employed	50.0%
Employed part time	–
Employed fulltime	50.0%
FAMILY INCOME (ANNUAL)	
Mean (standard deviation)	$66,313 ($29,317)
NUMBER OF CHILDREN PER HOUSEHOLD	
Mean	1.92
NUMBER OF ADOPTED CHILDREN PER HOUSEHOLD	
Mean	1.25
SOURCE OF ADOPTION	
Public child welfare agency	75.0%
Private (domestic)	16.7%
Private (international)	8.3%
ADOPTION SUBSIDY (MONTHLY)	
Mean (standard deviation)	$249 ($220)

TABLE 11–6

Characteristics of Spouses of Adoptive Parents Who Sorted and Rated (n = 8)

GENDER	
Male	100%
Female	–
AGE (YEARS)	
Mean (standard deviation)	48.9 (7.1)
RACE/ETHNICITY	
Caucasian	100%
EDUCATIONAL LEVEL	
Some college credit	37.5%
Bachelor's degree	50.0%
Master's degree	–
Doctoral degree	12.5%
EMPLOYMENT STATUS	
Employed fulltime	100%

The clusters

Seven clusters were identified from adoptive parents' qualitative statements. Sixty statements were generated, with cluster sizes ranging from 2 to 20 statements. The clusters presented with bridging factors from a low of .16 to a high of .66. These values are indicative of the tightness of this conceptual model. The seven clusters (named either by the participants or by the research team based on the statements in the concept clusters) were: "relating to the adoption agency" (.26), "relating to the biological family" (.66), "special issues stemming from the situation" (.61), "social issues and prejudice" (.55), "family integration" (.16), "positive parent–child interactions" (.38), and "rewards of adoption" (.20).

- *Cluster 1: Relating to the Adoption Agency.* This cluster focused on adoptive parents' challenges in dealing with their adoption agencies. Generally, statements in this cluster focused on a lack of services, the agency's dissemination of insufficient information, and limited communication between the adoptive family and adoption professionals. One statement, for example, was that adoptive parents faced "the challenge of getting good mental health care through Medicaid and through the limited post-adoption services offered."

- *Cluster 2: Relating to the Biological Family.* Adoptive parents identified unique issues in raising adopted children because the child has a different family of origin. The statements generated in the cluster indicated that adoptive parents either have a positive experience with their child's biological family (as evidenced by such statements as "maintaining a positive relationship with the child's birthparents") or a negative encounter in which adoptive parents view their child's biological family as an "interference."

TABLE 11–7

Characteristics of Children of Adoptive Parents Who Sorted and Rated (n = 23)

GENDER	
Male	73.9%
Female	26.1%
AGE (YEARS)	
Mean (standard deviation)	9.6 (5.7)
RACE/ETHNICITY	
Caucasian	65.2%
African American	13.0%
Hispanic	8.7%
Native American	–
Other	13.0%
RELATIONSHIP TO PARENT	
Birth child	26.1%
Adopted child	65.2%
Foster child	8.7%
BEHAVIORAL SPECIAL NEEDS?	
Yes	43.5%
No	56.5%
MEDICAL SPECIAL NEEDS?	
Yes	47.8%
No	52.2%
NUMBER OF PREVIOUS PLACEMENTS	
Mean (adopted/foster children only)	1.0
HOW LONG CHILD HAS LIVED IN HOME (YEARS)	
Mean (adopted/foster children only)	5.8

- *Cluster 3: Special Issues Stemming from the Situation.* This concept cluster reflected the various issues adoptive families face because of the nature of adoption. As examples, adoptive parents made statements that highlighted issues of cultural diversity and the need to understand the developmental cycles and issues particularly relevant for adopted children.

- *Cluster 4: Social Issues and Prejudice.* Adoptive parents identified the role society plays in relation to their experiences in raising adopted children. Adoptive parents noted that their own families and the general public have many different perspectives on adoption, ranging from curiosity to prejudice, depending on the circumstances of the particular adoption. One parent said a challenge she encountered in raising her adopted child was "explaining multiracial family composition to people outside the family."

Other adoptive parents noted social stigmatization that resulted in adopted "children being treated differently."

- *Cluster 5: Family Integration.* This concept cluster, which addressed family assimilation, had the lowest bridging factor in the cluster map, suggesting high cohesiveness of the statements. The statements showed that some adoptive families integrated relatively easily whereas others had more difficulty assimilating. Overall, adoptive parents seemed to view the family integration process in a realistic light, recognizing that they needed to be "patient" and "supportive" of their children through the integration process. This concept cluster also captured adoptive parents' feelings of anxiety, including "concerns regarding whether or not the child will accept you as a parent."

- *Cluster 6: Positive Parent–Child Interactions.* The predominant theme of this concept cluster was parent-child bonding. The parents' statements suggested a positive perspective of the bonding experience, as evidenced by comments such as, "children have a sense that they were chosen by their adoptive parents." A second theme was the importance that adoptive parents attributed to affirming their relationship with their child, as exemplified by the statement "convincing the child of the permanence of the family in spite of his past experiences."

- *Cluster 7: Rewards of Adoption.* Despite the difficult situations that can arise in the adoption process, this concept cluster highlighted the rewarding elements of adoption. Respondents' statements embodied concepts related to the positive experiences of adoptive parents. Statements included "satisfaction of seeing adoptive children develop and mature" and "seeing adoptive children thrive and grow within the new family and exceed the expectations of other people."

Ratings of the statements

As described earlier, participants were asked to rate each of the conceptual clusters using Likert scales, in which "1 = not very" and "7 = very."

- *Rating 1.1.* Participants were asked about each of the concept clusters: "How common do you think this experience or challenge is for adoptive parents?" There was wide variance between the highest and lowest rated clusters. Adoptive parents viewed rewards of adoption as extremely common with a rating of 6.45. Conversely, relating to the biological family (3.27) was seen as a relatively uncommon experience. The remaining clusters fell between these two values. Family integration (5.62), positive parent–child interactions (5.61), and special issues stemming from situation (5.25) were frequently experienced by adoptive parents (as evidenced by higher than average rating scores), while social issues and prejudice (4.78) and relating to the adoption agency (4.72) were perceived as less common (as reflected in lower scores). These findings, pictorially represented in Figure 11-1, are congruent with the notion that people view experiences at the micro-level as more relevant than pertinent issues further removed from them personally, such as issues at the macro-level.

- *Rating 1.2.* Adoptive parents also were asked to rate the statements on a seven-point scale based on how well adoption professionals have addressed the item. The cluster ratings ranged from a low of 3.07 to a moderate score of 4.63. Adoptive parents believed that adoption professionals had best addressed issues related to rewards of adoption (4.63) and that adoption professionals ignored many issues falling within the concept of relating to the adoption agency (3.07). The results are illustrated in Figure 11-2. As the moderate score of 4.63 exemplifies, adoptive parents generally perceived that adoption professionals had addressed their issues only to a limited extent.

Summary of the findings for Question 1

There was data consistency across the rating scales for Question 1. Despite the large rating variance between the scales (Rating 1.1 values 16 ranged from 6.45 to 3.27, and Rating 1.2 values ranged from 4.63 to 3.07), adoptive parents ranked the items in both scales similarly. Specifically, the cluster ratings for Rating 1.1 corresponded with the opinions expressed in Rating 1.2. Adoptive parents, for example, deemed rewards of adoption as a very common experience and stated that adoption professionals had addressed this notion well, particularly when compared to the issues in other clusters. Moreover, the rankings of the clusters based on the rating scores were very similar. The rankings in Rating 1.1 were Clusters 7, 5, 6, 3, 4, 1, and 2; the rankings in rating scale 1.2 were Clusters 7, 6, 5, 4, 3, 2, and 1. The similar rankings demonstrate the relative congruence between adoptive parents' views about the issues that are common and their views as to how well adoption professionals have addressed those issues.

Question 2

Question 2 asked adoptive parents what they did or what supports they used to cope with the challenges they faced in raising their adopted child.

The clusters

Adoptive parents' statements (56 in total) in response to this question grouped into seven clusters, ranging from 4 to 12 statements each. The clusters presented with bridging factors from .15 to .67. The seven clusters (named either by the participants or the research team based on the statements in the concept clusters) were: "support from within the family system" (.35), "social network" (.53), "self-education" (.55), "positive family environment" (.67), "religious or spiritual support" (.15), "support groups" (.41), and "professional supports" (.22).

- *Cluster 1: Support from Within the Family System.* The overarching theme of this cluster was the family as a social support network. Respondents, for example, referenced support from the "extended family," and described

FIGURE 11–1

Adoptive Parents Rating 1.1 Map

Rating 1: How common do you think this experience or challenge is for adoptive families?

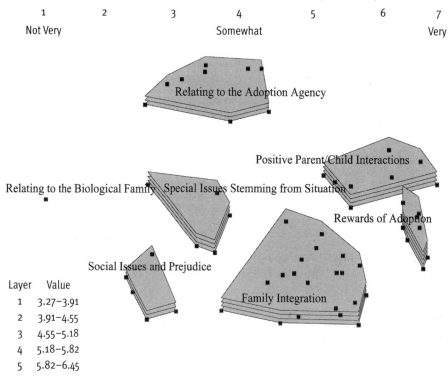

how the "husband and wife team together, to discuss decisions together, and support each other's decisions." Adoptive parents also highlighted the importance of integrating the child into the family by "reassuring the child that you love him and that he is a permanent part of the family."

- *Cluster 2: Social Network.* This cluster captured the role played by support systems external to the family in managing the challenges that adoptive parents encounter. Specifically, adoptive parents noted the usefulness of "school activities" and "leisure activities." Adoptive parents identified a range of social networks that assisted them in improving the quality of family interactions.

- *Cluster 3: Self-Education.* Adoptive parents indicated that taking a proactive role in self-education was a useful method for coping with the challenges that they experience. Cluster statements described such activities as "read[ing] about parenting" and "seek[ing] out information regarding adoption."

- *Cluster 4: Positive Family Environment.* Adoptive parents clustered statements together that illustrated a positive family environment as characterized by

FIGURE 11–2

Adoptive Parents Rating 1.2 Map

Rating 2: How well do you think the item has been addressed by the adoption professionals in your community?

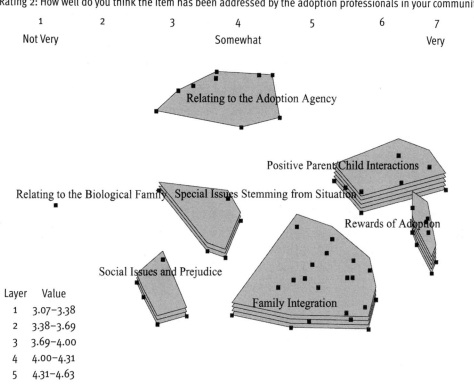

1	2	3	4	5	6	7
Not Very			Somewhat			Very

Layer   Value
1   3.07–3.38
2   3.38–3.69
3   3.69–4.00
4   4.00–4.31
5   4.31–4.63

warmth and consistency and open relationships within the adoptive family. Statements included adoptive parents' focus on being "very patient with the child" and "taking immediate action to correct problems."

- *Cluster 5: Religious or Spiritual Support.* This cluster included statements that highlighted spirituality as a coping mechanism for adoptive parents. The dominant themes in the cluster were the roles that faith, prayer, social support from the church, and a relationship with God played in adoptive parents' everyday lives. As evidenced by the low bridging number, adoptive parents clustered these statements together consistently. Further, the individual statement bridging factors, which ranged from .00 to .52, lent additional credence to the interconnectedness between spirituality and the methods that adoptive parents specifically use in coping with challenges.

- *Cluster 6. Support Groups.* This cluster focused on both formal and informal support groups for adoptive parents. Adoptive parents recognized the significance of maintaining and building emotional relationships with other adoptive parents. Support was viewed as reciprocal, as exemplified by the statement that adoptive parents "seek and give support to other adoptive families."

- *Cluster 7: Professional Supports.* Parents indicated that tangible supports, such as Medicaid, were helpful to them as they coped with the challenges they face as adoptive parents. Other statements focused on professional supports such as speech therapy, counseling, services provided by education professionals, and medical services, as well as the supports that adoption professionals provide to parents.

Ratings of the statements

As described earlier, participants were asked to rate each of the conceptual clusters using Likert scales.

- *Rating 2.1.* The first rating scale asked respondents to rate the importance of each item in assisting adoptive parents. Figure 11-3 shows that the highest average was 6.64 and the lowest was 4.93. In rank order, the following concepts were rated as important (based on average priority rating): "support from within the family system" (6.64), "religious or spiritual support" (5.53), "social network" (5.51), "positive family environment" (5.40), "self-education" (5.02), "professional supports" (4.95), and "support groups" (4.93). The high ratings associated with support from within the family system and religious or spiritual support (particularly when compared to the ratings for support groups and professional supports) highlight family solidarity and spiritual connection as cornerstones for families as they attempt to persevere through difficult times. These ratings infer that formal supports were perceived as necessary, although secondary to the relationships within the family unit.

- *Rating 2.2.* Adoptive parents also were asked to rate statements based on how well each item was supported or used by adoption professionals. Figure 11-4 shows that the cluster ratings ranged from a low of 2.20 to a high of 3.76. Generally, the ratings for this scale were very low, indicating that adoptive parents saw the need for improvement in the assistance provided by adoption professionals. In rank order (based on average priority ratings), the clusters received the following ratings: support from within the family system (3.59), professional supports (3.76), self-education (3.48), positive family environment (3.32), support groups (3.12), social network (2.52), and religious or spiritual support (2.20). These ratings suggest that adoptive parents believed adoption professionals had provided tangible services minimally to only adequately, as evidenced by the rating for professional supports. Adoptive parents felt adoption professionals had focused their energies on building support from within the family system and on self-education. The ratings infer that resources connected with religious or spiritual support (2.20) had been relatively untapped by adoption professionals.

FIGURE 11-3

Adoptive Parents Rating 2.1 Map

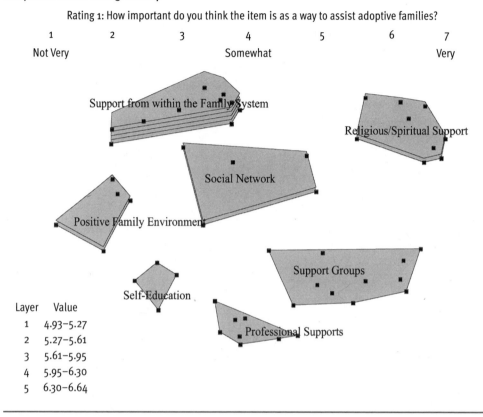

Rating 1: How important do you think the item is as a way to assist adoptive families?

| 1 | 2 | 3 | 4 | 5 | 6 | 7 |
| Not Very | | | Somewhat | | | Very |

Layer | Value
1 | 4.93–5.27
2 | 5.27–5.61
3 | 5.61–5.95
4 | 5.95–6.30
5 | 6.30–6.64

Summary of the findings for Question 2

A comparison of the data from Ratings 2.1 and 2.2 indicates some large disparities. Adoptive parents identified areas that could be enhanced by professionals in the adoption community. Cluster 1 (support from within the family system) had a rating scale difference of 3.05, suggesting that although adoptive parents deemed these items important, they believed that adoption professionals had not used resources in this cluster to the fullest potential. Cluster 2 (social network) had a difference of 2.99, suggesting that professionals had not wholly encouraged the development of social networks. Cluster 3 (self-education) had the second lowest rating scale difference (1.54), indicating that professionals in the adoption community are beginning to use this as a resource. Cluster 4 (positive family environment) had a 2.08 difference, suggesting that there is ample need for further development of resources in this area to promote a positive family environment. Cluster 5 (religious or spiritual support) had the largest rating scale difference at 3.33, demonstrating a great need for adoption professionals to support and use the spiritual aspect of most adoptive parents' lives. Cluster 6 (support groups) had a difference of 1.81 (the third lowest difference of all the clusters). This

FIGURE 11–4

Adoptive Parents Rating 2.2 Map

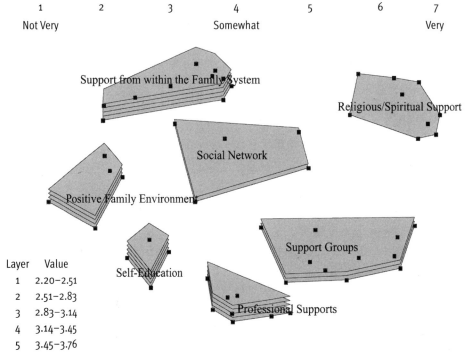

Rating 2: How well do you think the item has been supported and used by the adoption professionals in your community?

1	2	3	4	5	6	7
Not Very			Somewhat			Very

Support from within the Family System

Religious/Spiritual Support

Social Network

Positive Family Environment

Layer	Value
1	2.20–2.51
2	2.51–2.83
3	2.83–3.14
4	3.14–3.45
5	3.45–3.76

Self-Education

Support Groups

Professional Supports

cluster, surprisingly, was rated as the least important by adoptive parents. Finally, Cluster 7 (professional supports) had the lowest rating scale difference at 1.19, indicating that adoption professionals had been relatively attentive to items involving professional support, such as Medicaid.

There are some glaring incongruities between items that adoptive parents deemed important and their views of which items adoption professionals were supporting and using. In particular, adoptive parents stated that there was insufficient emphasis on support from within the family system and religious or spiritual support as viable methods of assisting families.

Question 3

The third question asked adoptive parents to identify the barriers they experienced in accessing postplacement services and supports.

The clusters

Four clusters were identified from the 44 statements of adoptive parents. Cluster sizes ranged from 5 to 19 statements. The clusters presented bridging factors from a low of

.24 to a high of .49. The four clusters (named either by the participants or by the research team based on the statements in the concept clusters) were "information on services" (.49), "availability and accessibility of services" (.37), "medical or behavioral service expenses" (.38), and "agency challenges" (.24).

- *Cluster 1: Information on Services.* Adoptive parents cited a lack of service information as a barrier to accessing postplacement services and supports. Specifically, statements indicated that adoptive parents "don't know who to talk to or where to start looking" and "there is a general lack of postplacement services and follow-up for children."

- *Cluster 2: Availability and Accessibility of Services.* Adoptive parents emphasized the lack of service availability and accessibility. They focused on the uneven distribution of services (with statements on the lack of availability of postadoption services in rural areas) and the fact that even when services were available, they often were inaccessible to the general public. One adoptive parent stated, "It's hard to get to appointments because the public transportation doesn't go as far as it's needed."

- *Cluster 3: Medical or Behavioral Service Expenses.* This cluster focused on the financial burden that many adoptive parents face, particularly in relation to the cost of medical and behavioral services and Medicaid limitations. Adoptive parents recognized the benefits of Medicaid, as reflected in the statement, "If counseling was needed, and Medicaid didn't pay, it would be difficult to have the service." Nonetheless, adoptive parents reported difficulties "finding a child psychiatrist that accepts Medicaid and new patients" and noted the lack of "seasoned mental health professionals" affiliated with Medicaid.

- *Cluster 4: Agency Challenges.* This cluster contained statements related to the challenges adoptive parents face as they attempt to work with their agencies. The bridging factor was .24, which demonstrated a cohesive concept. The overarching theme was that adoptive parents viewed the adoption agency as rather unresponsive to their needs. This perception manifested itself in several forms. First, adoptive parents suggested that current "training and other education courses for adoptive/foster parents do not address the real problems and issues facing adoptive families." Second, adoptive parents felt that "the agency is not aware of the scope of problems facing adoptive families." Finally, adoptive parents noted "worker caseloads are too high to allow individual attention for children and prompt delivery of services."

Ratings of the statements

As described earlier, participants were asked to rate each of the conceptual clusters using Likert scales.

- *Rating 3.1.* The first rating scale asked adoptive parents to rate the statements based on the importance of the identified barrier. Figure 11-5 shows that the cluster ratings ranged from 5.32 to 6.20, indicating that all of the barriers were moderately important to adoptive parents and should be addressed. In Cluster 1 (information on services), the average rating was 6.20, with a range of 6.45 to 5.91. Adoptive parents viewed lack of information regarding where to seek help as a major challenge to accessing postadoption services. In Cluster 2 (availability and accessibility of services), the average rating was 5.32, with a range of 5.91 to 4.00. In this cluster, the lack of local support groups was identified as a barrier to postplacement services, and the increase in gas prices was considered the easiest obstacle to overcome. Difficulties with Medicaid were viewed as a significant barrier in Cluster 3 (medical or behavioral service expenses), where the average rating was 5.54, with a range of 6.00 to 4.82. In Cluster 4 (agency challenges), the average rating was 5.42, with a range of 6.18 to 3.36. In this cluster, the two highest rated barriers were the lack of information for parents adopting privately and "worker's lack of knowledge regarding services that the child will be eligible to receive after the adoption." Having a set payment schedule for adoption subsidy was considered the least important obstacle facing adoptive parents.

- *Rating 3.2.* Adoptive parents also were asked to rate each statement based on how well a particular item had been addressed by adoption professionals in the community. Figure 11-6 shows that the cluster ratings ranged from a low of 2.71 to a high 3.10, scores that suggest that there is a significant need for improvement in all areas. The ratings for Cluster 1 (average 2.85, with a range of 3.36 to 2.55) indicated that adoption professionals are beginning to assist adoptive parents in learning how to access information about the services they need. The "lack of formal opportunities for postadoption services offered by the agency," however, was an area that adoptive parents believed still required greater attention from adoption professionals. The ratings for Cluster 2 (average 2.71, with a range of 3.45 to 1.91), which addressed service availability and accessibility, demonstrated that professionals in the adoption community recognized the issue of "no local adoptive support group," but efforts to provide such resources are still in the developing stage. Public transportation, rated 1.91 as a barrier, appears to require attention. The ratings for Cluster 3 (average 2.93, with a range of 3.27 to 2.45), regarding medical and behavioral service costs, indicated that the number of seasoned mental health professionals who accept Medicaid needs to be increased. Adoptive parents also reported ongoing "difficulties with medical insurance and service providers." The ratings for Cluster 4 (average 3.10, with a range of 3.73 to 2.36), regarding agency challenges, indicated that adoption professionals are beginning to address certain issues: Adoptive parents noted that adoption professionals are now "allowing siblings who were adopted to

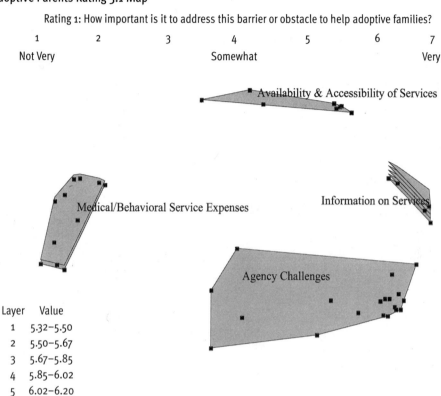

FIGURE 11–5

Adoptive Parents Rating 3.1 Map

Rating 1: How important is it to address this barrier or obstacle to help adoptive families?

1	2	3	4	5	6	7
Not Very			Somewhat			Very

Availability & Accessibility of Services

Medical/Behavioral Service Expenses

Information on Services

Agency Challenges

Layer	Value
1	5.32–5.50
2	5.50–5.67
3	5.67–5.85
4	5.85–6.02
5	6.02–6.20

different families to remain in contact," improving training and education courses, and providing adoption subsidy on a regular schedule, as evidenced by ratings of 3.73 in all three areas.

Summary of the findings for Question 3

There was a substantial difference between the ratings of the many barriers identified by adoptive parents and the extent to which adoptive parents perceived adoption professionals were addressing these barriers. Despite the difference in the overall averages (5.62 for rating scale 3.1 and 2.90 for rating scale 3.2), it is evident that adoption professionals are attempting to respond to the needs of adoptive parents. The greatest needs appear, however, to be in the areas of increased information regarding services and assistance with medical or behavioral service expenses.

Question 4

Question 4 asked adoptive parents about the ways that the barriers to postadoption services and supports could be overcome.

FIGURE 11-6

Adoptive Parents Rating 3.2 Map

Rating 2: How well has this item been addressed by the adoption professionals in your community?

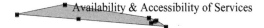

1	2	3	4	5	6	7
Not Very			Somewhat			Very

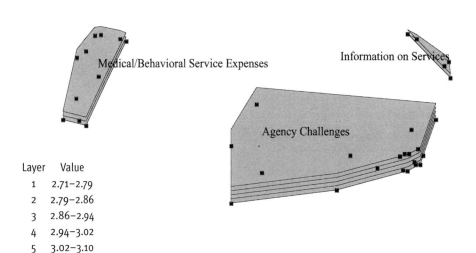

Layer	Value
1	2.71–2.79
2	2.79–2.86
3	2.86–2.94
4	2.94–3.02
5	3.02–3.10

The clusters

Five clusters were identified from the 50 statements made by adoptive parents. Cluster sizes ranged from 5 to 17 statements. The clusters presented bridging factors from a low of .19 to a high of .74. The five clusters (named either by the participants or by the research team based on the statements in the concept clusters) were "create or enhance agency services" (.26), "create or enhance support group options" (.19), "create or enhance training and education options" (.70), "create or enhance continuum of care" (.57), and "expanded financial supports" (.74).

- *Cluster 1: Create or Enhance Agency Services*. Adoptive parents identified several methods for overcoming barriers to postadoption services. Most suggestions focused on establishing a postadoption service unit, augmenting follow-up procedures, and increasing worker responsiveness to parents. Adoptive parents specifically suggested having a "contact person within the agency after the adoption is finalized for general questions and difficulties" and longitudinal follow-up that included "workers returning phone calls."

- *Cluster 2: Create or Enhance Support Group Options.* The low bridging number (.19) of this cluster reflected its conceptual cohesiveness. Adoptive parents clustered together statements about support groups, and a dominant theme was the need to create and enhance existing support groups. Adoptive parents also emphasized the importance of locating support groups in rural areas and other remote locations.

- *Cluster 3: Create or Enhance Training and Education Options.* In spite of the high bridging factor (.70), the general theme of this cluster was the need to increase training for adoptive parents and adoption professionals. Adoptive parents focused on the need for greater understanding of issues associated with "interracial adoption" and "behavioral problems."

- *Cluster 4: Create or Enhance Continuum of Care.* This cluster focused on the need to develop a broader continuum of care. Adoptive parents suggested that the continuum should include preventive measures, particularly if children have known family histories of substance abuse, residential treatment, and respite care. The development of such resources was seen as key to overcoming postadoption service barriers and ensuring permanency.

- *Cluster 5: Expanded Financial Supports.* Parents suggested that an increase in financial supports would ease some of the barriers that they faced in raising their adopted children. Adoptive parents specifically mentioned "better medical and dental coverage" and "more support and counseling for adoptive children."

Ratings of the statements

As described earlier, participants were asked to rate each of the conceptual clusters using Likert scales.

- *Rating 4.1.* The first scale asked adoptive parents to rate the statements regarding the importance of the approach in overcoming barriers they experienced. As Figure 7 shows, the cluster ratings ranged from 4.87 to 6.03, signifying that each of the clusters had more than moderate importance. In Cluster 1 (create or enhance agency services, with an average rating of 5.60 and a range of 3.73 to 6.55), adoptive parents rated one method quite highly: "the state could produce literature on all services that are available, how to obtain the service, and other relevant information." They rated monthly or quarterly "check-ups" by adoption professionals as relatively unimportant. In Cluster 2 (create or enhance support group options, with an average rating of 5.3 8 and a range of 4.18 to 6.00), adoptive parents rated a higher level of publicity for adoption support groups and available services as most important. In Cluster 3 (create or enhance training and education Options, with an average of 6.03 and a range 5.55 to 6.55), adoptive parents emphasized the importance of "better training for adoptive parents regarding the special needs of children who have been sexually abused." They regarded education as an important tool in overcoming access barriers to support resources. In Cluster 4 (create or enhance continuum of care, with an rating of 4.87 and a range of 4.87 to 6.27), adoptive parents identified a substantial need for "competent, seasoned mental health professionals that have experience with adoption issues on a sliding fee scale." In contrast, they did not perceive clothing allowances as important to overcoming obstacles. Finally, in Cluster 5 (expanded financial supports, with an average rating of 5.20 and a range of 3.73 to 6.45), adoptive parents identified the need for more extensive services for children with histories of sexual abuse.

- *Rating 4.2.* The second scale asked adoptive parents to rate the statements on how well each item had been addressed by adoption professionals. Figure 11-8 shows that the cluster ratings ranged from a low of 2.45 to a high of 2.82. The very low rating scores indicated that adoptive parents did not believe that adoption professionals had adequately addressed the five areas. Cluster 1, regarding agency services, had an average rating of 2.56 and a range of 2.00 to 3.36. Adoptive parents noted that adoption professionals were only mildly responsive in terms of returning phone calls, the item with the highest rating within the cluster. Cluster 2, regarding support group options, had an average rating of 2.74 and a range of 2.18 to 3.45. These ratings indicated that adoption professionals had not developed parent support groups well, especially in outlying locations. Cluster 3, regarding training and education, had an average rating of 2.82 with a range of 2.27 to 3.09. The ratings demonstrated that adoption professionals were only minimally acknowledging the importance of training and education options. Cluster 4, regarding a continuum of care, had an average rating of 2.45 with a range of 1.55 to 3.18. This cluster contained a variety of items which adoptive parents perceived as poorly addressed by adoption professionals. Cluster 5, regarding financial supports, had an average rating of 2.82 with a range of 2.27 to 3.36. Adoptive parents stated that adoption professionals had not adequately responded to families' needs for medical and dental coverage.

Summary of the findings for Question 4

On average, there was a difference of 2.74 between adoptive parents' ratings of the importance of each item as a way of overcoming the barriers to postadoption services and their perceptions of adoption professionals' efforts in assisting them in overcoming each of these barriers. Although there was clearly a discrepancy between the solutions suggested by adoptive parents and the actions taken by the professional community, there was commonalty. Adoptive parents, for example, viewed training and education as important methods for overcoming barriers and perceived these approaches as a priority for adoption professionals.

FIGURE 11-7

Adoptive Parents Rating 4.1 Map

Rating 1: How important do you think the Item is in assisting adoptive families to acess services?

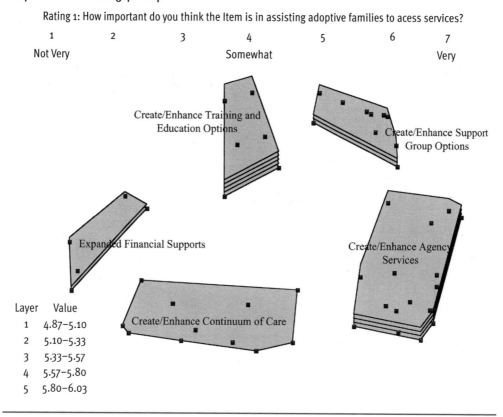

| 1 | 2 | 3 | 4 | 5 | 6 | 7 |
| Not Very | | | Somewhat | | | Very |

Create/Enhance Training and Education Options

Create/Enhance Support Group Options

Expanded Financial Supports

Create/Enhance Agency Services

Layer	Value
1	4.87–5.10
2	5.10–5.33
3	5.33–5.57
4	5.57–5.80
5	5.80–6.03

Create/Enhance Continuum of Care

Discussion

The adoption process is a time of change for both parents and the children. Adoptions, on the whole, are a time of joy and excitement as new families are created. Unsurprisingly, adoptive parents' statements centered around the rewards of the adoption, the importance of family integration, and the interactions that parents had with their children and their children with them. Although not specifically investigated in this study, these issues arise in considerations related to the success of adoption and the stabilization of adoptive families. In this study, approximately one-fourth of the children had behavioral problems, and the children had had an average of two placements before placement with the families who adopted them. Success in adoption can be defined, in its most simple form, as the child remaining in the home. As a result, the fact that adoptive families identified issues associated with this outcome as important is reasonable. This study showed that adoptive parents viewed concepts more closely related to the micro-level (the child, the home, and the adoption) as best addressed by adoption professionals. On the other hand, they viewed issues that were more macro-oriented

FIGURE 11-8

Adoptive Parents Rating 4.2 Map

Rating 2: How well do you think the item has been addressed by the adoption professionals in your community?

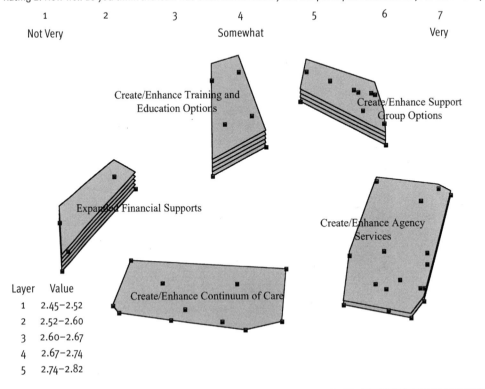

Layer	Value
1	2.45–2.52
2	2.52–2.60
3	2.60–2.67
4	2.67–2.74
5	2.74–2.82

(issues related to the adoption agency, professional service provision, and Medicaid) as inadequately addressed by adoption professionals.

Similarly, the supports that adoptive families viewed as important were distinctly different, depending on whether the supports were at the micro-level (familial) or at the macro-level (larger systemic support). Adoptive families perceived that they received only minimal support and that the greatest support came from the family system itself. A common theme in the responses to all four questions was the importance of support for adoptive parents: continuing support throughout the child's life and continuing even after the child reaches adulthood, support specific to their needs as adoptive parents, and support at both the formal and informal levels.

This study produced many important findings, but, like all research, it had several limitations. The findings represent the opinions, thoughts, and feelings of adoptive parents who participated in interviews and the sorting and rating sessions. As such, the findings cannot be generalized to the overall population of adoptive parents. In addition, the findings are cross-sectional and present a snapshot at the time of data collection. Data collected at other points in time may have produced different statements, clusters, or ratings. As a consequence, the ratings cannot be necessarily generalized to all adoptive parents, adopted children, or the adoption professionals who serve these families. Finally, the ratings provide only one picture of the subject groups and the challenges they face, their sources of support, and the methods that they use (or need) to overcome the identified barriers. The theoretical measures that were used sought participants' subjective views about what had occurred in the past and what should occur, as opposed to what actually has happened. Additional evaluation methods can and should be employed to gain a multifaceted view of the importance of families' needs and how best to address those needs.

Within these limitations, households without telephones were not represented in this study. Adoptive families living in poverty without an active telephone (families who arguably may be in the greatest need of postadoption services and supports) were not contacted. Self-selection bias (the characteristics potential subjects may have that lead to their inclusion or exclusion from the study) also affected this study. As an example, one adoptive parent briefly responded to the research staff by e-mail, expressing her regret that she did not have time to complete the sorting and rating task. Full-time employment and the challenges of raising an adopted child with special needs did not allow her the time to participate.

Finally, concept mapping can be a difficult process for participants, both in terms of the content and the actual tasks involved. Concept mapping requires specific cognitive abilities, including English literacy, sufficient reading comprehension, and the capacity for abstract thought. It is possible that some individuals who received information on the study did not understand the process fully and, as a result, did not participate. Data are not available to determine if the individuals who participated were significantly different from their respective adoption cohorts.

Recommendations

Based on the needs and ideas expressed by participants in this study, several recommendations are advanced:

1. *Continued support for adoptive families and adopted children should be provided.* Adoptive parents consistently noted that tangible supports for their family should not end when their child reaches 18 years old. Specifically, adoptive parents felt that their adopted children's eligibility for benefits (Medicaid and subsidies) should continue after they reach 18. They noted that some of their children, because of past experiences, are not at the same developmental or educational stage as their peers and continued support was key to their children's success as adults.

2. *Adoptive parents should be involved in the development of postadoption services and supports*. Parents want to be treated as partners in the adoption process. As experts on their own family situation, they should be treated as professionals in the helping system. Their continual involvement can promote success in making the changes that are needed in service programs and enhancing the success of adoptions.

3. *Social networking, both formal and informal, should be enhanced.* Social networks can be promoted through the development of a website for adoptive parents and adopted children. Such a website could provide a message board for parents and links with adoption professionals. Technology provides considerable flexibility and creativity for connecting groups who share common interests and needs.

4. *Greater emphasis should be placed on spirituality as support.* The study identified the valuable role of religion or spirituality as a means of support for adoptive families. Adoptive parents rated spirituality as second only to the family system as a support. Adoptive parents, however, ranked spirituality as the resource least well developed or used by adoption professionals. It is important to work holistically with families, and to that end, adoption professionals should move beyond the traditional biopsychosocial model and incorporate the spiritual needs of the family. Adoption professionals can partner with local churches and conduct workshops on adoption issues with congregations.

5. *Centralized information and referral systems should be developed.* Adoptive parents in this study highlighted the fact that there was no system that served as a central source of information and referral. A postadoption hotline staffed by adoptive parents and social workers is needed to provide families with information or refer families to services as needed.

6. *Mentoring programs should be established.* Mentoring programs can benefit adoptive families by helping them as they transition through the changes that are associated with adoption. Such programs often use volunteers to assist and provide support for families, with the goals of maintaining the family and ensuring child well being.

7. *Reality-based training should be provided.* In this study, some adoptive parents expressed their need for updated training on adoptive parenting. Such training should go beyond the traditional didactic approach used to prepare individuals to become adoptive parents. It should include such topics as the lifelong nature of adoption; what is "success" in adoption; the setbacks that can be anticipated; the factors that influence attachment and lead to adoption disruption; relationship building; developmentally appropriate and empirically based interventions; the differences in how adoptive families and biological families interact; discussion about adoption with the family's social support network of friends, family, and coworkers; and available resources. Such training should stress, particularly for new adoptive parents, that it is safe to ask questions and to acknowledge their struggles with the many issues associated with adoption.

Conclusion

Overall, the concept mapping process produced a significant amount of data that reflect adoptive parents' perceptions about the efforts of adoption professionals to assist and support them. The participants identified a number of concepts and ideas in connection with their postadoption needs. Yet, when asked how well adoption professionals were assisting them in meeting the challenges they faced, they gave professional efforts fairly low scores, reflecting their views that there is a need for improvement. As a theoretical measure, however, these data are the opinions of the respondents and that "real life" experiences may be significantly different. It may be as important, therefore, to educate the respondent populations on the actual situation as it is to address the situation itself. While some of the needed services exist, the adoptive parents may not be aware because of insufficient marketing. A dialogue may be initiated to identify areas for improvement, with a two-pronged effort: (1) education and communication between families and professionals regarding the issues identified in this study, and (2) specific attention to the needs that families perceive as inadequately addressed. Based on the data, adoption professionals and adoptive parents clearly are extremely invested in the success of adoptions. This dedication can act as a building block for future collaboration to improve existing adoption policies and practices.

References

Brown, J., & Calder, P. (1999). Concept mapping the challenges faced by foster parents. *Children and Youth Services Review, 21*(6), 481–495.

Biegel, D., Johnsen, J., & Shafran, R. (1997). Overcoming barriers faced by African-American families with a family member with mental illness. *Family Relations, 46*(2), 163–178.

Daughtry, D., & Kunkel, M. (1993). Experience of depression among college students: A concept map. *Journal of Counseling Psychology, 40*(3), 316–323.

Falconer, M., Cash, S., & Ryan, S. (2001). *Evaluation of community-based care in foster care and related services in Florida.* Tallahassee, FL: Department of Children and Families.

Galvin, P. (1989). Concept mapping for planning and evaluation of a Big Brother/Big Sister program. *Evaluation and Program Planning, 12*(1), 53–57.

Keith, D. (1989). Refining concept maps: Methodological issues and an example. *Evaluation and Program Planning, 12*(1), 75–80.

Kunkel, M., Cook, S., Meshel, D., Daughtry, D., & Hauenstein, A. (1999). God images: A concept map. *Journal for the Scientific Study of Religion, 38*(2), 193–202.

McDonald, T., Lieberman, A., Partridge, S., & Hornby, H. (1991). Assessing the role of agency services in reducing adoption disruptions. *Children and Youth Services Review, 13*, 425–238.

Pinderhughes, E. (1998). Short term placement outcomes for children adopted after age five. *Children and Youth Services Review, 20*(3), 223–249.

Tracy, E., Biegel, D., & Johnsen, J. (1999). *Impact of the family stability incentive fund program: A two year evaluative study.* Cleveland, OH: Cuyahoga County Community Mental Health Research Institute, Mandel School of Applied Social Sciences, Case Western Reserve University.

Trochim, W. (1989). An introduction to concept mapping for planning and evaluation. *Evaluation and Program Planning, 12*(1), 1–6.

U.S. Department of Health and Human Services (2001). *The AFCARS report: Interim fiscal year 1999 estimates as of June 2001.* [Online]. Accessed October 10, 2005, at http://www.acf.dhhs.gov/programs/cb/publications/afcars/june2001.htm

Valdez, G., & McNamara, J. (1994). Matching to prevent adoption disruption. *Child and Adolescent Social Work Journal, 11*(5), 391–403.

SECTION FOUR

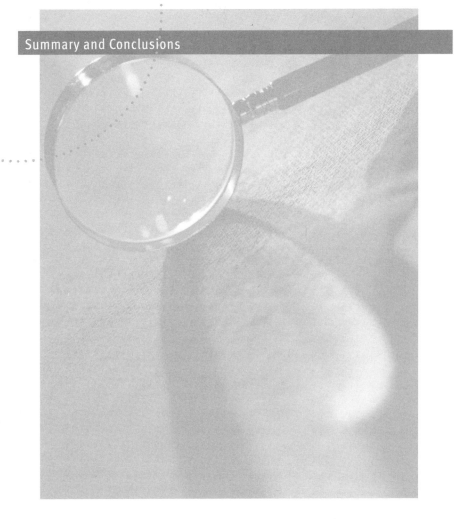

Summary and Conclusions

RESEARCH ON Postadoption Services:
IMPLICATIONS FOR
Practice, Program Development,
AND Policy

Madelyn Freundlich

As a result of recent policy and practice developments that have placed greater emphasis on adoption, attention has focused on the services and supports that children and families need following adoption. A growing body of research addresses the postadoption service needs of children and their families and the characteristics of effective programs. Most of these studies have considered the service needs of families who adopt children from the foster care system in this country, although others have recognized that families who adopt internationally often have similar needs (Albers, Reilly, & Rittner, 1997; Miller, Kierna, Mathera, & Klein-Gitelman, 1995). The emphasis on families who adopt children from foster care, however, reflects a recognition of the growing numbers adopted from the foster care system each year, the special needs of many of these children that have implications for postadoption services and supports, and the growing number of postadoption services programs that serve this group of families.

The number of children in foster care in the United States has remained at more than one-half million children each year (U.S. House of Representatives, 2005). In response to concerns about the number of children in care and the length of time that children remain in care, policy and practice have placed greater emphasis on timely permanency planning that ensures children return safely to their parents or other members of their extended families, or, if reunification is not possible, that they are provided with new families through adoption. The Adoption Assistance and Child Welfare Act of 1980 (P.L. 96-272) created the initial federal adoption policy framework. It explicitly recognized adoption as a permanency alternative for children in foster care, and it established the federal adoption assistance program to provide subsidies for children in foster care whose "special needs" posed challenges to their adoptions (Avery, 1998). The Adoption and Safe Families Act of 1997 (ASFA) added a framework that required more expeditious efforts to free children for adoption. ASFA established shortened time frames for seeking termination of parental rights (unless certain exceptions apply) and provided fiscal bonuses to states that increased the annual number of final-ized adoptions (U.S. Department of Health and Human Services [DHHS], 2000).

Since the enactment of ASFA and various states' implementation of innovative adop-tion initiatives, the number of adoptions of children in foster care has risen dramati-cally (DHHS, 2001). In fiscal year 2003, there were approximately 50,000 finalized adop-tions of children in foster care, a more than a two-fold increase in annual finalized adoptions over most of the 1980s and 1990s (DHHS, 2005; U.S. House of Representa-tives, 2005). Foster parents adopted the majority of these children, while kin and unre-lated families adopted smaller percentages (DHHS, 2005).

As adoption has come to be a viable permanency option and adoptions of children in foster care has increased, research increasingly has focused on the service needs of these children and their adoptive families. Based on the research, the majority of chil-dren in foster care (including children in care who are freed for adoption) clearly are affected by some combination of adverse factors (including histories of abuse and ne-glect, early deprivation, and prenatal alcohol and drug exposure) that significantly impact their physical health, mental health, and development (Barth & Berry, 1988; Rosenthal & Groze, 1992). The research also makes clear that many of the adoptive families of these children face a range of challenges and require both short- and long-term postadoption services and supports to meet their children's and their family's needs (Barth & Berry, 1988; Eheart & Power, 1995). Increasingly, research has focused on the nature and scope of these needs, the types of services and supports that most effectively respond to the challenges that adoptive families face, and the features of successful postadoption service programs.

This chapter reviews what is known from the research about the needs of families for postadoption services and supports, particularly families who adopt children from foster care. The first part draws on research that has identified the aspects of children's histories that affect their health, development, and psychosocial and school function-ing. The types of problems that children adopted from foster care often experience are also identified. This information provides an important foundation for understanding the needs of adoptive families for postadoption services and supports. The second part of the chapter examines the research-derived knowledge base as it informs practice, program development, and policy in the field of postadoption services. It first consid-ers the implications of the research for the overall design of postadoption services and the development of appropriate outcome measures to assess the impact of these pro-grams. It then considers the implications of research for program development, specifi-cally drawing on studies that have identified the key service needs of adoptive families and the barriers that families confront in obtaining needed services. Finally, the chap-ter considers the policy implications of research on postadoption services, with a focus on the issues related to funding and the availability and adequacy of subsidy and other mechanisms to support families' access to needed services. The chapter concludes with a consideration of directions for future research.

The Knowledge Base Regarding the Needs of Children Adopted from Foster Care

Research—much of it presented in this book—has provided the child welfare field with an understanding of the past experiences of children in foster care who are subsequently adopted and the types of problems that they bring with them or develop afterward. This understanding provides an essential foundation for practice, program development, and policy in the area of postadoption services.

A number of studies have sought to identify those aspects of children's histories that most powerfully affect their ongoing health, development, and well being. Two key features of children's histories have emerged from the research as particularly relevant to postadoption services: maltreatment and multiple placements while in foster care. Research consistently has found that large percentages of children adopted from foster care have experienced some type of maltreatment. Smith, in her Chapter 4 study of children served through the Illinois postadoption and guardianship program (all of whom had been adopted from foster care), found that a significant number had histories of abuse or neglect that placed them at risk of psychosocial problems and adjustment difficulties following adoption. Seventy-one percent of the children in her study had experienced some level of neglect (with 45% experiencing severe neglect), 43% had suffered from physical abuse, and 27% had been sexually abused. Similarly, Lenerz, Gibbs, and Barth found in their Chapter 5 study of children served through the Casey Family Services postadoption program (three-quarters of whom had been adopted from foster care) that one-half had experienced some form of maltreatment.

Studies also consistently have documented that large percentages of children adopted from foster care have had multiple placements while in out-of-home care. This finding is of concern because of the relationship that has been found between multiple placements in foster care and higher psychological risks for children, as well as greater risks of adoption disruption (Albers, Reilly, & Rittner, 1993; Wilson, 2000). In Chapter 11, Ryan found that the children in his study conducted in a Southern state (approximately 80% of whom had been in foster care) averaged two placements before joining their adoptive families. In Chapter 9, Fine, Doran, Berliner and Lieb found that the children in their Washington State study (all in foster care) had an average of three placements prior to joining their adoptive families. Lenerz, Gibbs, and Barth also found that one-third of the children in their study and Smith discovered that one-quarter of those in her Chapter 4 study had had more than one placement prior to their placements with their adoptive families.

Research further has contributed significantly to an understanding of the problems that children who are adopted from foster care experience—problems that have a direct bearing on the development and provision of effective postadoption services. In studies in which children adopted from foster care have comprised very high percentages or the totality of the adopted children studied, significant problems in several areas have been found.

Emotional and behavioral problems are most frequently identified by the research. Research consistently has found that adopted children are overrepresented among clinical populations of children with emotional and behavioral problems (Rosenthal & Groze, 1994; Smith & Howard 2001; Zill, 1996). Studies also document that the primary reason adoptive families seek postadoption services are their concerns about their children's emotional and behavioral problems (Lenerz, Gibbs, & Barth, Chapter 5; Smith, Chapters 4 and 8).

Several studies have focused on the incidence of emotional and behavioral problems either as independent factors or as problems that co-occur, recognizing that behavioral problems often are the manifestation of emotional problems (see Smith, Chapter 5). Festinger, for example, found that 34% of the children in her Chapter 2 study of children adopted from the New York City foster care system had emotional problems and 40% had behavioral problems. In her Chapter 1 study of children (all from foster care) and their adoptive families in Illinois, Howard found that the percentage of children with emotional problems ranged from 24% of the children adopted by kin to 46% of the children adopted by unrelated families, and that the percentage of children with behavior problems ranged from 43% of those adopted by kin to 55% of those adopted by unrelated families (with the percentages of children with emotional and behavioral problems adopted by foster families falling in between). Smith (Chapter 4) found that 43% of the adopted children in her Illinois study had a mental health diagnosis, as identified in the Diagnostic and Statistical Manual (DSM), while Lahti (Chapter 6) discovered, based on Child Behavior Checklist (CBCL) scores, that approximately one-half of the children served by the Maine postadoption program had a range of problems severe enough to warrant a referral to a mental health service provider. In studies that have examined the percentage of children with emotional or behavioral problems, Fine, Doran, Berliner, and Lieb (Chapter 9) found that 62% had one or both types of problems, and Smith (Chapter 8) found that 93% had problems of one or both types.

Research also documents relatively high rates of physical health problems and learning and other developmental disabilities among children adopted from foster care. Several researchers have found that children adopted from foster care demonstrate high levels of medical and other physical problems. Ryan (Chapter 11), for example, discovered that 30% of the adopted children in his study had medical needs, and Fine, Doran, Berliner, and Lieb (Chapter 9) found that an even higher percentage of adopted children (46%) had medical or physical health problems. Festinger (Chapter 2), who identified the medical and physical problems of the adopted children in her study with greater specificity, found that 24% of the children had medical problems, 10% had neurological problems, and another 7% had physical disabilities. Howard (Chapter 1) found that the proportion of children with chronic medical problems ranged from 11% of the children adopted by kin to 24% adopted by unrelated families, and that the proportion of children with physical disabilities ranged from 2% adopted by kin to 15% adopted by unrelated families (with the proportion of children adopted by foster families having these problems falling in between on both factors).

Similarly, research has documented a range of learning and other developmental disabilities among children adopted from foster care. Festinger (Chapter 2) found that

37% of the children in her study had learning disabilities. Fine, Doran, Berliner, and Lieb (Chapter 9) found that a lower percentage of children had learning disabilities (23%) but that 40% of the children in their study had sensory and developmental delays. Howard (Chapter 11) found that the proportion of children with learning disabilities ranged from 37% of the children adopted by kin to more than half (57%) adopted by unrelated families, and that the proportion of children with developmental delays ranged from 17% adopted by kin to one half (51%) adopted by unrelated families (with percentages for children adopted by foster families falling in between). Considering these problems in a somewhat different context, Smith (Chapter 4) found that 41% of the children in her Illinois study were placed in a special education setting.

This research provides critical information about the extent to which adopted children have experienced maltreatment in the past and multiple placements prior to adoption, and the extent to which they manifest emotional, behavioral, physical, and medical problems, and learning and other developmental disabilities. This body of knowledge provides an important foundation for understanding the needs of families for postadoption services. That understanding, however, also requires acknowledging other factors that bear on the postadoption experiences of children and families. Those factors include the nature of adoption as a way of forming families, a process that has its own unique dynamics and challenges; the situations of families who adopt children from foster care, particularly the extent to which their income levels, educational backgrounds, and existing support systems are adequate in assisting them to meet their children's needs; and aspects of the broader environment in which adoptive families live. Each of these factors is explored in the second section of this review.

Implications for Practice, Program Development, and Policy

Research on postadoption services has yielded many important findings for practice, program development, and policy. This knowledge base provides a strong foundation for strengthening postadoption services from each of these perspectives.

Implications for Practice

A number of studies have raised important practice issues with regard to postadoption services. Specifically, findings from research suggest that a family systems perspective is critical to effective postadoption services, that practice must recognize different types of adoptive families have different types of needs and postadoption services must be conceptualized accordingly, and that the outcomes for postadoption services must be comprehensively defined to reflect the variety and complexities of the concerns that cause adoptive families to seek assistance.

Postadoption services from a family systems perspective

One consistent theme that emerges from the research is that adoptive families' needs do not arise solely from the adopted child's problems or the family's concerns about the child, but, instead, these concerns extend more broadly to the entire family system. This research strongly suggests that postadoption services should not be designed with an exclusive focus on "fixing" the adopted child, even if (as the research also suggests) adoptive families frame the presenting problem in terms of the adopted child's emotional or behavioral difficulties or other child-focused issues.

In Chapter 8, Smith concluded that a family systems orientation is an effective approach to understanding and addressing the concerns of adoptive families. She found that even when families defined the presenting problems as child-focused, the issues invariably were more complex, involving problems at the child, family, and environmental levels. Many of the adoptive families in her study who sought postadoption services were struggling with the dynamics between their families and birthfamilies; with challenges to the marital relationship that had developed since adopting; with marital history issues such as infertility; and with aspects of the family that were contributing to the child's difficulties and that were undermining the family's ability to cope with the current challenges. Lenerz, Gibbs, and Barth (Chapter 5) similarly endorsed the importance of a family systems approach based on their findings, adding the facts that many families have biological children or have adopted more than one child, and that adoption-related issues often affect other children in the family.

In Chapter 3, Grand likewise emphasizes the importance of a family systems approach, noting that a service orientation that is exclusively child-focused emphasizes only the child's adaptation to the family and ignores issues related to the family's adaptation to the child. His research revealed that family systems issues may involve the marital dyad relationship, relationships among all family members (adults and children), and the family's connections with extended family and friends. He found that the quality of communication was a key family systems issue with implications for postadoption services, particularly with regard to adoption-related issues.

This body of research strongly suggests that practice must conceive postadoption services as supportive of the integrity of the adoptive family as a whole. Such an approach to the postadoption issues families face would recognize the importance of focusing not only on the child but also on the adoptive family and the wider community in which the family lives.

Practice recognition of differences among adoptive families

The research also highlights that different types of adoptive families may have different concerns and need different types of services and supports. Both Festinger (Chapter 2) and Howard (Chapter 1) examined the needs of different types of adoptive families. Festinger found that about one-half of the adoptive families in her study were kin and the remaining adoptive parents were either unrelated foster parents or families who had been recruited for waiting children. She also found that the adoptive families, as a group, were older (a mean of 55 years), of African American or Latino background, had limited educations, and had relatively low annual incomes. On average, however, kin were older than nonkin adopters, were more likely to be African American, and had substantially lower incomes (an annual average income of $8,000 compared to the average annual income of $17,000 for nonkin adopters). She also discovered that families' service needs (both services that families needed and how much of those services they needed) varied by services type and adoptive family type. Key family variables that were associated with services need were the families' racial and cultural backgrounds, level of education, the age of the parent at the time of adoption, and the employment status of the adoptive parent.

Howard also found that the three types of adoptive families whom she studied—kin, foster parent, and unrelated or "matched" adopters—differed on a number of variables. In findings similar to Festinger's, Howard learned that kin were more likely to head single-parent families, be African American, and have more limited incomes and educational backgrounds than foster parent and "matched" adoptive parents. Different types of families also expressed different types of concerns following adoption. Like Festinger, Howard found that differences in families' service needs were associated with families' demographic characteristics, including racial background, marital status, and educational level. Interestingly, however, particularly with kin, lower incomes were not necessarily associated with a higher level of perceived need.

This body of research suggests that practice should focus on the types of families who need postadoption services and the extent to which different types of families need and benefit from similar and different types of services and supports. Although differences among families may manifest across a variety of dimensions (an issue discussed later), at least one of the factors that distinguishes adoptive families (and, possibly, the nature of their needs for postadoption services and supports) is the extent and nature of any previous relationship the family had with the child. This research suggests that service needs vary among former foster parents who adopt (a group that continues to constitute a significant percentage of all adoptions of children in foster care) (DHHS, 2001), kinship families who adopt (who, as evaluations of guardianship programs suggest, are more often considering adoption and moving forward to adopt their relative children) (National Conference of State Legislatures, 2000), and unrelated adoptive families (who, in many communities, are being recruited in greater numbers as resources for waiting children in foster care) (Lakin & Whitfield, 1997).

Outcomes of postadoption services

From a practice perspective, research findings also have important implications for the development of outcomes that allow an assessment of the effect of postadoption service programs. The research suggests that practice should focus on developing a range of outcomes for postadoption services that reflect both the variety of issues families face and varying levels of problem intensity, determine which outcomes are appropriate for which adoptive families, and clearly identify the factors that limit the achievement of positive outcomes and examine the extent to which those factors can be mitigated.

First, the research suggests that practice should focus on developing a range of outcomes that are indicative of the effect of postadoption services. A fairly common outcome used by postadoption service programs is the rate of adoption dissolution among families served, a focus that is consistent with the ongoing research interest in the factors associated with disruption and dissolution and with adoption stability (Barth & Berry, 1988; Goerge, 1990; Rosenwald & Groze, 1992; Smith & Howard, 1991; Westhues & Cohen, 1990). Smith (Chapter 4), for example, noted that "keeping adoptive families together" was one of the primary goals of the Illinois postadoption service program that she studied. She found that this goal, which incorporated both physical factors and psychological commitment, was achieved by 94% of the families in her study. In 87% of the cases, children were still in the home at the conclusion of services, and in an additional 7% of cases, children were in out-of-home placements but were expected to return home. In connection with this outcome, she found that children adopted from foster care were no more likely to be placed out of home at the conclusion of postadoption services than were other adopted children, but their parents were more likely than the adoptive parents of other children to raise dissolution of the adoption as a possibility. This finding suggests that prevention of adoption dissolution is not only a key general outcome of postadoption services, but also may be an outcome of particular relevance for families for whom other alternatives can be successful but who have concluded that they should give serious consideration to dissolution.

Although research supports prevention of dissolution as a key outcome of postadoption services, it also suggests that other outcomes may be equally critical from the perspective of families who seek services. In her study, Smith (Chapter 8) examined a range of other postadoption services outcomes in the areas of child, parental, and family functioning. She found that from the perspective of parents, there were five areas of positive outcome achievement:

- Parents felt that they had developed a new perspective or understanding of their situation.

- Parents felt that they had strengthened their parenting abilities.

- The child's condition or behavior improved (including better performance in school, increased self-esteem, and greater comfort with adoption issues).

- The family climate improved.

- The family was able to link with needed resources.

Families tended to emphasize that they associated the primary benefits with their ability to move from seeing themselves as unable to cope (which carried with it highly negative emotions and negative perceptions of their children and themselves) to greater confidence in their parenting abilities, an enhanced acceptance and appreciation of their child, and a sense of hope for the future. Interestingly, Smith found that many of these outcomes were achieved through adoptive families' connections with other adoptive families rather than through clinically oriented services.

Similarly, Lahti, in Chapter 6, identified a range of key indicators of success in addition to reduced rates of adoption dissolution. These outcomes included reduced displacement (i.e., decreases in the number of days that a child was out of the home as a result of a problem), improved family functioning, improved child functioning and well being, greater access to and use of services, and high levels of satisfaction with services.

Second, research suggests that practice needs to focus more clearly on which interventions result in the most positive outcomes for different types of adoptive families.

The question of "what works and with whom" indicates the importance of assessing not only the effectiveness of various interventions but also service effectiveness in relation to the varying needs of different types of families. As Haugaard observed in Chapter 10, careful assessments are needed of service outcomes to test the effectiveness of different types of postadoption services for different types of adoptive families. These differences may be important as service needs and outcomes are explored, as indicated earlier, for kinship families, foster parent adopters, and adoptive families who are recruited and matched with waiting children. These differences also may be important as practice considers the potentially differing needs of single and married adopters and of families who fit the "traditional" definition of adoptive families and families considered "nontraditional," including gay and lesbian adoptive families. Finally, it is important to consider service needs and outcomes for adoptive families in general and adoptive families who, from a service delivery and research perspective, present more clinical issues.

Third, research informs an understanding of the factors that may limit the ability of families to achieve positive outcomes through postadoption services, a knowledge base on which practice can draw in the design and evaluation of these services. For example, in Chapter 8, Smith identified several factors that may affect the extent to which families realize improvements in their situations. Some of the limiting factors related to the quality of the services, including a limited knowledge base about the effective treatment of certain conditions and inadequate professional expertise on the part of postadoption services staff. Other factors were associated with program design (e.g., time limits on services) and the environment in which services are provided (e.g., an inadequate number of community resources). Other factors were associated with parental condition, including insufficient parental commitment to the adoption and parental incapacity, particularly in the form of advanced age and chronic or terminal health conditions. Finally, a limiting factor was associated with the child's status, particularly when the child has severe and irremediable difficulties.

Even in cases in which some of these limiting factors are present, however, research suggests that practice should examine how outcomes are defined so that the realities of the situation for each child and family are fully recognized. Smith (Chapter 8), for example, suggests that definitions of positive outcomes may fall along a continuum based on the nature of the child's needs. When the child's needs are severe, the most positive outcome may be that parents are able to understand and accept the child and find ways to optimize the child's development and the family's coping skills. When the child's needs are more moderate, considerable improvement may be possible in child and family functioning. Similarly, in situations in which a parent is of advanced age or affected by a debilitating or life threatening condition, the most positive outcome may be an alternative placement for the child while sustaining connections with the adoptive parent.

Implications for Program Development

Research also offers considerable guidance with regard to program development in the area of postadoption services. A number of studies have yielded information about the postadoption services being provided and the extent to which these services and supports "work" or do not "work" for adoptive families. This knowledge base provides key understandings about services that adoptive families need, the barriers they encounter in accessing needed services, and the qualities of postadoption service programs that they consider most important.

What adoptive families need from postadoption services

Research suggests that from the perspective of adoptive families, the effectiveness of postadoption services is associated with at least four factors at the program development level: the extent to which services and supports are specific to the needs of adoptive families, the types of services and supports that are provided, the extent to which preparation and ongoing educational services are integrated into the continuum of services, and the extent to which services and supports are available throughout the adopted child's life and continue into adolescence and adulthood.

• Services and supports specific to the needs of adoptive families

Research suggests that services and supports for adoptive families must be specific to the needs of these families. Underlying postadoption service programs are two key assumptions: (1) adoption is different in significant ways from parenting birthchildren and, therefore, the design and delivery of postadoption services must take these differences into account (Howard & Smith 1997); and (2) the histories of many adopted children (particularly children adopted from foster care who have experienced neglect, abuse, and attachment disruptions) have a significant impact on children and, therefore, have important implications for supports and services for families who adopt these children (see Chapter 8).

Research supports these assumptions, suggesting that adopted children and their families face issues unique to adoption. Smith (Chapter 8) found in her research that the children served through the Illinois program struggled with a number of adoption-related issues: low self-esteem associated with adoption and identity issues; depression and grief related to the losses at the heart of adoption; and as a consequence of these factors, difficulties regulating emotions. She also found certain themes in the difficulties that adoptive parents reported in raising children with complex histories of maltreatment and instability: the sense that parents were at the "end of their rope" in the face of intensified parenting stresses and frustrations related to the excessive and increasing demands in patenting children with significant emotional, behavioral, physical, and developmental problems.

• Types of postadoption services and support

A second key implication of the research relates to the nature of the provided services and supports. Barth, Gibbs, and Siebenaler (2001), in their review of adoptive families' needs for services, found that service needs fell into four major categories: educational and informational services, clinical services, material services, and support networks. The research suggests that in the area of educational and informational services, adoptive families need easily accessible information about services, supports, and resources, as well as parenting education, including practical help with children's needs. In the area of clinical services, adoptive families typically describe needs for counseling, including assistance with children's attachment issues; guidance in responding to their adopted children's emotional, behavioral, and developmental issues; crisis intervention services; counseling services for their children, including group services for older children; and specialized children's services, including outpatient drug and alcohol treatment. Key material services that adoptive families identify are adoption assistance (subsidies), medical coverage, and special medical equipment. Finally, adoptive families often identify as key support network services the following: support groups for parents; informal contact with other families who have adopted children with special needs; help lines; respite care and babysitting for other children in the family; and advocacy services, including assistance in negotiating the educational and mental health systems (Brown, 1996; Erich & Leung, 1998; Festinger, 2001; Fine, 2000; Groze, 1996a; Groze & Rosenthal, 1993; Kramer & Houston, 1999; Lenerz, 2000; McDonald, Propp, & Murphy, 2001; Marcenko & Smith, 1994; Meaker, 1989; Michigan Federation, 1999; Norris, 1990; Rosenthal & Groze, 1990; Rosenthal, Groze, & Morgan, 1996; Sedlak, 1991; Smith & Howard, 1999).

Recently, research has attempted to clarify which of these many types of services are most useful and meaningful to adoptive families. Some studies have found that adoptive parents need and benefit from a combination of concrete and clinical services. Festinger (Chapter 2), for example, found that adoptive families identify a range of services as "most needed," including information services, after school services, educational services (such as tutoring and special education services), clinical services, health services, housing assistance (more often identified by kin adoptive parents than by other adopters), home assistance, vocational or educational training, and legal assistance. Lenerz, Gibbs, and Barth (Chapter 5) found that adoptive families served through the Casey Family Services postadoption services program most frequently used family systems counseling, case advocacy, group services for both children and adults, and postadoption services workshops.

Other research has found that adoptive families, while recognizing the value of and their needs for professional services, often express the need for more informal supports. Ryan (Chapter 11), for example, found that adoptive families identified needs for a mix of postadoption services. When asked what supports they used to cope with challenges, the adoptive families in his study not only identified professional supports but also emphasized the importance of a range of informal supports, including the family itself, their social network, and religious and spiritual supports. Similarly, Festinger (Chapter 2) found that adoptive families' needs for social network support was particularly great. Her findings lead to a recommendation that greater emphasis be placed on developing foster or "resource" parent cluster groups as a model for meeting families' needs for social network support. In line with these findings, Lahti (Chapter 6) concluded that families needed services more in line with an educational and supportive model than services provided in accordance with a more therapeutic model.

• Importance of preparation and continuing education

In several studies, adoptive parents have reported that they were not well prepared for the challenges that they encountered following adoption and that they needed more reality-based training and educational programs (Festinger, Chapter 2; Ryan, Chapter 11). Howard (Chapter 1) found that all three types of adoptive families who participated in her study—kinship, adoptive families, foster parent adoptive families, and matched adoptive families—reported a need for more thorough preparation and ongoing educational services following adoption. From a program development perspective, these findings have important implications for the design and delivery of a continuum of educationally oriented services for adoptive families.

• Continuing services and supports

Research on postadoption services consistently has concluded that adoption is a significant experience with lifelong effects for adoptive families (Barth & Berry, 1988; Lenerz, Gibbs, & Barth, Chapter 5; Smith & Howard, 1994). Studies have shown that the challenges in adoption, particularly when children have special needs, do not disappear readily or in predictable fashion; that adoptive families experience successive achievements and setbacks; and that the needs of adoptive families for services may increase over time (Groze, 1996b; Rosenthal & Groze, 1994). Lenerz, Gibbs, and Barth, for example, found in their evaluation of the Casey Family Services postadoption program that families sought services long after their adoptions were finalized and often returned to the program for additional services after the original contact. In some cases, identity-related issues that had not previously emerged for adopted children arose in adolescence, triggering a need for services. Their study and others (see Groze, 1996b; Rosenthal & Groze, 1994) indicate that postadoption services are likely to be most effective and relevant for adoptive families when they are made available beyond the initial postadoption phase.

Barriers that adoptive families encounter in obtaining postadoption services

Research suggests, in yet other findings with important implications for program development, that adoptive families confront a range of barriers in accessing postadoption services and supports (Barth & Berry, 1988; Eheart & Power, 1995). Among the barriers adoptive parents most consistently identify are limited information about and the high costs of needed services. Both Festinger (Chapter 2) and Ryan (Chapter 11) found that adoptive families often feel cut off and helpless once they adopt, unable to obtain information about the services they need. Ryan and Fine (Chapter 11), Doran, Berliner, and Lieb (Chapter 9) also found that adoptive families face particular challenges in meeting the expenses associated with medical and behavioral services for their children. In their study of the availability and level of subsidy for families who adopted children from foster care in Washington State, Fine and colleagues found that a number of adoptive families identified cost as one of the key barriers to services. Families reported paying significant sums for a range of needed services, including mental health treatment, respite care, medical services, special education (including developmental services and tutoring), physical and occupational therapy, and home adaptations to accommodate their adopted children's physical disabilities.

These findings are consistent with those of other studies that have focused on adoptive families' use of respite care. These studies demonstrate that although adoptive families frequently need respite, only a small percentage of families actually use this service because they do not believe that it is available, cannot find qualified respite case providers, or cannot afford the service (Commonwealth of Kentucky, 1993; Owens-Kane & Barton, 1999; Walsh, 1991). It is noteworthy that informational and financial barriers have been identified in several surveys of other types of families whose children have special needs or who are attempting to cope with high levels of stress. Soderland, Epstein, Quinn, Cumblad, and Petersen (1995), for example, found that parents of children with emotional and behavioral problems often cited informational and financial barriers to service. Staudt (1999) found that parents who were surveyed after they received intensive family preservation services often complained about informational barriers.

Involvement of adoptive parents and adopted persons in postadoption services

One quality of postadoption services from a program development perspective that the research has hinted at but not fully explored is the involvement of adoptive parents and adopted persons in the development of postadoption services. Some studies that have surveyed adoptive parents on their postadoption service needs and the extent to which those needs have been met have suggested that adoptive parents' perspectives are essential in ensuring that postadoption services are effective and responsive (Becker & Loch, 1995). Research, however, has not closely examined the extent to which adoptive parents have been involved in this area, the nature of their role, or the effect of their participation on program quality. In a similar vein, Grand (Chapter 3) pointed out that the voice that is rarely heard in adoption research is that of the adoptee—an observation that is equally applicable to the role typically played by adopted persons in the development of postadoption services. Although some adoption agencies report that they consult with adult adoptees on practice and program issues (personal communication, Jill Cole, Director of International Adoption, Spence Chapin Services for Families and Children, April 10, 2002), adoptees' involvement in postadoption program development appears to continue to be quite limited.

As research tentatively suggests, adoptive parents and adopted persons likely have much to contribute to the design, implementation, and development of postadoption services. There are practice models for the involvement of adoptive parents and adoptees that could be used to strengthen the design and delivery of postadoption services. In several states, for example, postadoption services have been developed based on information directly obtained from adoptive families through surveys, focus groups, and advisory boards (Casey Family Services, n.d.).

In sum, research has shown that adoptive families' needs are multidimensional and may arise at each developmental stage for the family and the adopted person. From a program development perspective, the research makes clear the need for flexible programming that permits families to return for services when needed and does not limit the extent to which they may receive services (Lenerz, Gibbs, and Barth, Chapter 5). It further demonstrates that adoptive families of all types (whether kin, foster parent, or matched adoptive families) desire postadoption services and support that they can access quickly and without stigma (Howard, Chapter 1).

Implications for Policy

The research suggests that from a policy perspective, at least two issues warrant closer attention: the extent to which adoptive families have adequate financial supports to meet the needs of their children, and the extent to which current policy and funding frameworks appropriately recognize families' needs for postadoption services and provide the resources that are necessary to develop, implement, and sustain effective programs.

With regard to the financial support of adoptive families, subsidies provide critical financial assistance for many families who adopt children with special needs and, equally if not more importantly, provide children with access to health care coverage through Medicaid (see National Adoption Assistance Training, Resources, and Information Network, 1999/2000). Subsidies make it possible for many families to adopt children with physical, mental health, and developmental needs who could not otherwise afford to do so (Avery & Mont, 1992). At the same time, a number of studies have highlighted the relationship between subsidies and postadoption stability (Avery & Mont, 1992; Barth, 1993; Sedlak, 1991). Barth and Berry (1991), for example, compared stable and disrupted adoptions and found that families with stable placements received higher levels of subsidy and that the highest rate of dissolution occurred among families who received no subsidy whatsoever. The importance of subsidies is further highlighted by the relatively low incomes of many adoptive families of children with special needs. In Illinois, for example, Howard and Smith (2000) found that 41% of all adoptive families had incomes under $25,000 and 56% had incomes under $35,000. Howard (Chapter 1) and Festinger (Chapter 2) both found that kin adoptive parents had particularly low incomes and that many kin families identified problems related to the adequacy of financial support for their children.

Given the current research-based understanding of the critical role of subsidy in supporting adoptive families and promoting adoption stability, a fuller exploration of approaches from a policy perspective is essential to ensure that subsidy programs operate effectively on behalf of children adopted from foster care. As Fine, Doran, Berliner and Lieb (Chapter 9) note, a better understanding is needed of how adoptive families actually use adoption assistance and whether the level of subsidy that they receive is adequate to the tasks that adoptive families face.

An additional policy issue that the research raises is the extent to which subsidies should be tied to the child's needs for services or should encompass some consideration of families' levels of resources and financial ability to support the children they may adopt. Federal law directs a consideration of children's needs alone (Avery, 1998), while recommendations about subsidy eligibility often focus on the special needs of children and not on eligibility criteria regarding their adoptive parents (see Casey Family Services, n.d.). Law and advocacy take this position in large part because of concerns that children will be denied subsidy and Medicaid coverage if their adoptive parents are determined to have sufficient independent resources to meet their children's needs. Howard (Chapter 11), however, raised the question whether subsidy determinations should consider, particularly in the case of kinship care families whose incomes tend to be extremely low, the financial situation of the adoptive family as at least one factor in subsidy determinations. This issue has become particularly relevant as more kinship families are being asked to consider adopting relative children in their care and are giving serious consideration to this option (Testa, 1997; 1999).

The research raises an additional issue in connection with the adequacy of subsidy in the context of adoptive families' multifaceted needs. Fine, Doran, Berliner and Lieb found that although subsidy was a viable resource for families in Washington State, many families who received subsidies for their children nevertheless faced significant challenges in paying for services that their children needed, particularly services not covered by Medicaid or private insurance. This reality suggests that policy must take a more expansive view of financing strategies with regard to services that respond to the range of physical health, mental health (including the need for residential treatment services), developmental, and educational needs of children adopted from foster care. It cannot be assumed that subsidy and Medicaid coverage, standing alone, will be adequate to meet the many needs of some children.

The second policy implication raised by the research is the extent to which current funding frameworks recognize the full scope of families' needs for postadoption services and provide the necessary resources for the development, implementation, and maintenance of such programs. Research suggests that the adoptive families of children from foster care (as well as some children from other countries) need a broad continuum of community-based services that begin with sound preparation, extend through preventive services, and include a range of educational and informational, clinical (including highly intensive mental health interventions), material, and supportive services (Casey Family Services, n.d.). A careful analysis of federal, state, and local funding sources is needed to determine the levels at which resources currently are used, assess the extent to which existing resources could be more fully and effectively used, and identify the gaps in fiscal support for key components of postadoption services that need to be addressed. Such an analysis necessarily must extend to the major federal funding streams that are being used and possibly could be mobilized more effectively, including Titles IV-B and IV-E of the Social Security Act, Medicaid, discretionary grant funding through the Adoption Opportunities Program, funding for mental health services through the Comprehensive Community Mental Health Services for Children Program, and funding for developmental and educational services through the Individuals with Disabilities Education Act (Oppenheim, Gruber, & Evans, 2000).

State and local funding also must be included in the analysis of financial supports for postadoption services. Several states have developed innovative policy approaches to the funding of post adoption services, approaches that can serve as models for communities that have not yet developed effective financing strategies. Oregon, for example, has put policies into place that provide adoption subsidies to all children adopted from foster care, irrespective of children's eligibility under Title IV-E of the Social Security Act or the Supplemental Security Income (SSI) program (Casey Family Services, n.d.) Virginia has established a "client fund" that permits each adoptive family to request funds each year (a maximum of $500) for such services as respite care, special camps for their children, tutoring, and copayments for health insurance (Casey Family Services, n.d.).

Conclusion

The research-derived knowledge base regarding postadoption services provides a wealth of information that can significantly enhance practice, program development, and policy in this field. The research has contributed to an understanding of the past experiences of children who are adopted from foster care—histories that include maltreatment and multiple placements during their stays in foster care. These factors have important implications for children's subsequent health, development, and ability to attach to their adoptive families, whether those families are kin, children's former foster families, or families who were recruited and matched with them.

Importantly, research also provides a foundation for understanding "what works" in postadoption services. It contributes important knowledge on practice issues related to the conceptualization of postadoption services and the types of outcomes that may be anticipated from such services. Research also provides an understanding on which program development may be based, particularly in relation to the nature and scope of services that adoptive families need and the barriers they encounter in obtaining needed services. Finally, from a policy perspective, research provides a foundation for further analyses about the adequacy of financial supports for adoptive families and the extent to which current funding frameworks recognize families' needs for postadoption services and support the development of such programs.

Although the current research-based knowledge base contributes significantly to practice, program development, and policy, there is much that remains to be understood. Far more work is needed, for example, in examining the "what works and for whom" question in relation to different types of adoptive families. A fuller understanding is needed with regard to the effectiveness of different services and service delivery strategies for adoptive families of different racial and cultural backgrounds and "nontraditional" families, including gay and lesbian families. The "what works and for whom" question also needs to be examined in relation to adopted children whose special needs fall along a continuum from relatively mild to severe. Particularly in relation to services for children with significant mental health problems, the knowledge base related to effective interventions is limited. At the same time, more comprehensive evaluations are needed of current postadoption services and program models. More needs to be understood about the extent to which current services appear to be effective and how they might be made more effective through different service delivery strategies, as well as the extent to which current models provide the best approaches to serving adoptive families.

References

Albers, E. C., Reilly, T., & Rittner, B. (1993). Children in foster care: Possible factors affecting permanency planning. *Child & Adolescent Social Work Journal, 10*(4), 329–341.

Avery, R. J. (1998). Adoption assistance under P.L. 96-272: A policy analysis. *Children and Youth Services Review, 20*(1–2), 29–55.

Avery, R. J., & Mont, D. M. (1992). Financial support of children involved in special needs adoption: A policy analysis. *Journal of Policy Analysis and Management, 11*, 419–441.

Barth, R. P., & Berry, M. (1988). *Adoption and disruption: Rates, risks, and responses.* New York: Aldine de Gruyter.

Barth, R. P., & Berry, M. (1991). Preventing adoption disruption. *Prevention in Human Services, 9*, 205–222.

Barth, R. P., Gibbs, D. A., & Siebenaler, K. (2001). *Assessing the field of post-adoption services: Family needs, program models, and evaluation issues.* Washington, DC: U.S. Department of Health and Human Services.

Becker, R. L., & Loch, H. M. (1995). *Resources for adoptive parents. Program evaluation.* St. Paul, MN: Wilder Research Center.

Casey Family Services. (n.d.). *Strengthening families and communities: An approach to post-adoption services, a white paper.* Shelton, CT: Casey Family Services.

Commonwealth of Kentucky. (1993). *Strategic plan for post legal adoption services in Kentucky.* Frankfort, KY: Department of Social Services.

Eheart, B. K. & Power, M. B. (1995). Adoption: Understanding the past, present, and future through stories. *The Sociological Quarterly, 36*, 197–216.

Erich, S., & Leung, P. (1998). Factors contributing to family functioning of adoptive children with special needs: A long term outcome analysis. *Children and Youth Services Review, 20*(1/2), 135–150.

Festinger, T. (2001). *After adoption: A study of placement stability and parents' service needs.* New York: Shirley M. Ehrenkranz School of Social Work, New York University.

Fine, D. N. (2000). *Adoptive family needs assessment: Final report.* Salem, OR: Oregon Post Adoption Resource Center, Oregon Department of Human Resources.

Goerge, R. M. (1990). The reunification process in substitute care. *Social Service Review (September)*, 422–457.

Groze, V., & Rosenthal, J. A. (1993). Attachment theory and the adoption of children with special needs. *Social Welfare Research and Abstracts, 29*(2), 5–12.

Groze, V. (1996a). *Successful adoptive families: A longitudinal study of special needs adoption.* Westport, CT: Praeger.

Groze, V. (1996b). *Successful adoptive families.* Westport, CT: Praeger.

Howard, J. A., & Smith, S. L. (1997). *Strengthening adoptive families: A synthesis of post-legal adoption opportunities grants.* Normal, IL: Illinois State University.

Kramer, L., & Houston, D. (1999). Hope for the children: A community-based approach to supporting families who adopt children with special needs. *Child Welfare, 78*(5), 611–636.

Lakin, D. & Whitfield, L. (1997). Adoption recruitment: Meeting the needs of waiting children. In R. J. Avery (Ed.), *Adoption policy and special needs children* (pp. 107–126). Westport, CT: Greenwood Publishing Group.

Lenerz, K. (2000). Evaluating post-adoption services: Knowledge from the past, plans for the future. *Dialog, 1*(3), 2–3.

Marencko, M. O., & Smith, L. K. (1991). Post-adoption needs of families adopting children with developmental disabilities. *Children and Youth Services Review, 13*(5/6), 413–424.

McDonald, T. P., Propp, J. R., & Murphy, K. C. (2001). The post-adoption experience: Child, parent, and family predictors of family adjustment to adoption. *Child Welfare, 80*(1), 71–94.

Meaker, P. P. (1989). *Post-placement needs of adoptive families: A study of families who adopt through the Texas Department of Human Services.* Master's thesis, The University of Texas at Arlington. On file at the Evan B. Donaldson Adoption Institute, New York, NY.

Michigan Federation of Private Child and Family Agencies. (1999). *Survey of adoptive parents regarding post-adoption services: Final report.* Lansing, MI: Michigan Federation of Private Child and Family Agencies.

Miller, L. C., Kierna, M. T., Mathera, M. I., & Klein-Gitelman, M. (1995). Developmental and nutritional status of internationally adopted children. *Archives of Pediatric Adolescent Medicine, 149,* 40–44.

National Adoption Assistance Training, Resource and Information Network. (1999/2000). *State adoption subsidy profiles.* St. Paul, MN: North American Council of Adoptable Children.

National Conference of State Legislatures. (2000). *A place to call home: Adoption and guardianship for children in foster care.* Denver, CO: National Conference of State Legislatures.

Norris, K. (1990). *Montana post-adoption center.* Helena, MT: Montana Adoption Resource Center.

Oppenheim, E., Gruber, S., & Evans, D. (2000). *Report on post adoption services in the states.* Washington, DC: The Association of Administrators of the Interstate Compact on Adoption and Medical Assistance, APHSA.

Owens-Kane, S., & Barth, R. P. (1999). *Evaluating a family support service: An empirical study of respite care outcomes.* Berkeley, CA: University of California, School of Social Work.

Rosenthal, J. A., & Groze, V. (1990). Special needs adoption: A study of intact families. *Social Service Review, 64,* 475–505.

Rosenthal, J. A., & Groze, V. (1992). *Special needs adoption: A follow-up study of intact families.* New York: Praeger.

Rosenthal, J. A., & Groze, V. (1994). A longitudinal study of special-needs adoptive families. *Child Welfare, 73*(6), 689–706.

Rosenthal, J. A., Groze, V., & Morgan, J. (1996). Services for families adopting children via public child welfare agencies: Use, helpfulness, and need. *Children and Youth Services Review, 18*(1/2), 163–182.

Sedlak, A. J. (1991). *Study of adoption assistance impact and outcomes: Phase II report.* DHHS Contract No. 105-89-1607. Rockville, MD: Westat.

Smith, S., & Howard, J. (1991). A comparative study of successful and disrupted adoptions. *Social Service Review, 65*(2), 248–265.

Smith, S. & Howard, J. (1994). *The adoption preservation project.* Normal, IL: Illinois State University, Department of Social Work.

Smith, S. L., & Howard, J. A. (1999). *Promoting successful adoptions: Practice with troubled families.* Thousand Oaks, CA: Sage Publications.

Smith, S. L. & Howard, J. A. (2001). *A comparative study of adopted and birth children.* Springfield, IL: Illinois Department of Children and Family Services.

Soderland, J., Epstein, M. H., Quinn, K. P., Cumblad, C., & Petersen, S. (1995). Parental perspectives on comprehensive services for children and youth with emotional and behavioral disorders. *Behavioral Disorders, 20*(3), 157–170.

Staudt, M. (1999). Barriers and facilitators to use of services following intensive family preservation services. *The Journal of Behavioral Health Services & Research, 26*(1), 39–49.